THE GUITAR GRIMOIRE®

PROGRESSIONS & IMPROVISATION

BY ADAM KADMON

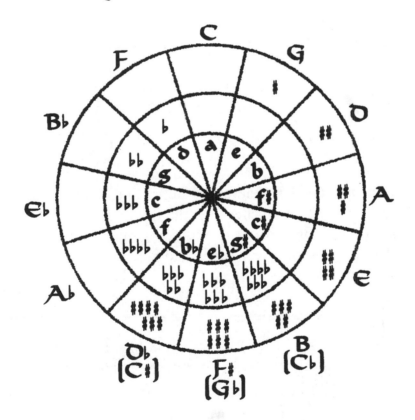

Produced by

⭐®METATRON INC.

for

CARL FISCHER®
65 Bleecker Street, New York, NY 10012

ISBN 0-8258-3197-0

Well, as far as I can tell this wraps up the reference series. The next task will be method books. I apologize to to all my Guitar Grimoire devotees who have been patiently waiting for this book which took four years to create. The countless phone calls and letters from people letting me know that they were waiting. My publisher kept driving me nuts, "where is the progressions volume?"

You have no idea how glad I am to finish this book and get it out of my hair. The truth of the matter is, over the course of the last four years I started the progressions book about ten times. At one point we had like 180 pages done, but something just wasn't right. But alas, good things come to those who wait and I can now say this is another book that I would have loved to have as I was learning, therefore I know that others will derive benefit from it too.

This book is dedicated to all the Guitar Grimoire devotees
who have been patiently awaiting its completion.

Happy Pickings.

A.K.

For more information on **The Guitar Grimoire®** Series and other music instructional products
by Adam Kadmon check out the following Web sites:
http://www.guitargrimoire.com
http://www.adamkadmon.com

gri·moire \grє m'wär\ *n* (*rhymes with guitar*)
[F., book of magical formulas]:
magician's manual

CONTENTS

THE BUILDING BLOCKS OF MUSIC

In order to understand progressions, one must understand the basics of harmony and theory. Music is sound. But for now imagine that is is a set of 12 equal blocks (fig. 1). The distance from one block to the next is a half-step. From block 1 to block 2 is a half-step, from 8 to block 9 is a half-step, etc.

fig. 1   *fig. 2*

7 of these 12 tones or blocks have been given positions of "major" importance (fig. 2). Looking at the diagram we only see 7 numbers, but there are still 12 tones or blocks. The empty blocks are reserved for flats ♭ and sharps ♯ . The distance from block 1 to the first empty block is still a half-step. The blocks that are numbered are the tones that make up the Major scale.

The various combinations of half-steps are called intervals. Basically, an interval is the distance between two tones. The names of the intervals are then divided into two sets: the majors and the perfects. The majors are 2, 3, 6, and 7; the perfects are 1, 4, 5, and 8. 1 would be a unison, such as two instruments playing the same note. An 8 would be the octave. Altering the intervals with flats or sharps changes them from major and perfect into minor, diminished, and augmented (fig. 3).

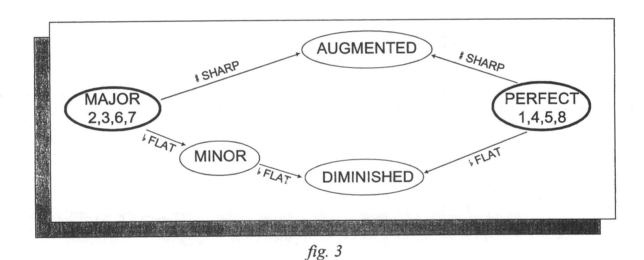

fig. 3

In essence:
- Flat a major — get a minor
- Flat a minor — get a diminished
- Flat a perfect — get a diminished
- Sharp a major — get an augmented
- Sharp a perfect — get an augmented

The entire set of major and perfect intervals are called diatonic intervals.

Let's look at an easy way for memorizing interval distances by counting the amount of blocks. There are 12 building blocks within the Major scale. Therefore, an interval has to consist of so many building blocks. We'll demonstrate first with a major 2nd. There are 3 blocks in a major 2nd (fig. 4), but the distance from the 2 to the 3 is also a major 2nd (fig. 5).

fig. 4   *fig. 5*

Fig. 6 is a complete chart of intervals showing you a breakdown in building block format. Also observe, the chart tells you how many half- and whole steps make up each interval.

```
1     1 BLOCK = UNISON .................................................(0 STEPS)
1  ♭2    2 BLOCKS = MINOR 2nd ...................................(½ STEPS)
1     2    3 BLOCKS = MAJOR 2nd ...............................(1 WHOLE STEP)
1        ♭3    4 BLOCKS = MINOR 3rd ...........................(1½ STEPS)
1          3    5 BLOCKS = MAJOR 3rd ........................(2 WHOLE STEPS)
1            4    6 BLOCKS = PERFECT 4th ..................(2½ STEPS)
1              ♭5    7 BLOCKS = DIMINISHED 5th ...............(3 WHOLE STEPS)
1                5    8 BLOCKS = PERFECT 5th .............(3½ STEPS)
1                  ♭6    9 BLOCKS = MINOR 6th ..............(4 WHOLE STEPS)
1                    6    10 BLOCKS = MAJOR 6th ..............(4½ STEPS)
1                      ♭7    11 BLOCKS = MINOR 7th ........(5 WHOLE STEPS)
1                        7    12 BLOCKS = MAJOR 7th ..........(5½ STEPS)
```

fig. 6

Now let's look at all the individual components of the Major scale in building block breakdown (fig. 7).

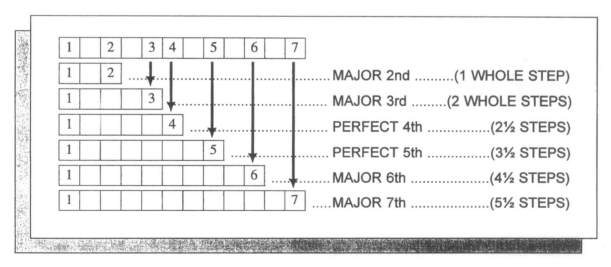

fig. 7

We can clearly see here the individual intervals. We have a 2nd, 3rd, 4th, 5th, 6th, and 7th. With the block diagram we can also see exactly how many steps make up each interval.

Using the same building block breakdown method, we can also analyze the intervallic relationship between the intervals themselves.

Fig. 8 clearly shows us the distance of the intervals from the intervals. For instance, from the major 2nd to the major 3rd is a major 2nd or a whole step. From the 3rd to the 4th is a minor 2nd or a half-step, etc.

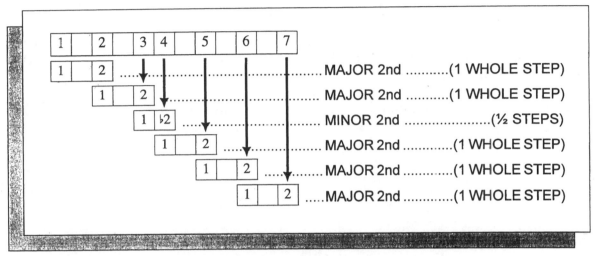

fig. 8

In studying the altered intervals, many of them will look differently on paper and in theory, but sonically, they are the same (fig. 9).

1			♭3	1						♭5	1							♭6	1								♭7
1			#2	1						#4	1							#5	1								#6

fig. 9

Notice the numbers to the right of each set above are different between the upper and the lower, yet each has the same number of blocks. The minor 3rd is the same as the augmented 2nd, the diminished 5th is the same as the augmented 4th, the minor 6th is the same as the augmented 5th, and the minor 7th is the same as the augmented 6th.

In the next example, the diminished 7th (a double-flat 7th) is the same as the major 6th in sound; although in theory, they also are two very different intervals (fig. 10).

1									6
1									♮7

fig. 10

The complete group of intervals which make up the scale, in this case the Major scale, can be theoretically repeated infinitely in both directions; although, in practice there are only so many octaves the human ear can hear (fig. 11).

← | 1 | | 2 | | 3 | 4 | | 5 | | 6 | | 7 | 1 | | 2 | | 3 | 4 | | 5 | | 6 | | 7 | → *fig. 11*

This is the mathematics of music theory. It is important that you memorize the numerics behind the building blocks, in order to form a solid foundation for your musical creations.

SCALES AND MODES

A scale is a sequence of tones comprised of varying intervals. Modes can be described as scale inversions. The Major scale has 7 modes, because it has 7 tones. The 1st mode of any modal system is the scale itself. For many scales, the individual modes have been given names because they are used as scales themselves.

The modes of the Major scale are the Ionian, Dorian, Phrygian, Lydian, Mixolydian, Aeolian, and Locrian. The Major scale is the Ionian mode (Major scale = Ionian). Of all the scales, the Major is the only one that has a different name for the 1st mode.

The II mode of any scale is based upon the 2nd tone of the main scale, in this case the Major scale. A mode uses the exact tones of the main scale; however, what was a 2 becomes a 1, what was a 3 becomes a 2, etc. (fig. 12).

1	2	3	4	5	6	7	1	2	3	4	5	6	7
	1	2	b3	4	5	6	b7						

fig. 12

The process then continues for the other modes. For the III mode, the 3 becomes the 1, the 4 becomes the 2, etc. (fig. 13).

1	2	3	4	5	6	7	1	2	3	4	5	6	7
		1	b2	b3	4	5	b6	b7					

fig. 13

For the IV mode, the 4 becomes the 1, the 5 becomes the 2, etc. (fig. 14).

1	2	3	4	5	6	7	1	2	3	4	5	6	7
			1	2	3	#4	5	6	7				

fig. 14

For the V mode, the 5 becomes the 1, the 6 becomes the 2, etc. (fig. 15).

1	2	3	4	5	6	7	1	2	3	4	5	6	7
				1	2	3	4	5	6	b7			

fig. 15

For the VI mode, the 6 becomes the 1, the 7 becomes the 2, etc. (fig. 16).

1	2	3	4	5	6	7	1	2	3	4	5	6	7
					1	2	b3	4	5	b6	b7		

fig. 16

For the VII mode, the 7 becomes the 1, the 1 becomes the 2, the 2 becomes the 3, etc. (fig. 17).

1	2	3	4	5	6	7	1	2	3	4	5	6	7
						1	b2	b3	4	b5	b6	b7	

fig. 17

For a more thorough study on scales refer to **The Guitar Grimoire - Scales & Modes** and **The Guitar Grimoire - A Notated Intervallic Study of Scales.**

CHORDS

A chord defined is 3 or more tones played simultaneously; an interval can be considered a 2 tone chord, as in a Power chord. A basic chord "formula" is to use every other tone of the scale. For example, a Major chord contains 1, 3, 5. A Major 7th chord is 1, 3, 5, 7 (fig. 18).

Major Scale	1		2		3	4		5		6		7
Major Chord	1				3			5				↓
Major 7th △7	1				3			5				7

fig. 18

What about those big fancy chords like 9ths, 11ths, and 13ths? Using 2 octaves of our Major scale, we can clearly see that a 9th is a 2nd, an 11th is a 4th, and the 13th is a 6th (fig. 19). This should help remove the mystery behind big chords.

Major Scale	1		2		3	4		5		6		7	1		2		3	4		5		6		7
Major 9th	1				3			5				7			9			↓						
Major 11th	1				3			5				7			9			11				↓		
Major 13th	1				3			5				7			9			11				13		

fig. 19

To play inversions merely bounce the lowest tone up an octave (fig. 20).

Major Scale	1		2		3	4		5		6		7	1		2		3	4		5		6		7
Major Chord	1				3			5				↓					3							
1st Inversion					3			5				1					↓							
2nd Inversion								5				1					3							

fig. 20

CHORD NAMING

Certain guidelines help musicians communicate. To understand numeric chord formulas, you must understand the chord naming system in this text. In fig. 21 the 7 symbols denote the status of specific tones within the chord. Flat and sharp symbols are used when altering any other tones. Do not use - and + as flats and sharps.

CHORD NAMING CHART

	SYMBOL	DENOTES STATUS OF	CHANGE	RESULT	NAME	EXAMPLE & FORMULA
3 tone	−	3	b	b3	MINOR	C− = 1, b3, 5
	+	5	#	#5	AUGMENTED	C+ = 1, 3, #5
	°	3,5	b	b3,b5	DIMINISHED	C° = 1, b3, b5
4 tone	△	7	same	7	DELTA	C△ = 1, 3, 5, 7
	7	7	b	b7	DOMINANT	C7 = 1, 3, 5, b7
	∅	3,5,7	b	b3,b5,b7	HALF-DIMINISHED	C∅ = 1, b3, b5, b7
	°7	7 of ∅	extra b	bb7	DIMINISHED 7th	C°7 = 1, b3, b5, bb7

fig. 21

POLYCHORDS, SLASHCHORDS, & SUBSTITUTIONS

Comparing interval maps of the C Major scale and C△13 chord in fig. 22 we see that the 9th, 11th, and 13th are actually a 2nd, 4th, and 6th.

There is another way of looking at 9ths, 11ths, and 13ths known as polychords & slashchords. Polychords are the generic formula and slashchords are the pitch translation. For a detailed study of polychords & slashchords we recommend the books **Guitar Grimoire Chords & Voicings** and **Guitar Grimoire Chord Encyclopedia**.

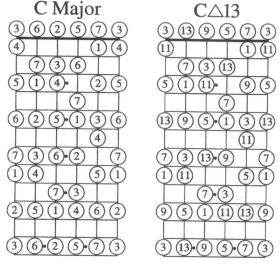

fig. 22

Let's take a △13 polychord formula (fig. 23) then convert it to a slashchord formula.

fig. 23

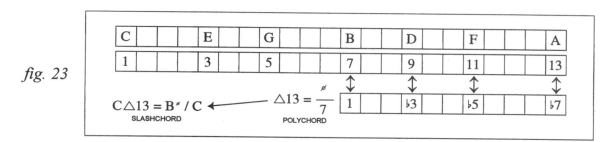

The slashchord formula for the polychord above is Bø / C. Start by playing a Bø chord which is a 1, ♭3, ♭5, ♭7. Without changing the fingering of the Bø play it over a C note. Let's analyze what the Bø becomes on a C△13 interval map.

What was a 1 on the Bø interval map is now the 7 on the C△13 interval map. What was ♭5 now becomes the 11, what was the ♭7 on the Bø is now the 13th, and what was the ♭3 is now the 9th (fig. 24).

1, ♭3, ♭5, ♭7 starting on B...   played over a C becomes ...   a 7, 9, 11, 13 which is a C△13

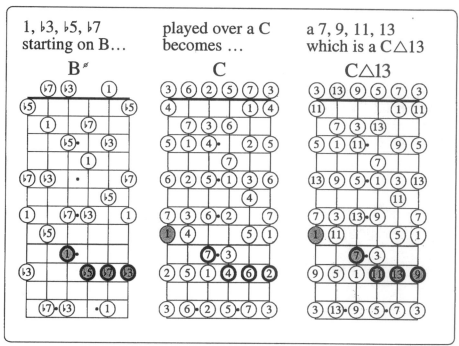

fig. 24

SUBSTITUTIONS

C△13

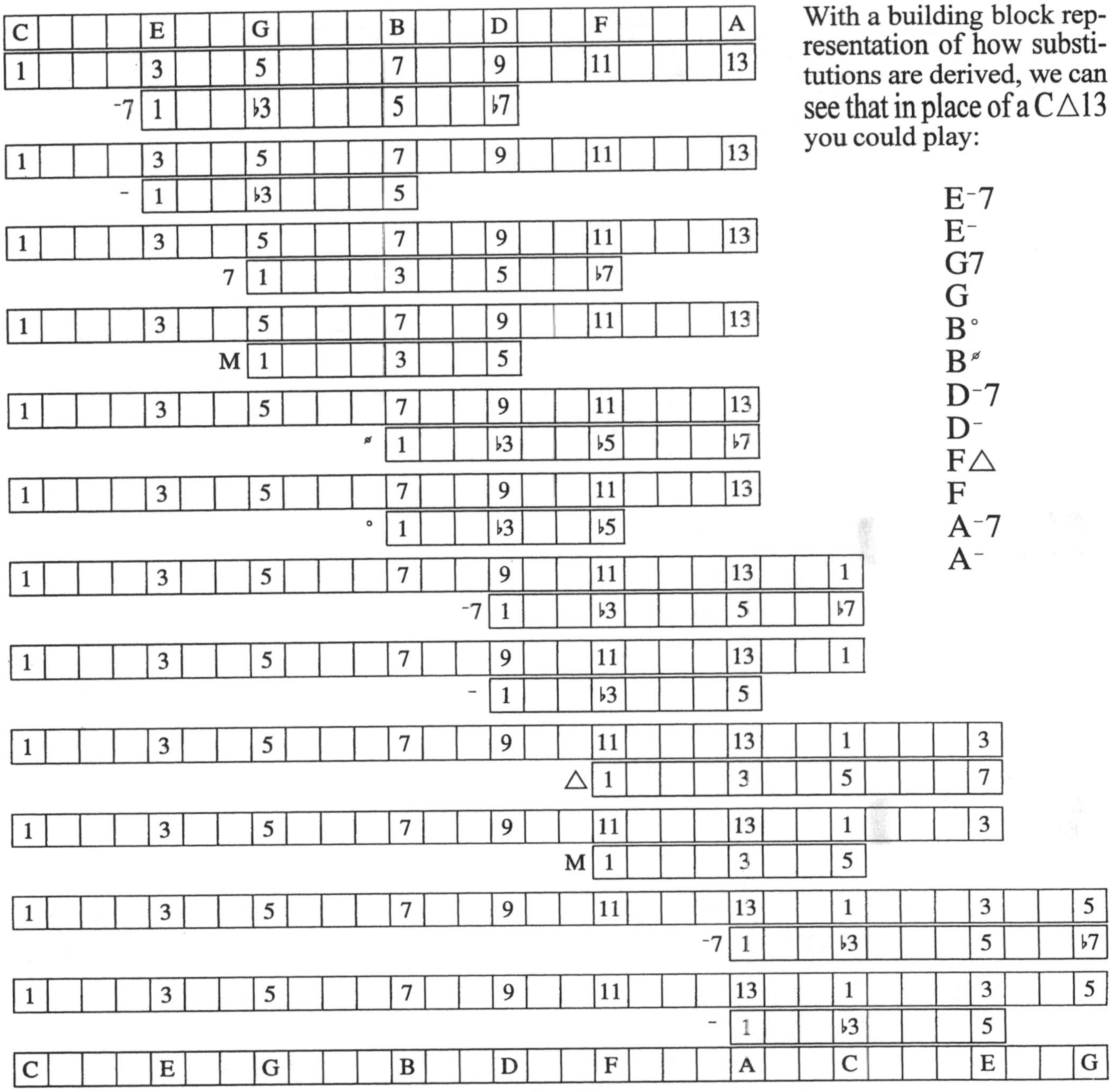

With a building block representation of how substitutions are derived, we can see that in place of a C△13 you could play:

E-7
E-
G7
G
B°
Bø
D-7
D-
F△
F
A-7
A-

fig. 25

Any one of the above mentioned chords will work over the C△13 (fig. 25). Observe that the tones of the substitutions are contained in the original chord or its extended version. That is the secret to the mystery of substitutions.

However, some may find this a bit tricky to understand. **The Guitar Grimoire - Chords & Voicings** and **The Guitar Grimoire - Chord Encyclopedia** contain diagrams known as chord interval maps. The interval maps make it easier to substitute chords.

PROGRESSIONS

Now that we have set the foundation with a brief study of scales, modes, chords, and substitutions, we are now ready to tackle progressions. Let's start with the Major scale and its modes (fig. 26).

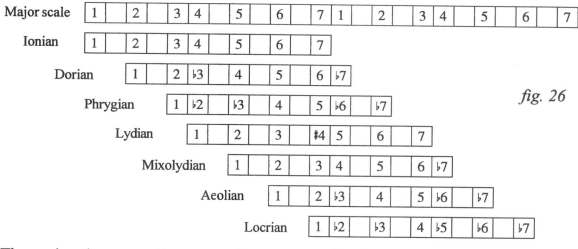

fig. 26

Then using the every other note rule we extract the chords from the modes (fig. 27).

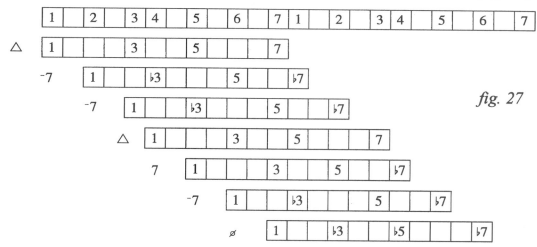

fig. 27

Now we assign pitch to our formula. We will use the key of C for this example (fig. 28).

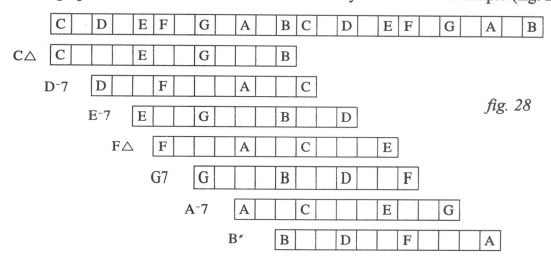

fig. 28

What we have is the first progression type known as the Diatonic Progression. Diatonic means you are using the notes of the scale to derive your chords, in this case the Major scale in the key of C.

In "measure" format the progression looks like this (fig 29):   *fig. 29*

CΔ   D⁻7   E⁻7   FΔ   G7   A⁻7   B⁻   CΔ

Now when we extract the chords from the modes of the Major scale for the purpose of creating progressions, the intervallic positions become scale tone degrees and are marked with roman numerals.   *fig. 30→*

1	2	3	4	5	6	7
I	II	III	IV	V	VI	VII

Therefore the I position will always be understood to be a major 7, the II position will always be a minor 7, the III position will always be a minor 7 etc. so on and so forth (fig. 31).

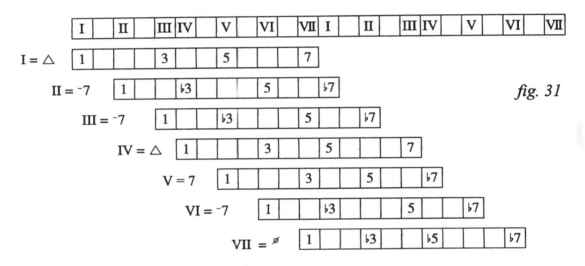

fig. 31

The same diatonic progression from above in scale tone degree "measure" format is demonstrated in fig. 32. This method of scale tone degree format is also known as baseline. Professional musicians most of the time write out their progressions in this way so that the progressions are "generic" allowing them to add pitch on the fly as many times the same tune will have to be played in different keys for different singers.

fig. 32

I   II   III   IV   V   VI   VII   I

When scale tone degrees have other symbols added then the chord is played accordingly (fig. 33↓).

I⁺   II♭5   III7⁺   IV⁻Δ   V7♭5   VI⁻   VII⁻   IΔ

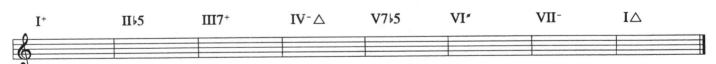

The above baseline progression is demonstrated in the key of "C" so you can see the alterations (fig. 34↓).

C⁺   D♭5   E7⁺   F⁻Δ   G7♭5   A⁻   B⁻   CΔ

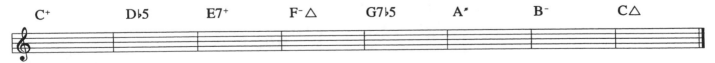

Even though the scale tone degrees are standard such as I = Δ, II = ⁻7 etc., some people will still write them out as IΔ, II⁻7 etc.

We also use the same method to derive simple diatonic progressions using triads. Starting with the Major scale and its modes again (fig. 35):

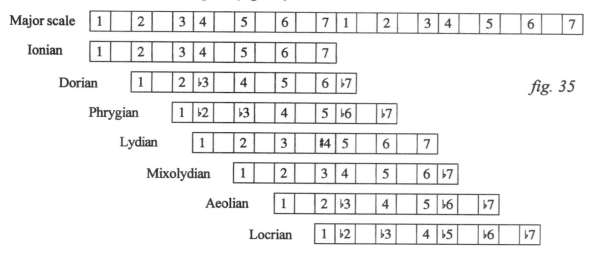

fig. 35

Then using the every other note rule we extract the chords from the modes (fig. 36).

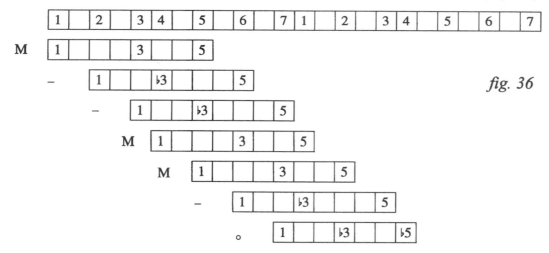

fig. 36

Now we assign pitch to our formula. We will use the key of C for this example (fig. 37).

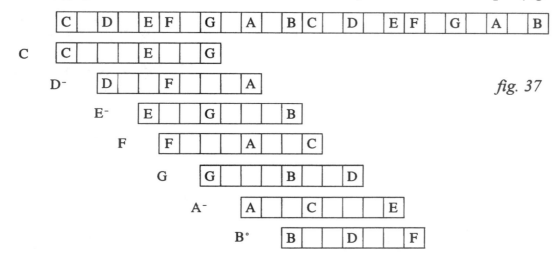

fig. 37

What we have is a diatonic progression using triads in the key of C.

CIRCLE OF FIFTHS

The next type of progression is known as circle progressions. Before we can understand circle progressions we must be able to understand the circle of fifths (fig. 39).

The "Circle of Fifths" demonstrates the relationship of the scale tone degrees (fig. 38) to each other in fifths (fig. 39) .

On the circle of fifths you see 12 positions like the 12 positions of a clock. These 12 positions represent the 12 building blocks of music, the 7 scale tone degrees and the 5 enharmonic degrees. Unlike a clock whose numbers flow consecutively 1, 2, 3, 4, 5 etc. the positions on the circle of fifths are I, V, II, VI, etc. In other words they move in fifths.

To better understand the Circle of Fifths, let's string several octaves of building blocks together as in the figure below. Space allows for three octaves only (fig. 40).

Notice that one fifth is made up of 8 blocks. The numbers in bold below appear in the circle of fifths diagram above (start at I on top and follow clockwise).

1	2	3	4	5	6	7
I	II	III	IV	V	VI	VII

fig. 38

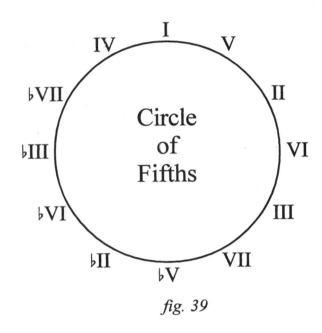

fig. 39

COUNTING FIFTHS:
STEP 1: start at the " I "
STEP 2: count one 5th (8 blocks)
STEP 3: continue counting where left off

1	2	3	4	5	6	7
I	II	III	IV	V	VI	VII

one octave = 12 blocks

1	2	3	4	5
I	II	III	IV	V

5th = 8 blocks

three octaves ↓

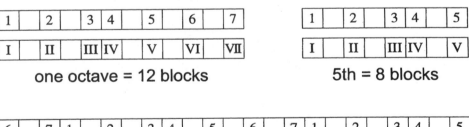

fig. 40

We ran out of space in the previous example by putting the octaves in a straight line. We can loop seven octaves end to end, to form a complete circle. In the diagram below (fig. 41) the emphasized tones are the fifths. This is another way of demonstrating a "Circle of Fifths".

The Circle of Fifths gets its name from moving in a clockwise direction around the circle from the top or the I starting point. In a counterclockwise direction, the emphasized tones become fourths, which also contain 8 building blocks starting from the I descending to the IV. This is an *inverted* fifth.

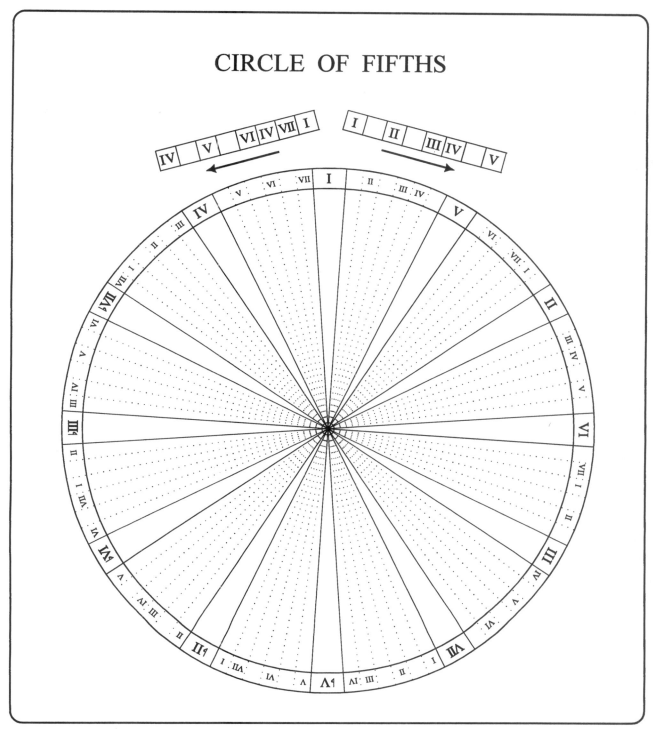

fig. 41

Now that you know that each position is a fifth, what about the relationship to other positions. For example, if you take any position as a starting point then skip a position, that is a whole tone or step. This holds true for any position on the circle of fifths. Fig 42 demonstrates this. This works in both directions.

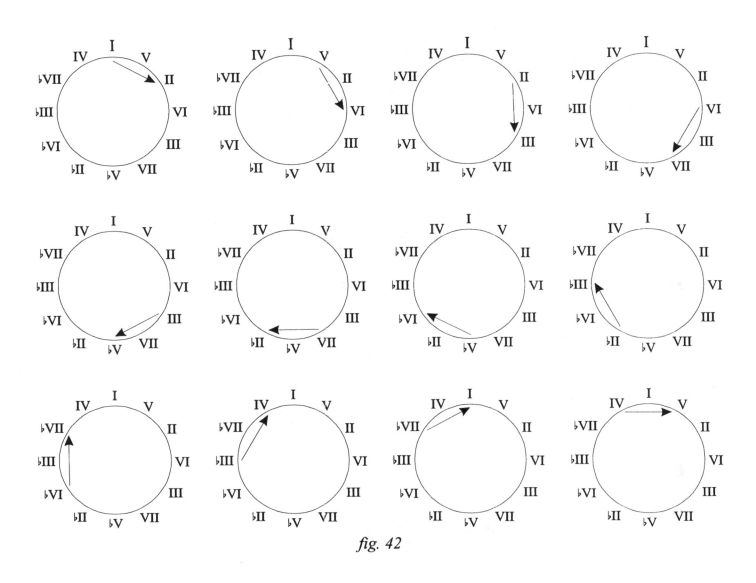

fig. 42

If we take any position as our starting point and skip two positions clockwise we have a sixth. This holds true regardless of which position you start on (fig. 43).

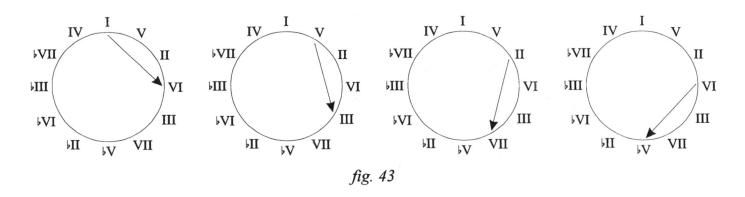

fig. 43

This works in reverse as well, however, you get a minor third. Bear in mind, though, that a minor third is an inverted sixth (fig. 44).

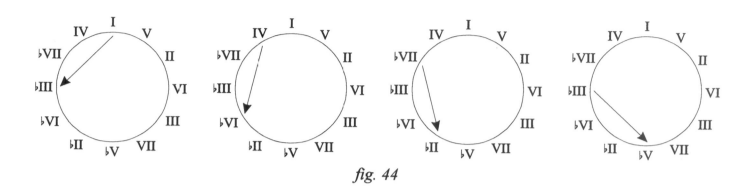

fig. 44

Now if you take any starting position and skip three positions clockwise, what you have is a major third or two whole tones or steps. Again this works whatever position you start from (fig. 45).

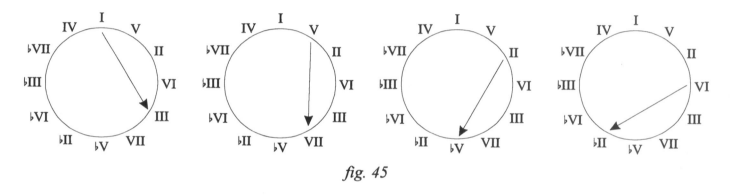

fig. 45

This works in reverse too. If you skip three positions from your starting point counterclockwise you get a minor sixth. A minor sixth is an inverted third (fig. 46).

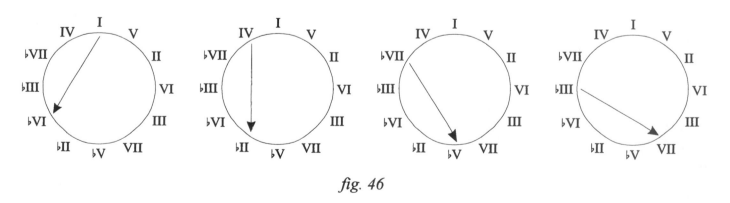

fig. 46

If we skip four positions clockwise from our starting point we have a seventh or five and a half steps. Again this holds true regardless of where you start (fig 47).

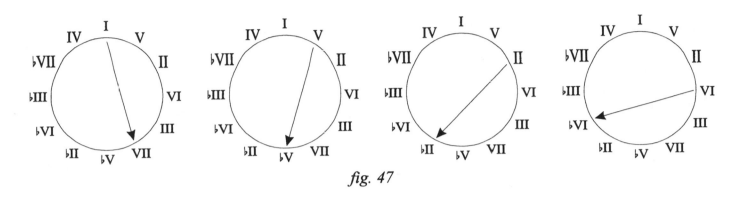

fig. 47

If we skip four positions counterclockwise we get a minor second or a half-step. A minor second is an inverted seventh (fig.48).

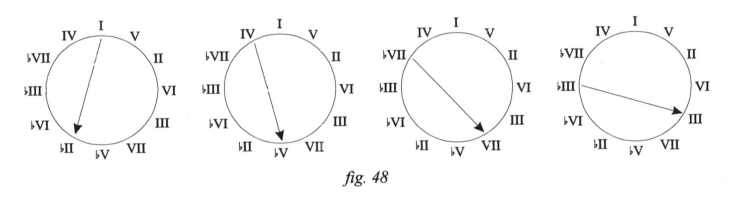

fig. 48

And if we shoot directly across from our starting point we get a flatted fifth (fig. 49).

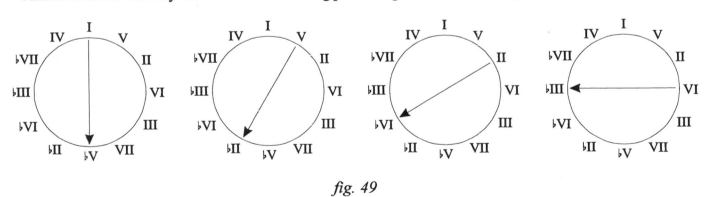

fig. 49

CIRCLE PROGRESSIONS

Now that we understand the circle of fifths we can start on the next type of progression known as circle progressions. In jazz and popular music you hear musicians talking about the II, V, I. The II, V, I is the first basic circle progression derived from the circle of fifths. Observe the diagram on the right, we start at the II position on the circle and move counterclockwise to the V position then to the I position (fig. 50).

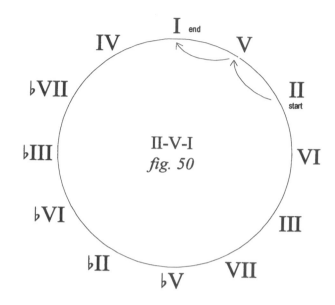

Now we move to the next basic circle progression which is the VI, II, V, I. The same principal applies here. We start at the VI position and move counter-clockwise to the II position then to the V position and end up at the I position (fig. 51).

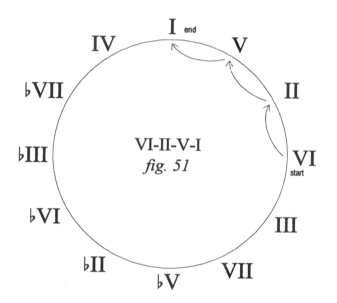

Once again the next in line for the basic circle progressions is the III, VI, II, V, I. We start at the III position and move counter-clockwise to the VI position then to the II position then to the V position then we end up at the I position (fig. 52).

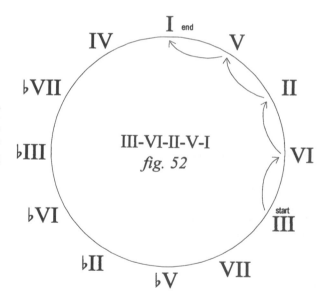

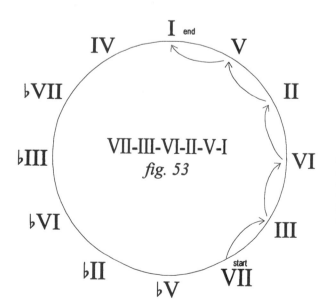

The next basic circle progression is the VII, III, VI, II, V, I. We start at the VII position and just like the other progression move counterclockwise to the III position then to the VI position then to the II postition then to the V position and end up at the I position (fig. 53). See a pattern taking place? Good.

The last of the basic circle progressions throws us a curve ball. Instead of starting at the ♭V position and continuing counterclockwise, it starts at the IV position then shoots across to the VII position and from the VII continues counter-clockwise along the circle of fifths as the other progressions on the previous page. This is the IV, VII, III, VI, II, V, I (fig. 54).

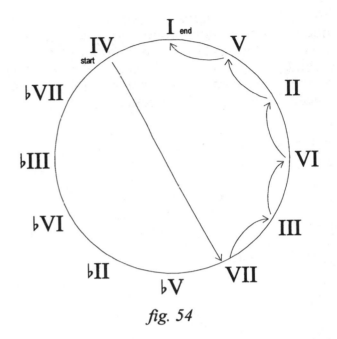

fig. 54

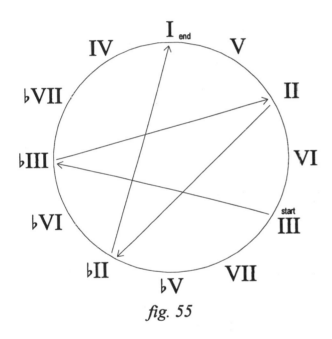

fig. 55

The next type of progression is the chromatic progression. But as far as I'm concerned, the chromatic progression comes from the circle of fifths too (fig. 55).

Circle progressions can be combined with chromatic progessions in creating songs as figure 56 demonstrates.

In fact, you can combine circle, diatonic, and chromatic progessions when creating songs.

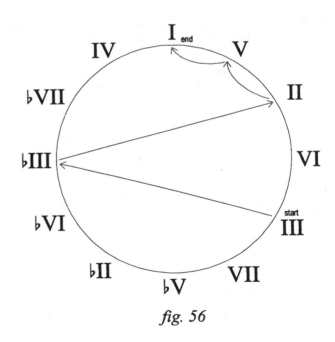

fig. 56

When creating progressions you are not limited to just using circle progressions like II-V-I etc. or diatonic or chromatic progressions. You can use any root motion. Your patterns can be symmetric or very methodical or highly random. In the first example we have a root motion of second, fifth, second, fifth, second, fifth, etc. In the next three examples we have symmetrical patterns as the basis for our root motion, namely a star, a triangle, and a square (fig. 57). These can be called "Scale Tone Degree" progressions.

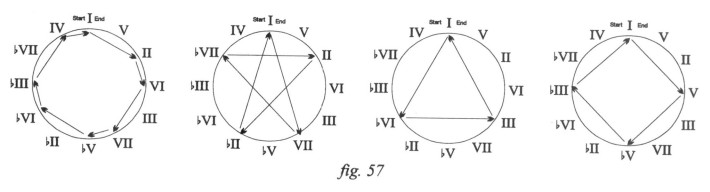

fig. 57

In the next four examples we have totally random root motion (fig. 58).

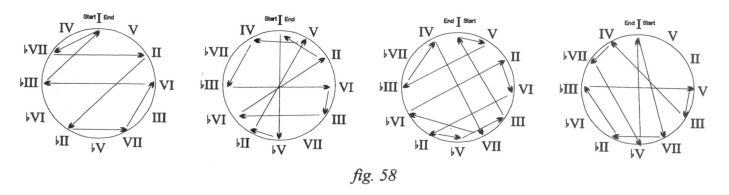

fig. 58

When creating these "Scale Tone Degree" progressions picture an X and Y axis. The X axis represents the root motion and the Y axis represents the chord alterations (fig. 59).

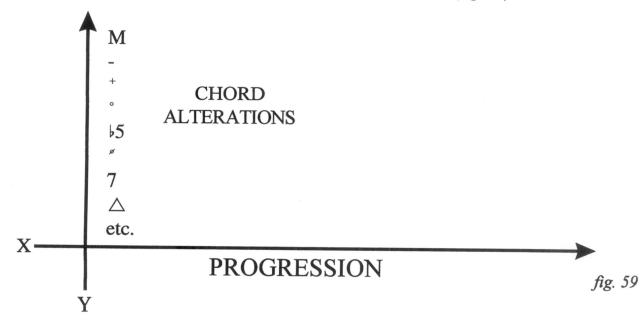

fig. 59

Let's make a progression on the circle of fifths then we'll transfer our root motion to "measure" format (fig. 60 & fig. 61).

Next we'll add chord alterations (fig. 62). In fact the same "scale tone degree" progression can yield many progressions even though the root motion is the same. Each progression will sound totally different than the other. Then you have 12 different keys to play with.

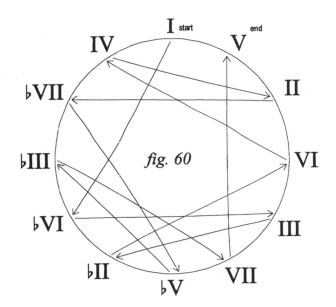

fig. 60

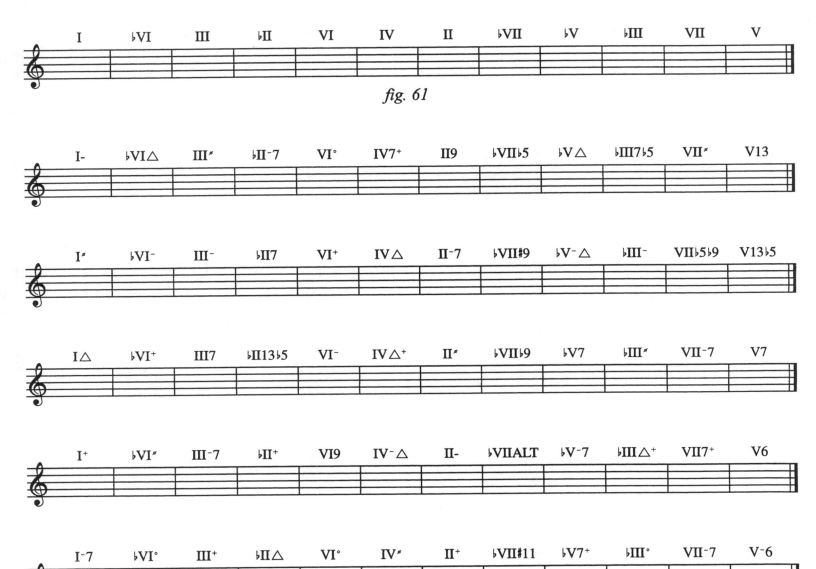

fig. 61

fig. 62

Let's take the first alteration and add pitch. We'll do it in seven different keys (fig.63). Just one root motion or scale tone degree progression can yield hundreds of progressions between alterations and pitch. We've included a bunch of scale tone degree progressions starting with four measure progressions to keep you busy. Most of all you now know how to make your own.

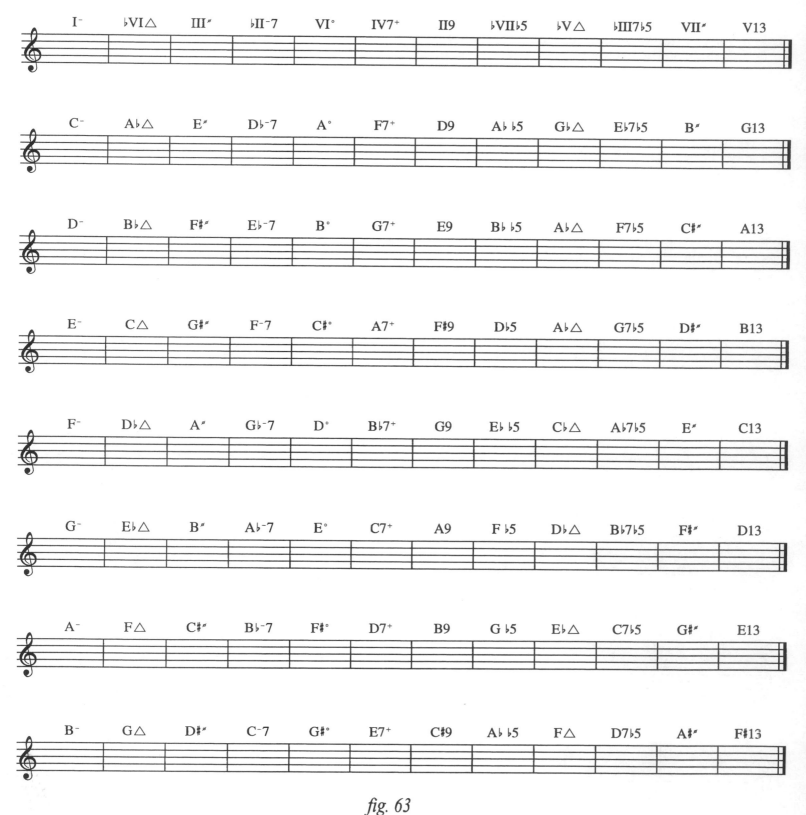

fig. 63

20

4 MEASURE SCALE TONE DEGREE PROGRESSIONS

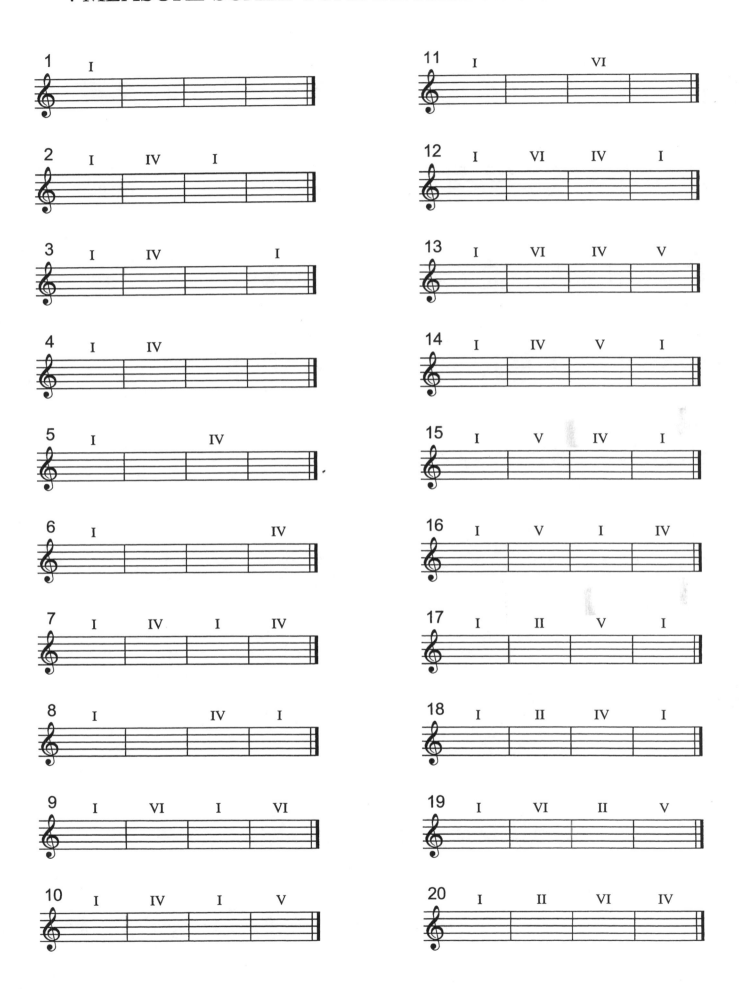

4 MEASURE SCALE TONE DEGREE PROGRESSIONS

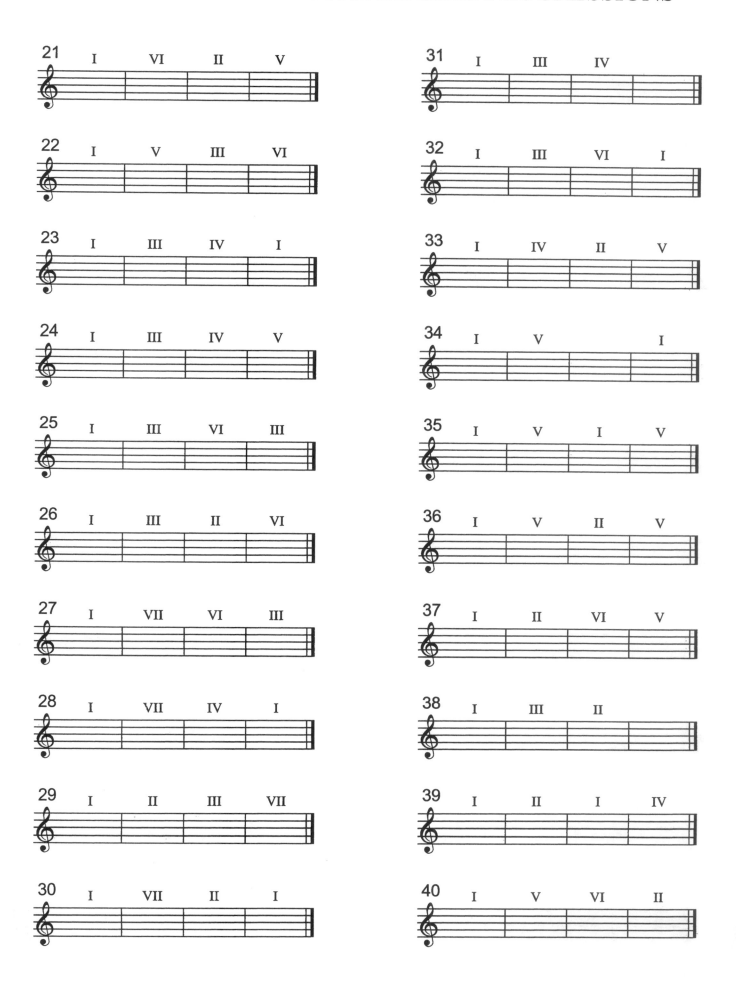

4 MEASURE SCALE TONE DEGREE PROGRESSIONS

SCALE TONE DEGREE PROGRESSIONS

ADD CHORD TYPES: M (maj) ⁻ (min) ⌀ (half-dim) 7 (dom) ⁺ (aug) ° (dim) with extensions / variations

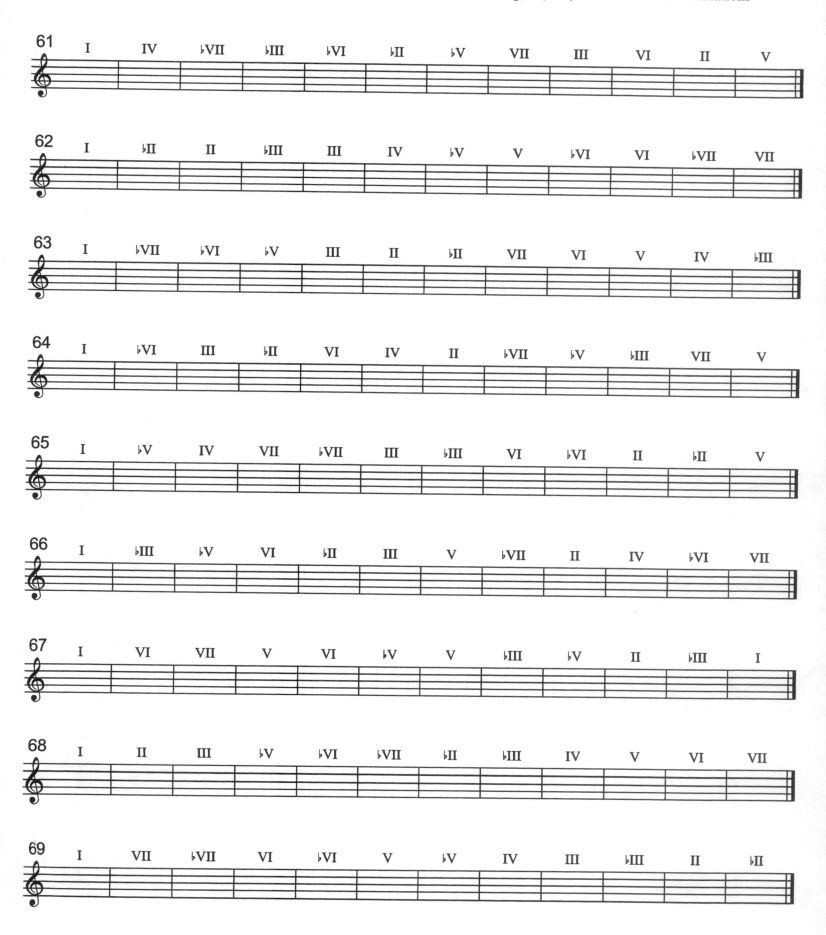

SCALE TONE DEGREE PROGRESSIONS

ADD CHORD TYPES: M (maj) – (min) ᵍ (half-dim) 7 (dom) ⁺ (aug) ° (dim) with extensions / variations

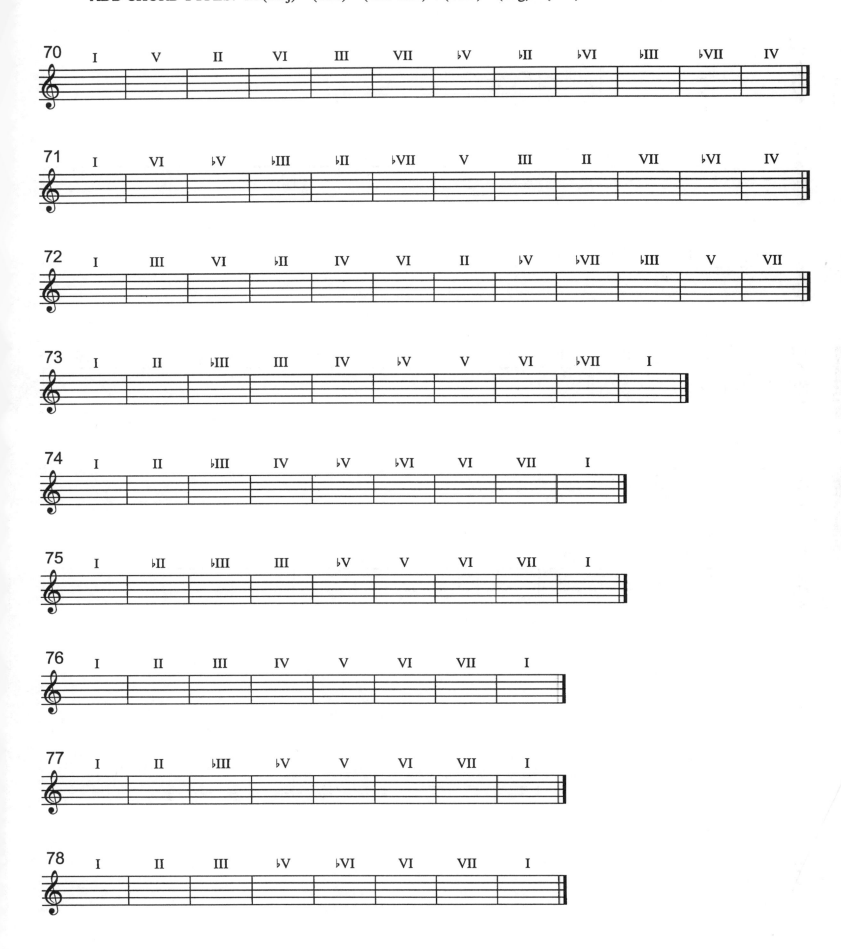

SCALE TONE DEGREE PROGRESSIONS

ADD CHORD TYPES: M (maj) ⁻ (min) ø (half-dim) 7 (dom) ⁺ (aug) ° (dim) with extensions / variations

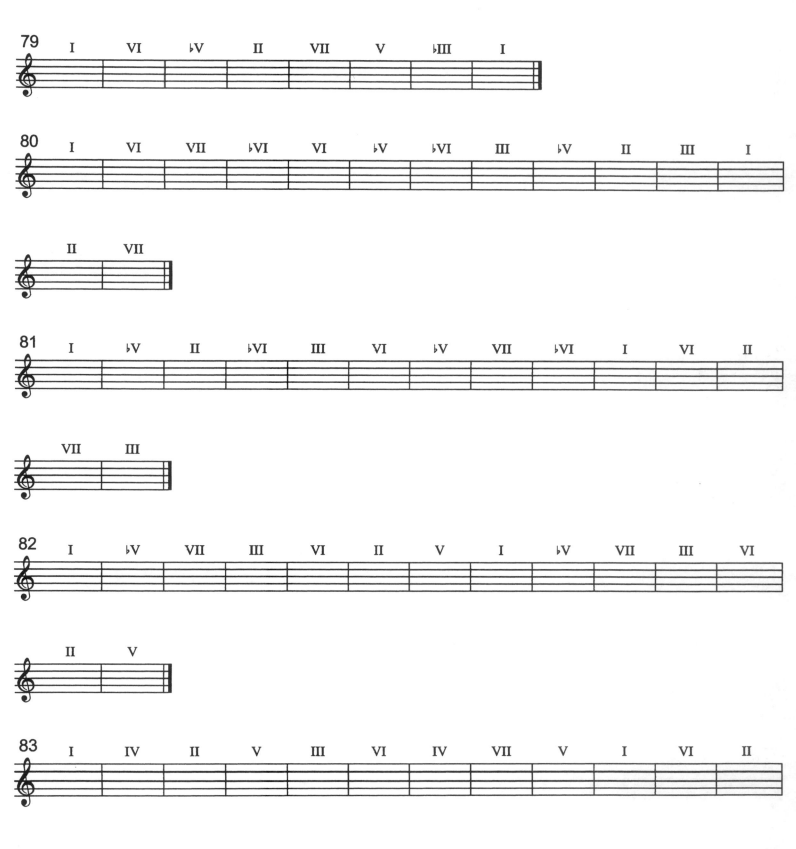

SCALE TONE DEGREE PROGRESSIONS

ADD CHORD TYPES: M (maj) ⁻ (min) ⁰̸ (half-dim) 7 (dom) ⁺ (aug) ° (dim) with extensions / variations

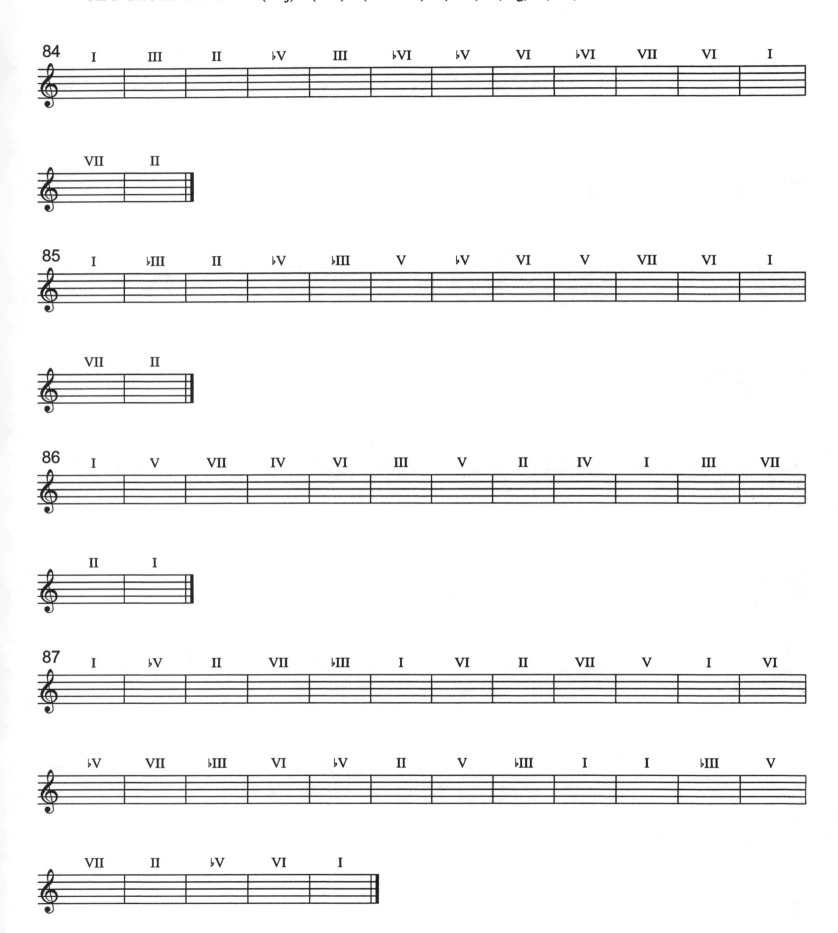

SCALE TONE DEGREE PROGRESSIONS

ADD CHORD TYPES: M (maj) ⁻ (min) ⁿ (half-dim) 7 (dom) ⁺ (aug) ° (dim) with extensions / variations

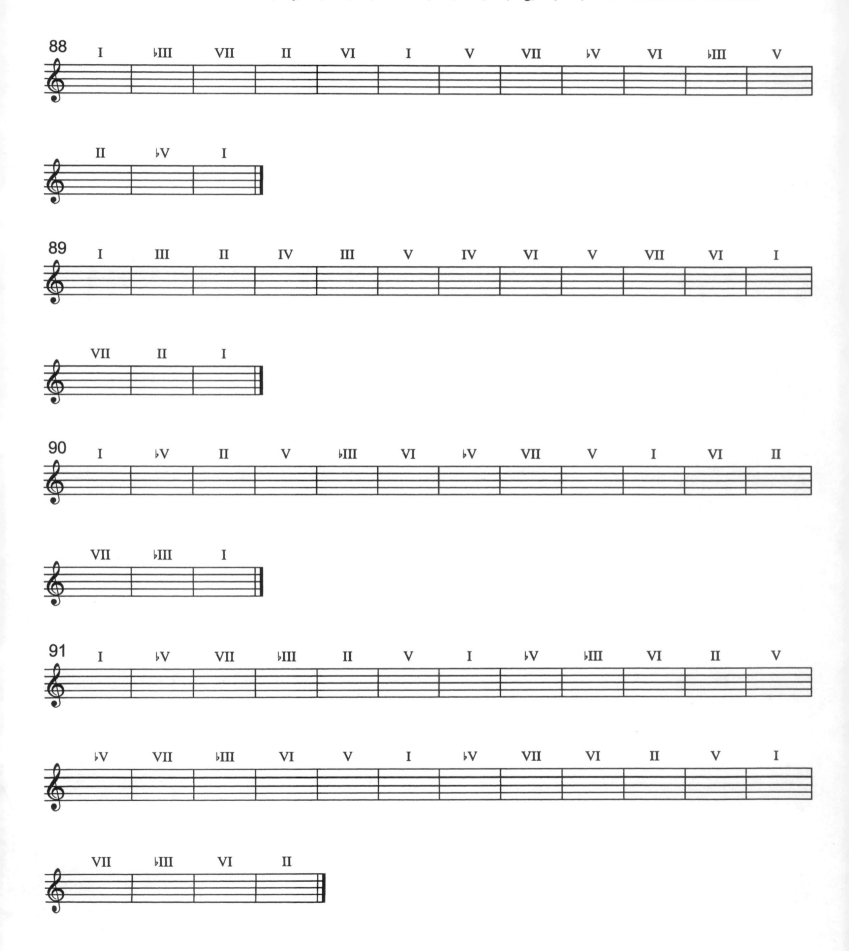

SCALE TONE DEGREE PROGRESSIONS

ADD CHORD TYPES: M (maj) ⁻ (min) ø (half-dim) 7 (dom) ⁺ (aug) ° (dim) with extensions / variations

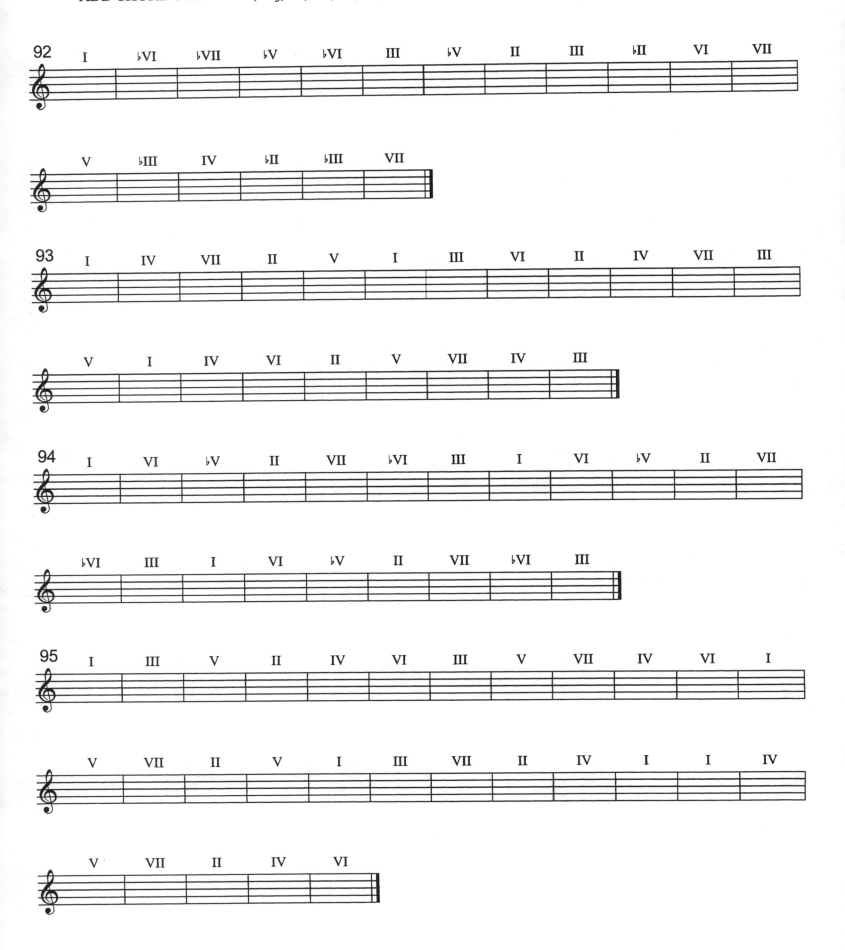

SCALE TONE DEGREE PROGRESSIONS

ADD CHORD TYPES: M (maj) ⁻ (min) ⌀ (half-dim) 7 (dom) ⁺ (aug) ° (dim) with extensions / variations

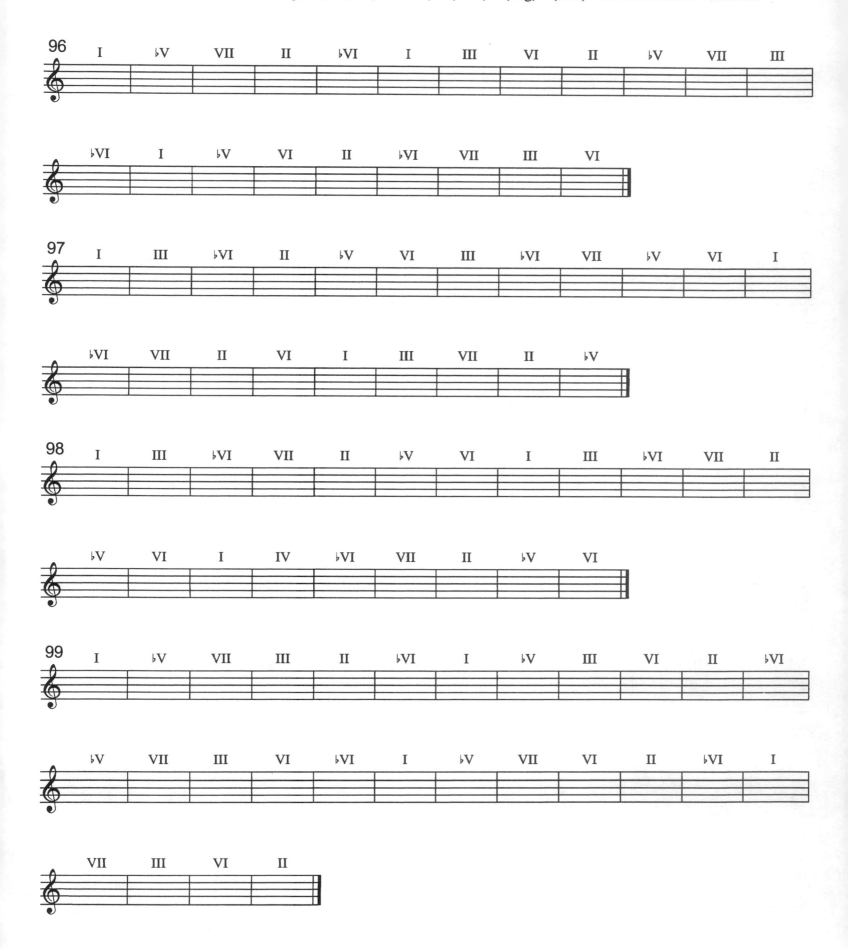

SCALE TONE DEGREE PROGRESSIONS

ADD CHORD TYPES: M (maj) ⁻ (min) ⌀ (half-dim) 7 (dom) ⁺ (aug) ° (dim) with extensions / variations

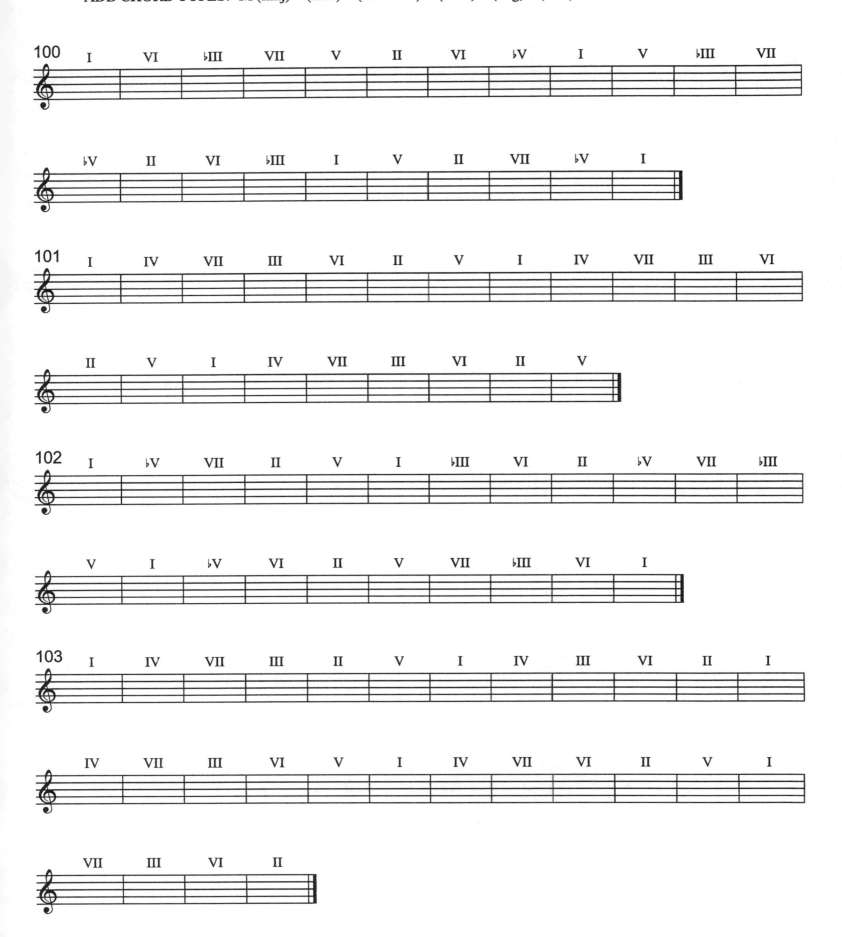

SCALE TONE DEGREE PROGRESSIONS

ADD CHORD TYPES: M (maj) ⁻ (min) ⌀ (half-dim) 7 (dom) ⁺ (aug) ° (dim) with extensions / variations

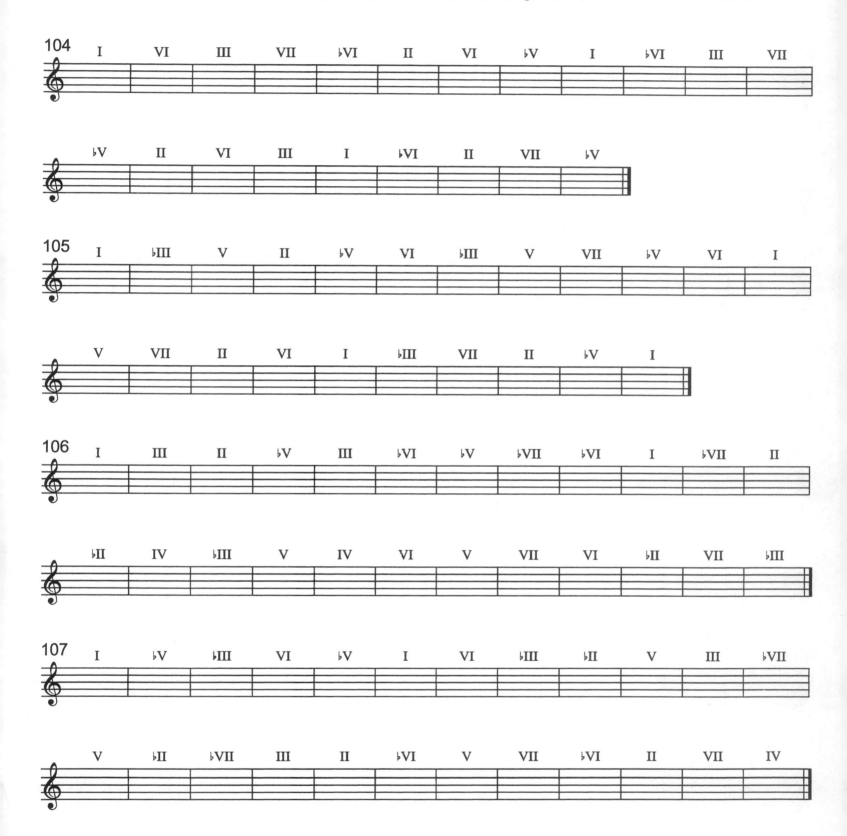

SCALE TONE DEGREE PROGRESSIONS

ADD CHORD TYPES: M (maj) ⁻ (min) ⌀ (half-dim) 7 (dom) ⁺ (aug) ° (dim) with extensions / variations

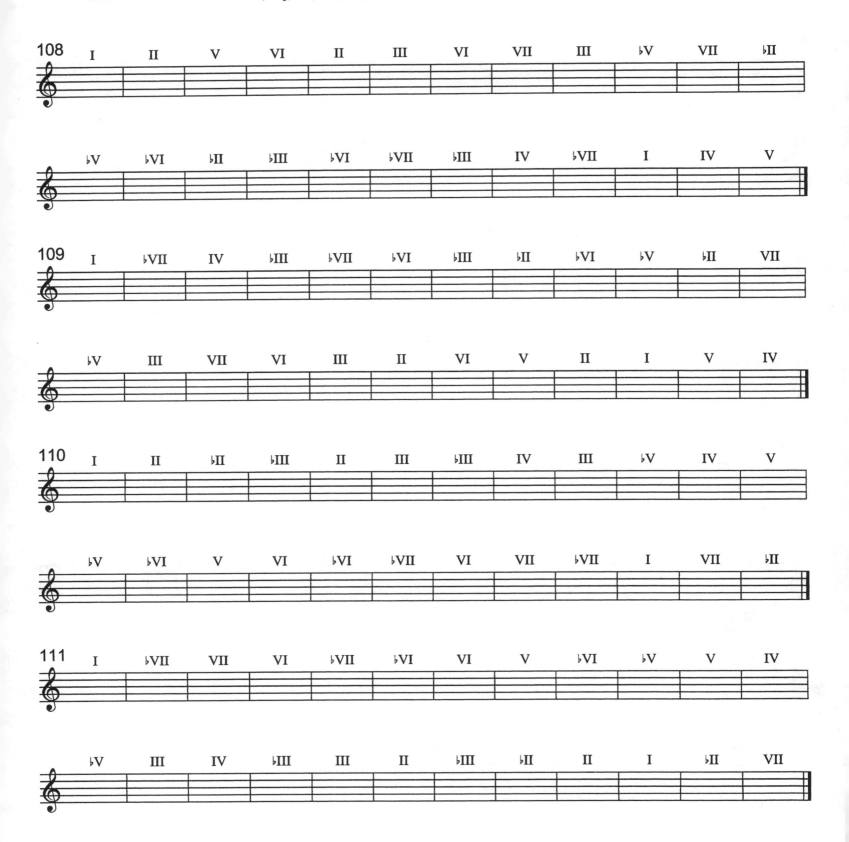

SCALE TONE DEGREE PROGRESSIONS

ADD CHORD TYPES: M (maj) ⁻ (min) ᵡ (half-dim) 7 (dom) ⁺ (aug) ° (dim) with extensions / variations

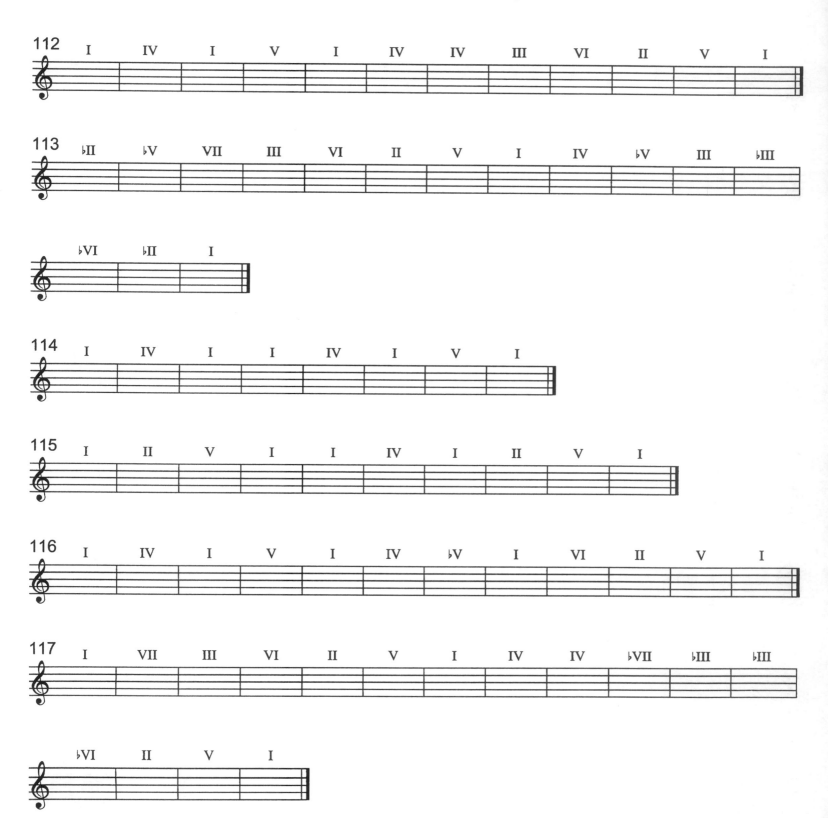

SCALE TONE DEGREE PROGRESSIONS

ADD CHORD TYPES: M (maj) ⁻ (min) ⁿ (half-dim) 7 (dom) ⁺ (aug) ° (dim) with extensions / variations

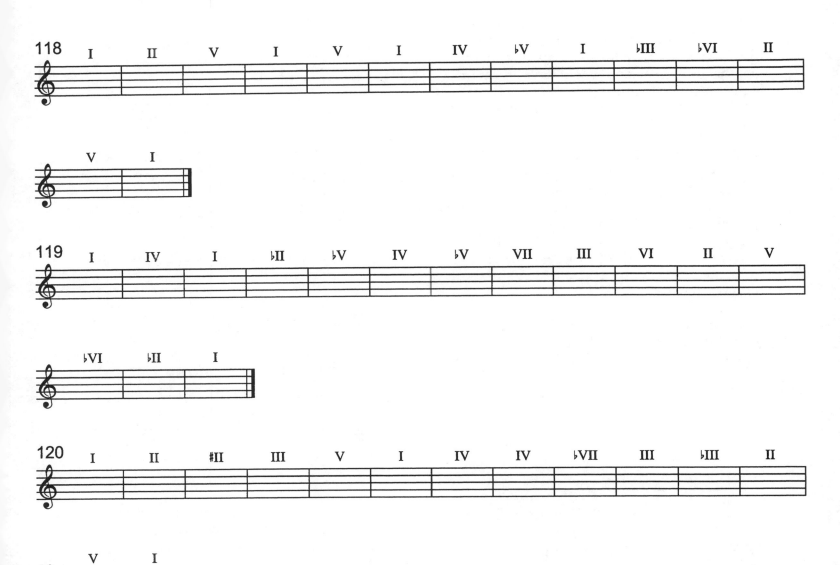

INSTANT SONG CREATOR - THE A A B A METHOD

The method of creating progressions using the "X & Y" axis alterations of scale tone degree progressions is great for creativity, but chances are that only a select few will have an ear that can appreciate them. If you want a larger listening audience you have to keep your music simple.

In this section there are a whole slew of four measure progressions voiced in straight Major & Minor open voicings.

Here's how it works. There is a method of creating songs known as the A A B A method. "A" represents a short progression, usually four measures, and "B" represents a short progression.

What this means is, you play the progression, repeat it, play the next progression and return to the first progression (fig.64).

But you are not limited to A A B A combinations.

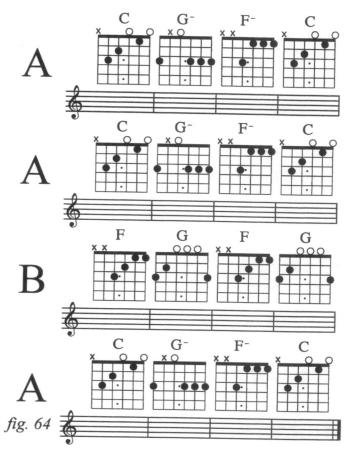

fig. 64

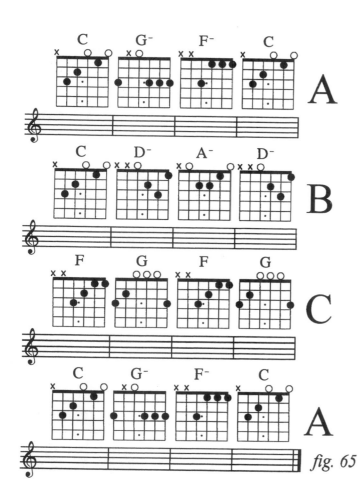

fig. 65

The example to the left (fig. 65) demonstrates an A B C A combination. Observe that the second line is different from the A A B A example above.

You can do A B B A combinations, or A B A B combinations, or A B C D combinations, or A B A C combinations. Get the picture?

The only limitations are those that you place upon yourself.

Remember, the "A", the "B", the "C", the "D", of the A A B A etc., represent progressions and not pitch.

In essence, the A A B A means, little progressions strung together to make a big progression. In other words, a song.

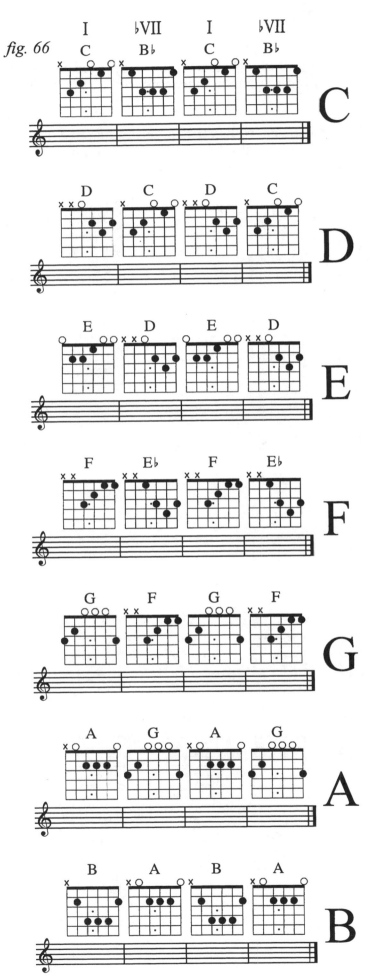

fig. 66

The four measure progressions in this section are graphed out in two columns per page. Each column is one progression graphed out in the keys of C,D,E,F,G,A,B, using open chord voicings. At the very top of each column is the baseline or root motion. See figure 66.

This section is then divided into sub-sections, as in,

> progressions that start on the I chord
> progressions that start on the II chord
> progressions that start on the III chord
> progressions that start on the IV chord
> progressions that start on the V chord
> progressions that start on the VI chord
> progressions that start on the ♭VII chord

In case you are wondering why it's the ♭VII and not the VII chord, the ♭VII chord for this type of progression sounds better.

Notice that progressions starting on the II thru ♭VII chord sub-sections, are still listed as C,D,E,F,G,A,B.

When you are creating a song with these progressions, all sub-section choices, I, II, III, etc. (in other words A A B A combinations), must be from the same key in order to stay in key, unless you are changing the key of the song for the last verse and chorus.

As you get more familiar with these progressions you can revoice them or extend them. A major can become a major seventh or you can use a dominant seventh or sixth or augmented etc. Whatever alteration you make depends upon your creativity. You will be the judge as to whether it sounds good or not. Of course, if you think it sounds good and people start throwing rotten fruit at you, you might have to reconsider the alterations you have made.

CHORDS USED IN 4 MEASURE PROGRESSIONS

The chord voicings in this section are open chord voicings, which means they are played in the open position, by the nut, and incorporate open strings. A few of the voicings, however, do not have open strings.

On the following pages, for the benefit of the beginner, each chord has the fingering mapped out. Then the intervallic formula is mapped out with the translation into the note, or pitch, equivalent next to it. Last but not least the chord voicing as it appears in notation.

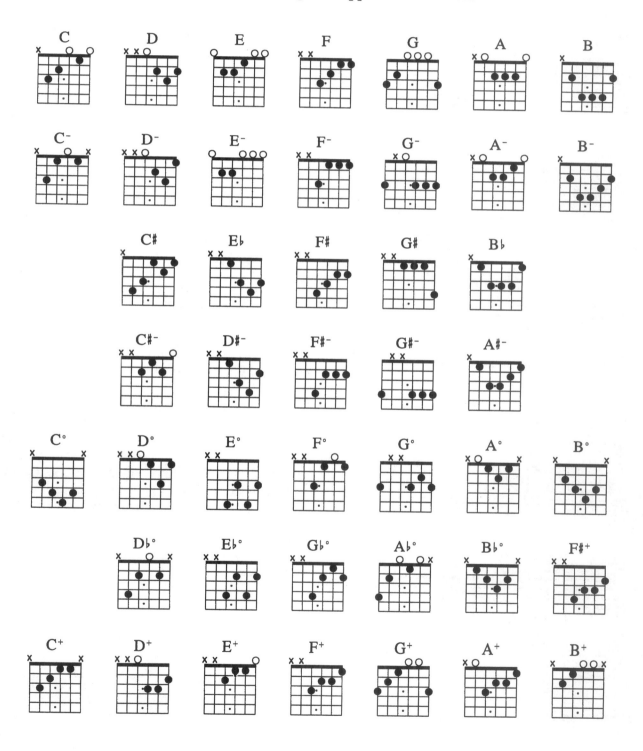

C

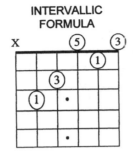

FINGERING   INTERVALLIC FORMULA   NOTES

D

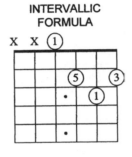

FINGERING   INTERVALLIC FORMULA   NOTES

E

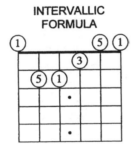

FINGERING   INTERVALLIC FORMULA   NOTES

F

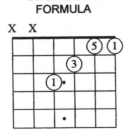

FINGERING   INTERVALLIC FORMULA   NOTES

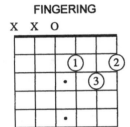
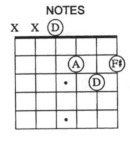
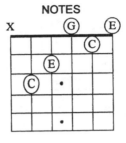

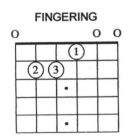
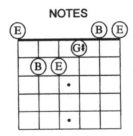

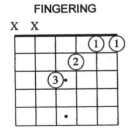
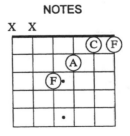

G

FINGERING

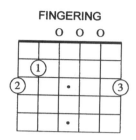

INTERVALLIC FORMULA

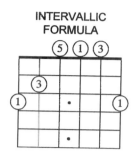

NOTES

A

FINGERING

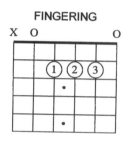

INTERVALLIC FORMULA

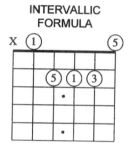

NOTES

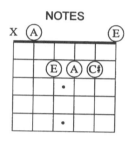

B

FINGERING

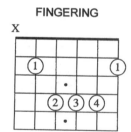

INTERVALLIC FORMULA

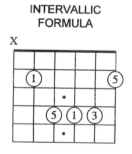

NOTES

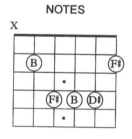

C⁻

FINGERING

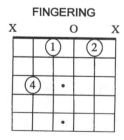

INTERVALLIC FORMULA

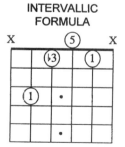

NOTES

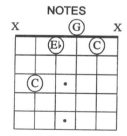

D⁻

FINGERING
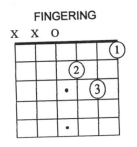

INTERVALLIC FORMULA
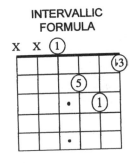

NOTES

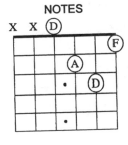

E⁻

FINGERING
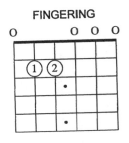

INTERVALLIC FORMULA
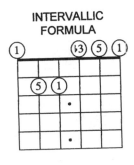

NOTES
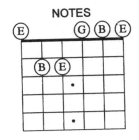

F⁻

FINGERING
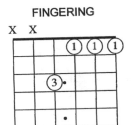

INTERVALLIC FORMULA
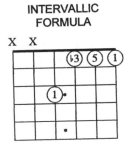

NOTES
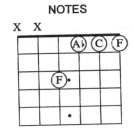

G⁻

FINGERING
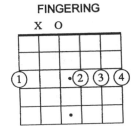

INTERVALLIC FORMULA
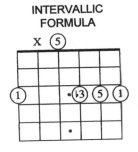

NOTES
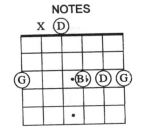

41

A⁻

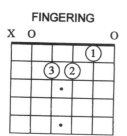

FINGERING

X O   O

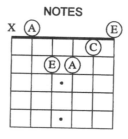

INTERVALLIC
FORMULA

X ①   ⑤
             ♭3
⑤ ①

NOTES

X Ⓐ   Ⓔ
             Ⓒ
Ⓔ Ⓐ

B⁻

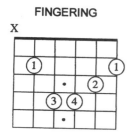

FINGERING

X

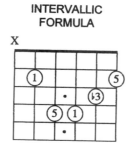

INTERVALLIC
FORMULA

X

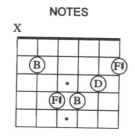

NOTES

X

C#

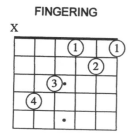

FINGERING

X

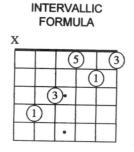

INTERVALLIC
FORMULA

X

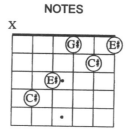

NOTES

X

E♭

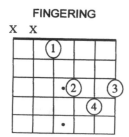

FINGERING

X X

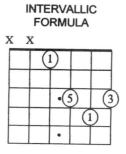

INTERVALLIC
FORMULA

X X

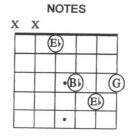

NOTES

X X

F#

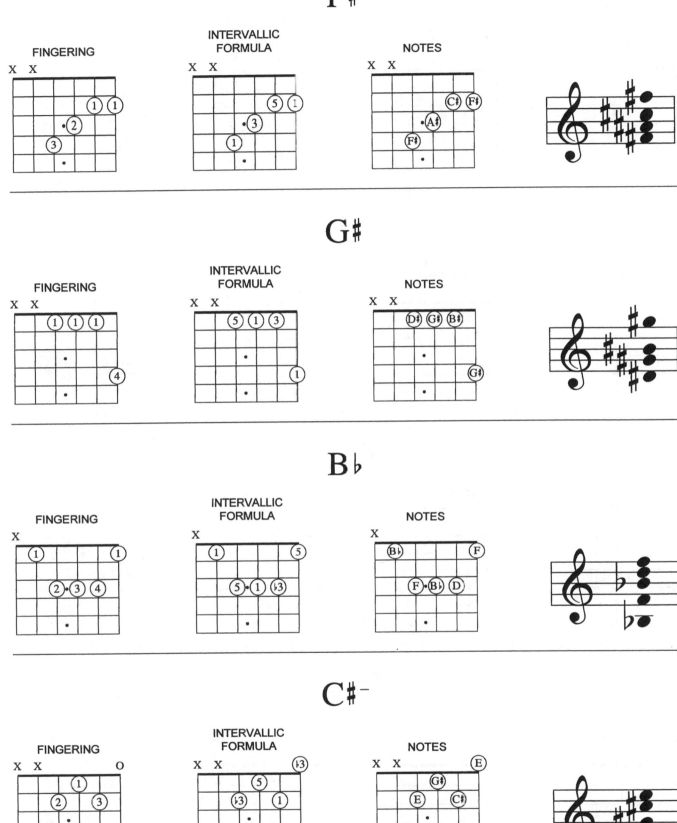

FINGERING

INTERVALLIC FORMULA

NOTES

G#

FINGERING

INTERVALLIC FORMULA

NOTES

B♭

FINGERING

INTERVALLIC FORMULA

NOTES

C#⁻

FINGERING

INTERVALLIC FORMULA

NOTES

D#−

FINGERING	INTERVALLIC FORMULA	NOTES	
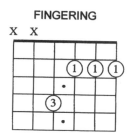	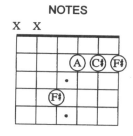		

F#−

FINGERING	INTERVALLIC FORMULA	NOTES	
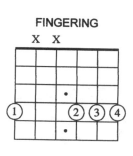	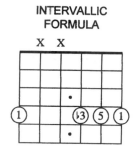	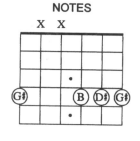	

G#−

FINGERING	INTERVALLIC FORMULA	NOTES	
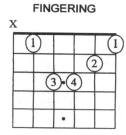	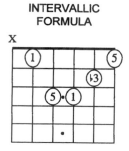	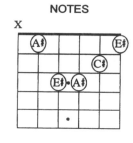	

A#−

FINGERING	INTERVALLIC FORMULA	NOTES	
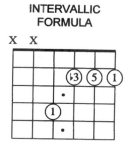			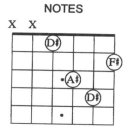

C°

FINGERING	INTERVALLIC FORMULA	NOTES

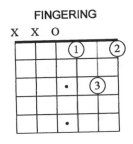 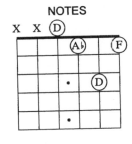 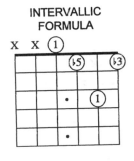

D°

FINGERING	INTERVALLIC FORMULA	NOTES

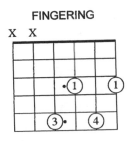 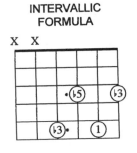 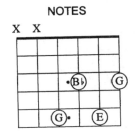 

E°

FINGERING	INTERVALLIC FORMULA	NOTES

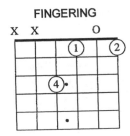 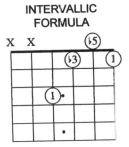 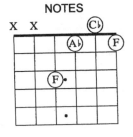 

F°

FINGERING	INTERVALLIC FORMULA	NOTES

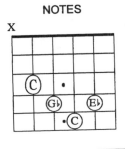  

G°

FINGERING

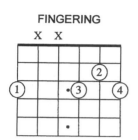

INTERVALLIC
FORMULA

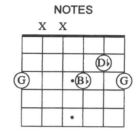

NOTES

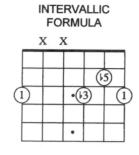

A°

FINGERING

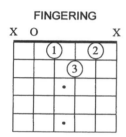

INTERVALLIC
FORMULA

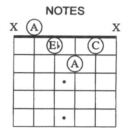

NOTES

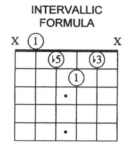

B°

FINGERING

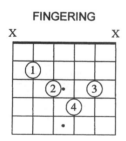

INTERVALLIC
FORMULA

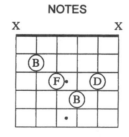

NOTES

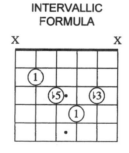

D♭°

FINGERING

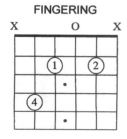

INTERVALLIC
FORMULA

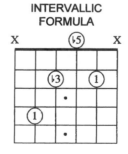

NOTES

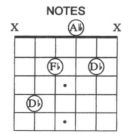

46

E♭°

FINGERING
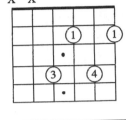

INTERVALLIC FORMULA
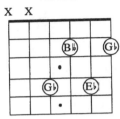

NOTES
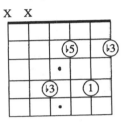

G♭°

FINGERING
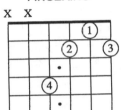

INTERVALLIC FORMULA
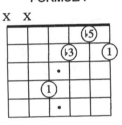

NOTES
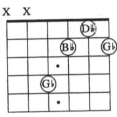

A♭°

FINGERING
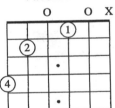

INTERVALLIC FORMULA
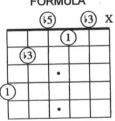

NOTES
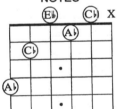

B♭°

FINGERING
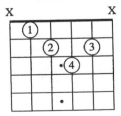

INTERVALLIC FORMULA
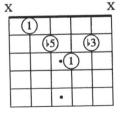

NOTES

C⁺

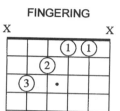

FINGERING

INTERVALLIC FORMULA

NOTES

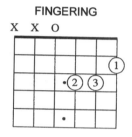 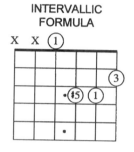  

D⁺

FINGERING

INTERVALLIC FORMULA

NOTES

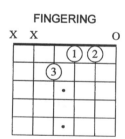 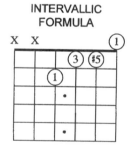 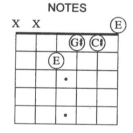 

E⁺

FINGERING

INTERVALLIC FORMULA

NOTES

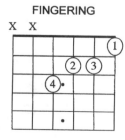 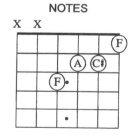 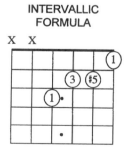 

F⁺

FINGERING

INTERVALLIC FORMULA

NOTES

G⁺

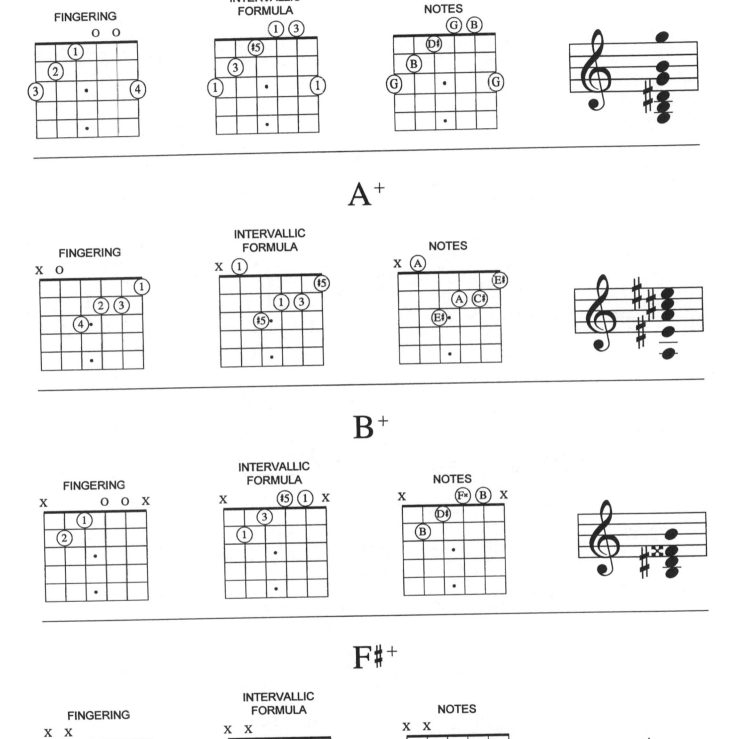

4 MEASURE PROGRESSIONS STARTING AT I

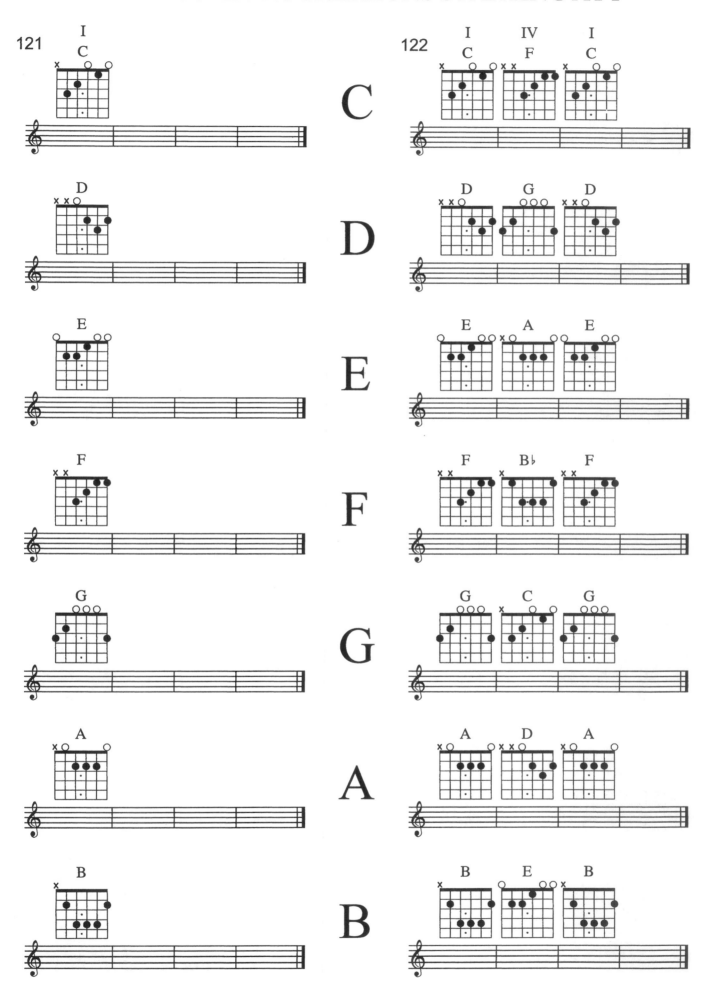

4 MEASURE PROGRESSIONS STARTING AT I

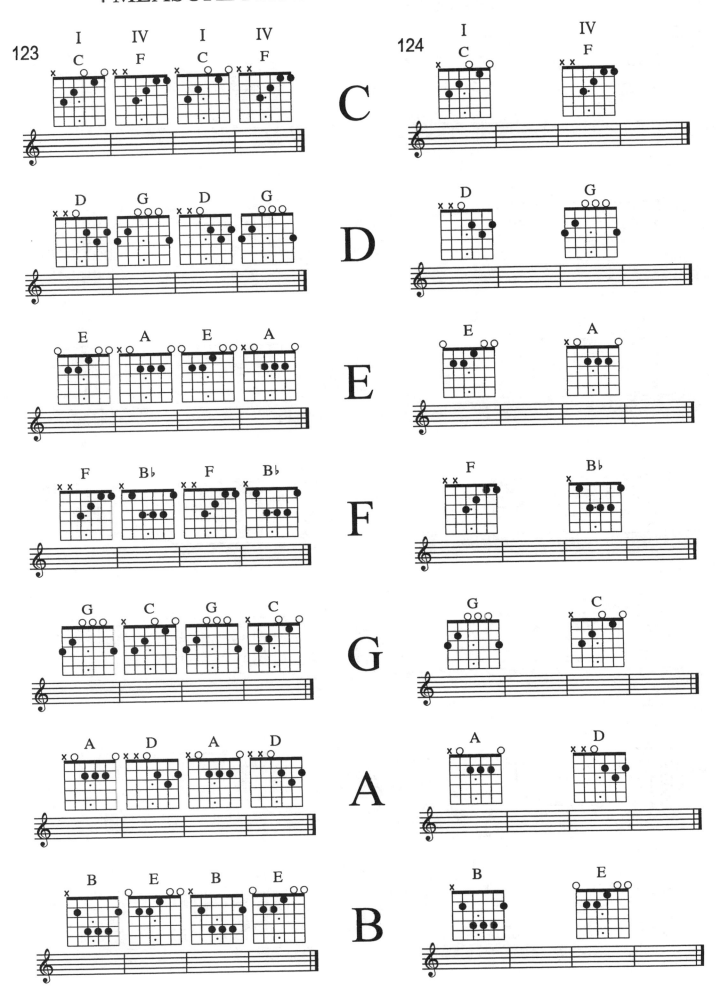

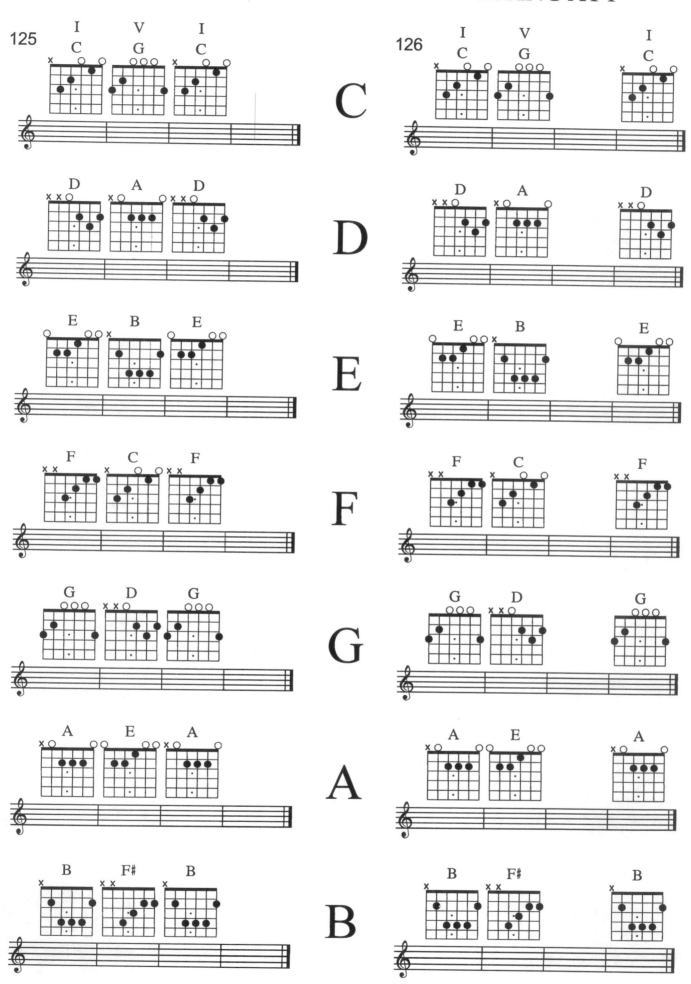

4 MEASURE PROGRESSIONS STARTING AT I

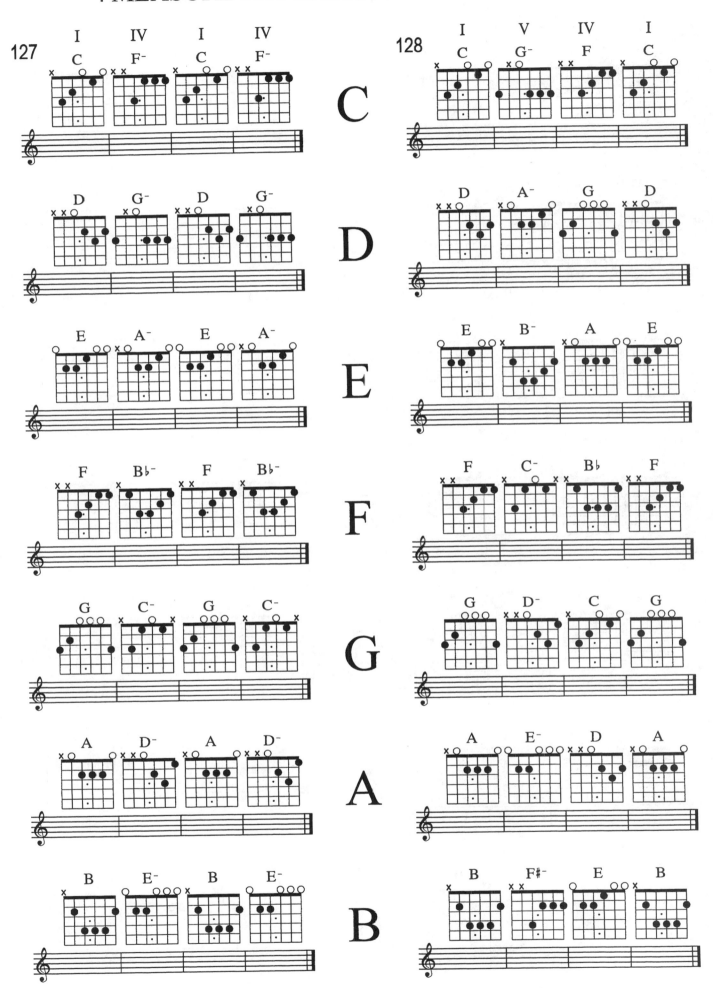

4 MEASURE PROGRESSIONS STARTING AT I

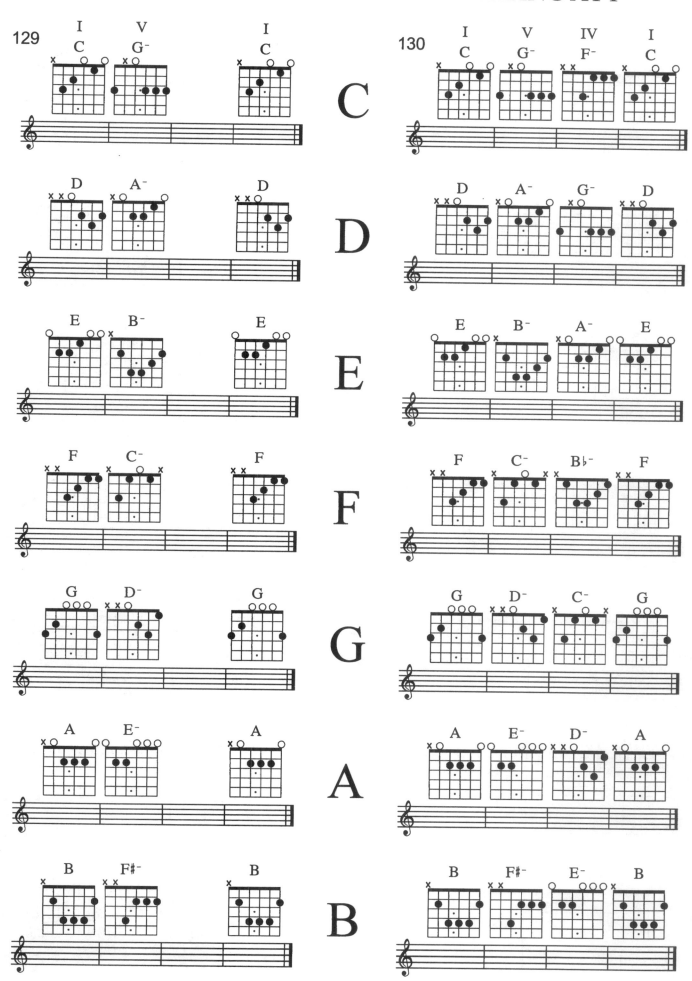

4 MEASURE PROGRESSIONS STARTING AT I

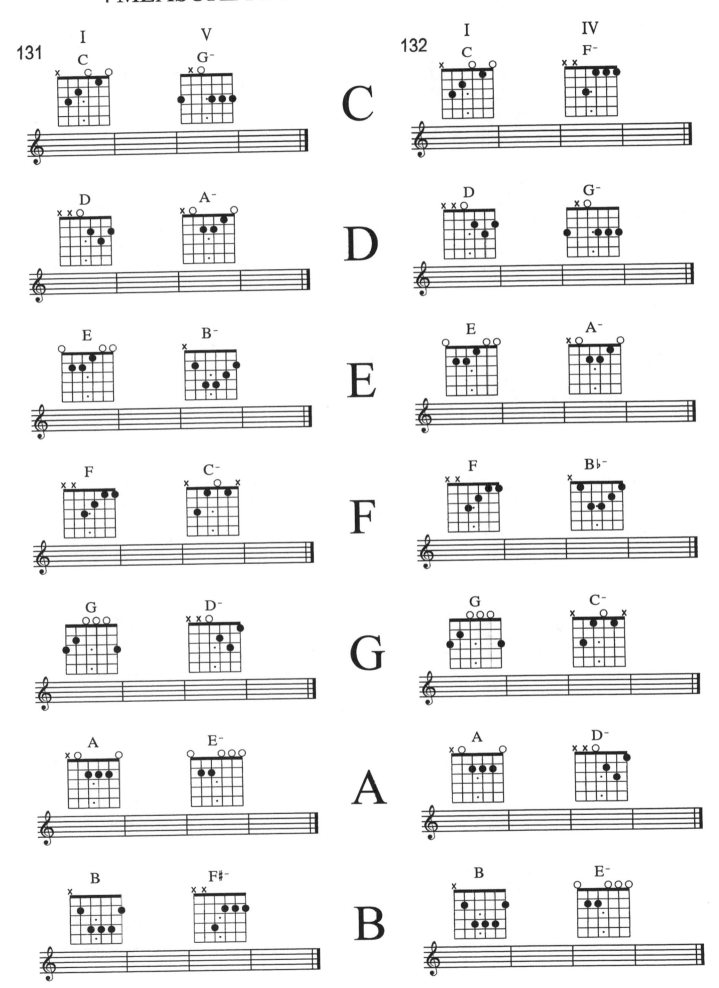

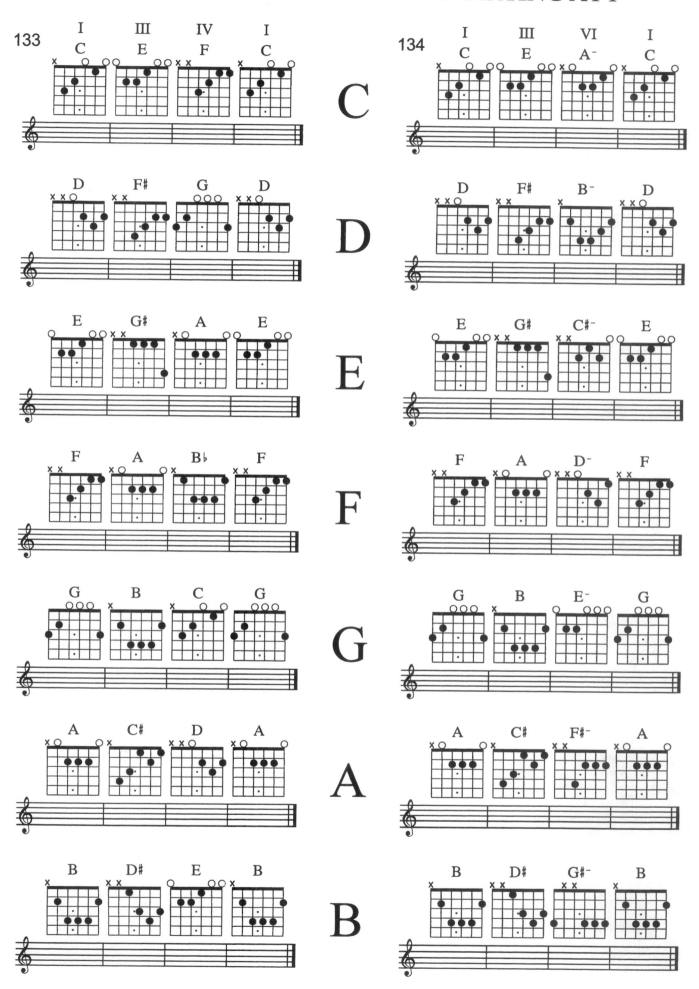

4 MEASURE PROGRESSIONS STARTING AT I

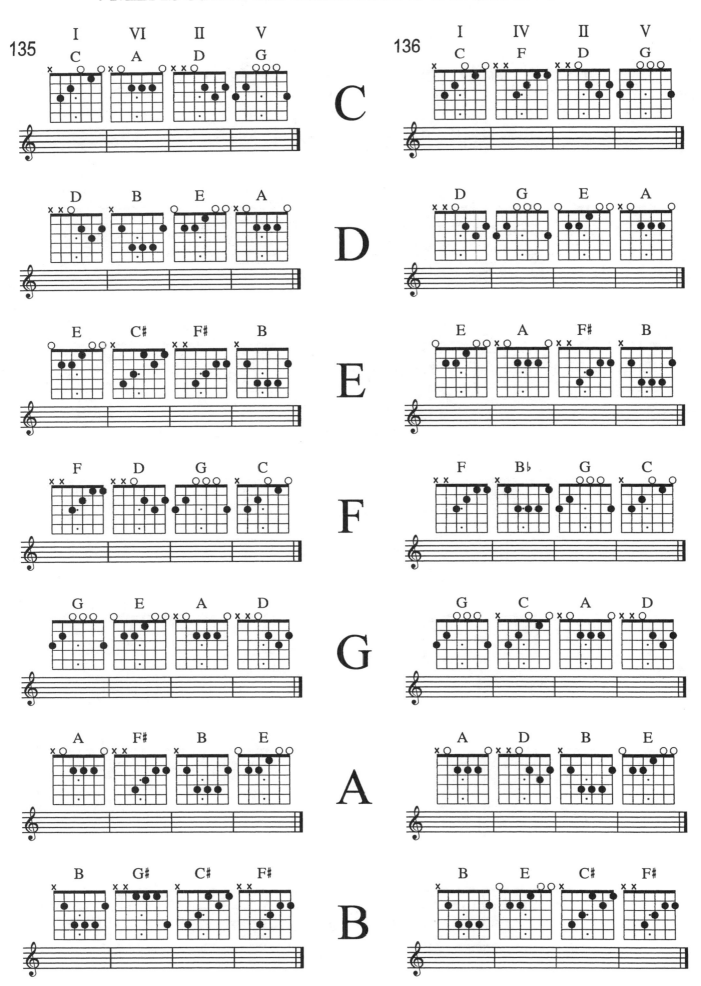

4 MEASURE PROGRESSIONS STARTING AT I

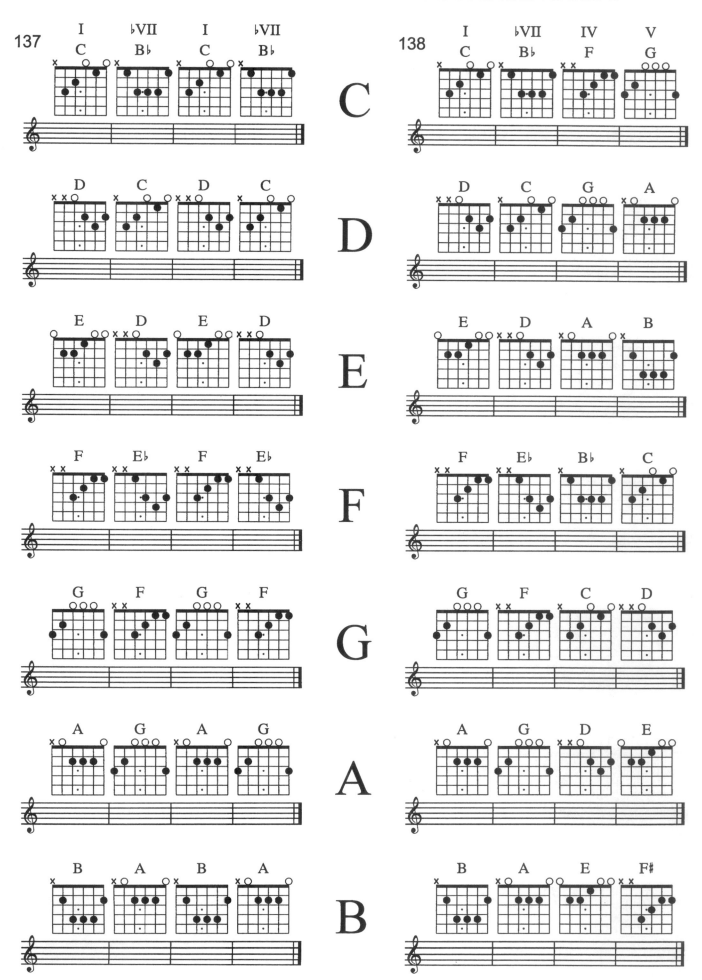

4 MEASURE PROGRESSIONS STARTING AT I

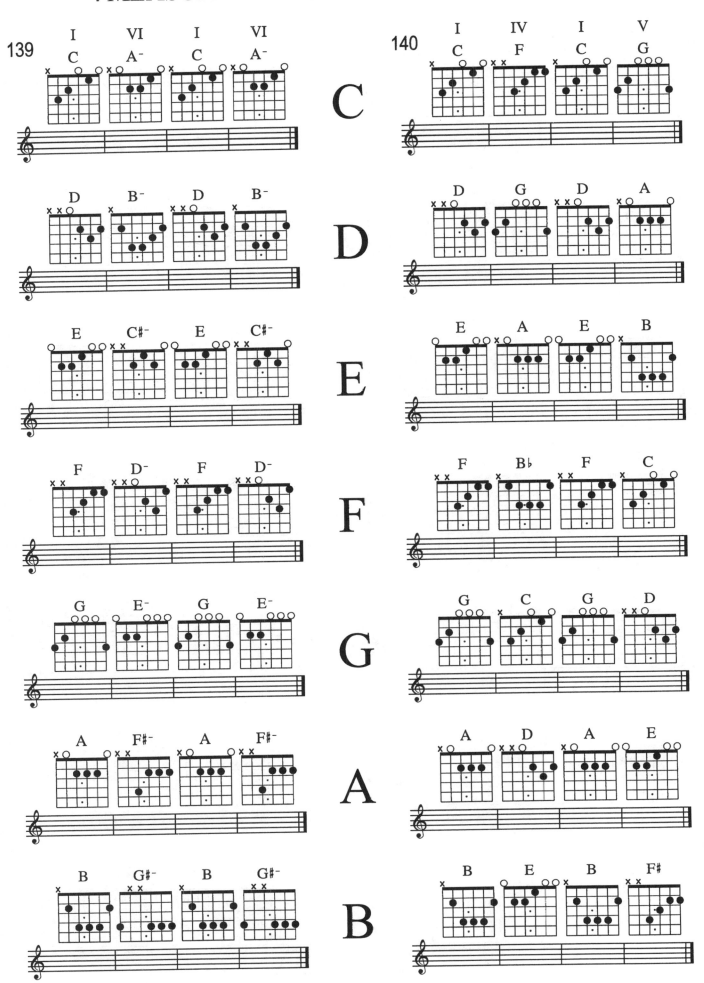

4 MEASURE PROGRESSIONS STARTING AT I

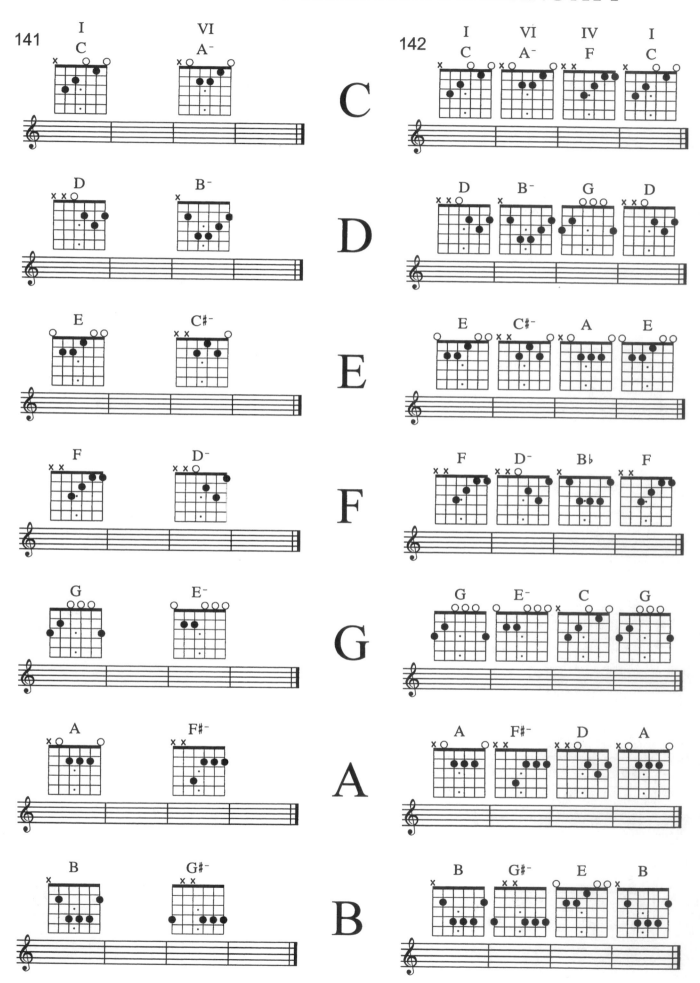

4 MEASURE PROGRESSIONS STARTING AT I

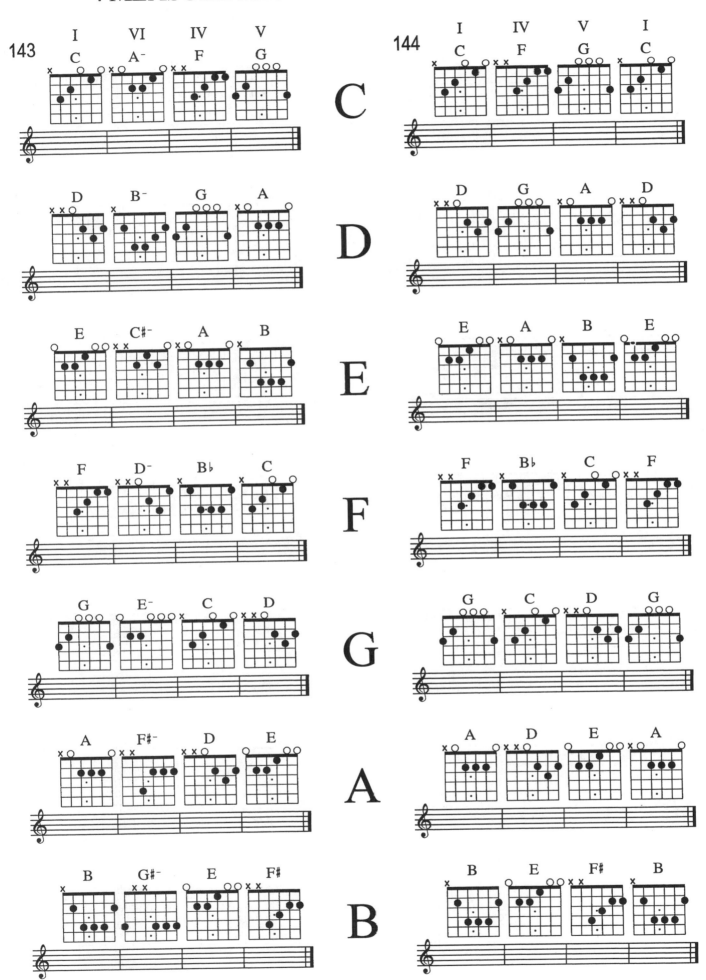

4 MEASURE PROGRESSIONS STARTING AT I

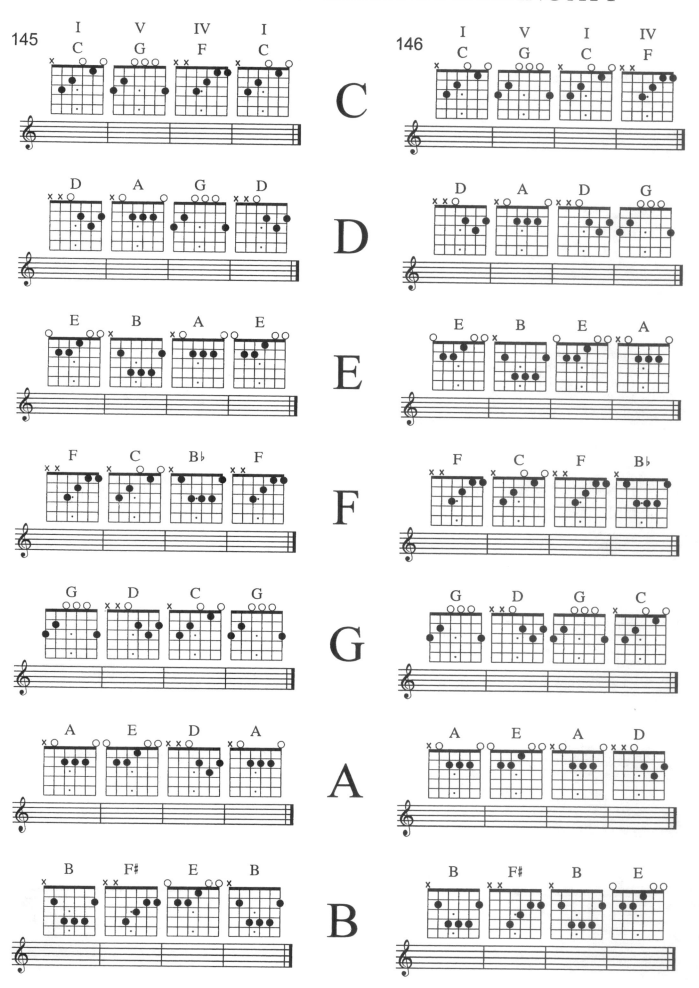

4 MEASURE PROGRESSIONS STARTING AT I

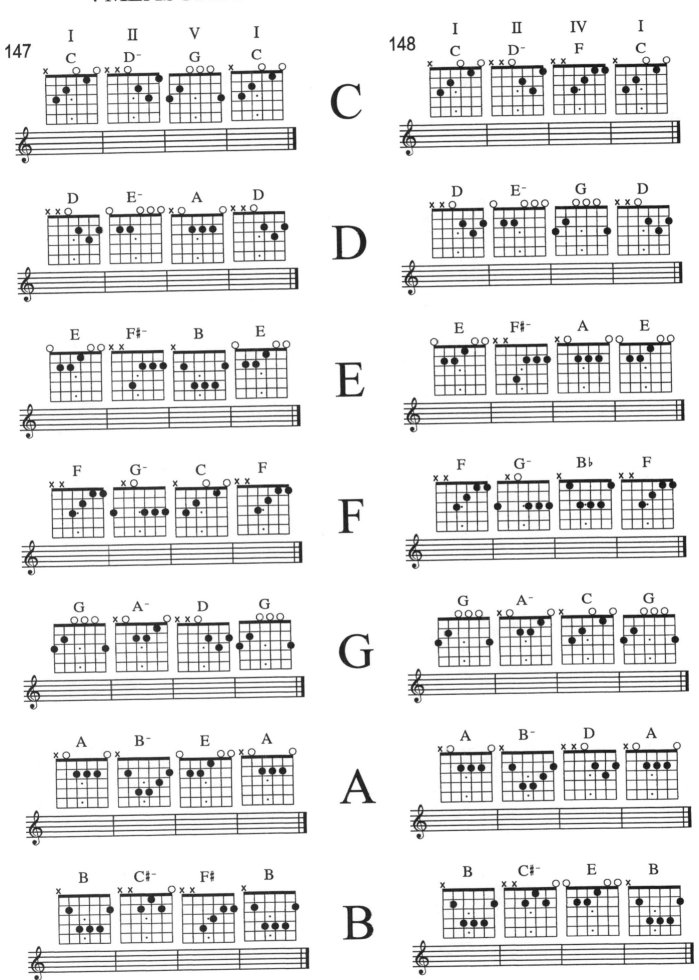

4 MEASURE PROGRESSIONS STARTING AT I

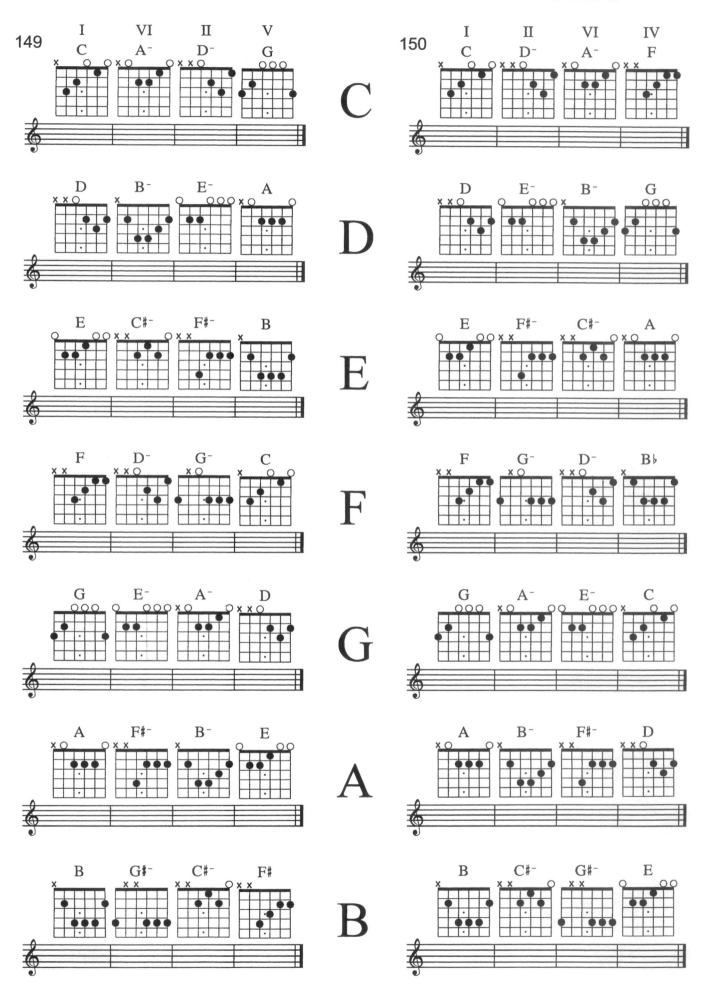

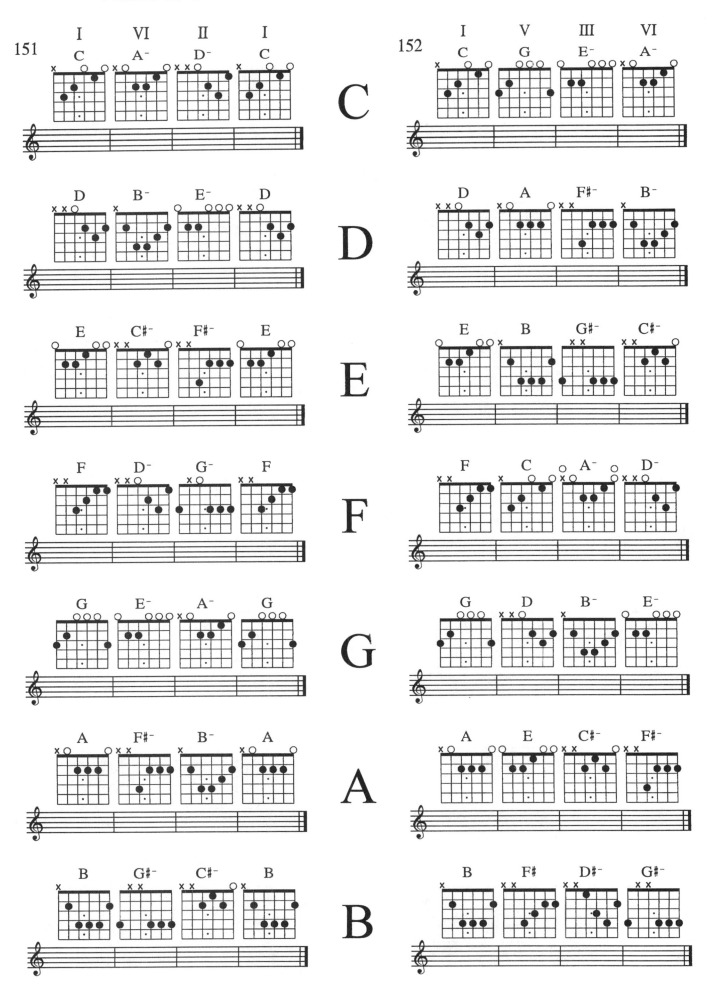

4 MEASURE PROGRESSIONS STARTING AT I

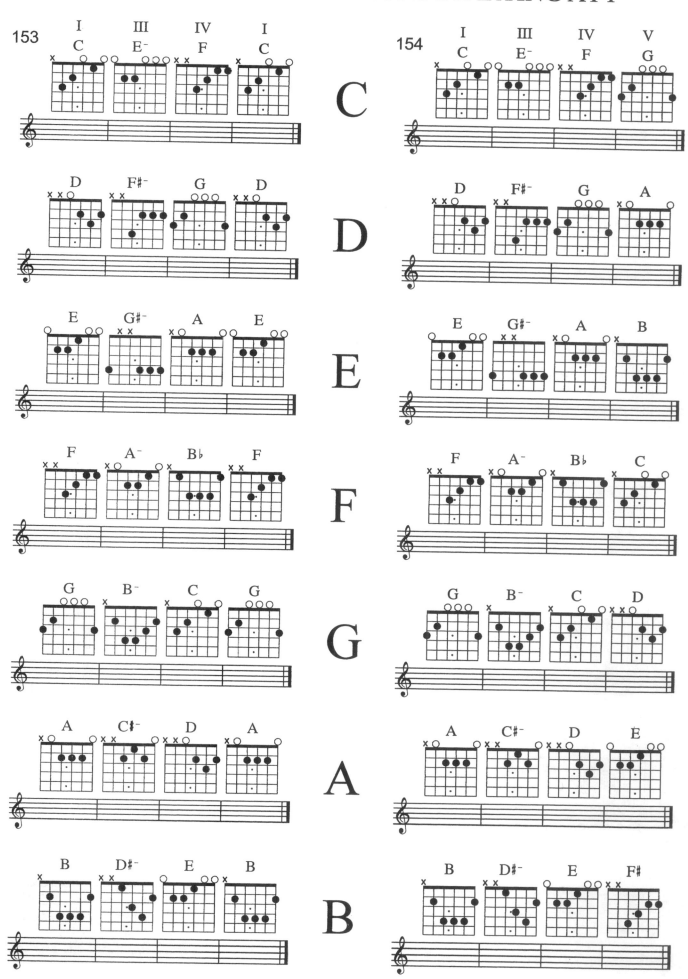

4 MEASURE PROGRESSIONS STARTING AT I

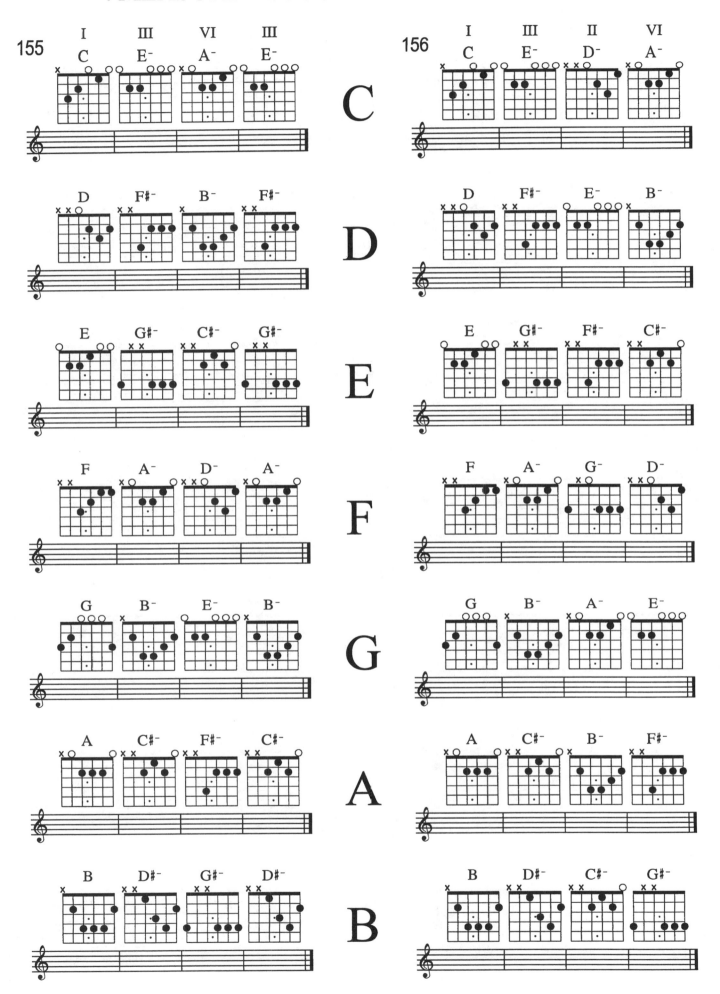

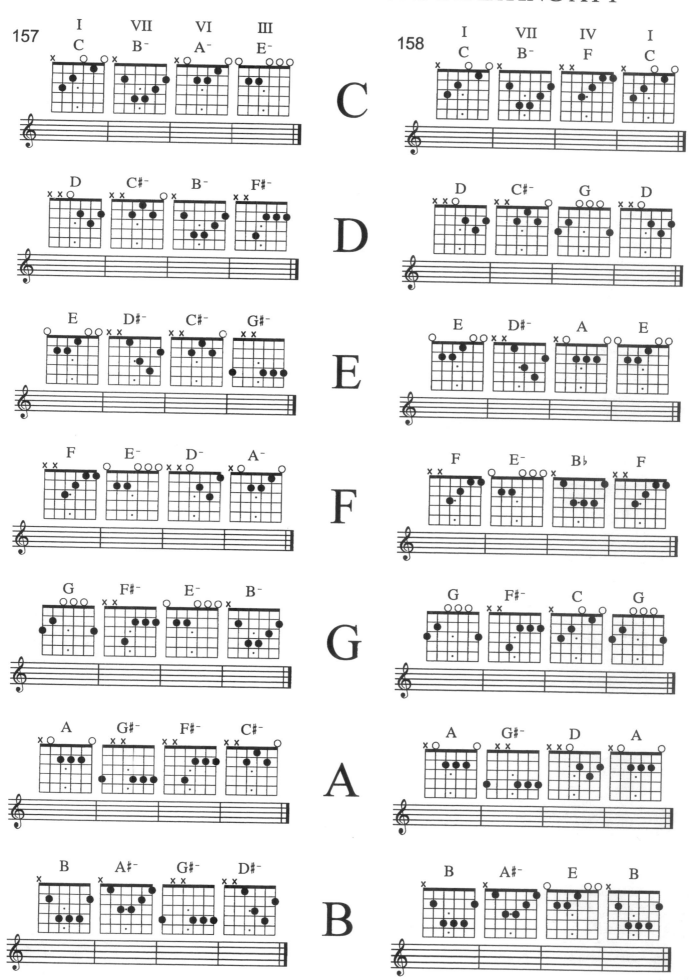

4 MEASURE PROGRESSIONS STARTING AT I

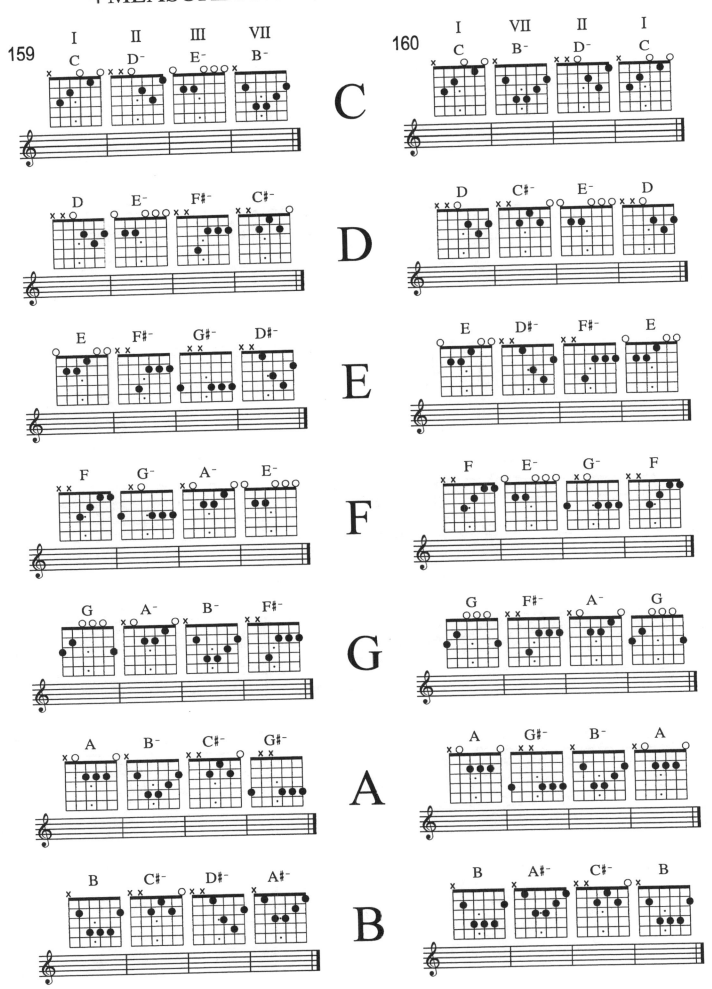

4 MEASURE PROGRESSIONS STARTING AT I

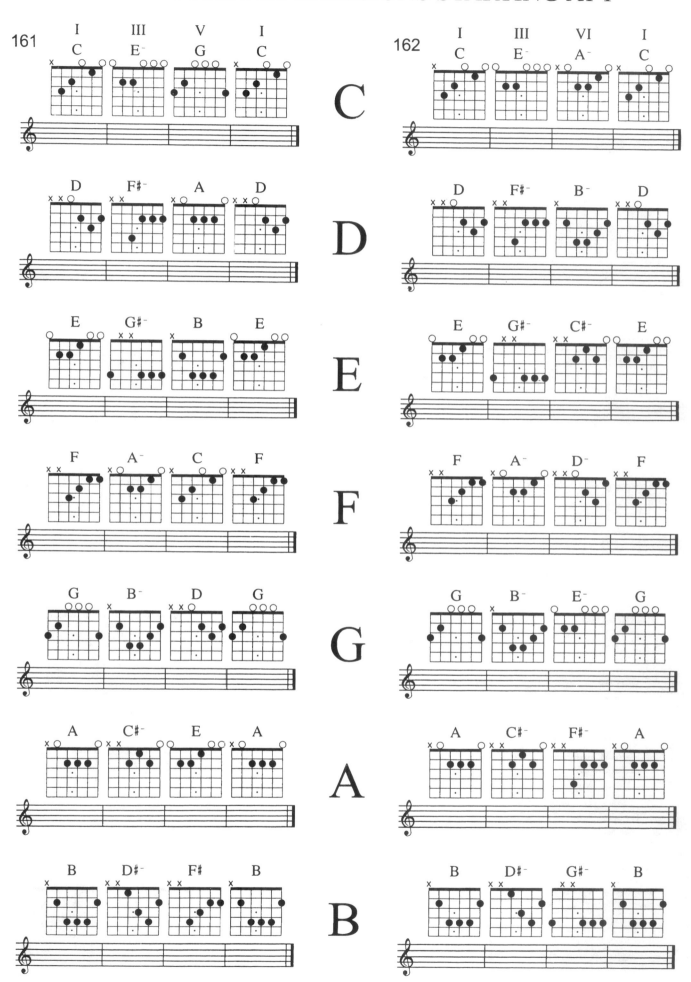

4 MEASURE PROGRESSIONS STARTING AT I

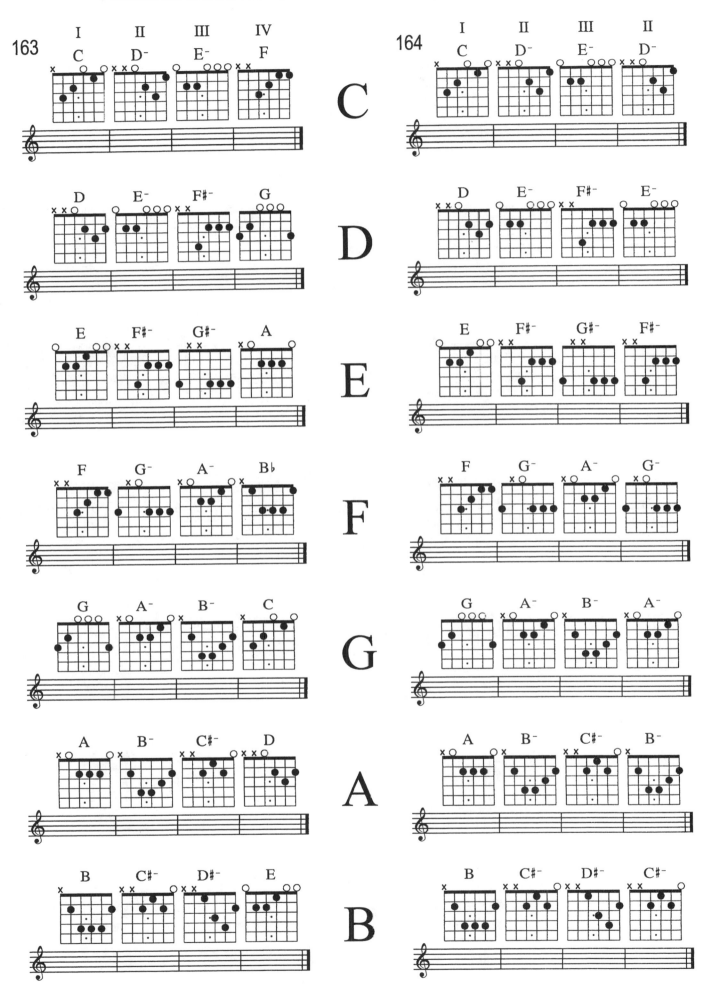

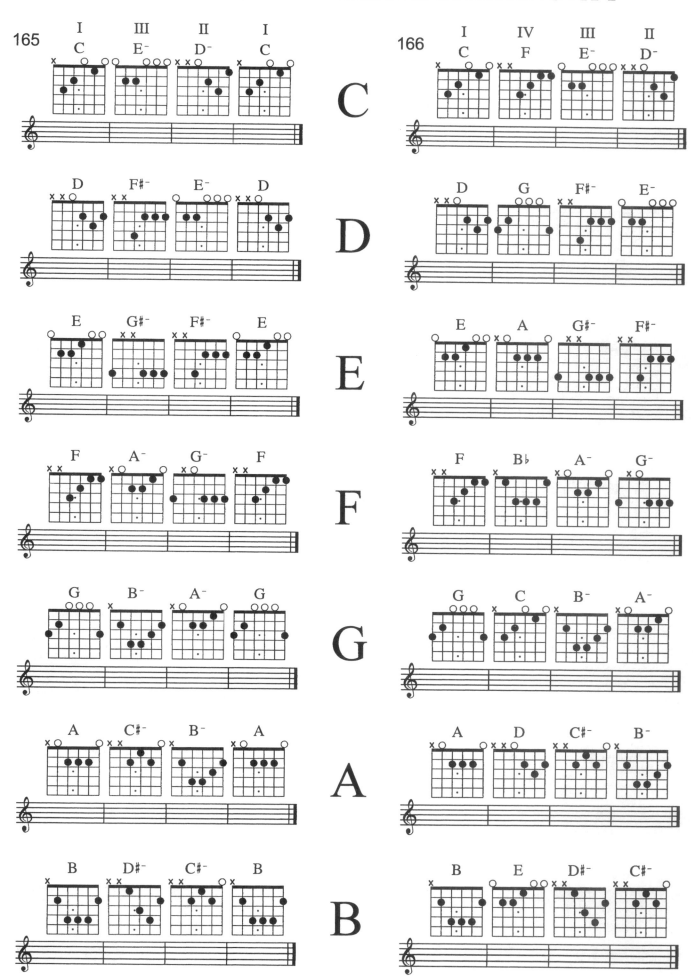

4 MEASURE PROGRESSIONS STARTING AT I

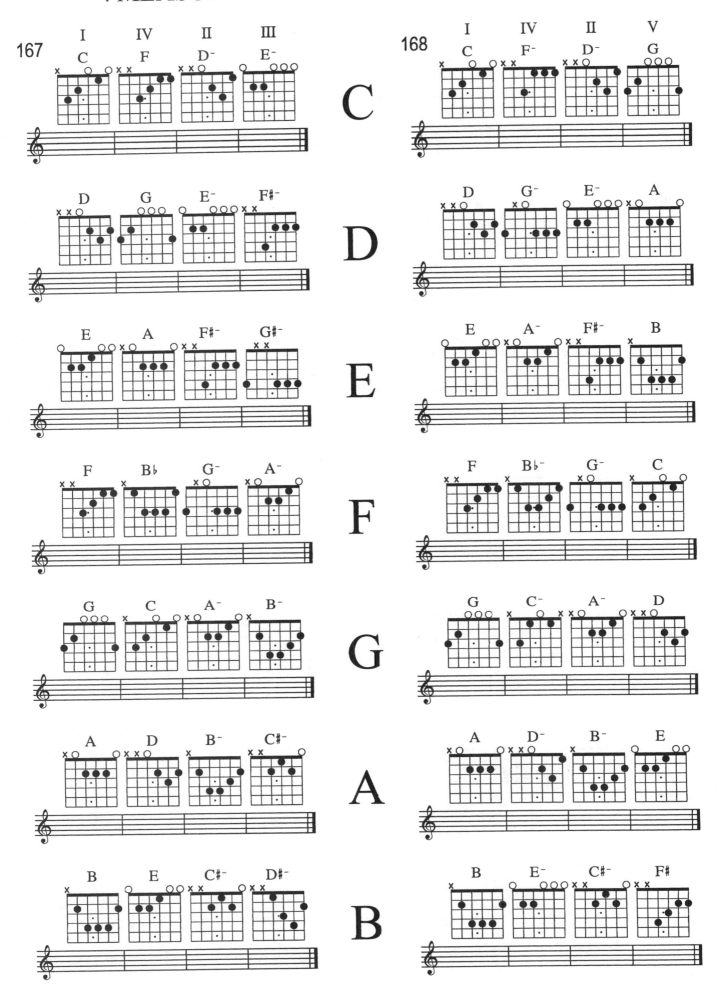

4 MEASURE PROGRESSIONS STARTING AT I

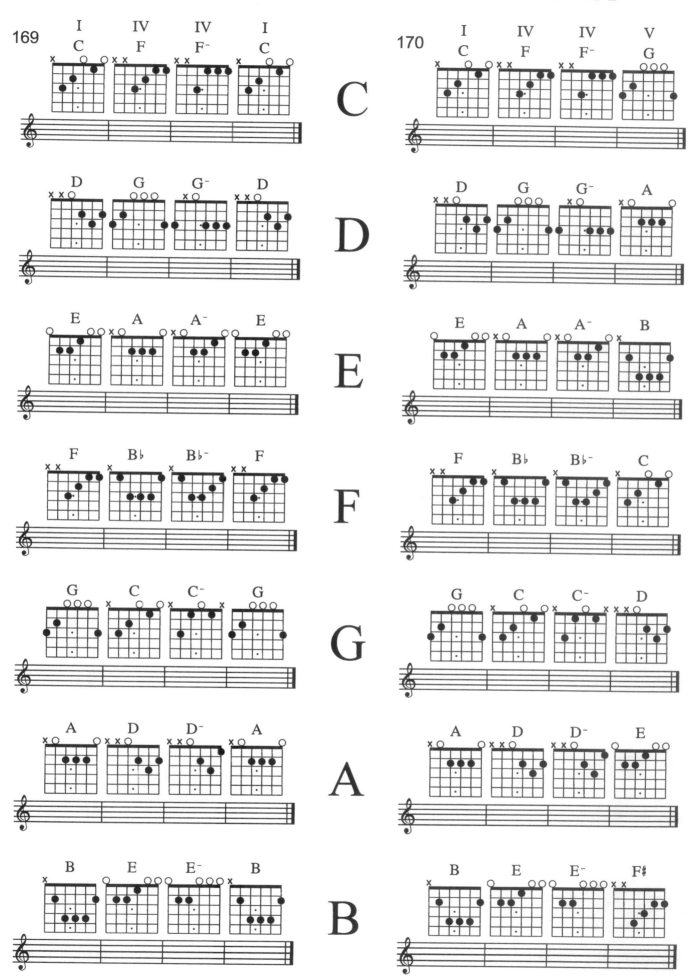

4 MEASURE PROGRESSIONS STARTING AT I

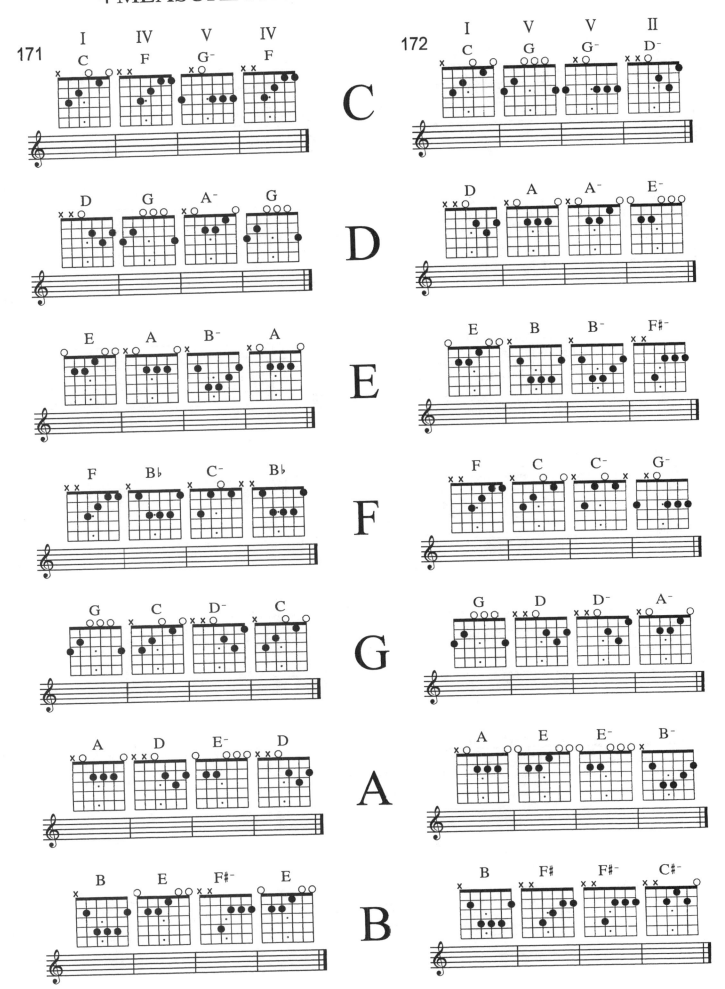

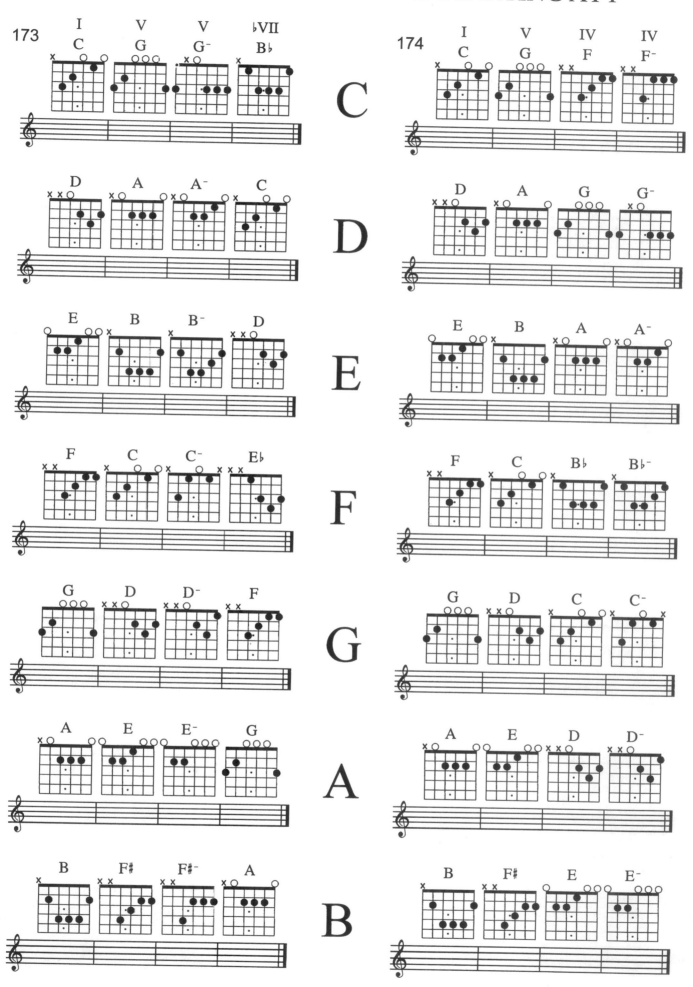

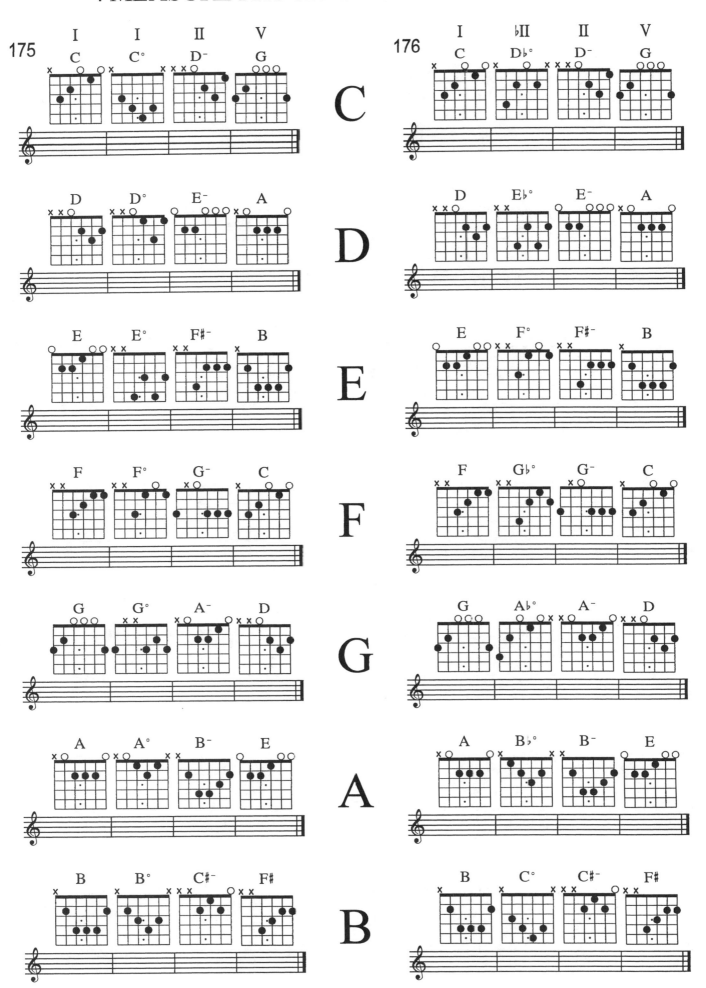

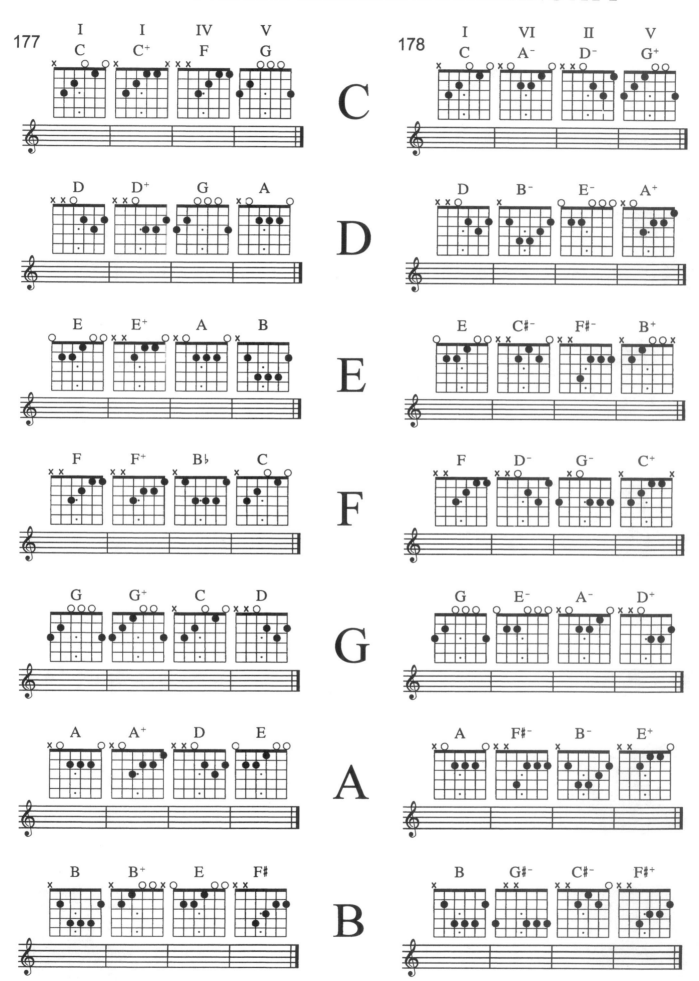

4 MEASURE PROGRESSIONS STARTING AT I

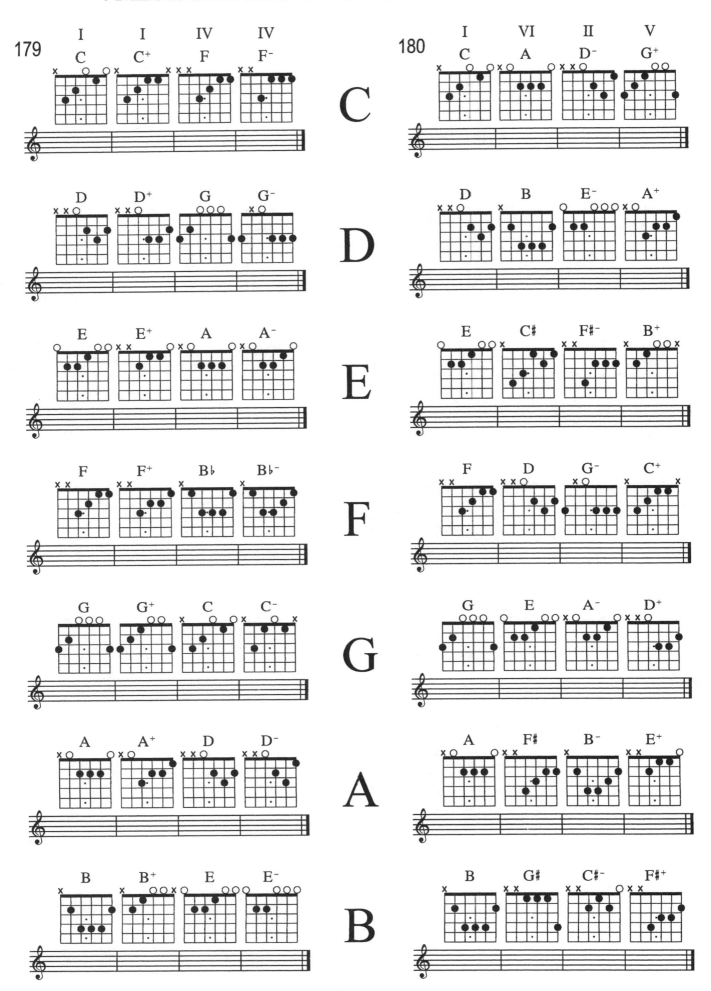

4 MEASURE PROGRESSIONS STARTING AT I

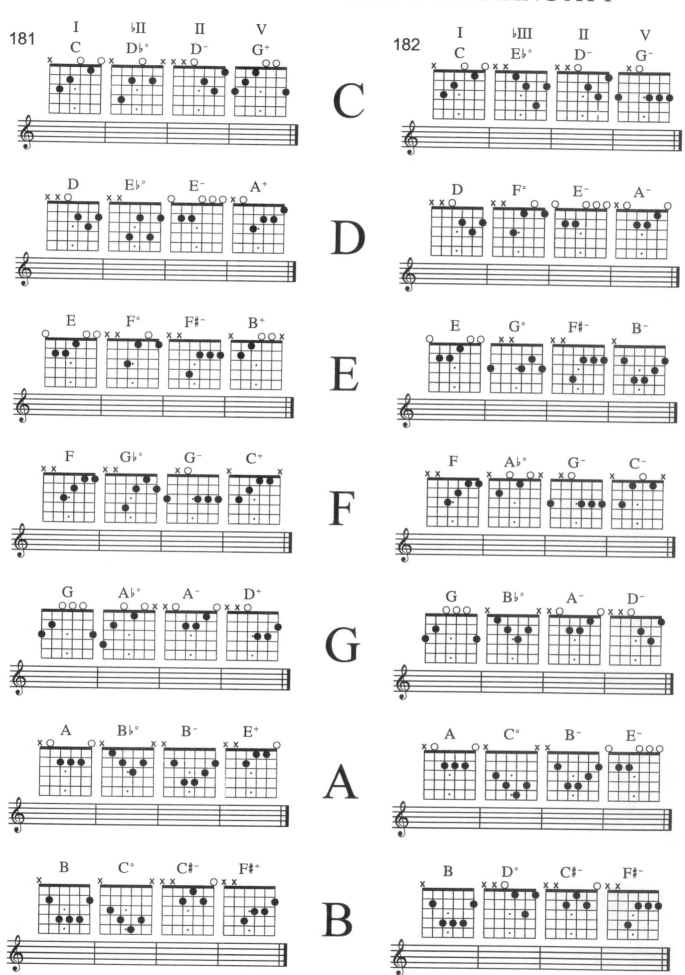

4 MEASURE PROGRESSIONS STARTING AT II

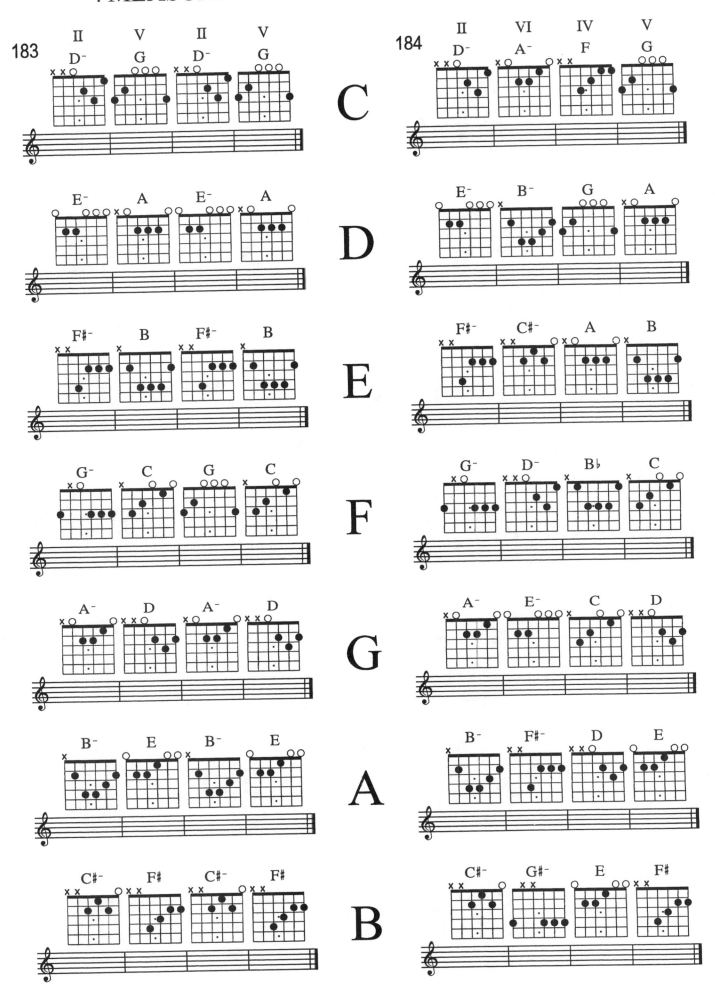

4 MEASURE PROGRESSIONS STARTING AT II

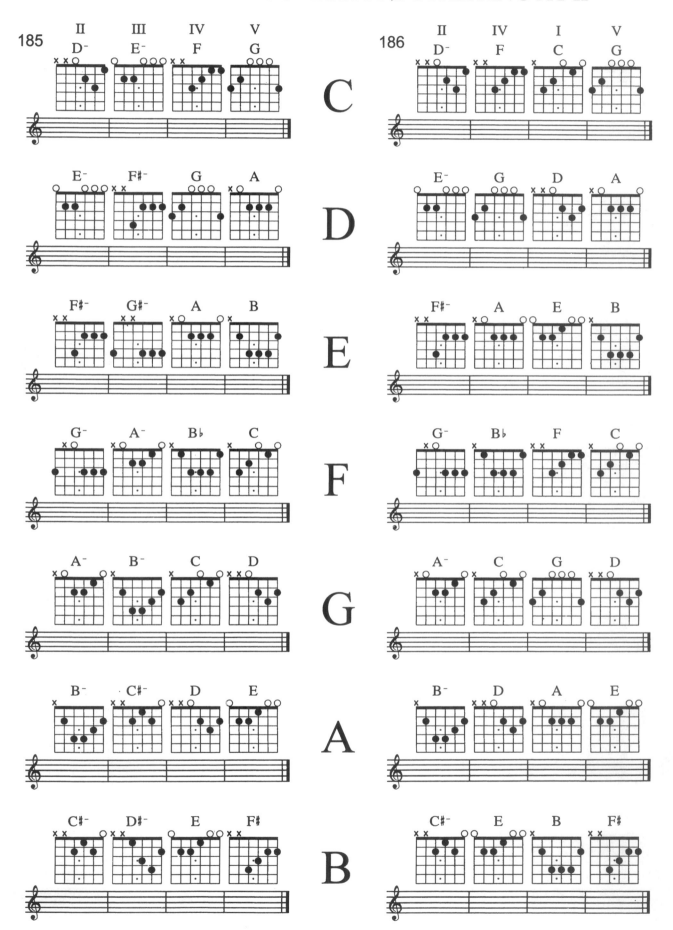

4 MEASURE PROGRESSIONS STARTING AT II

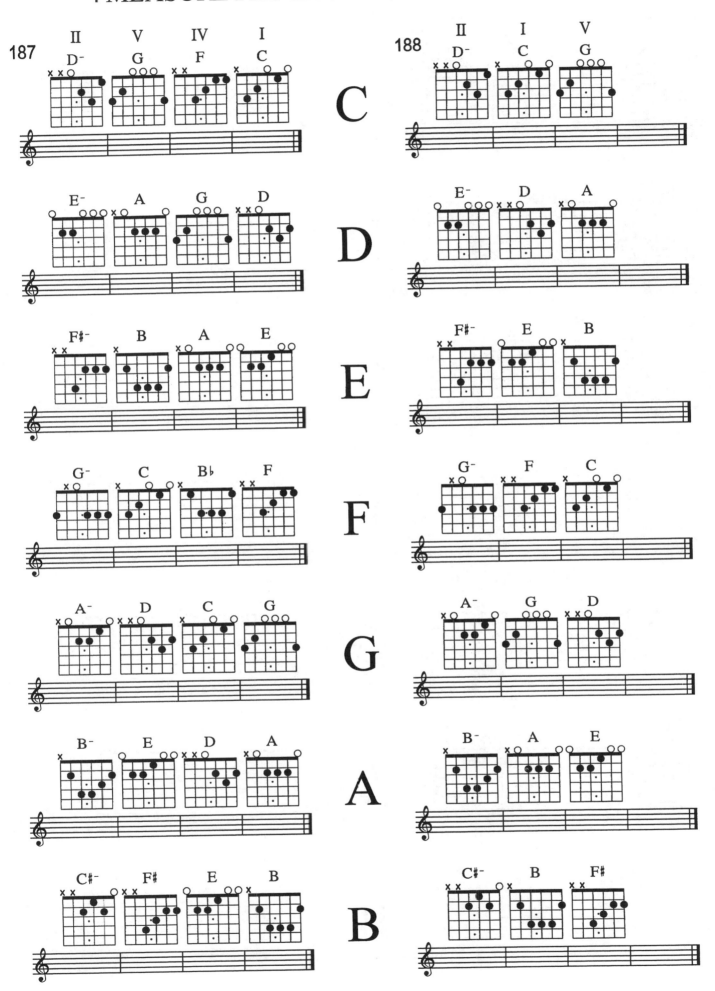

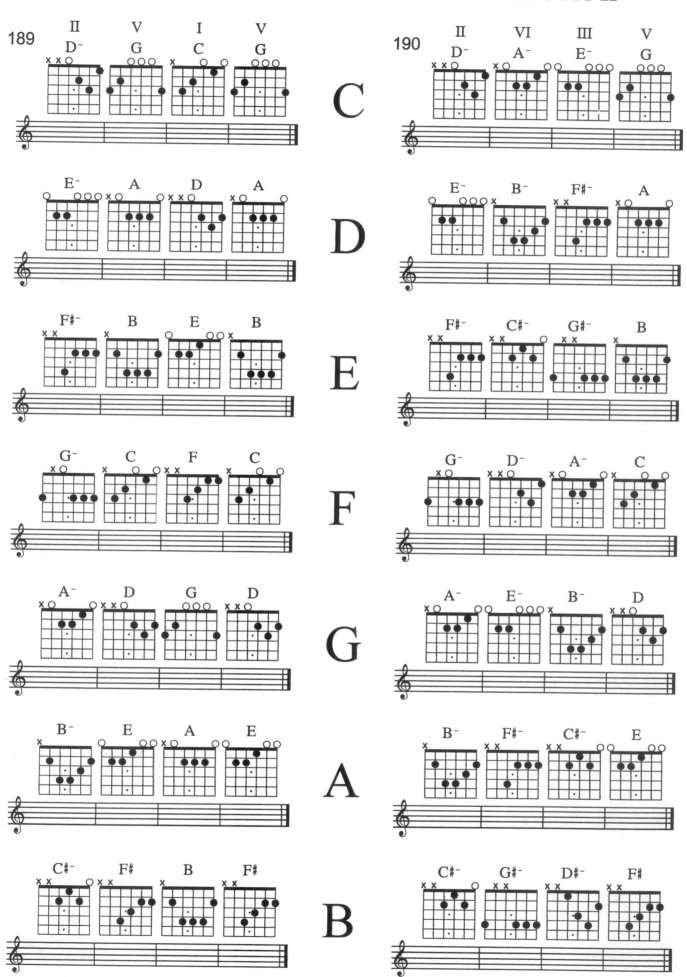

4 MEASURE PROGRESSIONS STARTING AT II

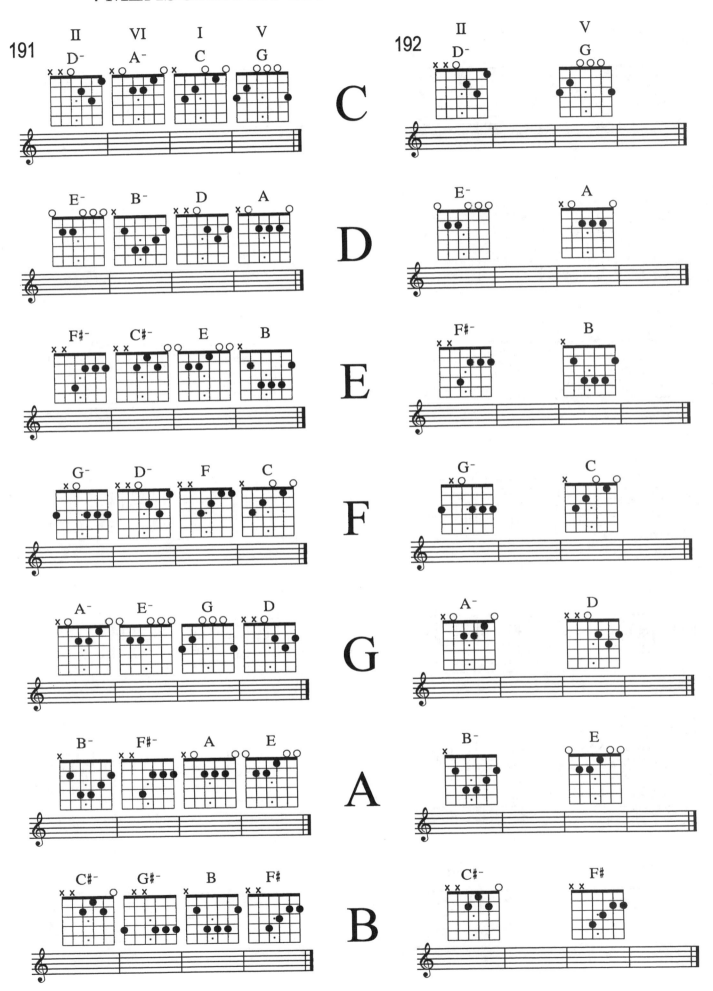

4 MEASURE PROGRESSIONS STARTING AT II

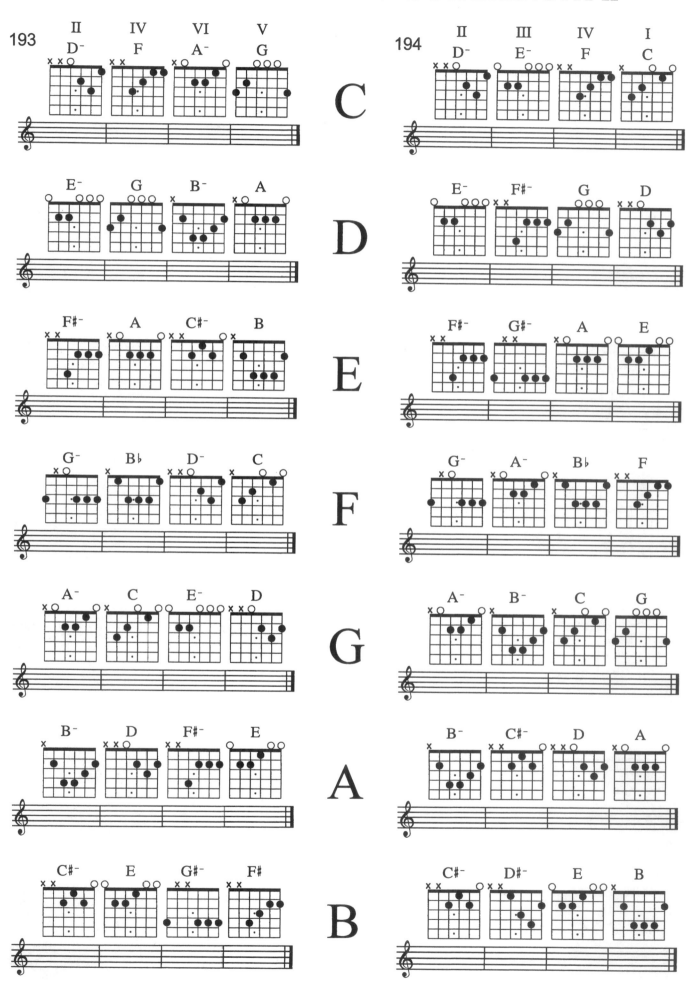

4 MEASURE PROGRESSIONS STARTING AT II

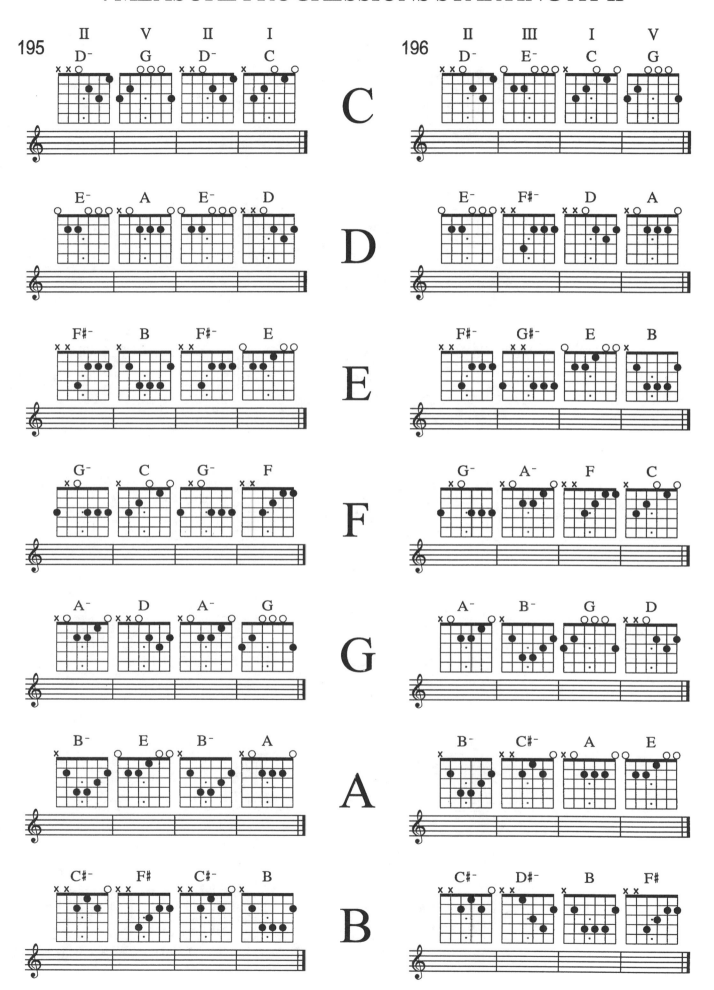

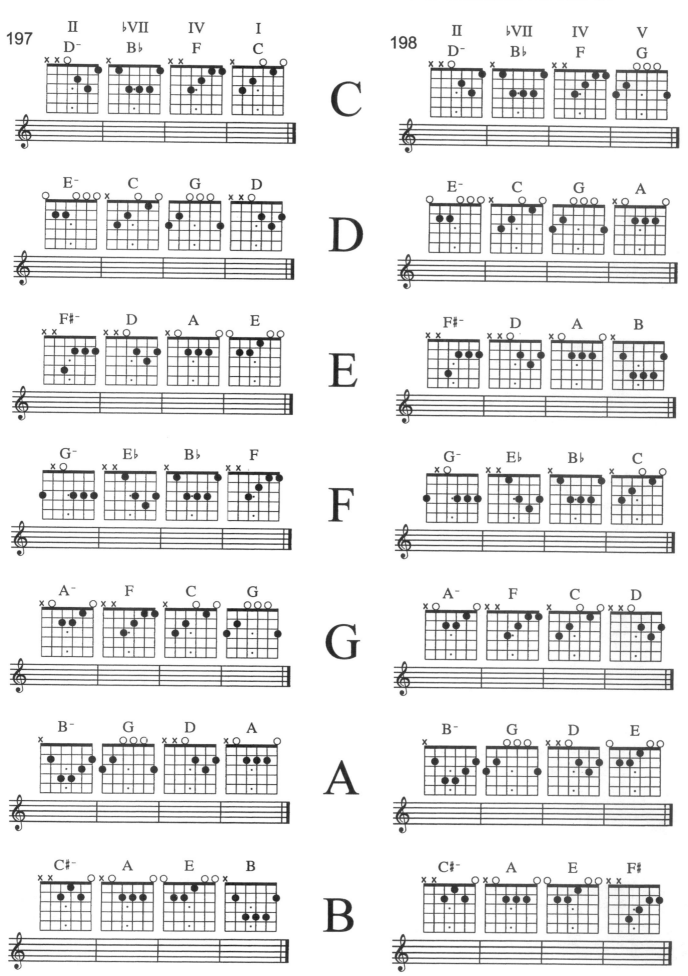

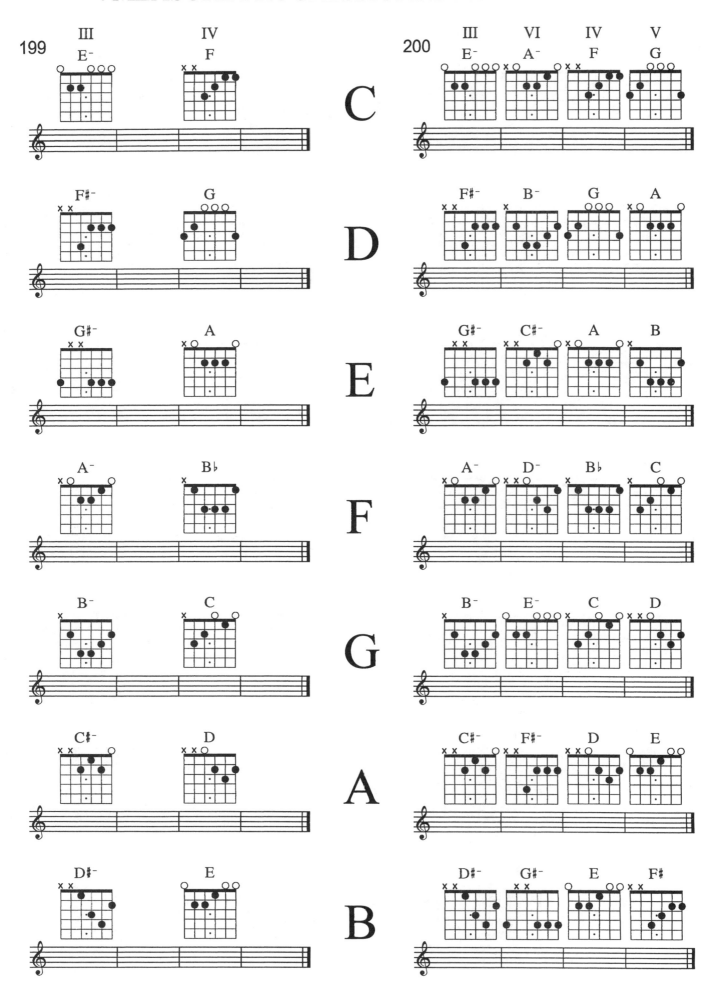

4 MEASURE PROGRESSIONS STARTING AT III

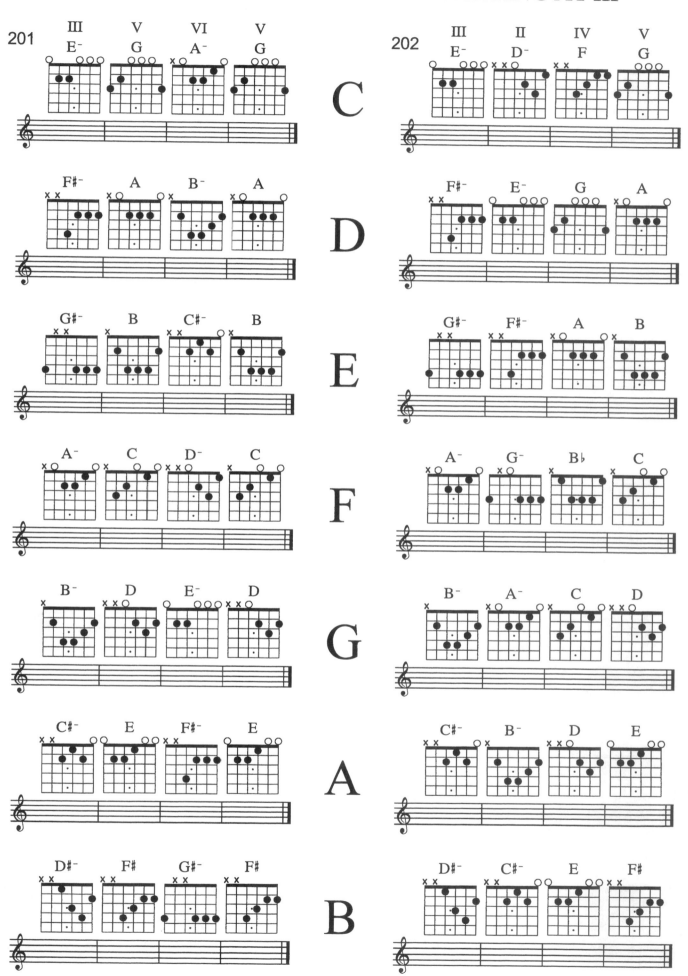

4 MEASURE PROGRESSIONS STARTING AT III

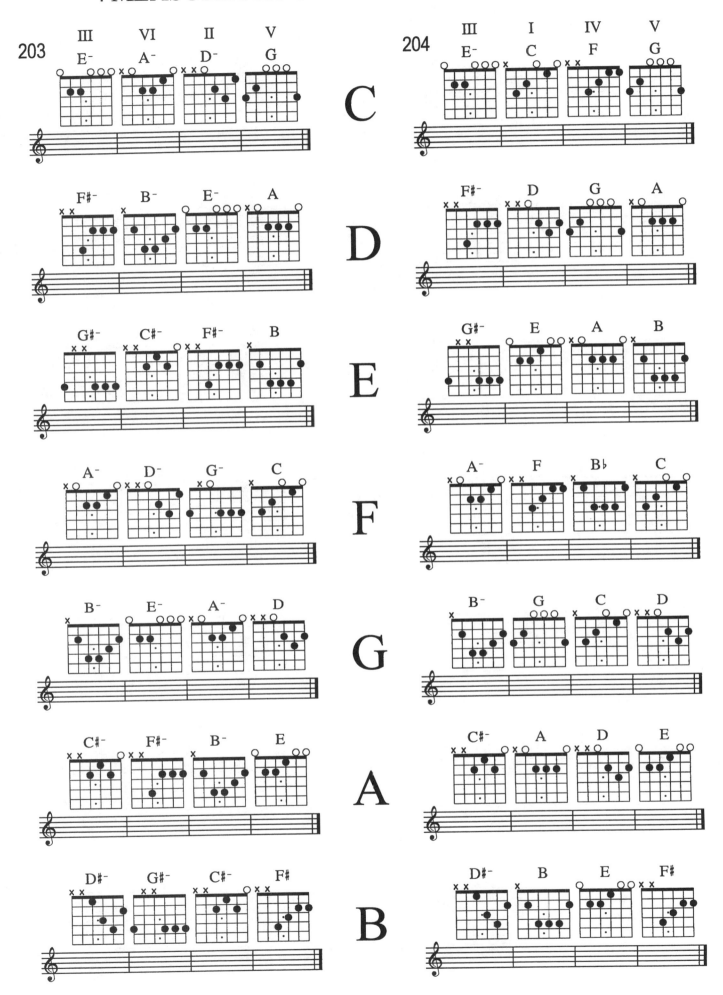

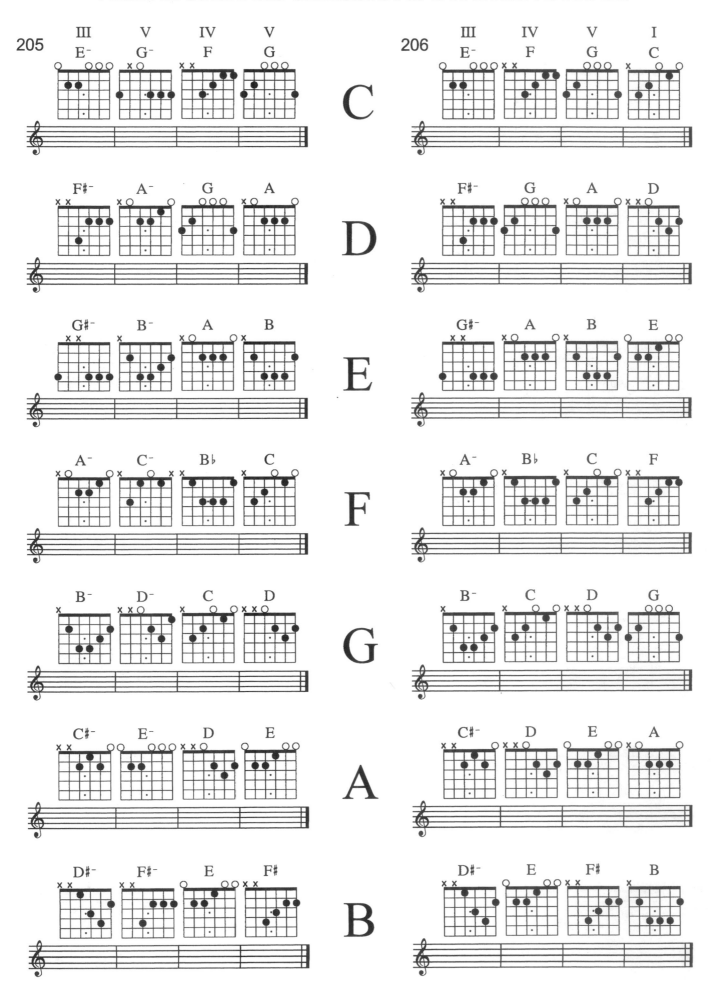

4 MEASURE PROGRESSIONS STARTING AT III

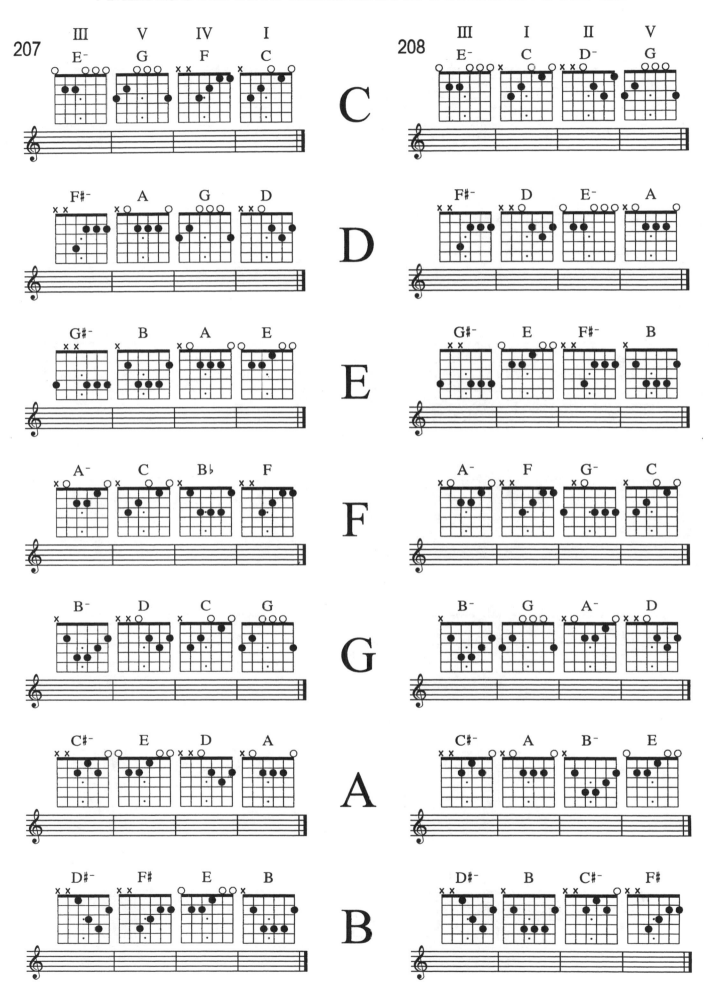

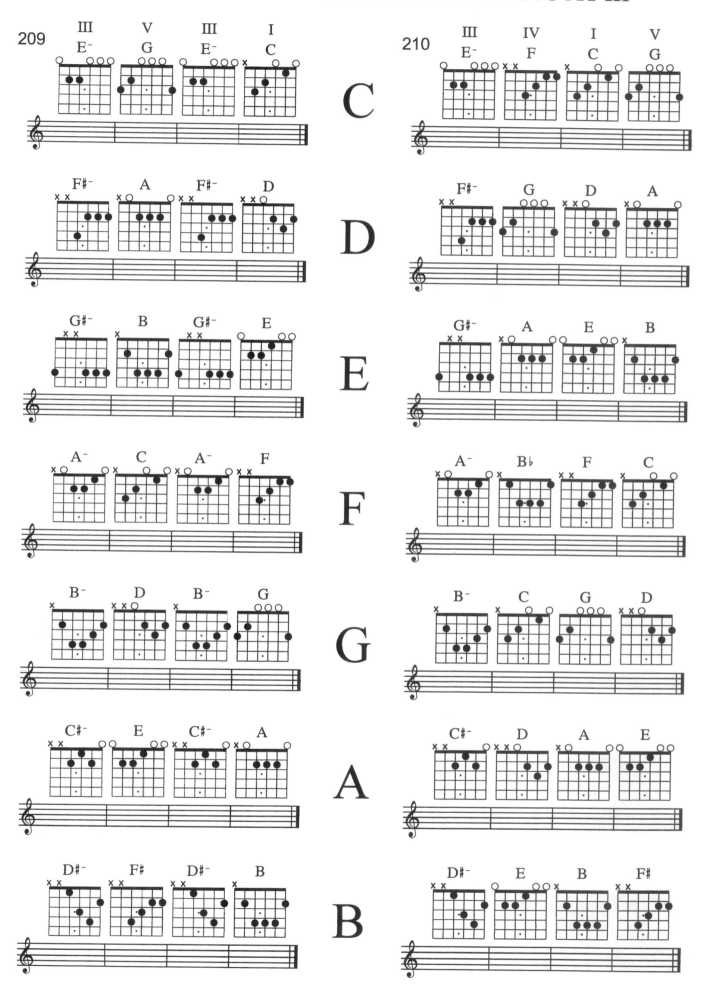

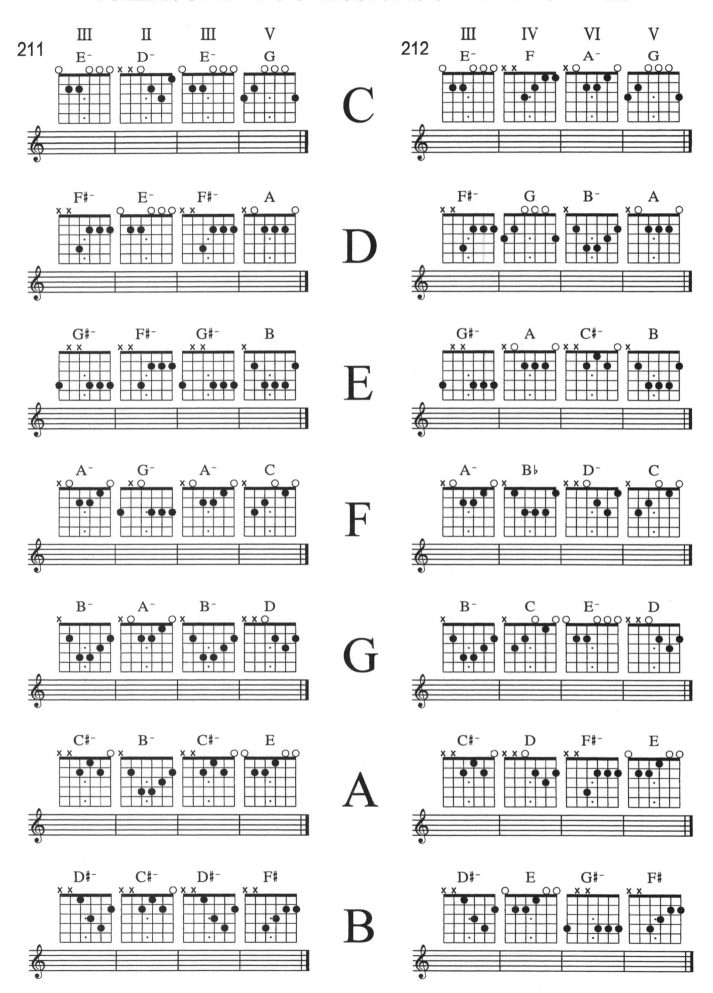

4 MEASURE PROGRESSIONS STARTING AT III

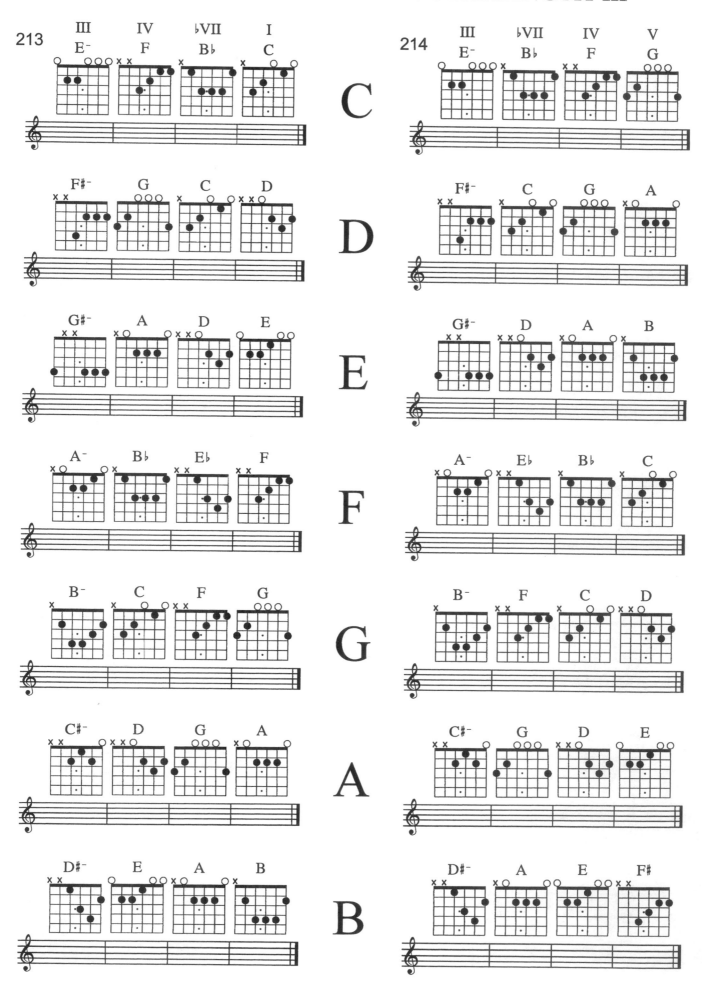

4 MEASURE PROGRESSIONS STARTING AT III

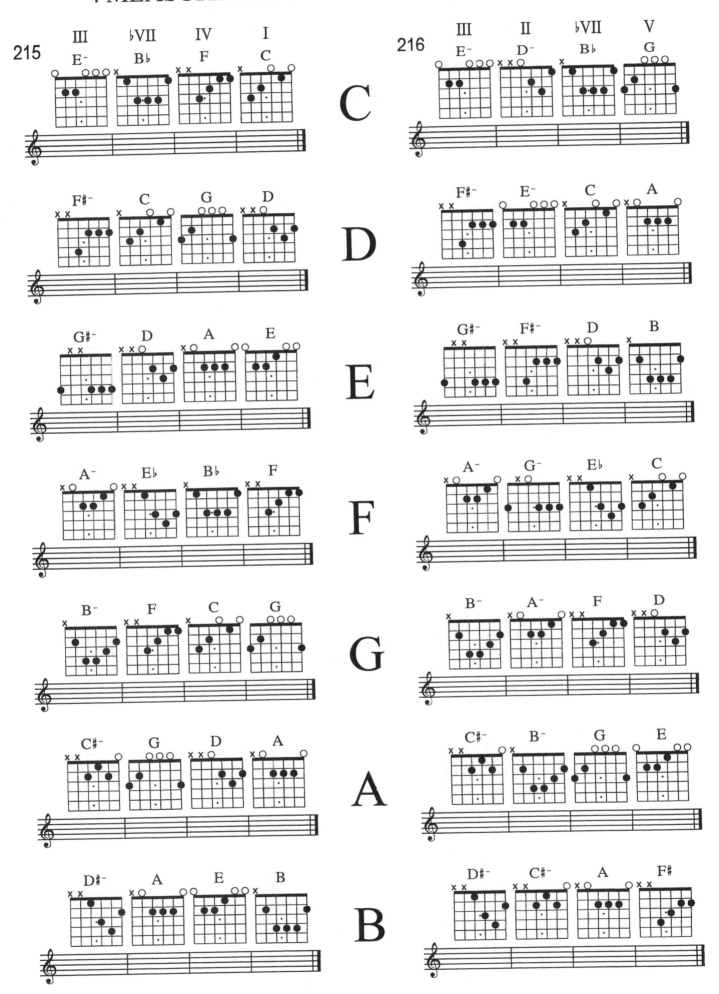

4 MEASURE PROGRESSIONS STARTING AT IV

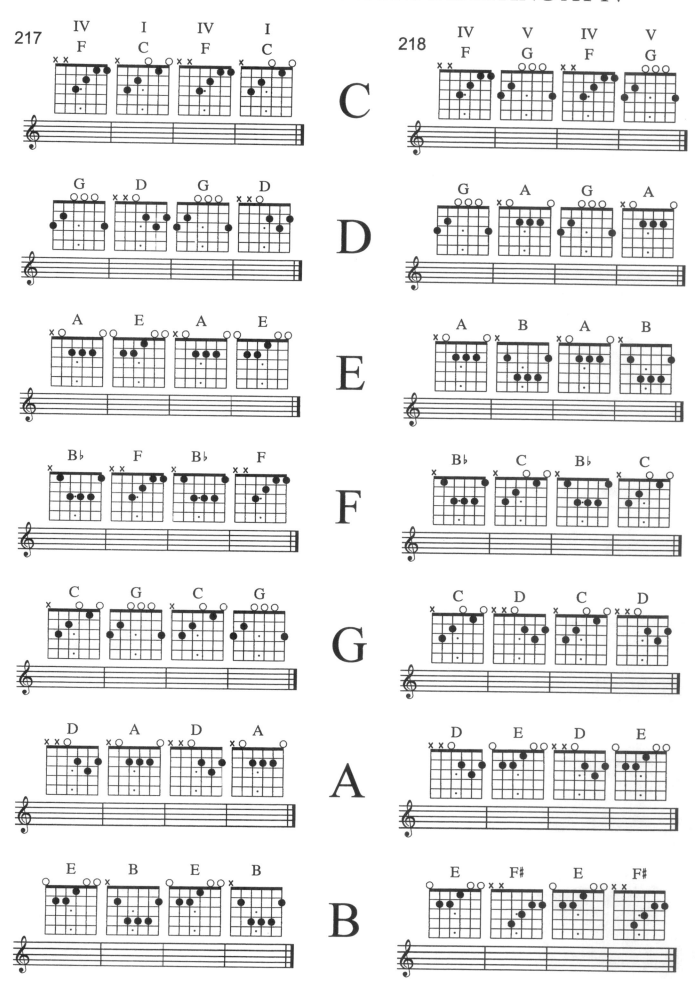

4 MEASURE PROGRESSIONS STARTING AT IV

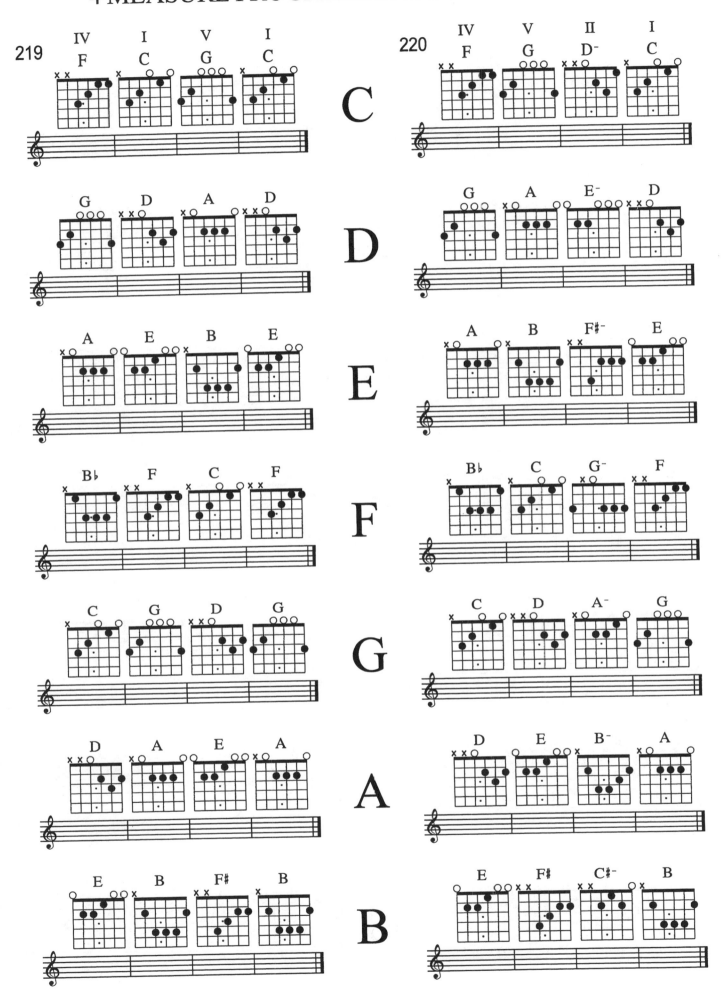

4 MEASURE PROGRESSIONS STARTING AT IV

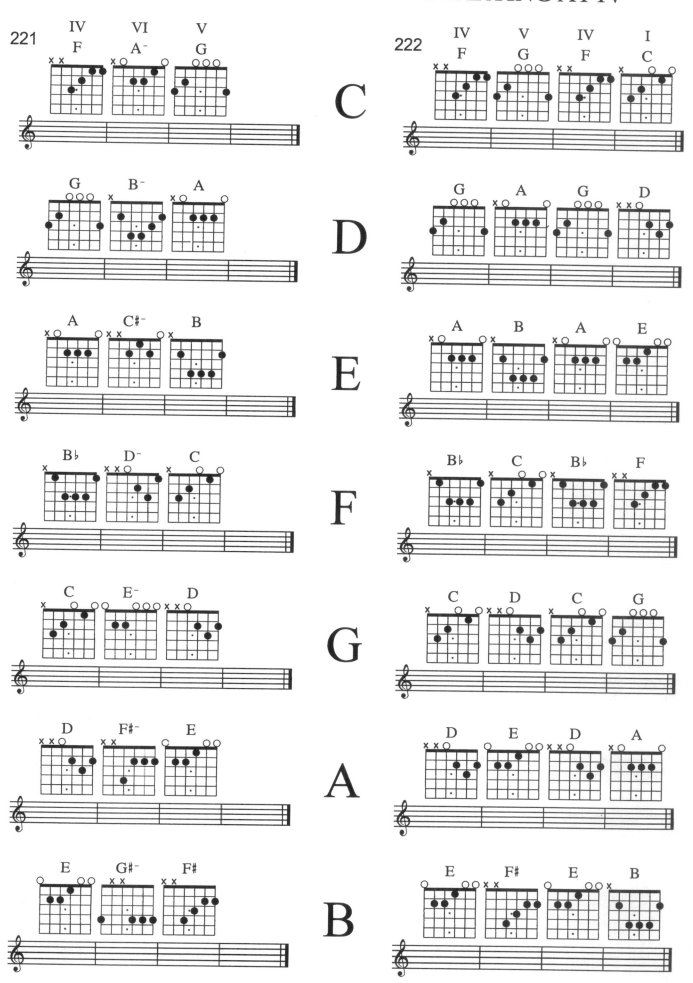

4 MEASURE PROGRESSIONS STARTING AT IV

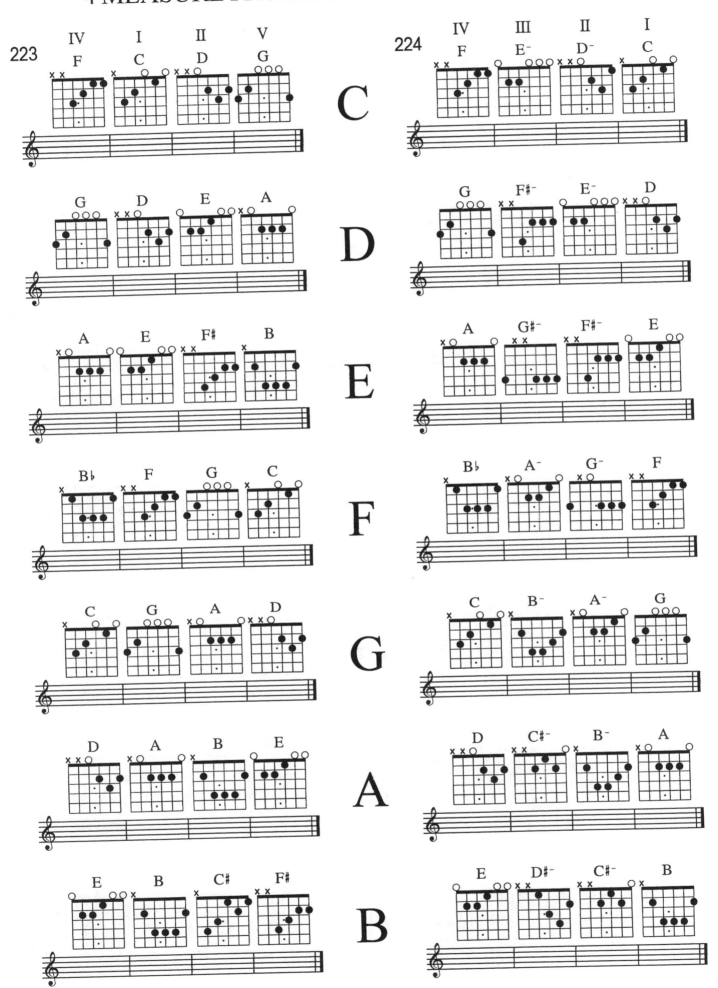

4 MEASURE PROGRESSIONS STARTING AT IV

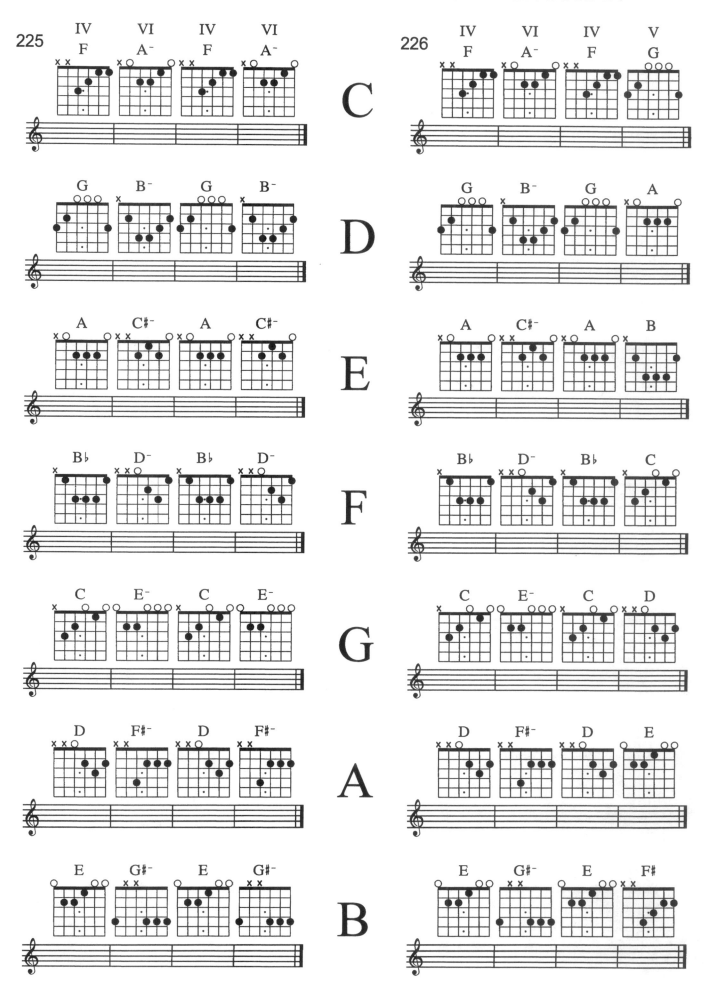

4 MEASURE PROGRESSIONS STARTING AT IV

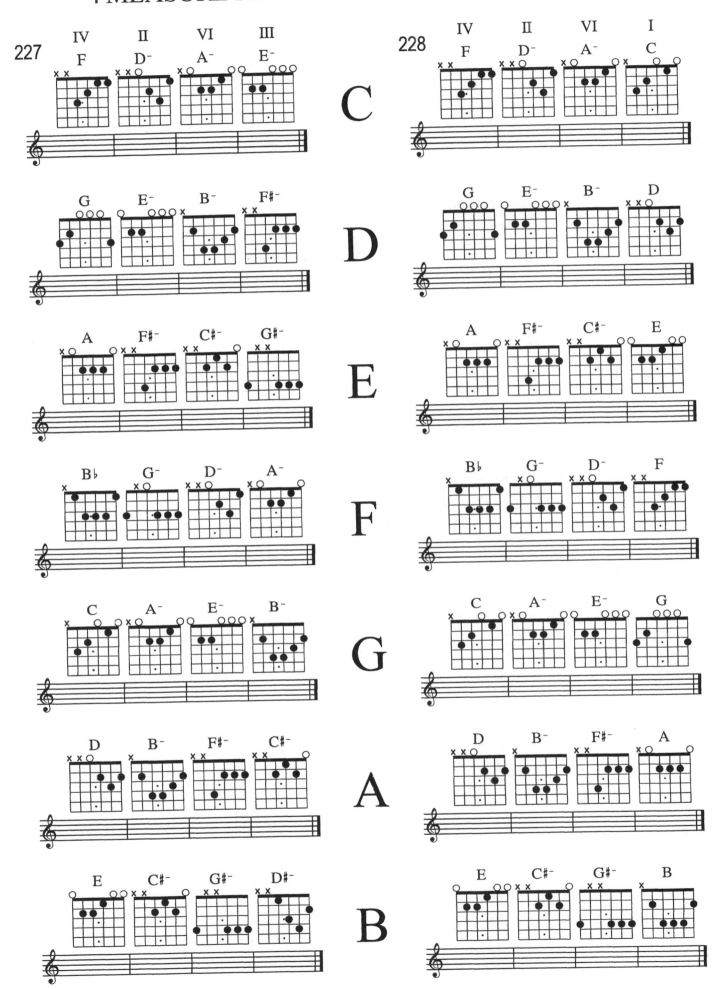

4 MEASURE PROGRESSIONS STARTING AT IV

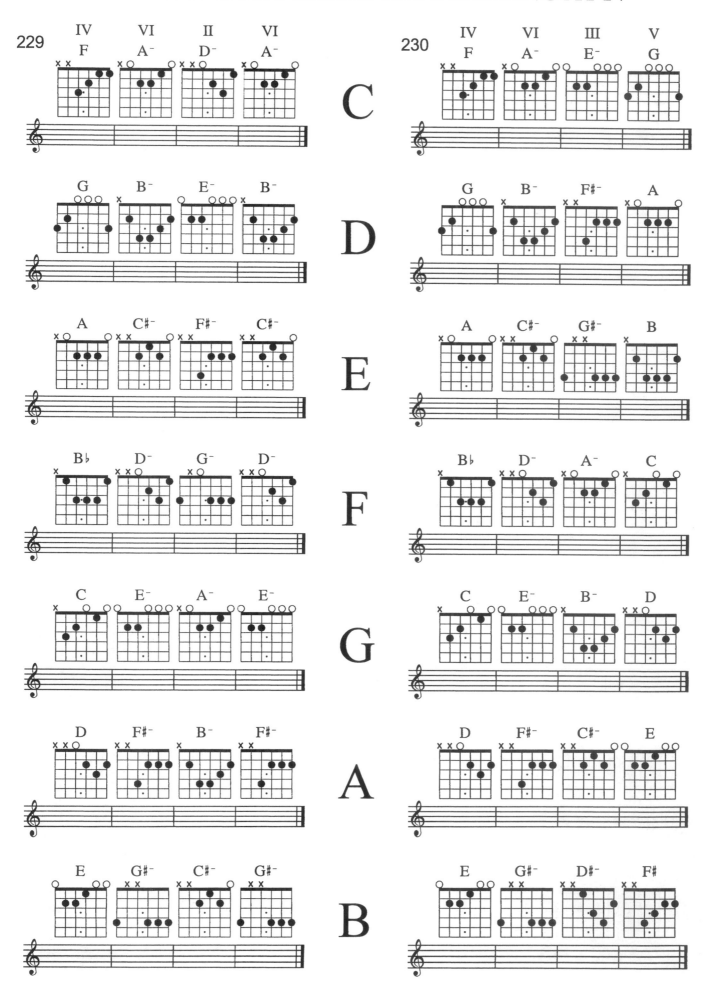

4 MEASURE PROGRESSIONS STARTING AT IV

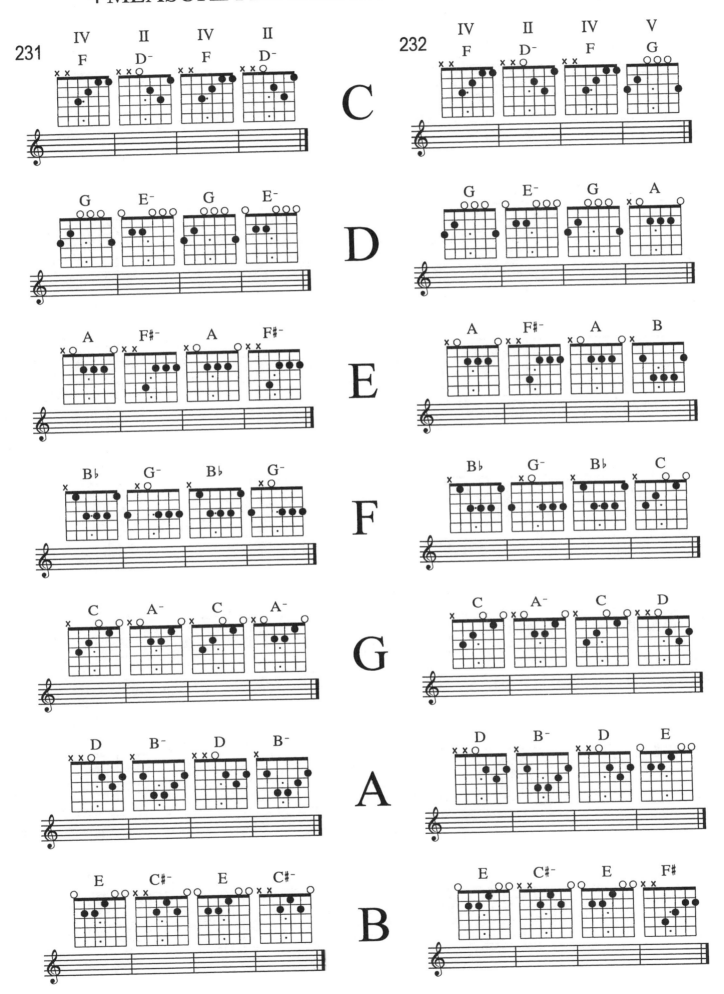

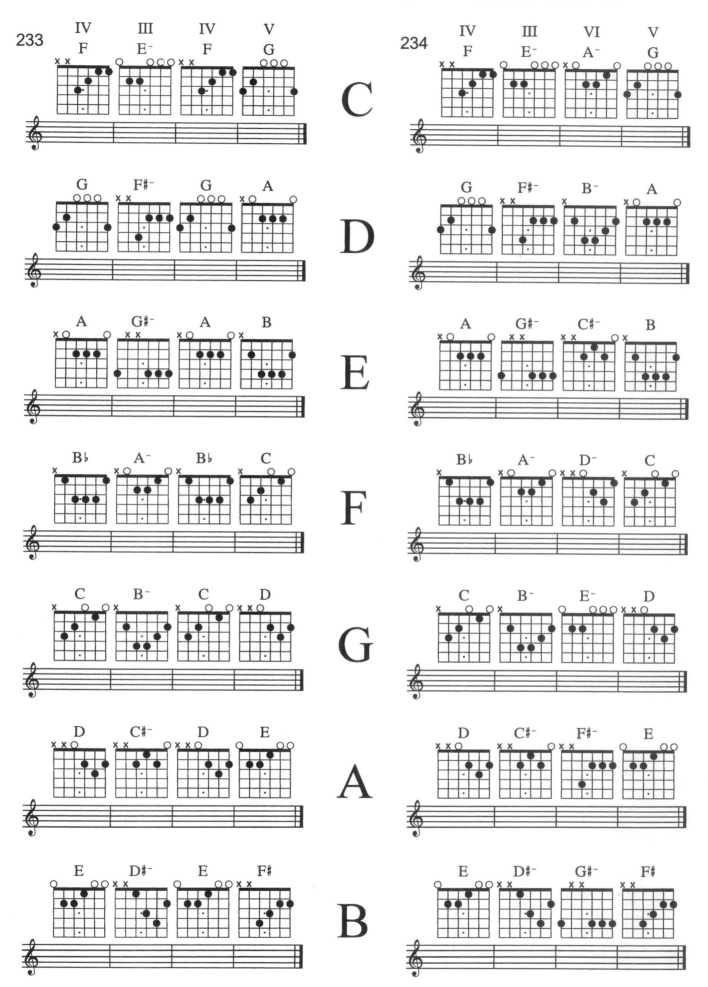

4 MEASURE PROGRESSIONS STARTING AT IV

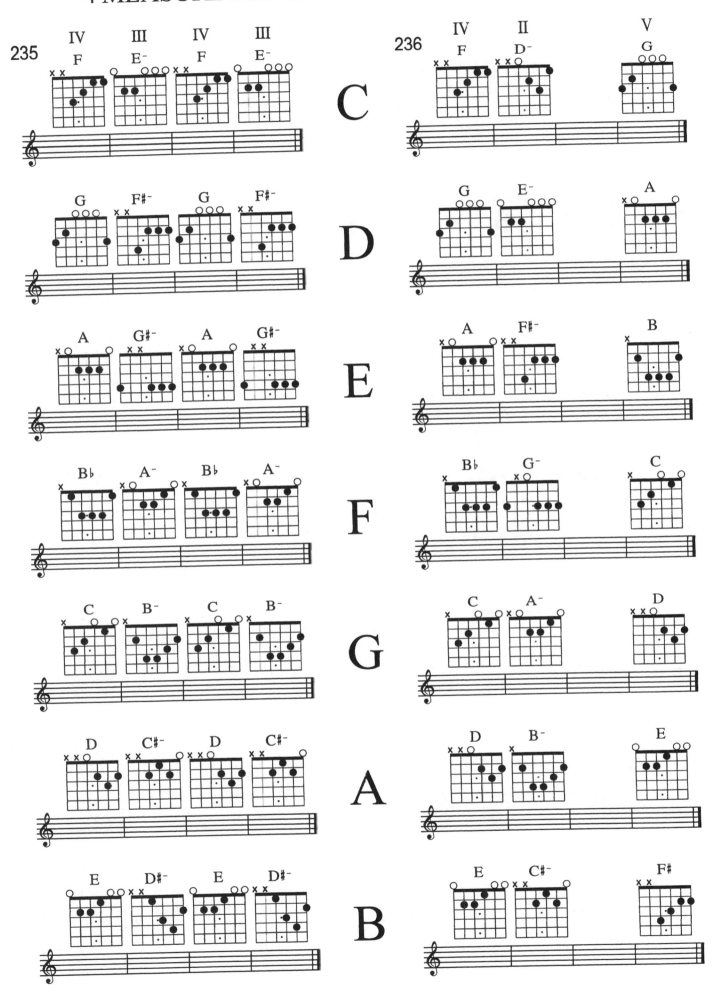

4 MEASURE PROGRESSIONS STARTING AT IV

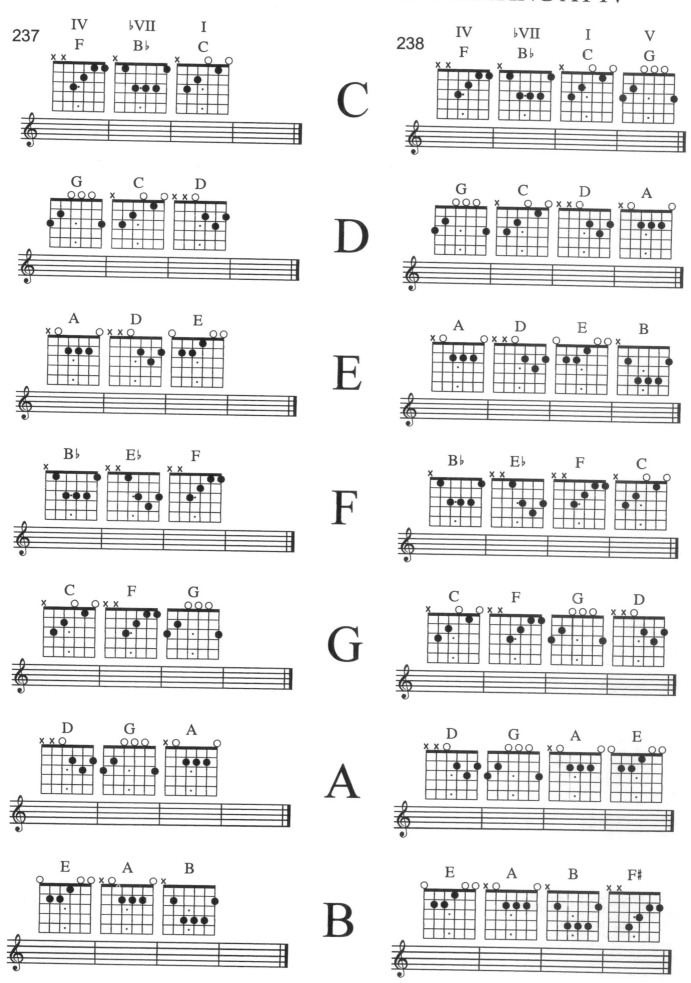

4 MEASURE PROGRESSIONS STARTING AT IV

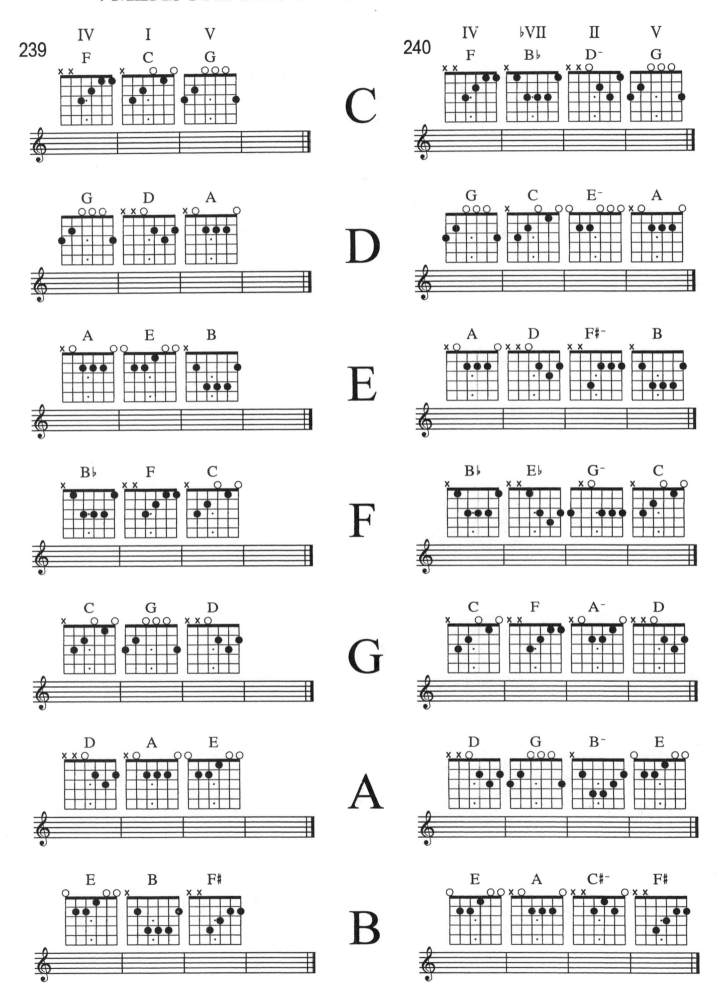

4 MEASURE PROGRESSIONS STARTING AT IV

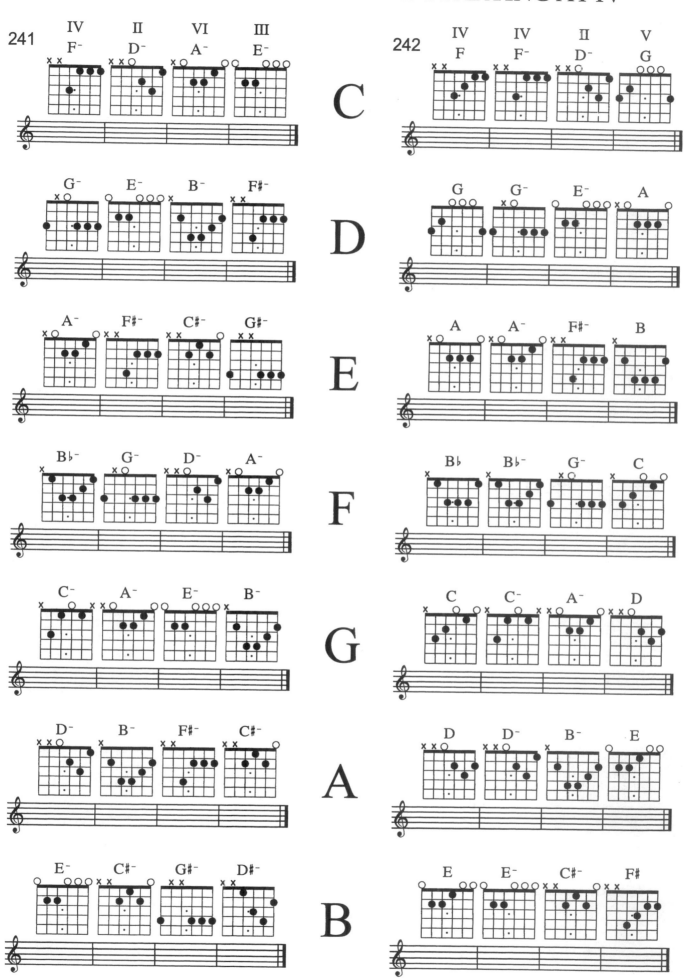

4 MEASURE PROGRESSIONS STARTING AT IV

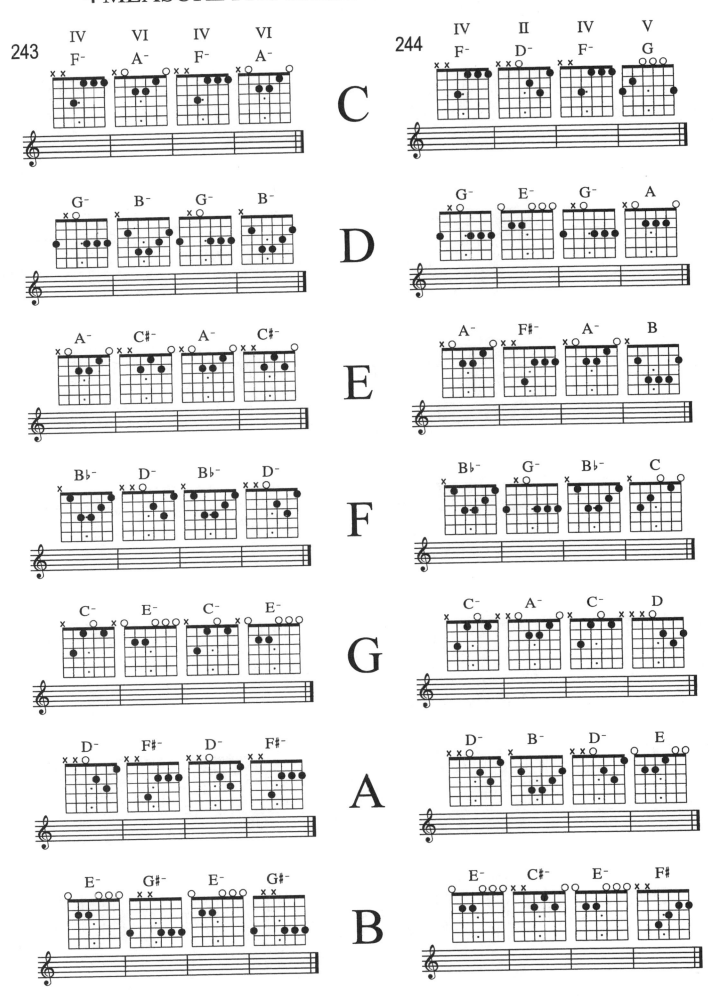

4 MEASURE PROGRESSIONS STARTING AT IV

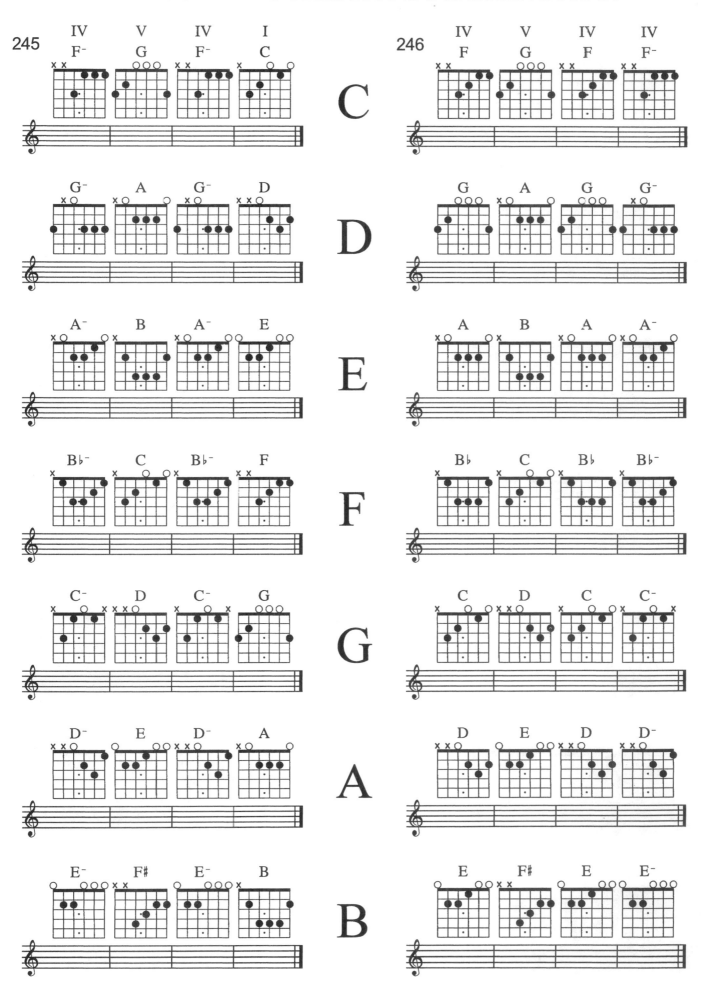

4 MEASURE PROGRESSIONS STARTING AT IV

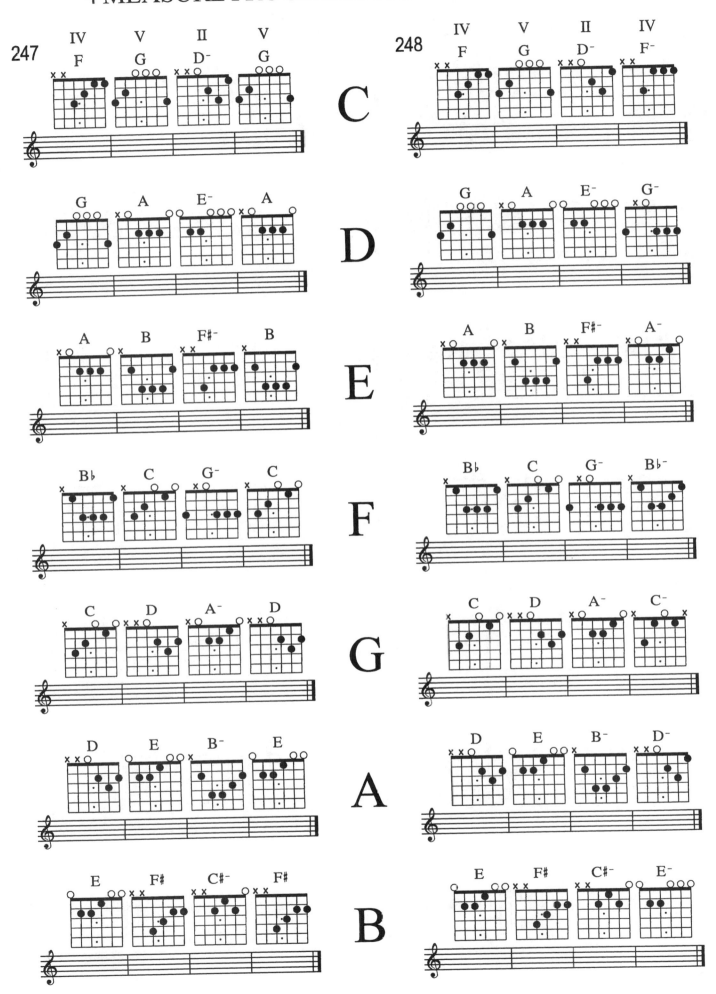

4 MEASURE PROGRESSIONS STARTING AT IV

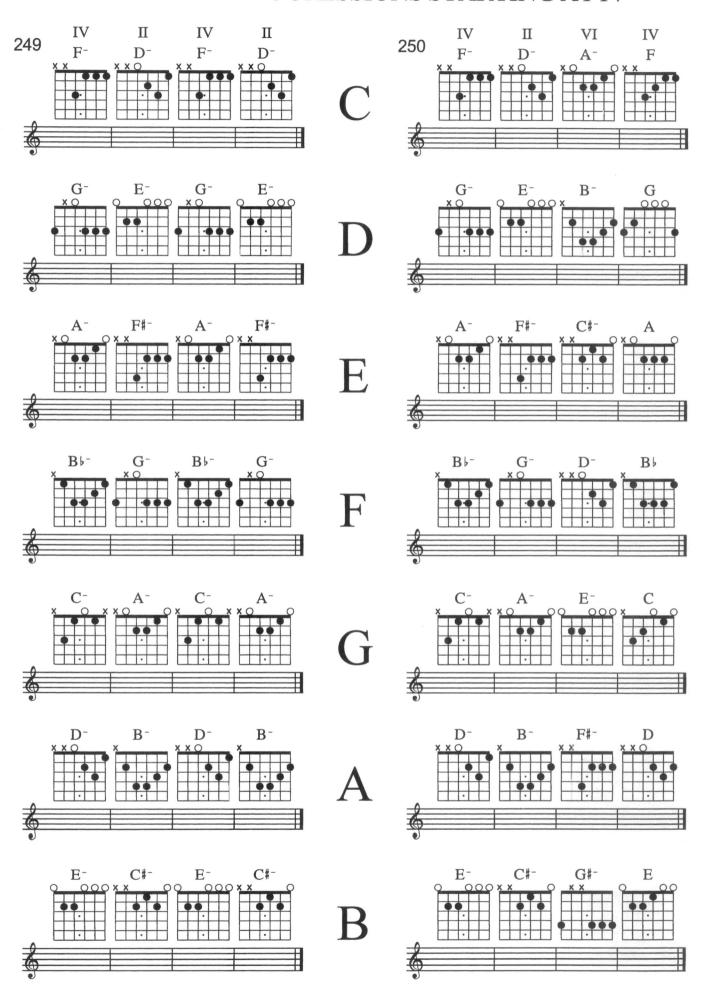

4 MEASURE PROGRESSIONS STARTING AT IV

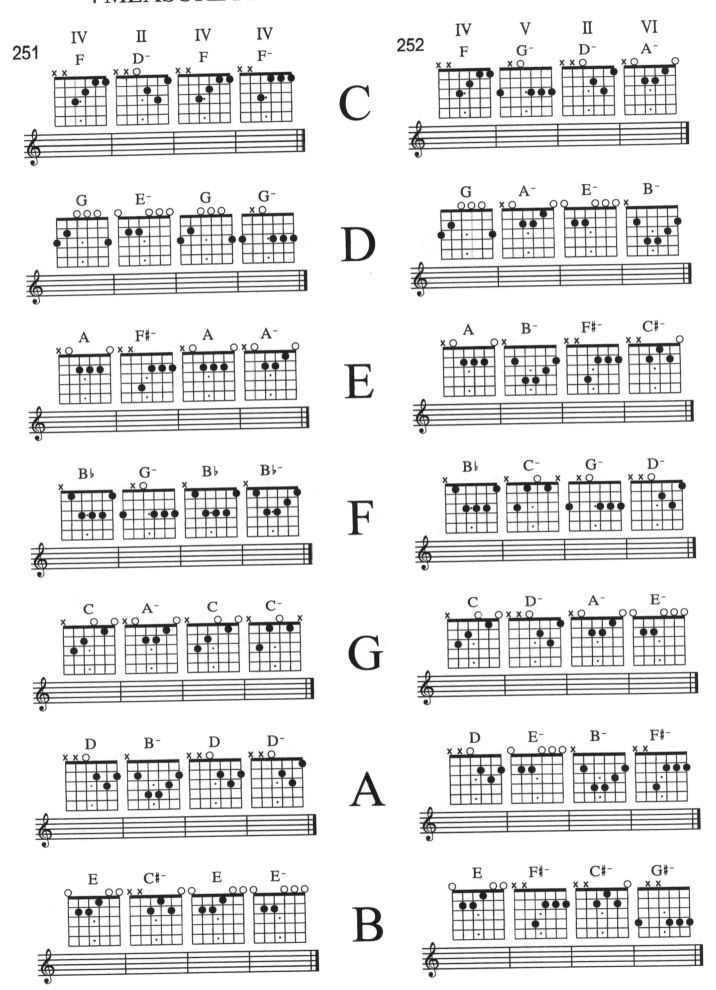

4 MEASURE PROGRESSIONS STARTING AT V

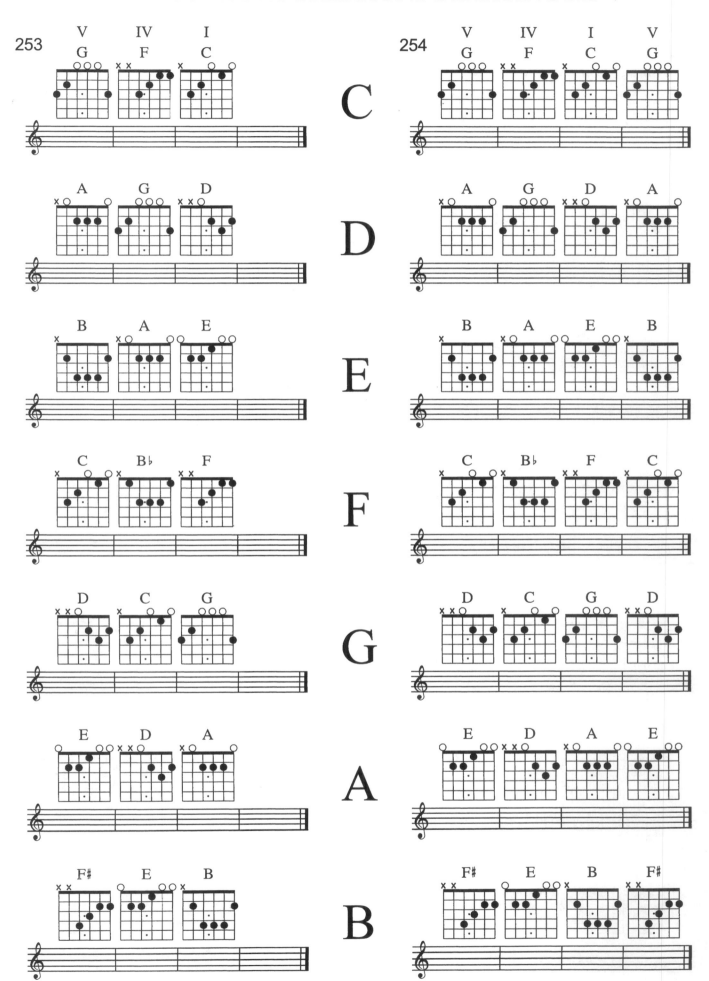

4 MEASURE PROGRESSIONS STARTING AT V

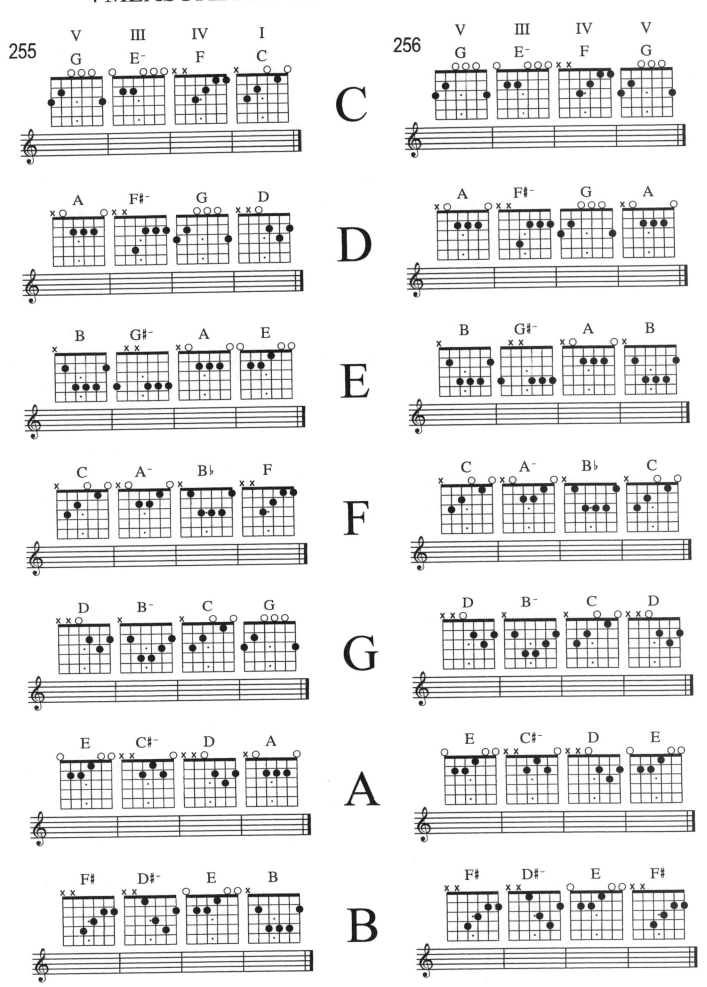

4 MEASURE PROGRESSIONS STARTING AT V

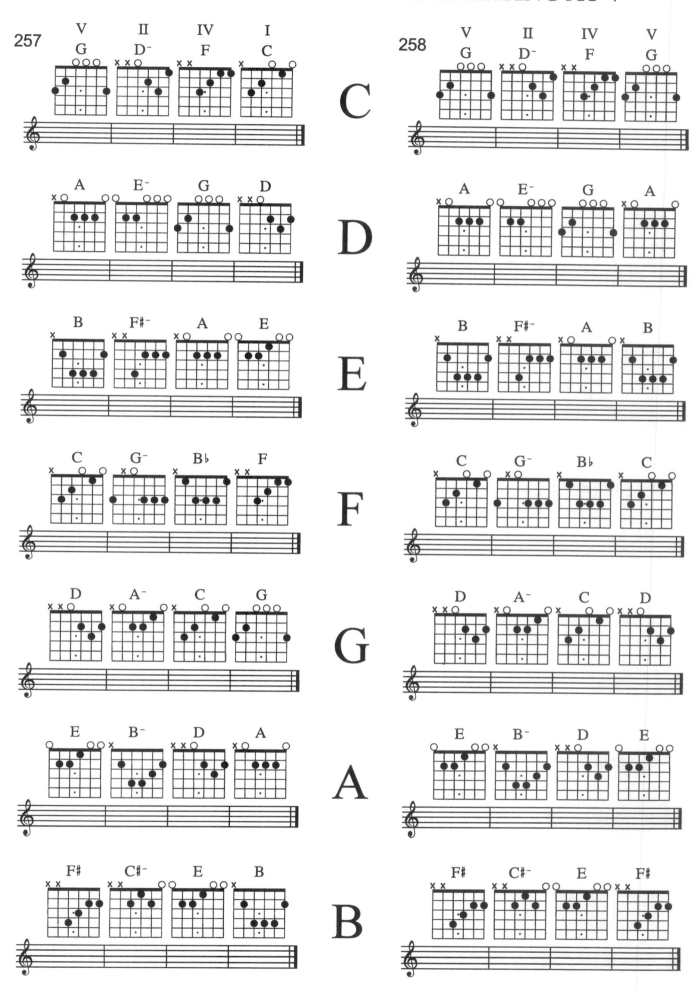

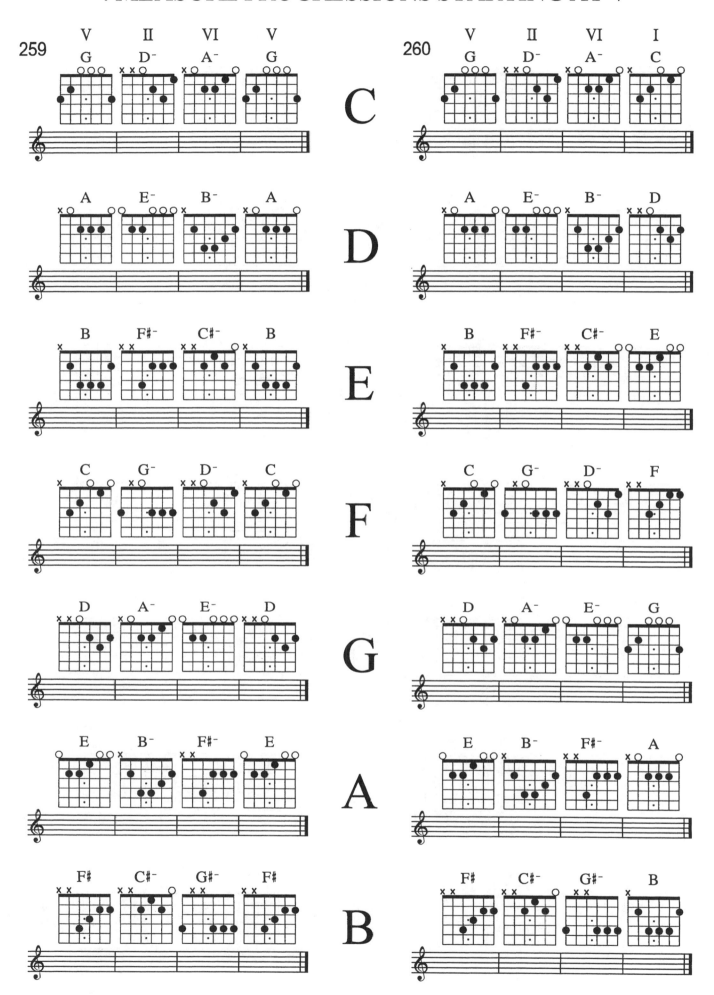

4 MEASURE PROGRESSIONS STARTING AT V

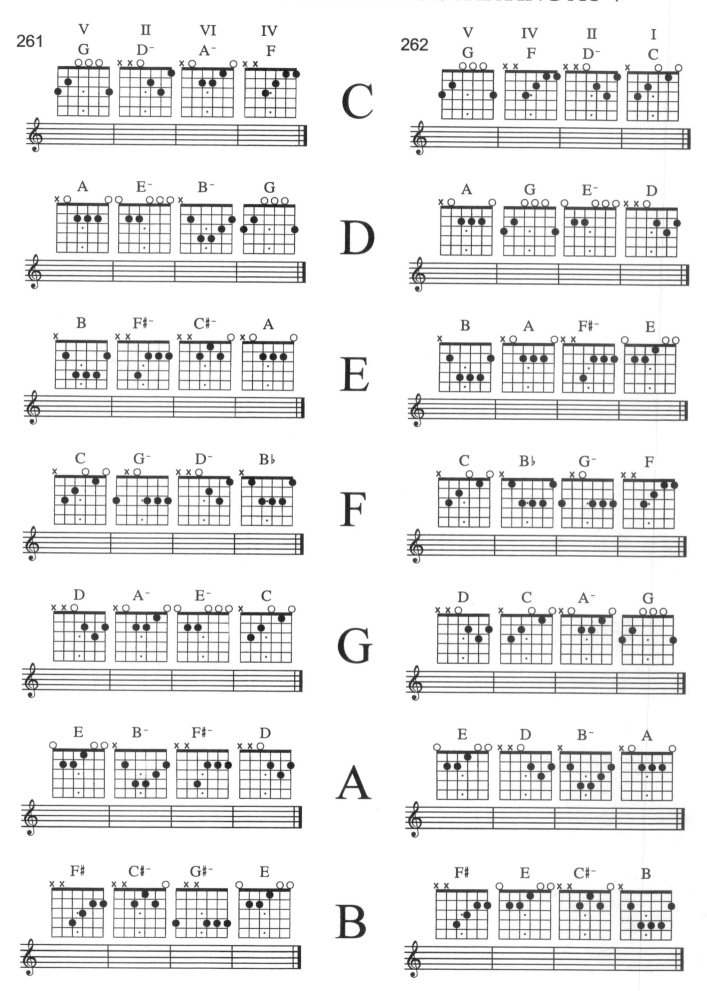

4 MEASURE PROGRESSIONS STARTING AT V

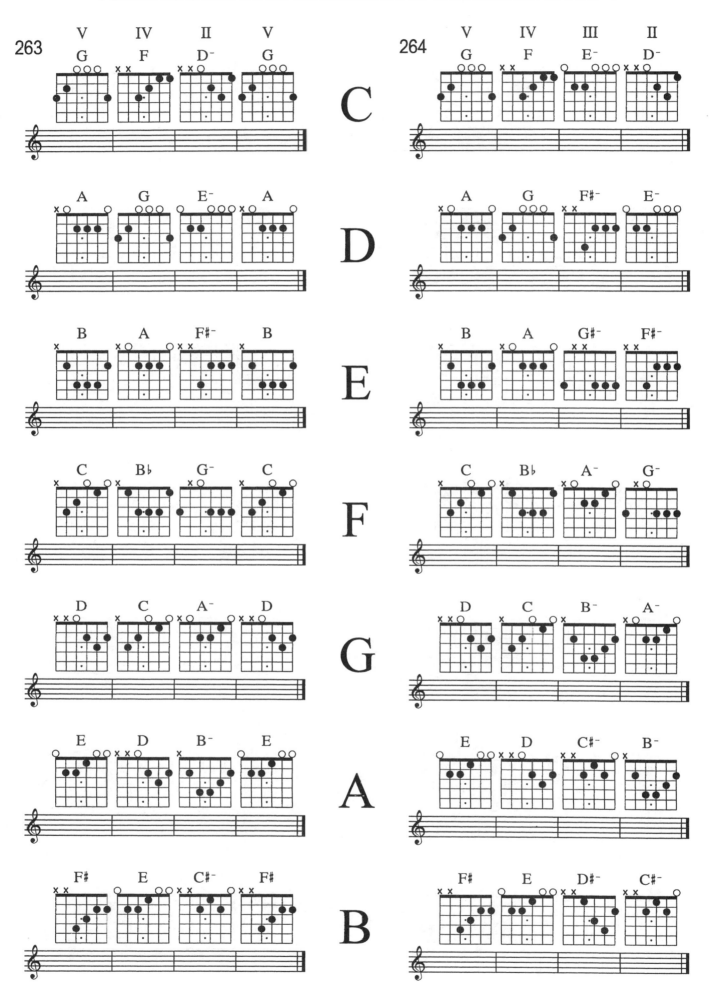

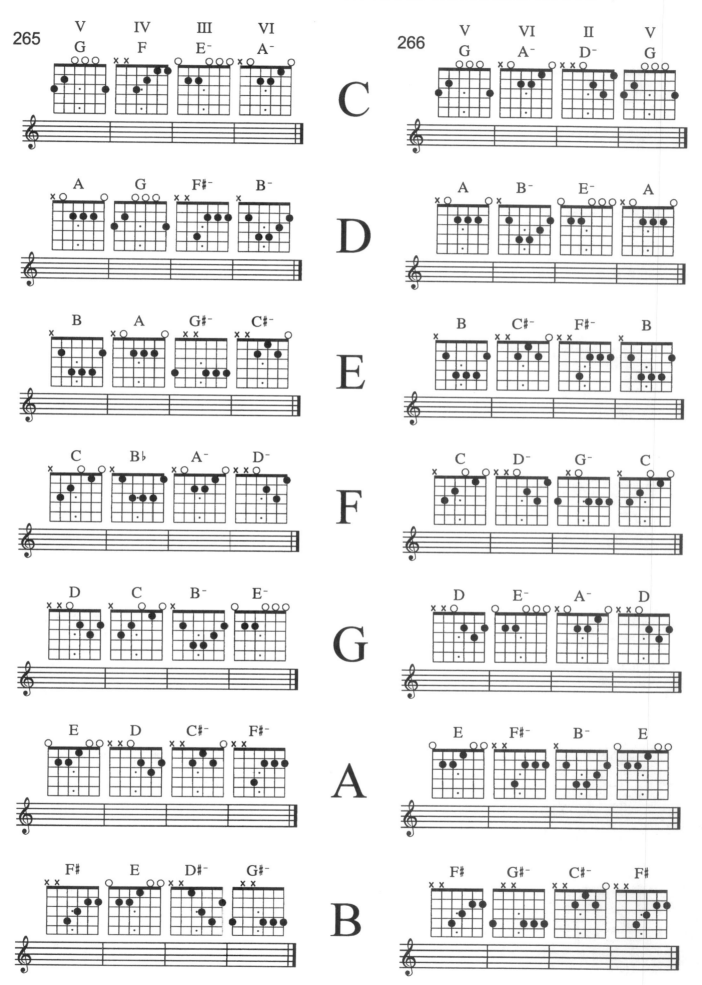

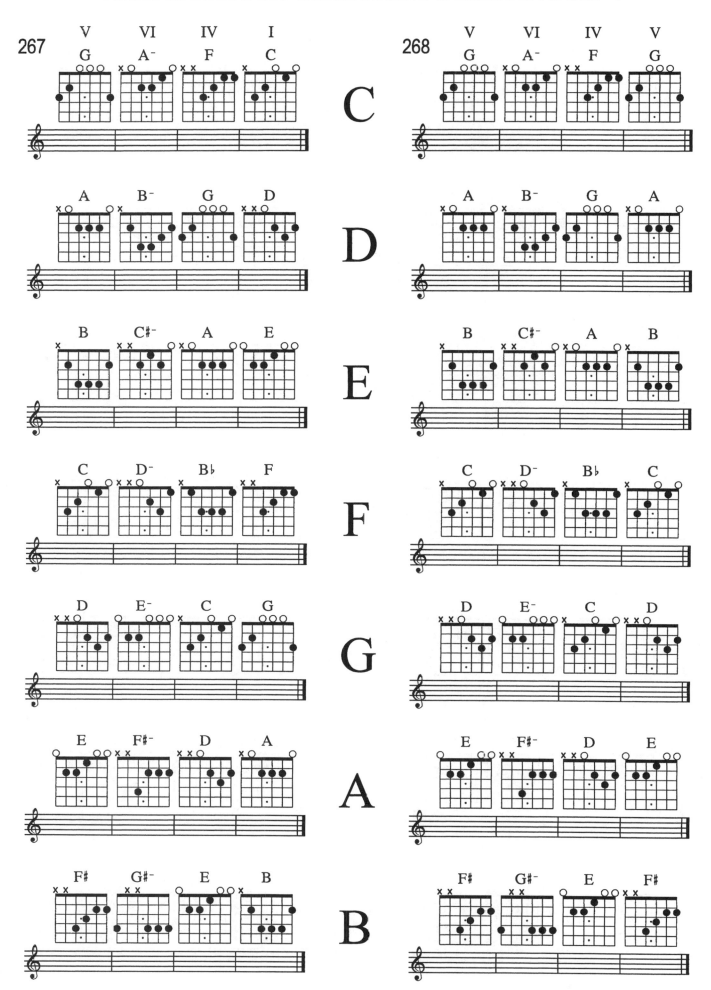

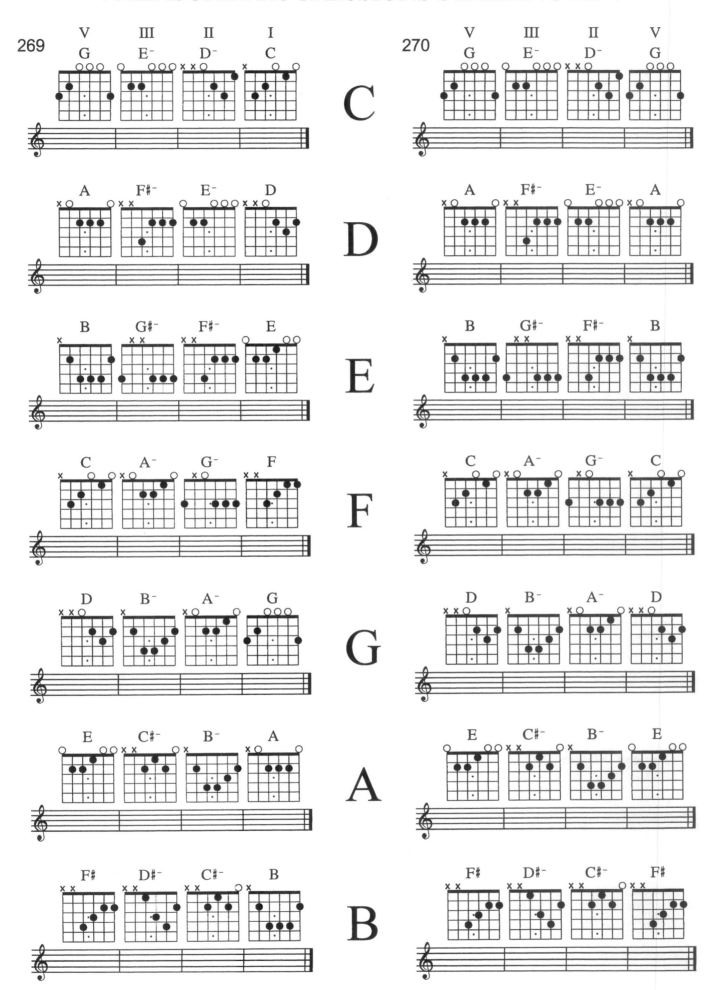

4 MEASURE PROGRESSIONS STARTING AT V

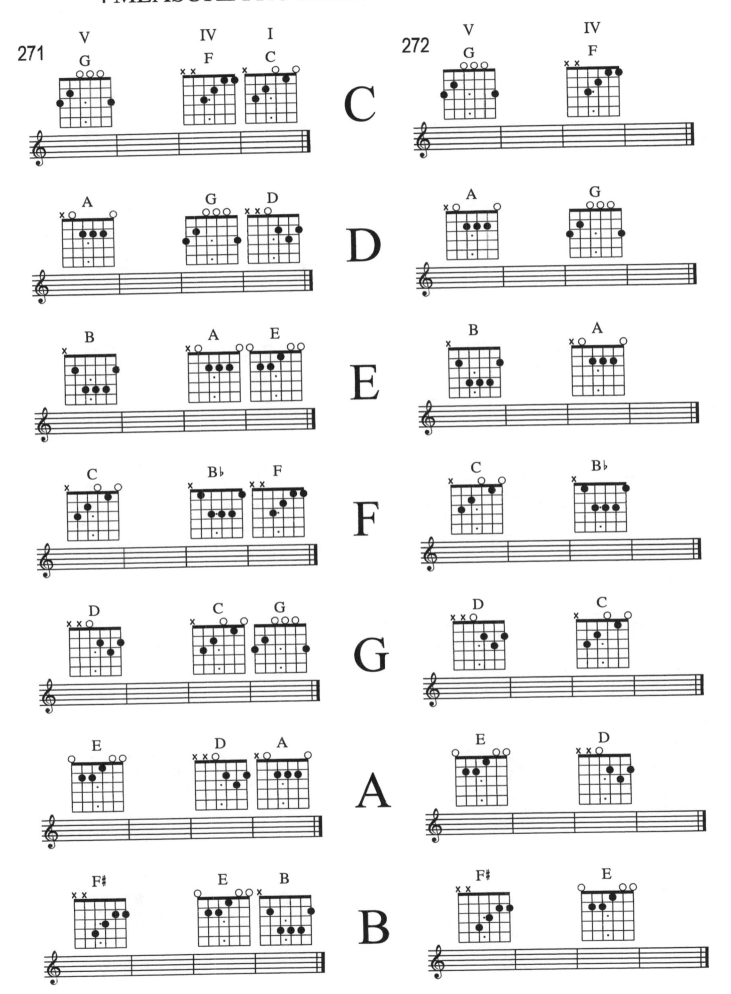

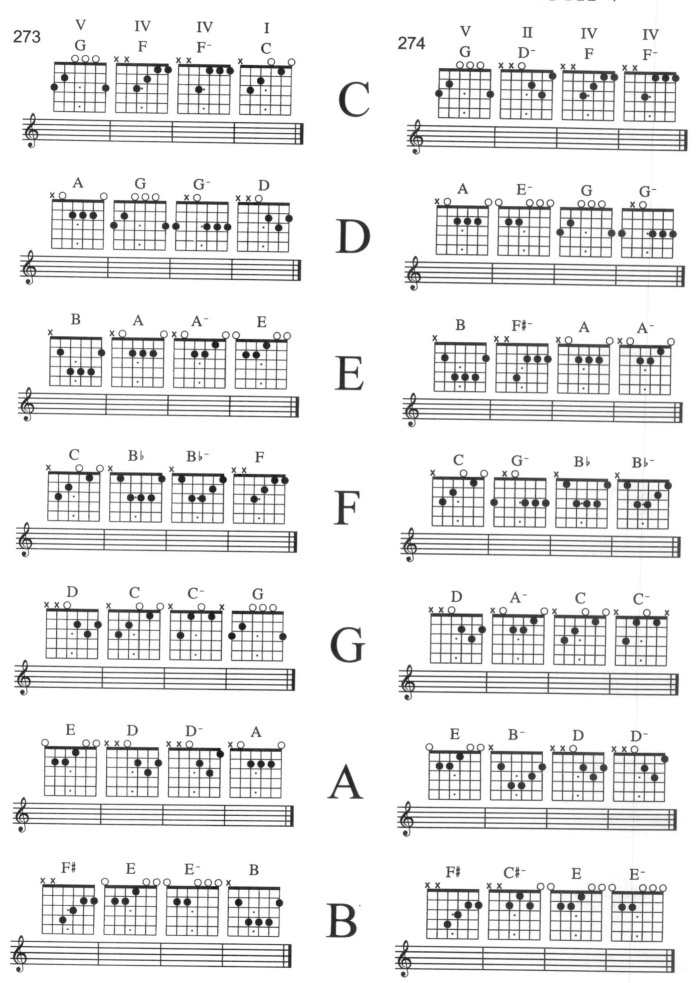

4 MEASURE PROGRESSIONS STARTING AT V

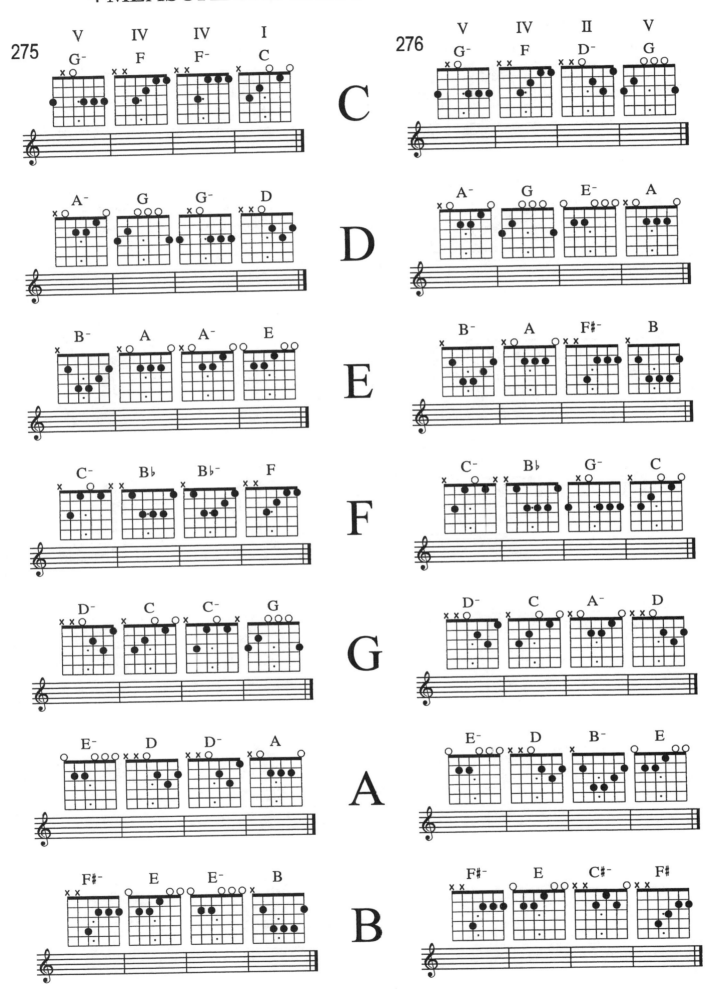

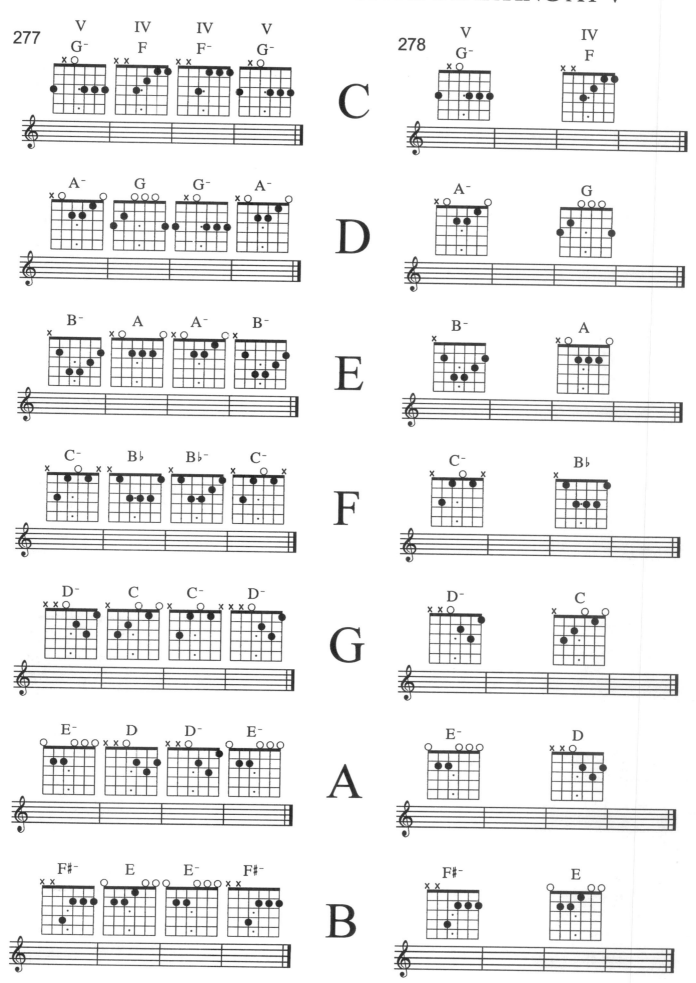

4 MEASURE PROGRESSIONS STARTING AT V

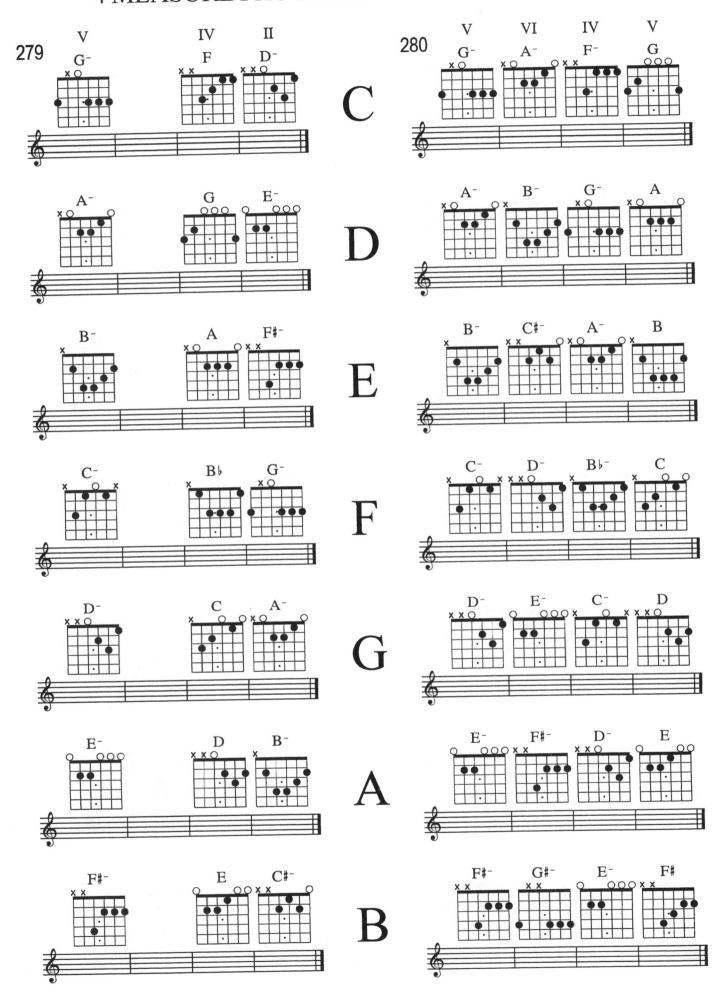

4 MEASURE PROGRESSIONS STARTING AT VI

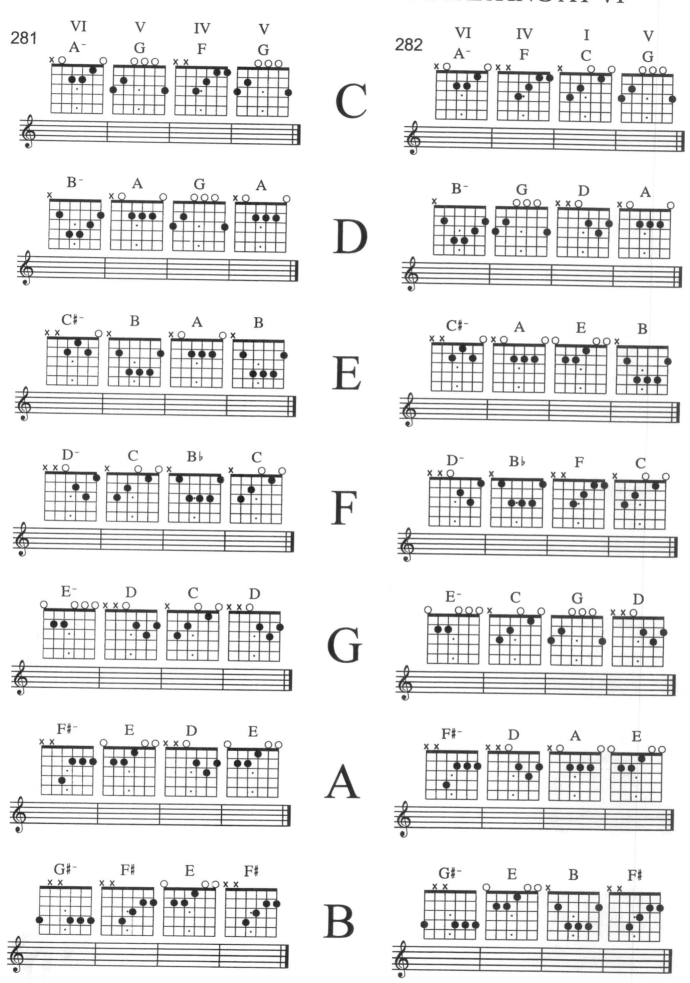

4 MEASURE PROGRESSIONS STARTING AT VI

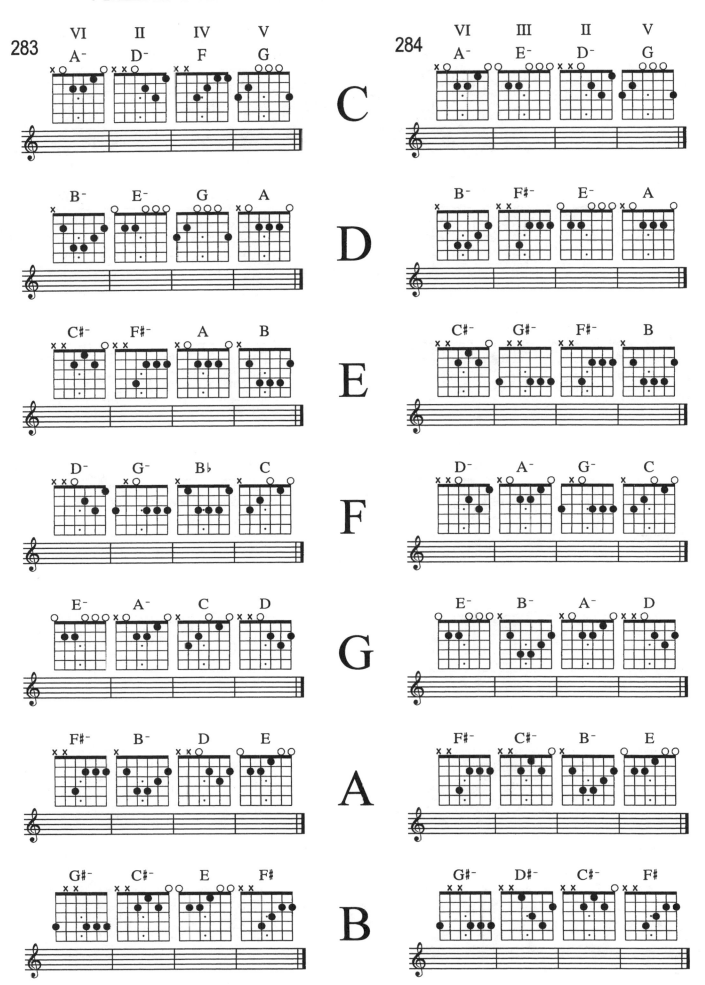

131

4 MEASURE PROGRESSIONS STARTING AT VI

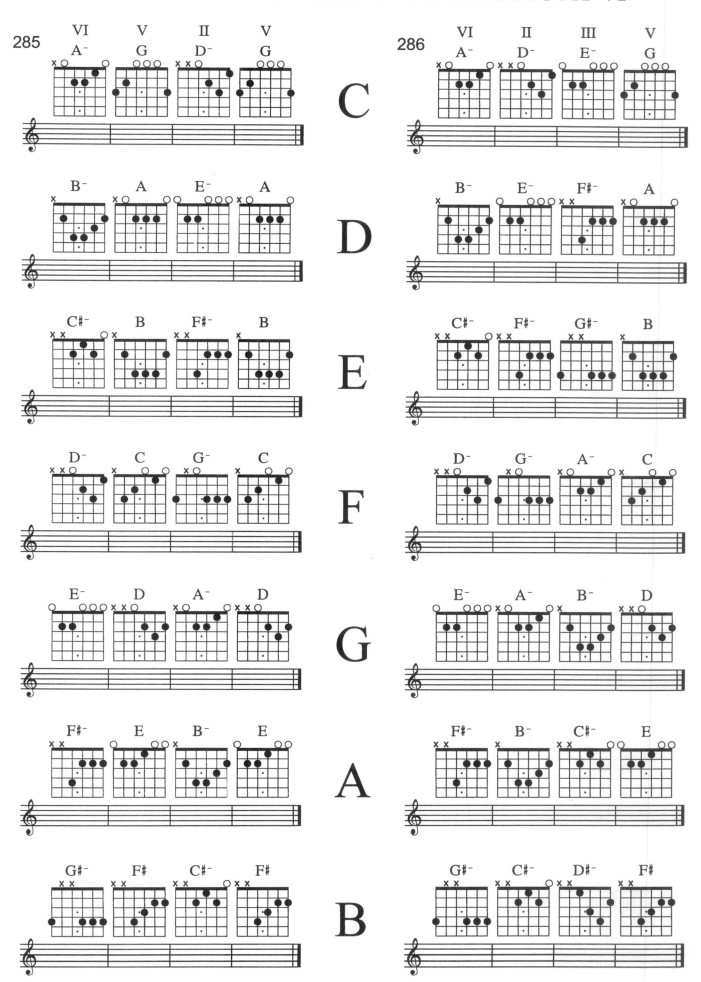

4 MEASURE PROGRESSIONS STARTING AT VI

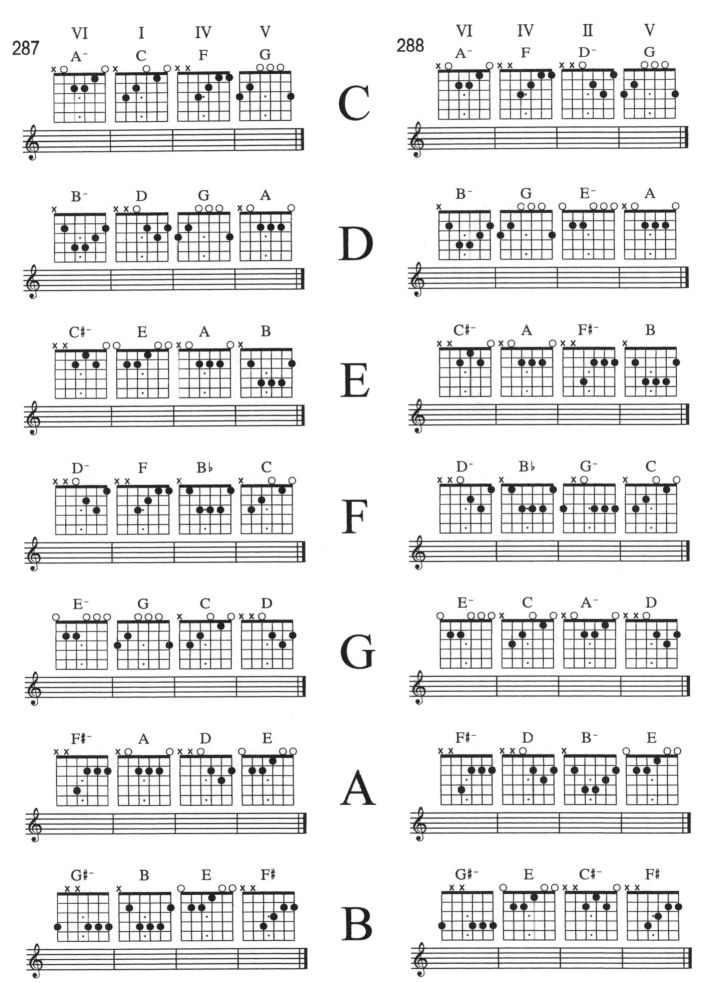

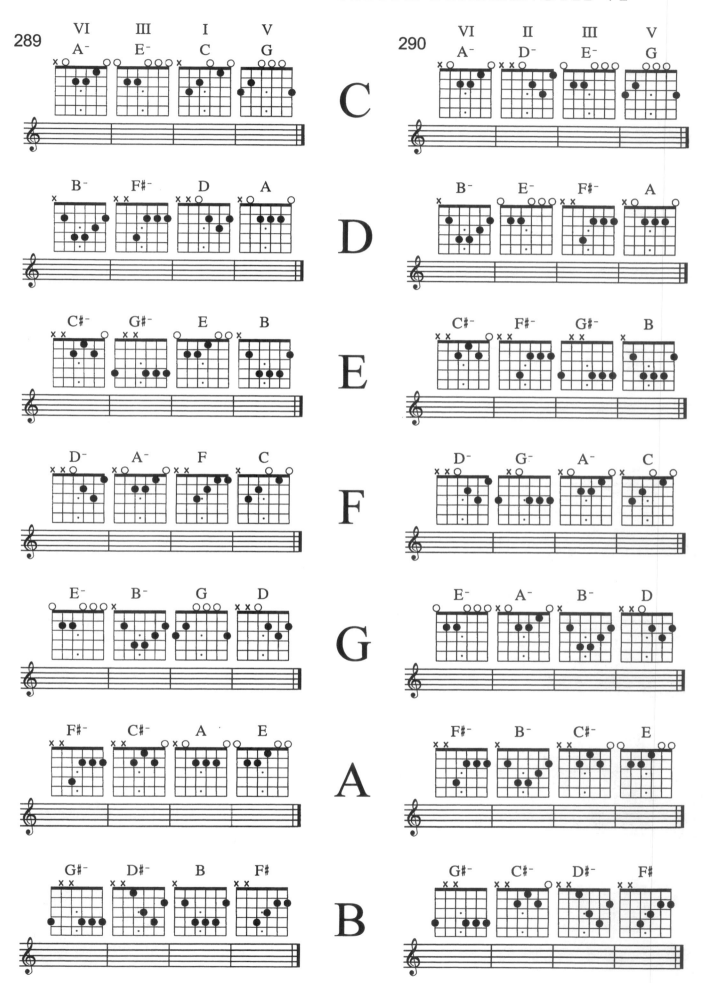

4 MEASURE PROGRESSIONS STARTING AT VI

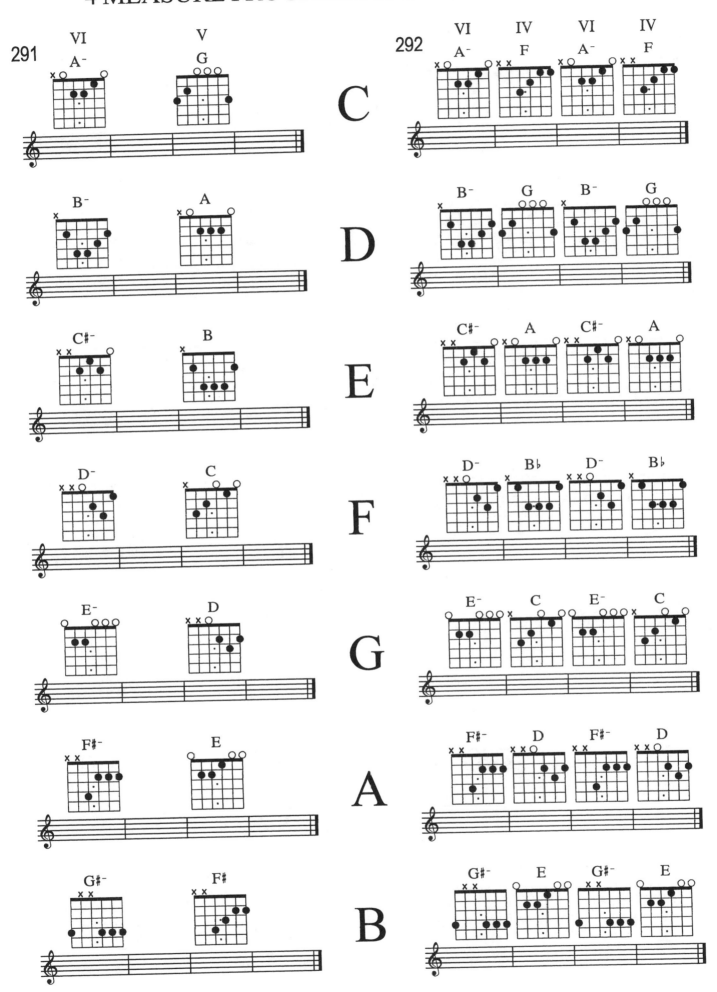

4 MEASURE PROGRESSIONS STARTING AT VI

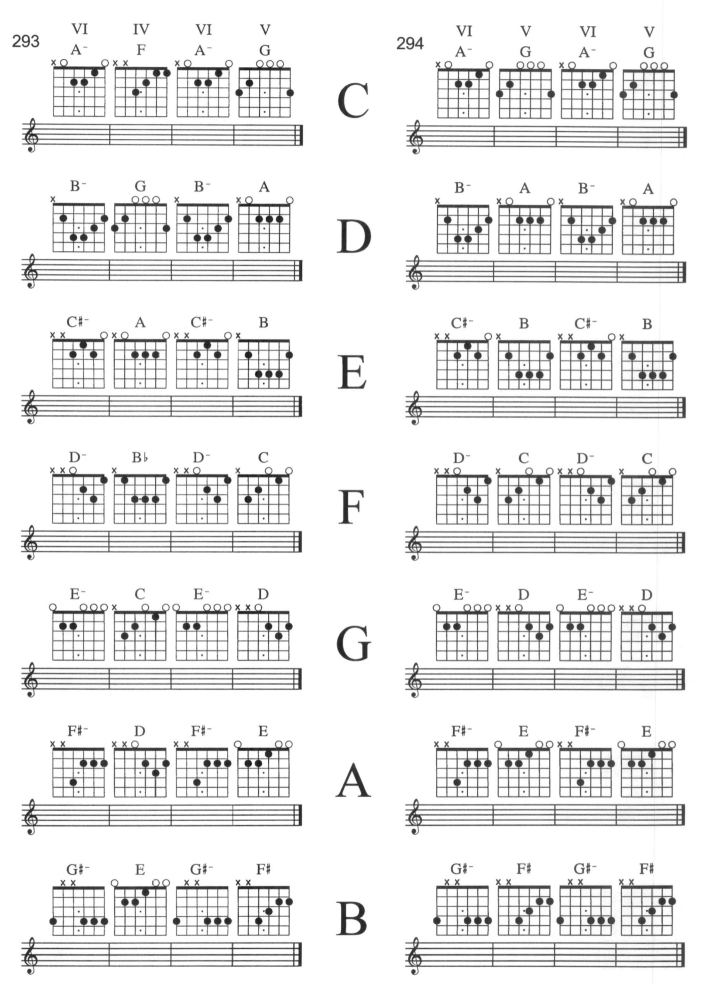

4 MEASURE PROGRESSIONS STARTING AT VI

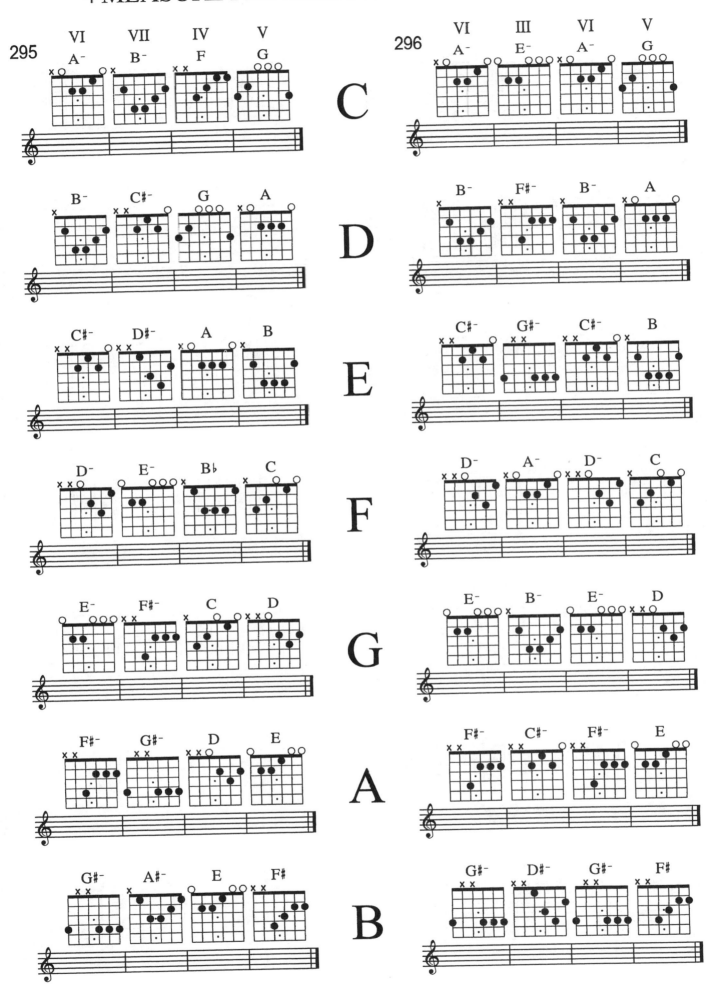

4 MEASURE PROGRESSIONS STARTING AT VI

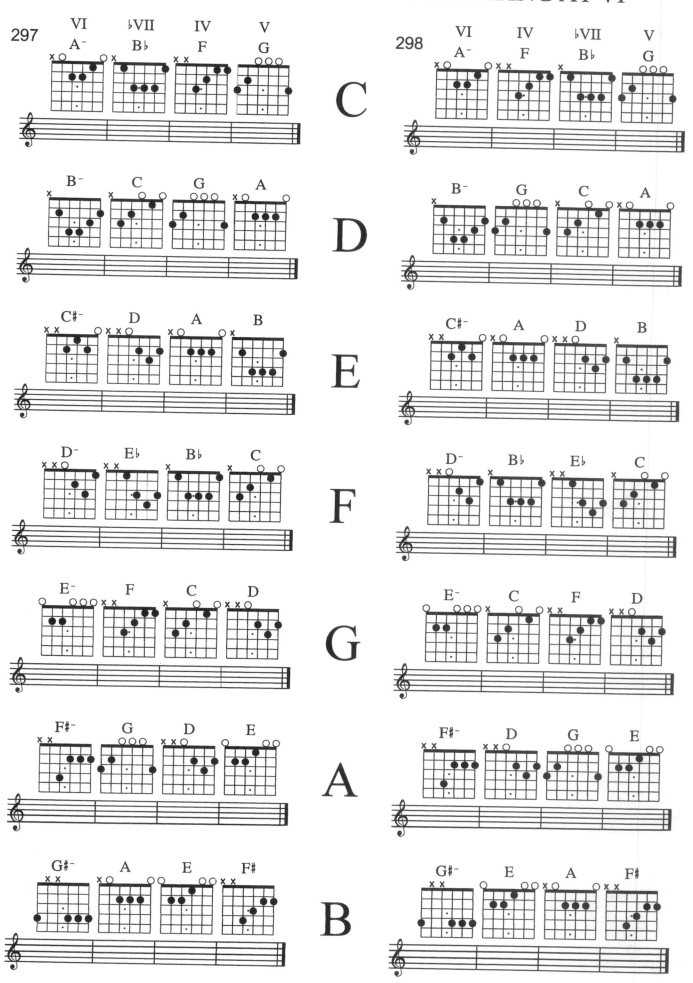

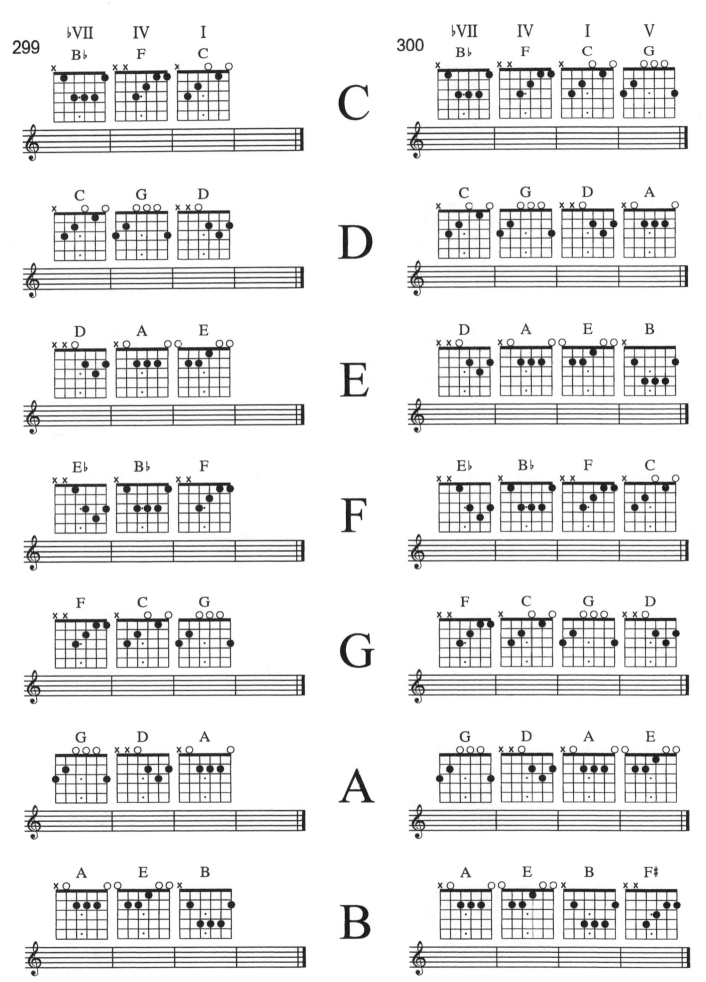

4 MEASURE PROGRESSIONS STARTING AT ♭VII

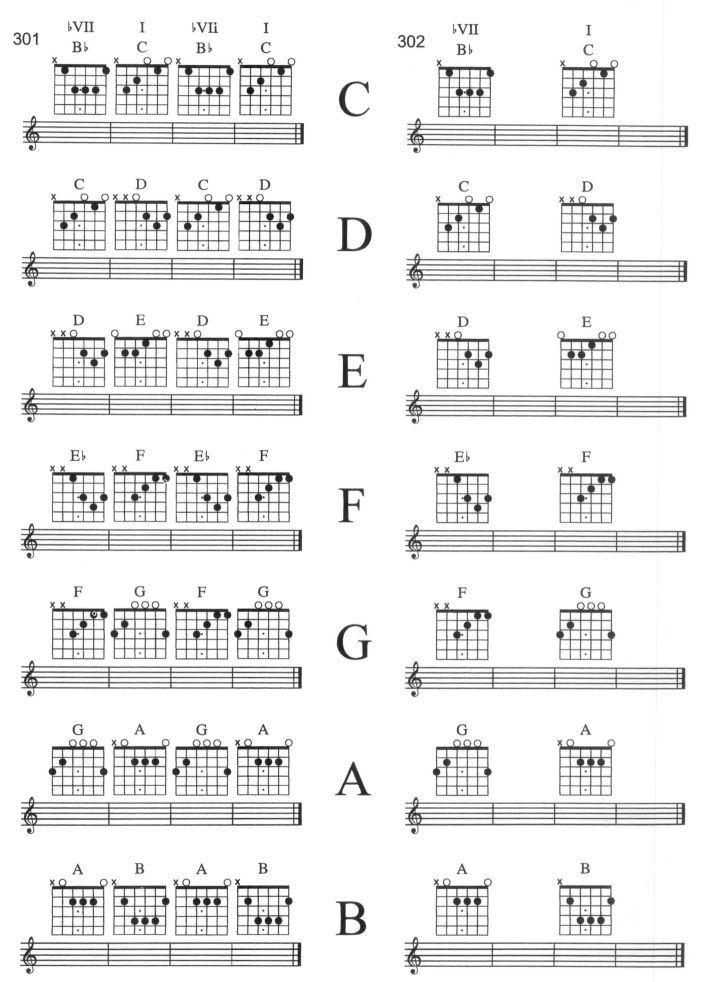

4 MEASURE PROGRESSIONS STARTING AT ♭VII

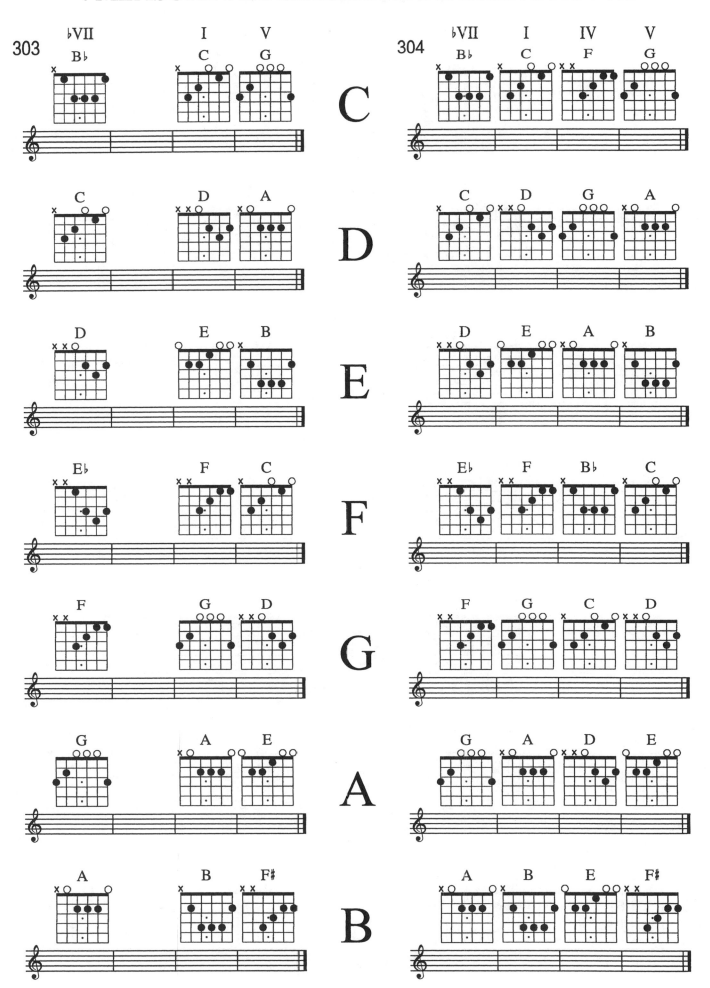

4 MEASURE PROGRESSIONS STARTING AT ♭VII

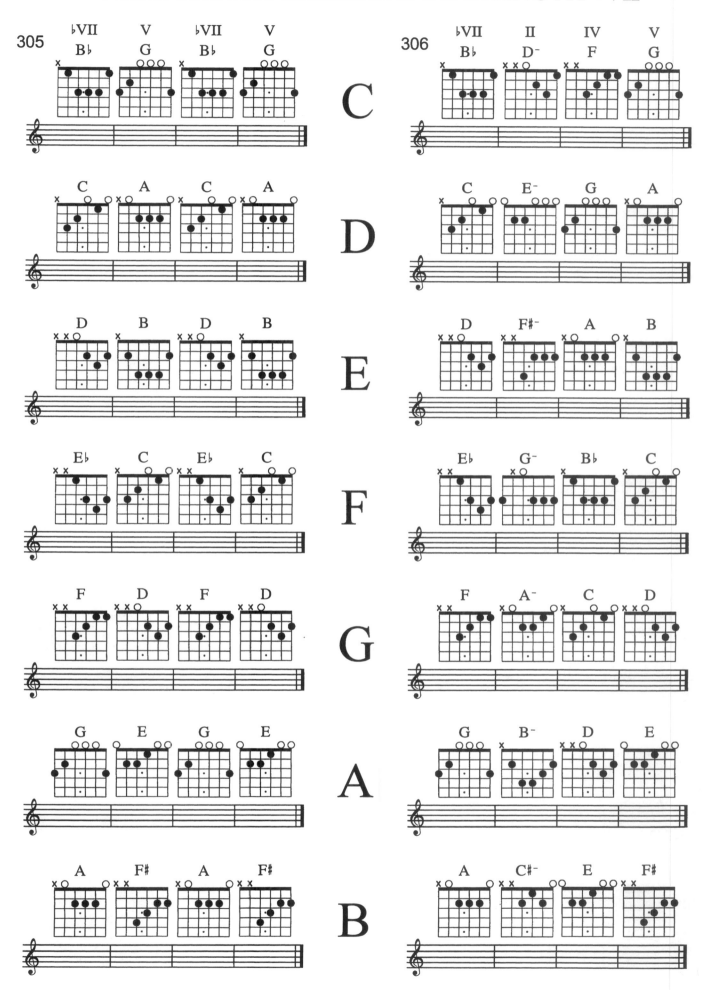

SOLOING AND COMPATIBILITY

In order to solo over progressions we need to understand scales, chords, and scale-chord compatibility. Well we've covered the basics of scales and chords so you're two thirds of the way there. In fact, when we extracted the chords from the modes to learn our first diatonic progression we demonstrated scale-chord compatibility. In essence, the scale we use to solo over the chord must contain the tones of that chord and visa versa. For a more in depth study of compatibility check out **The Guitar Grimoire Chords & Voicings.**

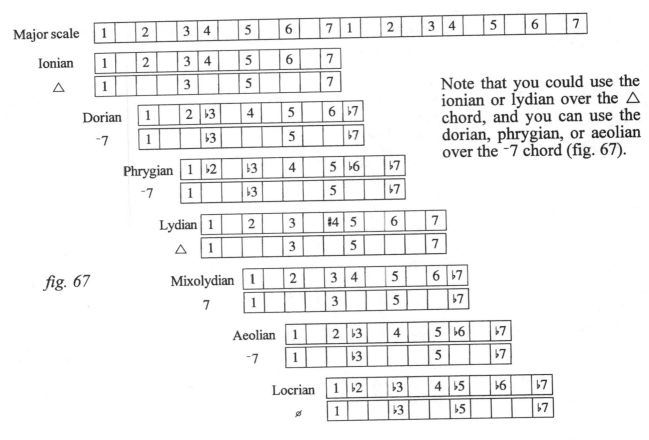

Note that you could use the ionian or lydian over the △ chord, and you can use the dorian, phrygian, or aeolian over the ⁻7 chord (fig. 67).

fig. 67

Our starting point for improvising or soloing over progressions is the one chord jams that were so popular in the late 60's and 70's. In fact they're still used in concert a lot, because they are so much fun and the crowd soaks it up. Anyway if we are doing a jam in A Minor, we use the A minor pentatonic to solo. Or we can use one of the minor modes (dorian or aeolian) (fig. 68).

A MINOR PENTATONIC

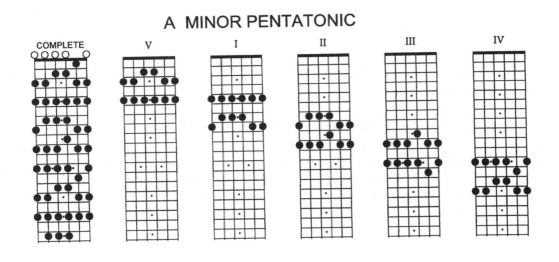

fig. 68

That's fine for one chord jams, but what about when you are changing chords? Alright, let's start with a basic 12 bar blues progression. This would be a 12 measure progression with a I, IV, V root motion (fig. 69).

fig. 69

We'll do it in the key of A using basic triad open chord voicings. This means that the chord voicings use open strings (fig. 70).

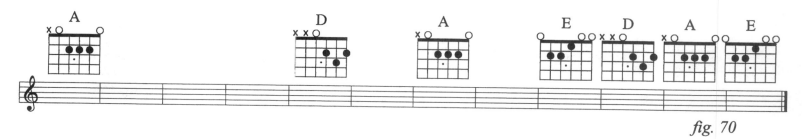

fig. 70

Well, for the "bluesy" sound you can still use the minor pentatonic scale over that progression. The only thing to remember is that when you are playing over the IV chord you will place your emphasis on the 4 tone. When you are playing over the V chord your emphasis will be on the 5 tone. Looking at the interval map for the minor pentatonic in the key of A, you can see it a little better (fig. 71).

For a much better demonstration of this, check out the **Guitar Grimoire: Progressions and Improvisation** video. You can demonstrate things easier on video than in a book.

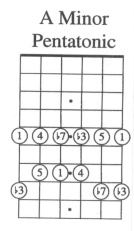

A Minor
Pentatonic

fig. 71

When you are trying to generate a country, or southern rock sound that's a different matter. First of all you will be using major pentatonics. However, you must use the corresponding petatonic for whatever chord you are playing. In other words, when you are playing an "E", you play a E major pentatonic. And when you are using an "A", you would use an A major pentatonic. And when you are playing a "G" you will use a G Major pentatonic, etc. But if you play a minor chord you will use the corresponding minor pentatonic.

The same holds true when soloing with mixolydians, as in, you play the corresponding scale chord combination, E & E, A & A, etc.

On the following pages are examples of basic 12 bar progressions with open chord voicings in the keys of C, D, E, F, G, A, B. At the top of the page are four variations of the same basic progression. At the bottom of the page are corresponding major pentatonic "windows" for soloing. What I mean is, staying in the same position while changing scales. On the facing page are the mixolydian "windows". Observe that all of the 12 bar progressions, including their variations, are merely combinations of four measure progressions pieced together.

12 BAR PROGRESSIONS: KEY OF C

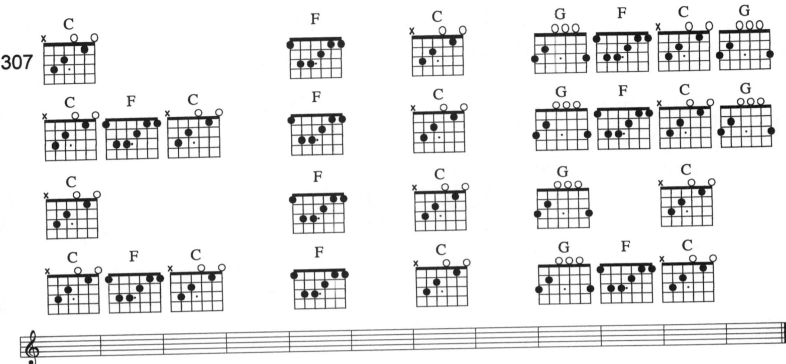

307

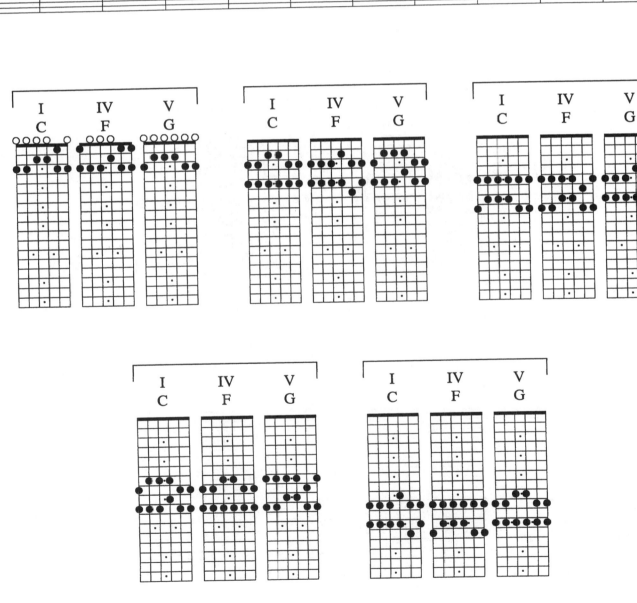

MIXOLYDIAN SOLOING PATTERNS: KEY OF C

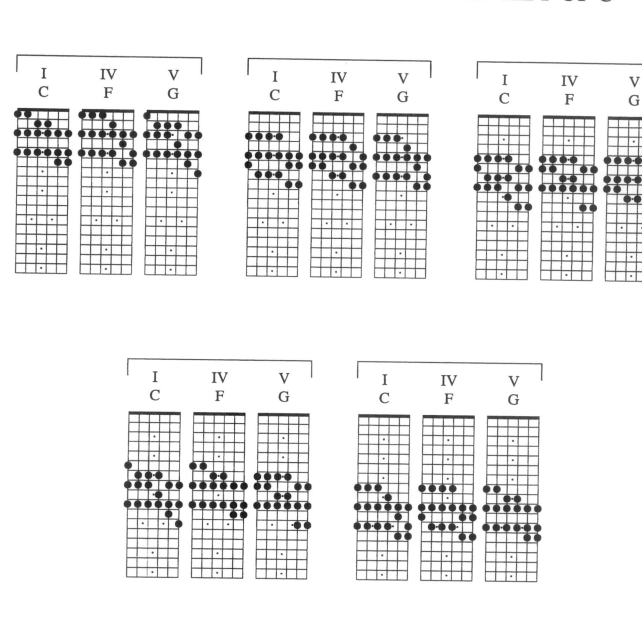

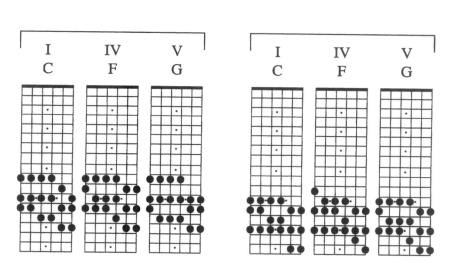

12 BAR PROGRESSIONS: KEY OF D

308

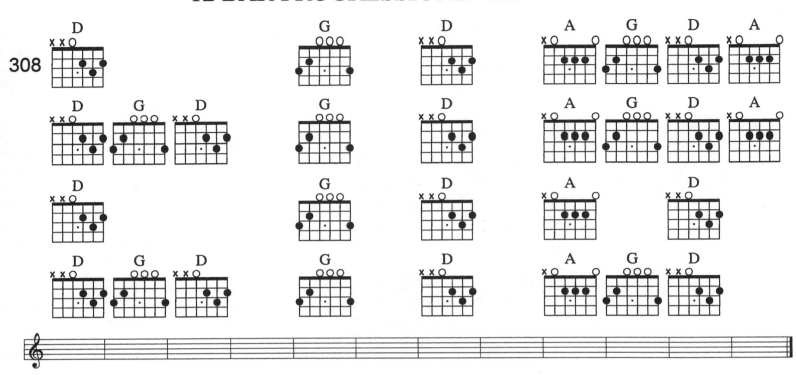

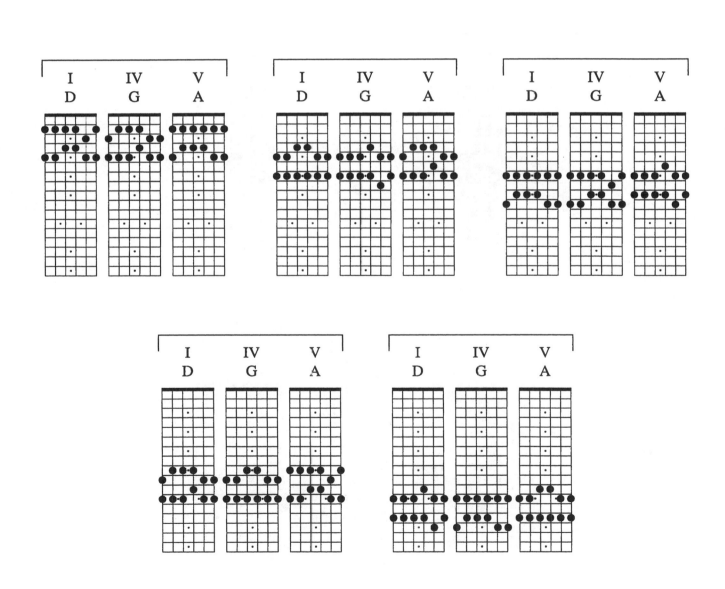

MIXOLYDIAN SOLOING PATTERNS: KEY OF D

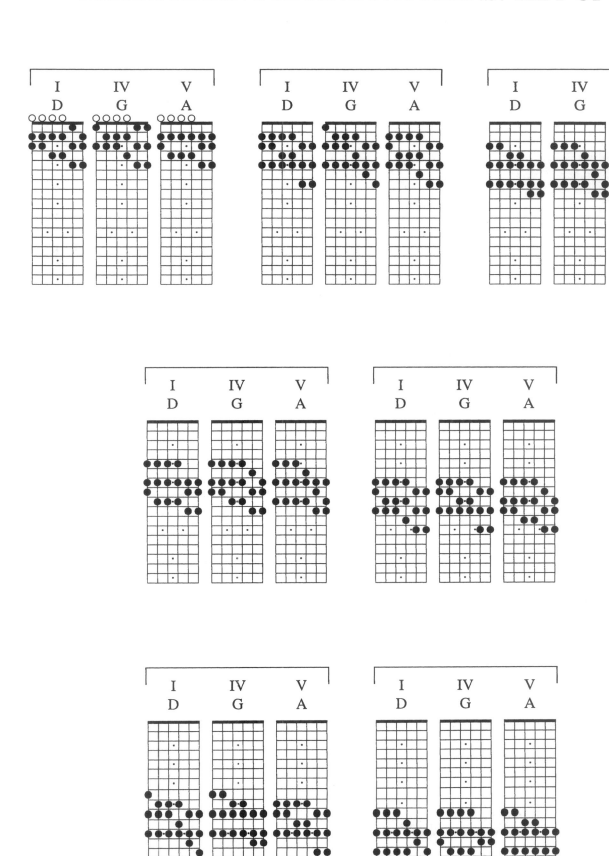

12 BAR PROGRESSIONS: KEY OF E

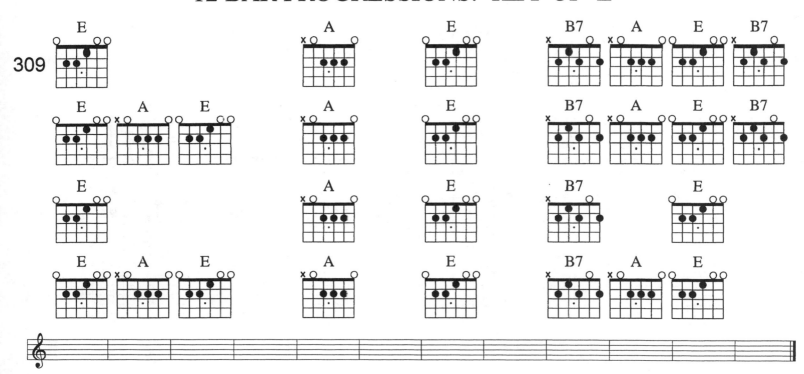

309

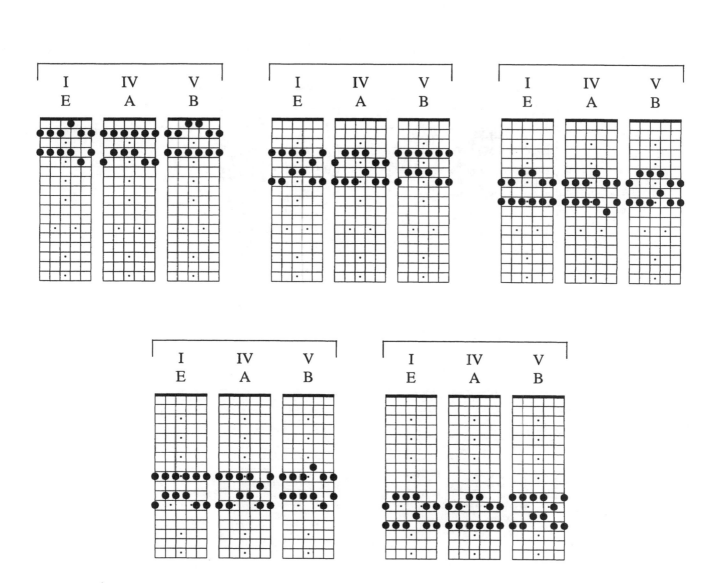

MIXOLYDIAN SOLOING PATTERNS: KEY OF E

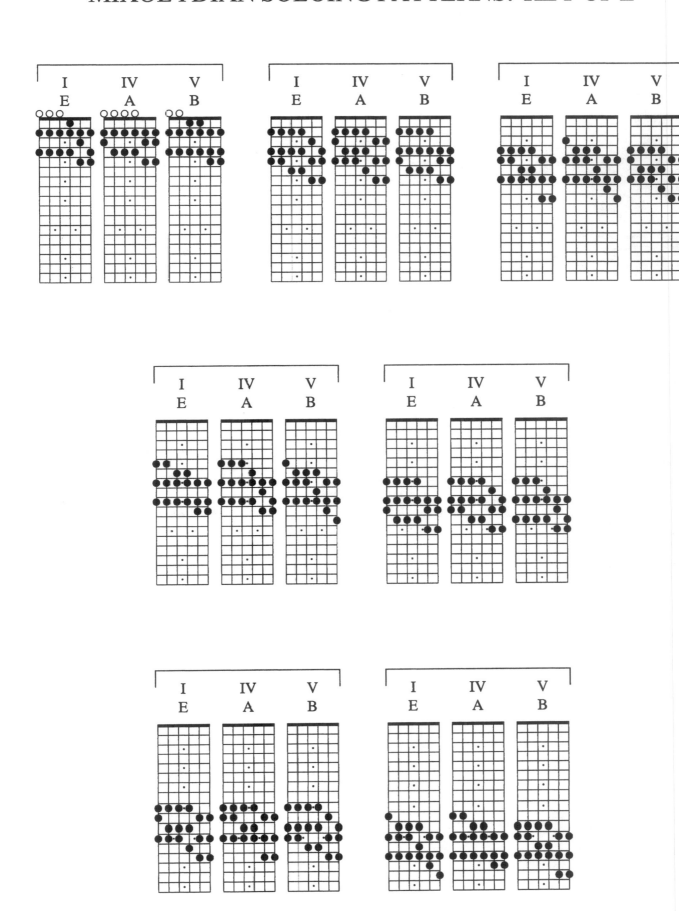

12 BAR PROGRESSIONS: KEY OF F

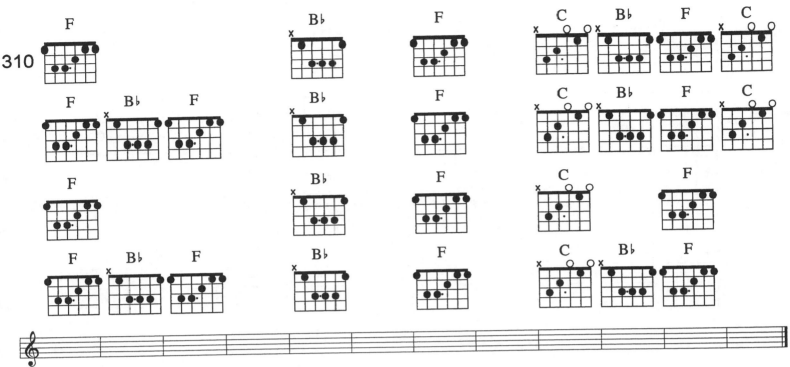

310

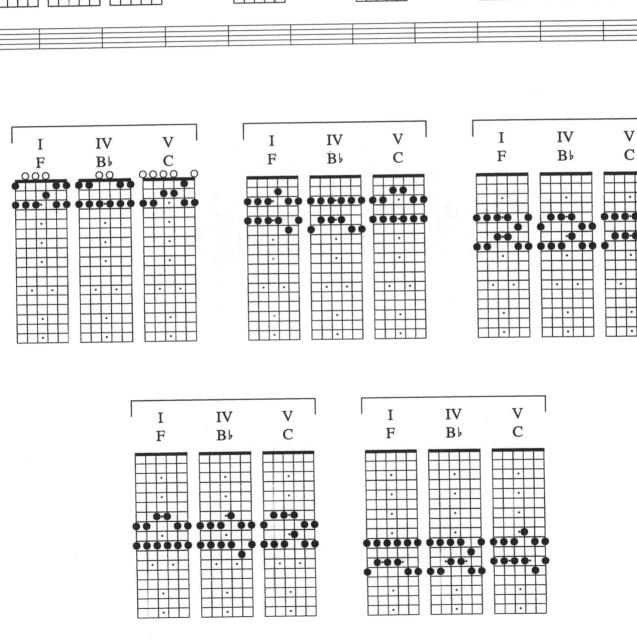

MIXOLYDIAN SOLOING PATTERNS: KEY OF F

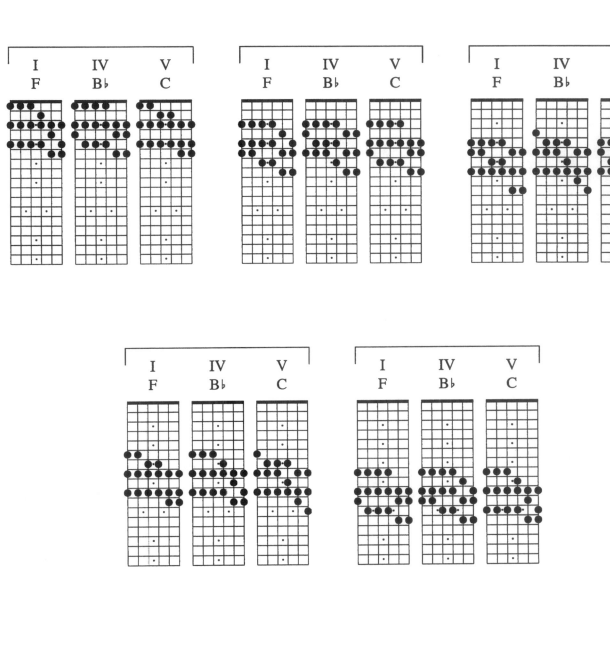

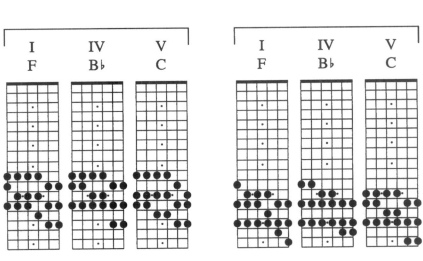

12 BAR PROGRESSIONS: KEY OF G

311

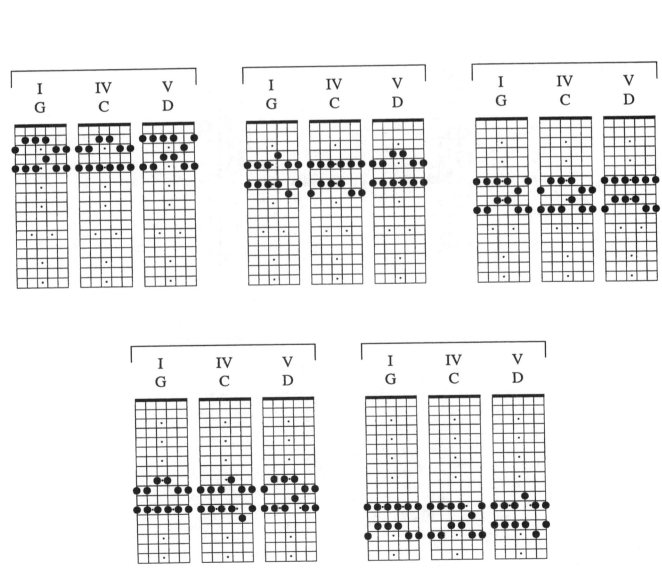

MIXOLYDIAN SOLOING PATTERNS: KEY OF G

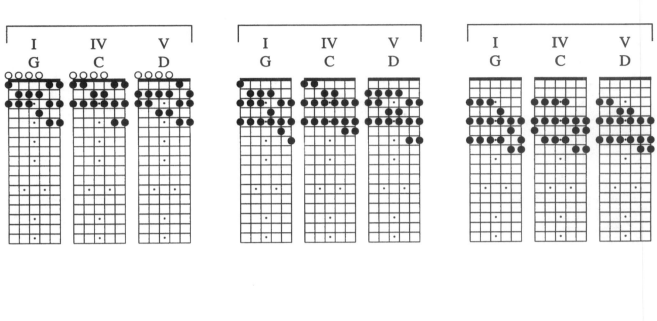

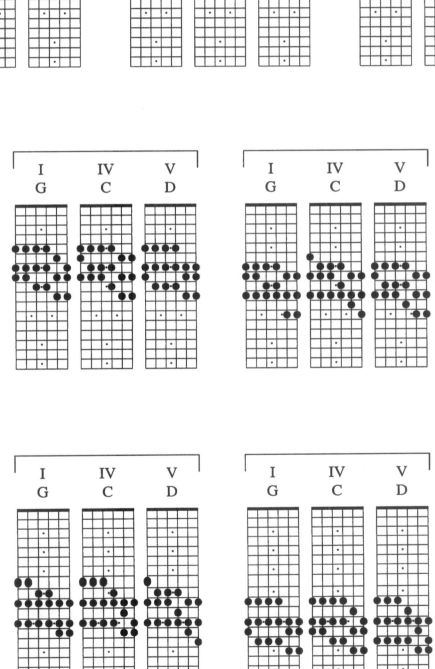

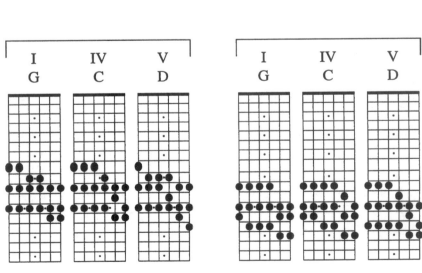

12 BAR PROGRESSIONS: KEY OF A

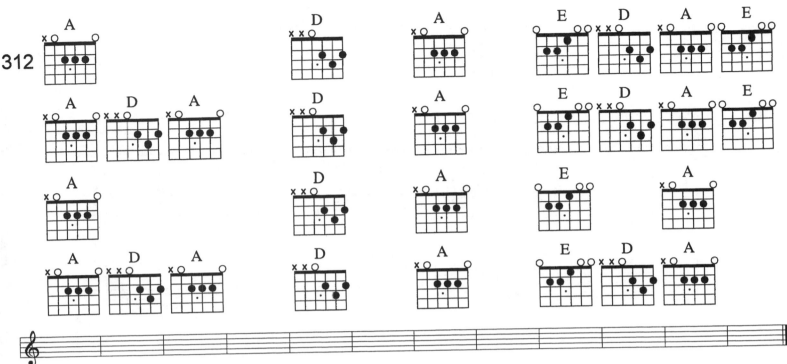

312

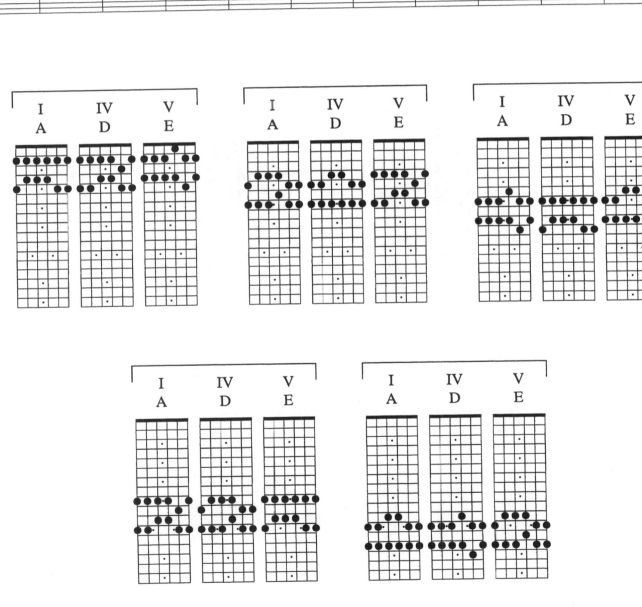

MIXOLYDIAN SOLOING PATTERNS: KEY OF A

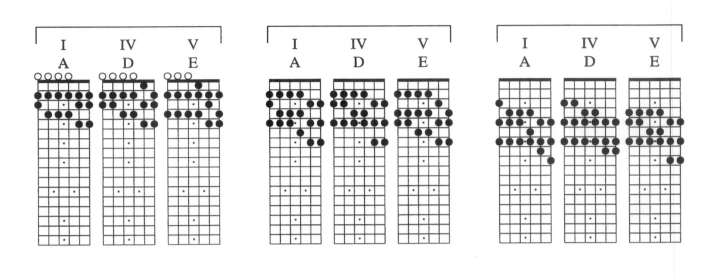

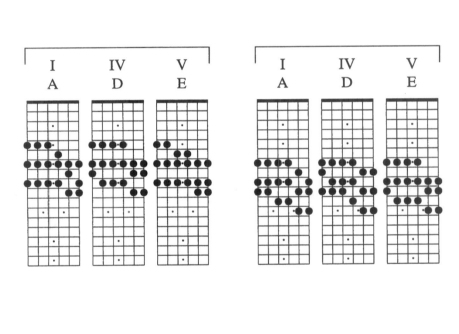

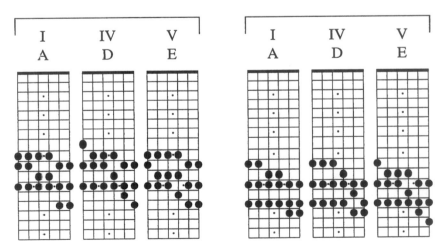

12 BAR PROGRESSIONS: KEY OF B

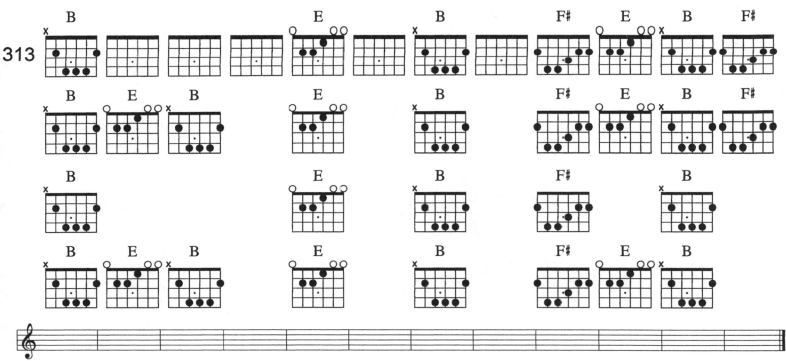

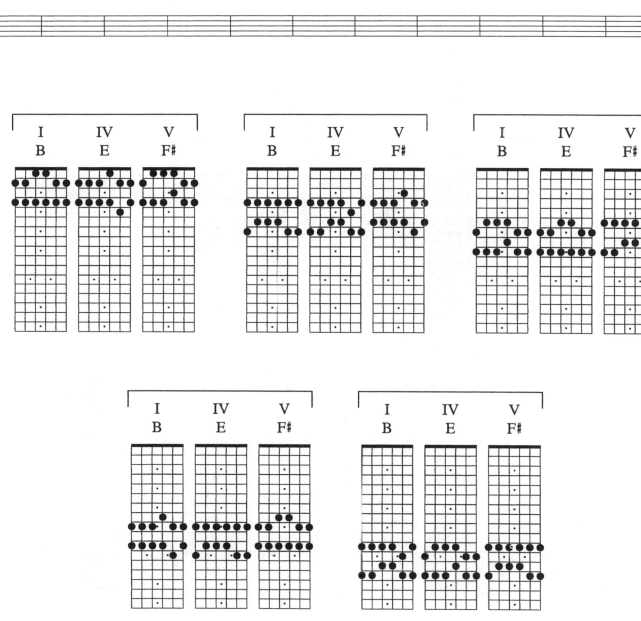

MIXOLYDIAN SOLOING PATTERNS: KEY OF B

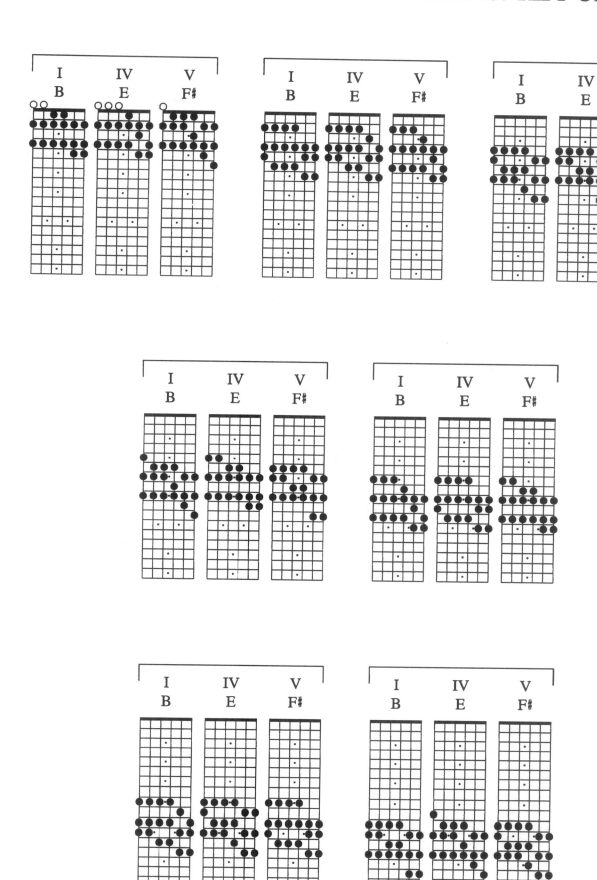

WINDOW SOLOING

What about mixing major and minor chords, then soloing over them? Good question. Let's start by building a song. We'll take four 4 measure progressions. One from the I section, one from the II section, one from the IV section, and one from the V section all in the key of "C" (fig. 72).

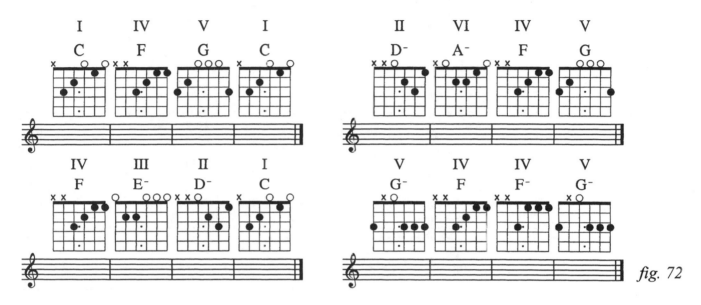

fig. 72

When we put them together our song looks like this (fig. 73).

On the following pages are charts graphed out in the keys of C, D, E, F, G, A, B for soloing without changing positions, or what I call soloing within a "window" (fig. 74).

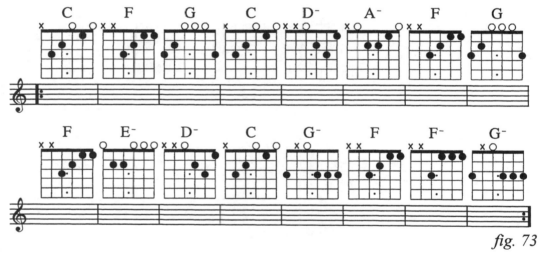

fig. 73

Each scale pattern is listed as a major with its relative minor beneath. If you will notice on our soloing chart for our song, you will see that C and A⁻ are the same, as are F and D⁻, as are G and E⁻ etc.

These patterns are taken from the key of C chart.

fig. 74

SOLOING PATTERNS

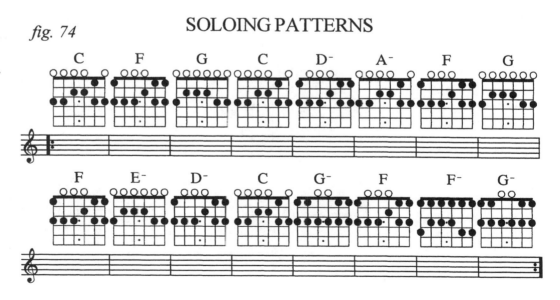

159

WINDOW SOLOING: KEY OF C

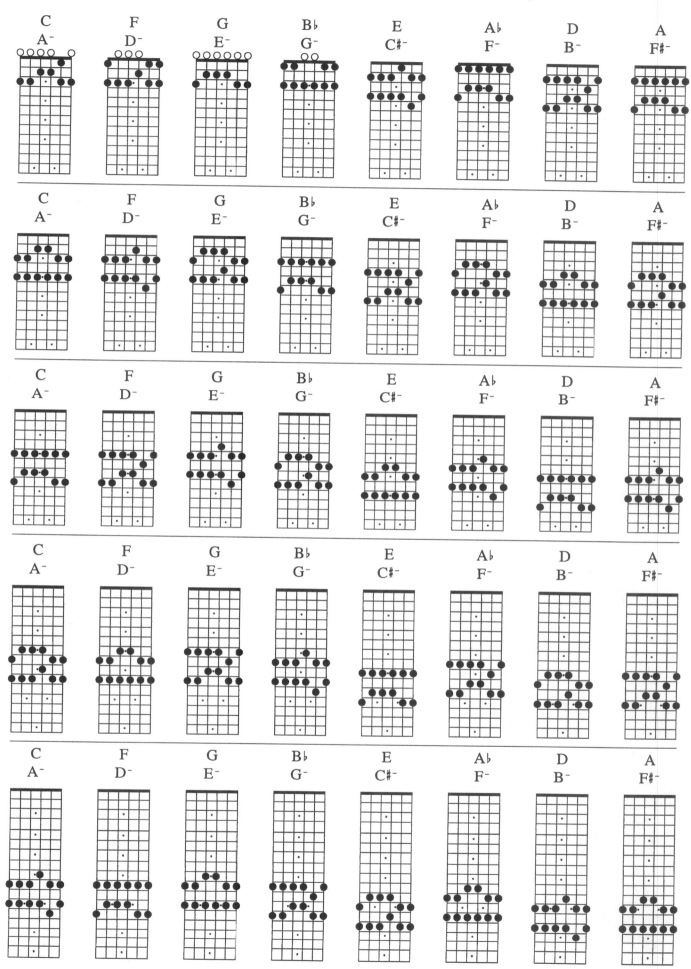

WINDOW SOLOING: KEY OF D

WINDOW SOLOING: KEY OF E

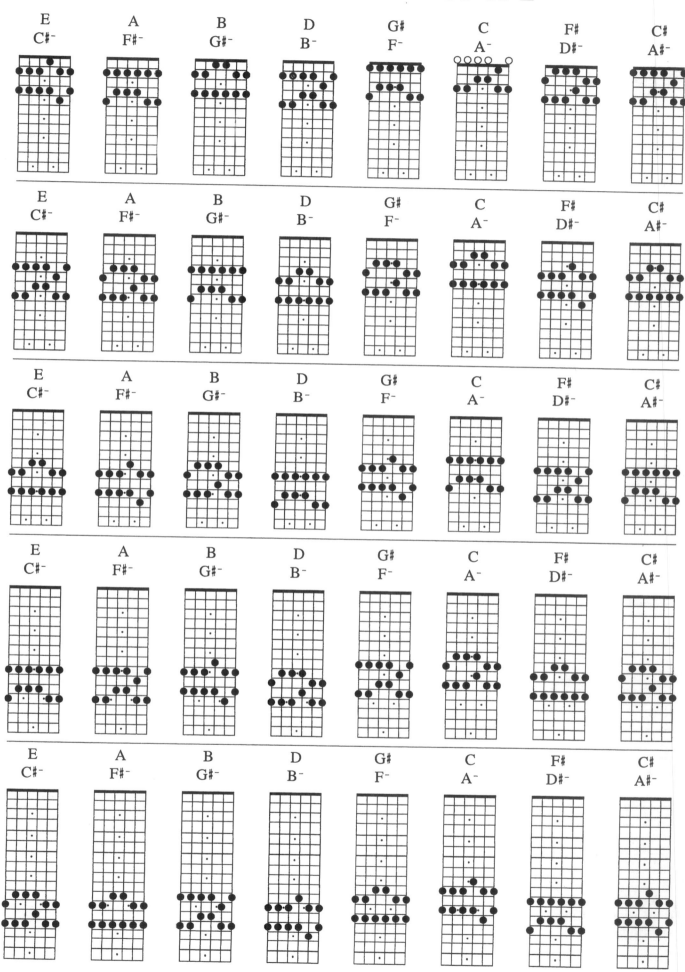

162

WINDOW SOLOING: KEY OF F

F	B♭	C	E♭	A	D♭	G	D
D-	G-	A-	C-	F♯-	B♭-	E-	B-

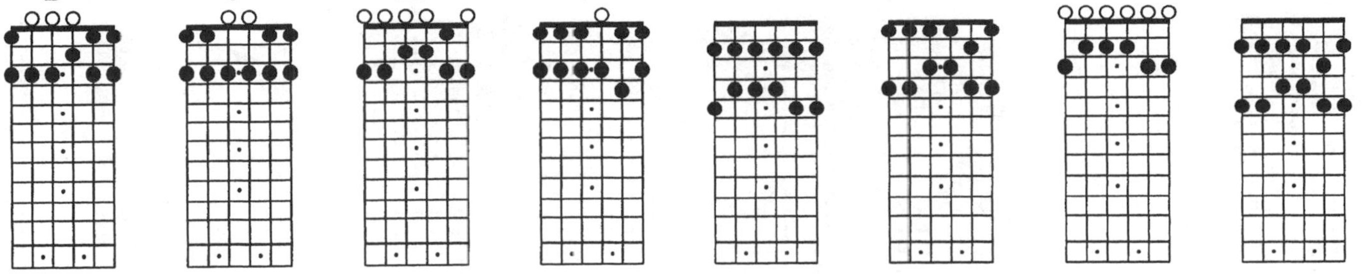

F	B♭	C	E♭	A	D♭	G	D
D-	G-	A-	C-	F♯-	B♭-	E-	B-

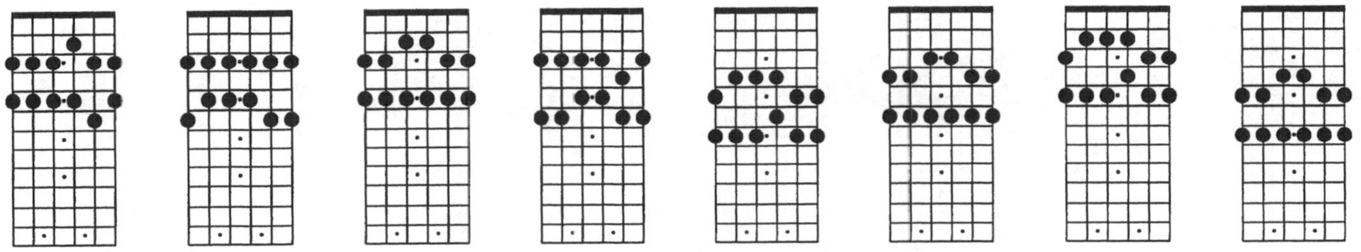

F	B♭	C	E♭	A	D♭	G	D
D-	G-	A-	C-	F♯-	B♭-	E-	B-

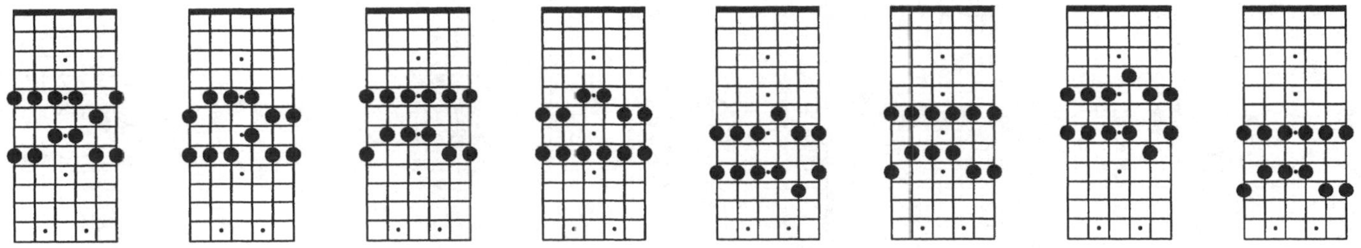

F	B♭	C	E♭	A	D♭	G	D
D-	G-	A-	C-	F♯-	B♭-	E-	B-

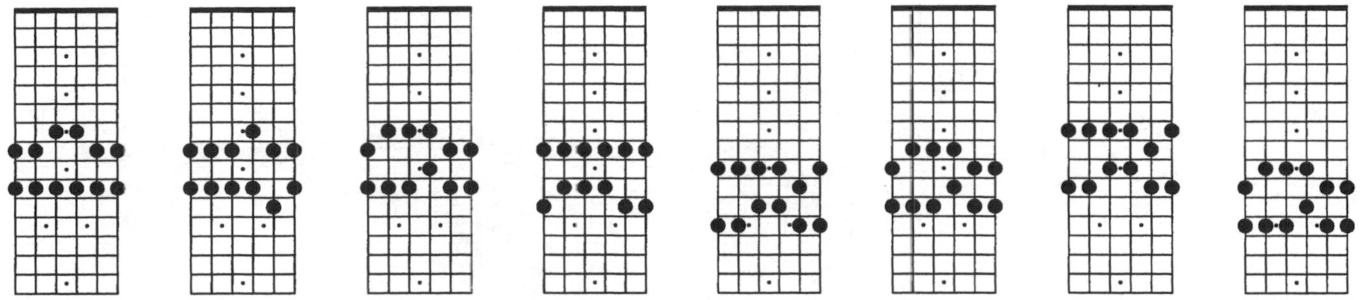

F	B♭	C	E♭	A	D♭	G	D
D-	G-	A-	C-	F♯-	B♭-	E-	B-

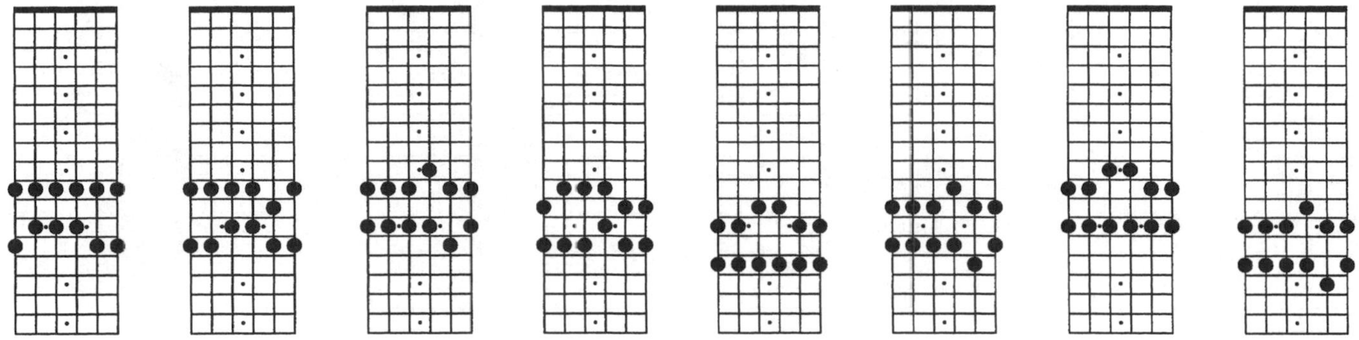

WINDOW SOLOING: KEY OF G

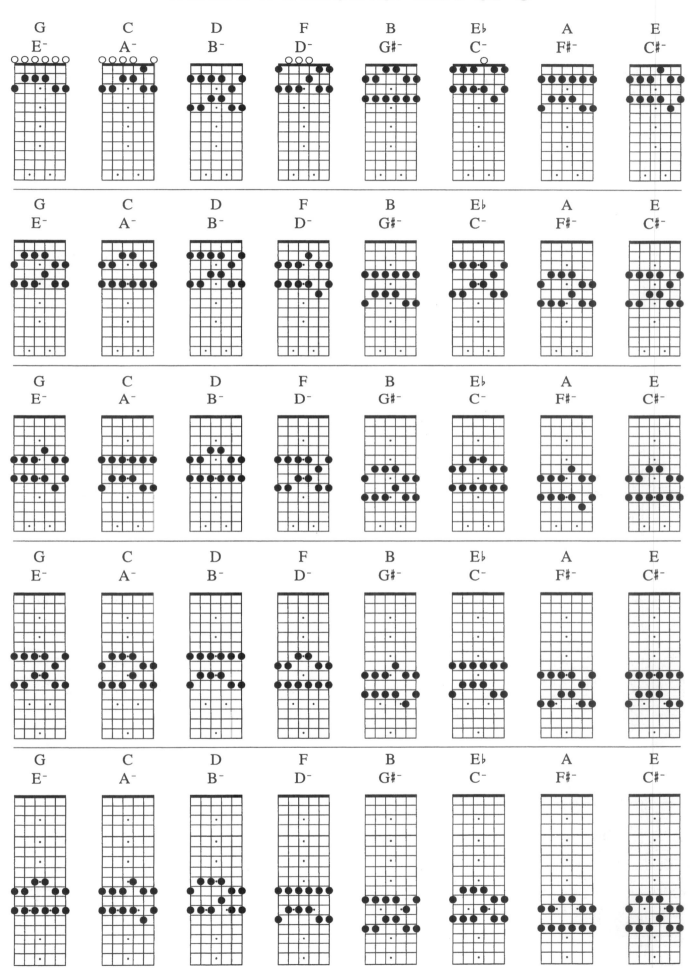

164

WINDOW SOLOING: KEY OF A

WINDOW SOLOING: KEY OF B

SOLOING OVER DIATONICS AND CIRCLE PROGRESSIONS

On the following pages are graphed out the diatonic chords in open voicings for the keys of C, D, E, F, G, A, B just like the example below.

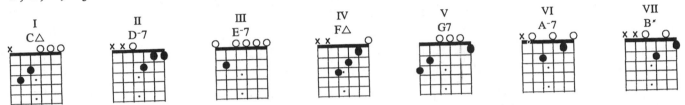

They are then arranged in circle progression sequence and bracketed off in the various circle segments. In other words, II V I, VI II V I, III VI II V I, VII III VI II V I, and IV VII III VI II V I.

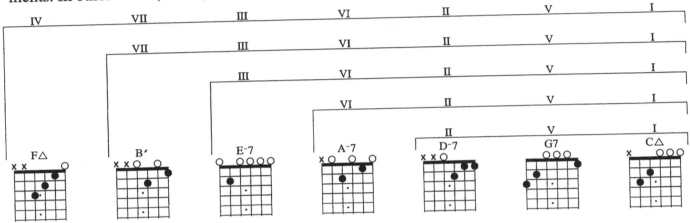

If you'd map out the individual progressions they would look like this.

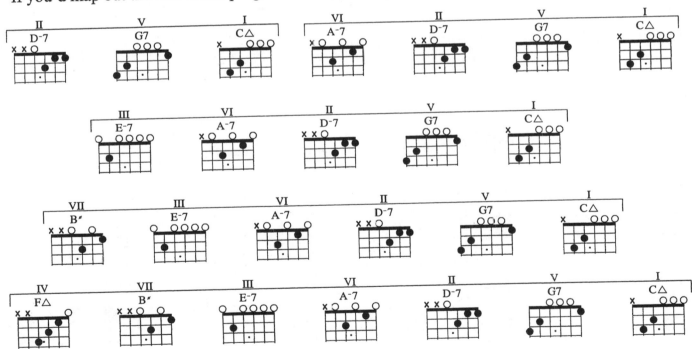

Beneath the bracketed diagram are the patterns of the appropriate Major scale. Any of the patterns will work over any of the chords.

DIATONIC PROGRESSION: KEY OF C

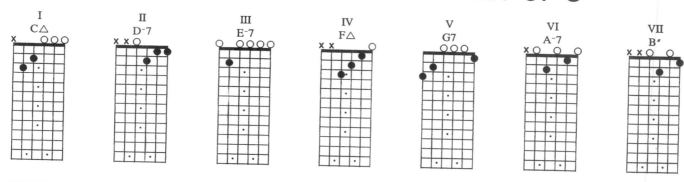

CIRCLE PROGRESSIONS: KEY OF C

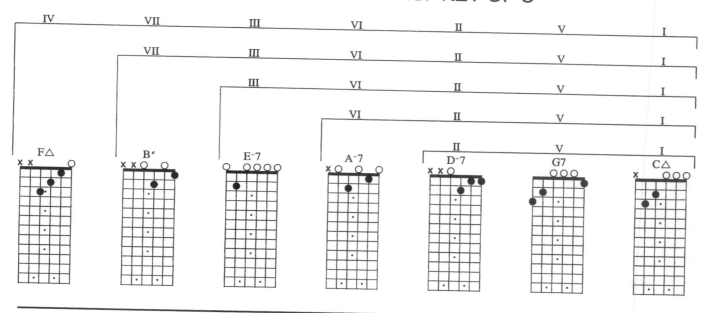

C MAJOR = D DORIAN ~ E PHRYGIAN ~ F LYDIAN ~ G MIXOLYDIAN ~ A AEOLIAN ~ B LOCRIAN

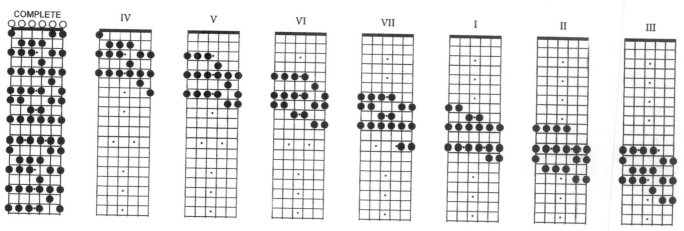

DIATONIC PROGRESSION: KEY OF D

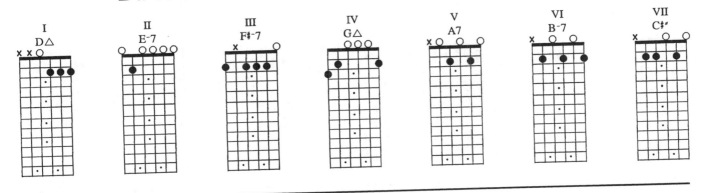

CIRCLE PROGRESSIONS: KEY OF D

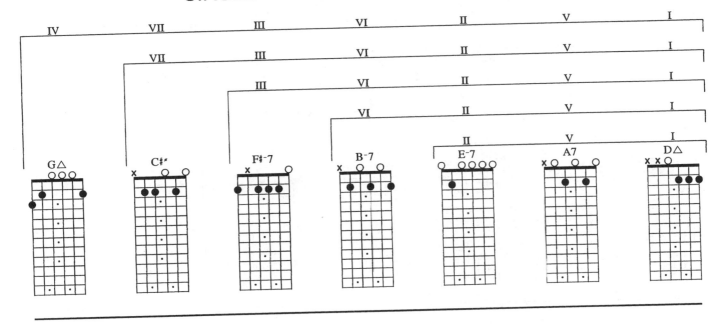

D MAJOR = E DORIAN ~ F♯ PHRYGIAN ~ G LYDIAN ~ A MIXOLYDIAN ~ B / C♭ AEOLIAN ~ C♯ / D♭ LOCRIAN

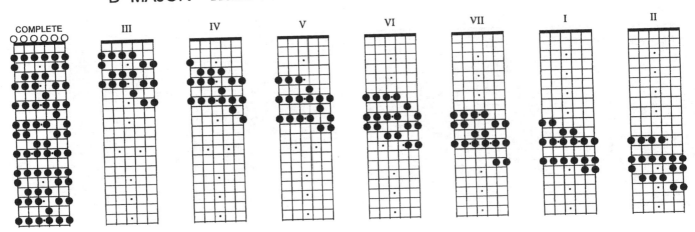

DIATONIC PROGRESSION: KEY OF E

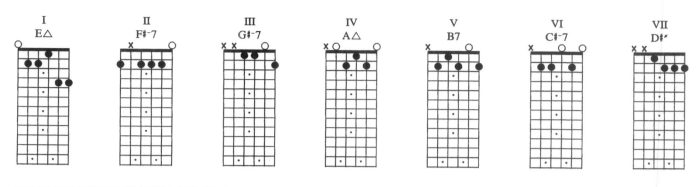

CIRCLE PROGRESSIONS: KEY OF E

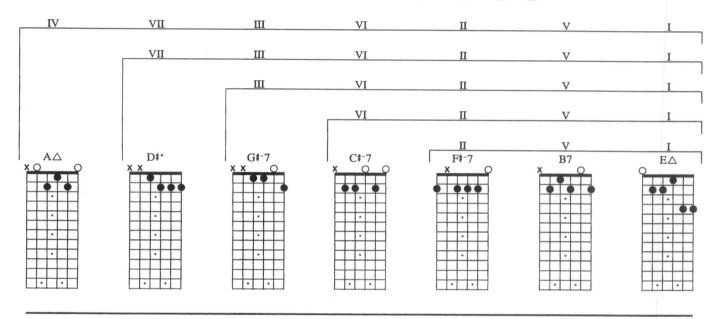

E MAJOR = F# DORIAN ~ G# PHRYGIAN ~ A LYDIAN ~ B MIXOLYDIAN ~ C# AEOLIAN ~ D# LOCRIAN

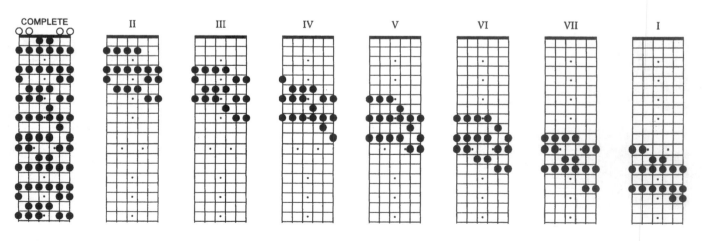

DIATONIC PROGRESSION: KEY OF F

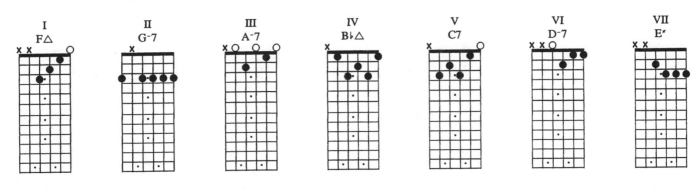

CIRCLE PROGRESSIONS: KEY OF F

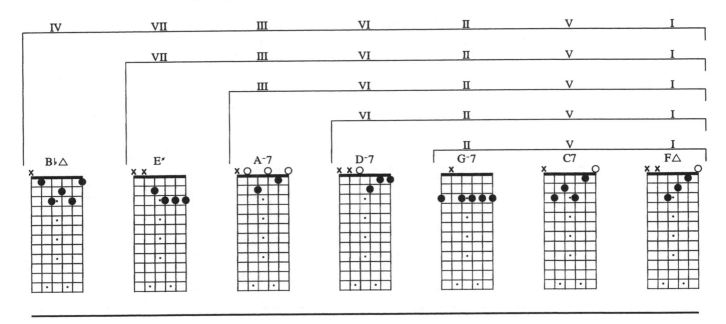

F MAJOR = G DORIAN ~ A PHRYGIAN ~ B♭ LYDIAN ~ C MIXOLYDIAN ~ D AEOLIAN ~ E LOCRIAN

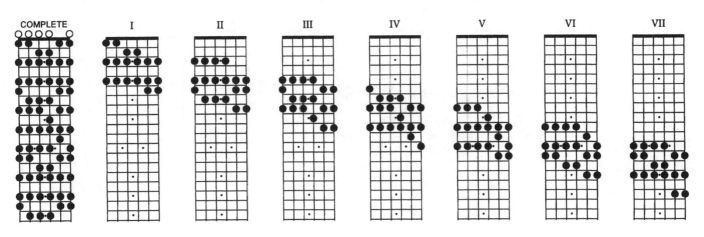

DIATONIC PROGRESSION: KEY OF G

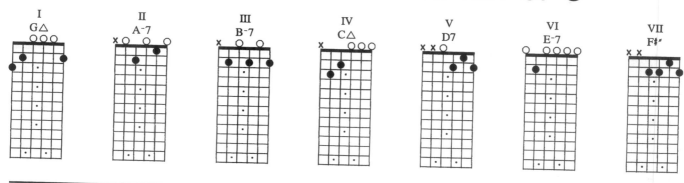

CIRCLE PROGRESSIONS: KEY OF G

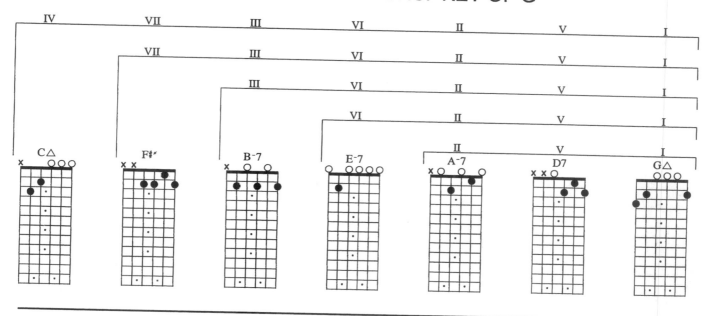

G MAJOR = A DORIAN ~ B PHRYGIAN ~ C LYDIAN ~ D MIXOLYDIAN ~ E AOELIAN ~ F# LOCRIAN

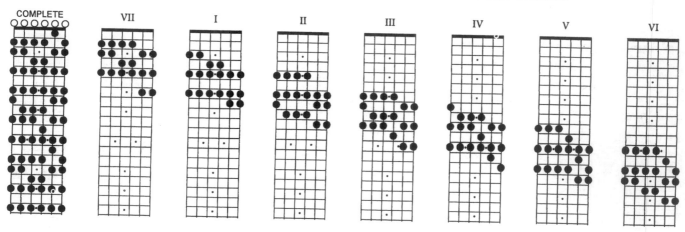

DIATONIC PROGRESSION: KEY OF A

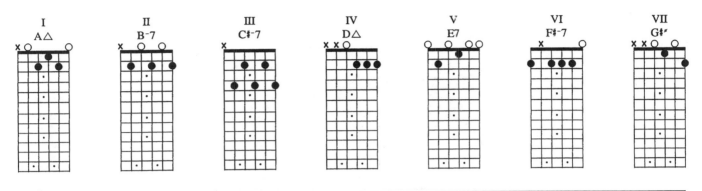

CIRCLE PROGRESSIONS: KEY OF A

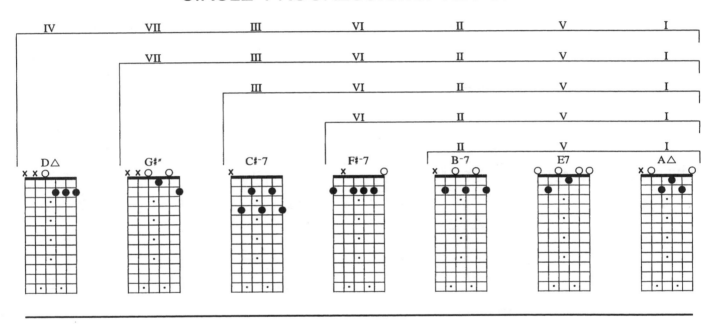

A MAJOR = B DORIAN ~ C♯ PHRYGIAN ~ D LYDIAN ~ E MIXOLYDIAN ~ F♯ AEOLIAN ~ G♯ LOCRIAN

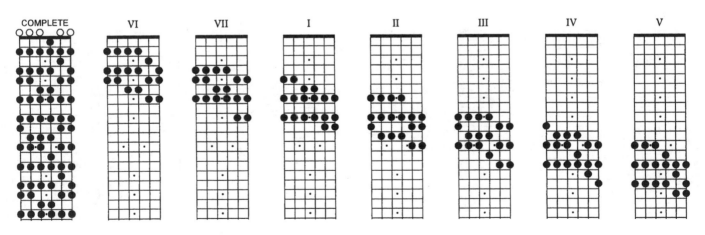

DIATONIC PROGRESSION: KEY OF B

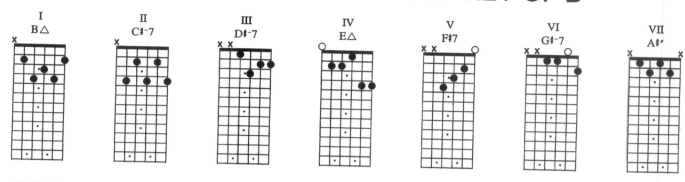

I B△	II C#-7	III D#-7	IV E△	V F#7	VI G#-7	VII A#°

CIRCLE PROGRESSIONS: KEY OF B

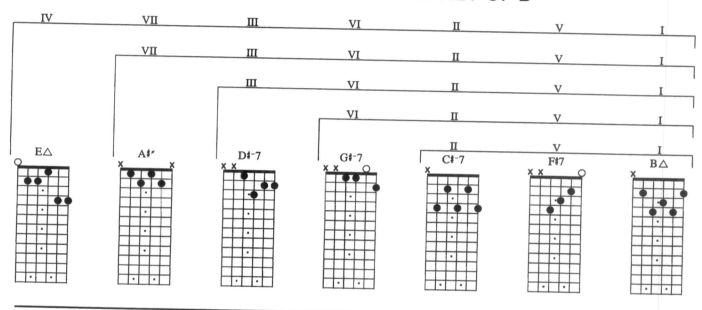

IV	VII	III	VI	II	V	I
VII	III	VI	II	V	I
III	VI	II	V	I
VI	II	V	I

E△	A#°	D#-7	G#-7	C#-7	F#7	B△

B / C♭ MAJOR = C# DORIAN ~ D# PHRYGIAN ~ E LYDIAN ~ F# MIXOLYDIAN ~ G# AEOLIAN ~ A# LOCRIAN

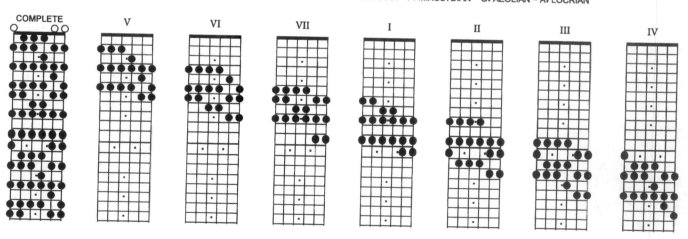

COMPLETE	V	VI	VII	I	II	III	IV

174

IMPROVISING OVER SCALE TONE DEGREE PROGRESSIONS

Now we tackle the task of improvising, or soloing over random scale tone degree progressions. Let's take one of the scale tone degree progressions from that chapter.

| I | ♭VI | III | ♭II | VI | IV | II | ♭VII | ♭V | ♭III | VII | V |

Next, we'll add our alterations:

| I- | ♭VI△ | III″ | ♭II-7 | VI° | IV7+ | II9 | ♭VII♭5 | ♭V△ | ♭III7♭5 | VII″ | V13 |

Then we'll add pitch, let's use the key of C. By the way there are charts at the back of the book that can help you do that.

| C- | A♭△ | E″ | D♭-7 | A° | F7+ | D9 | A♭♭5 | G♭△ | E♭7♭5 | B″ | G13 |

Now we have to voice our chords on the guitar. If you don't quite know how to do this yet, the books **The Guitar Grimoire Chords & Voicings** and **The Guitar Grimoire Chord Encyclopedia** can help. Using the interval maps and voicings from those books our progression now takes on a different look. This is just one of countless possibilities for voicing these chords.

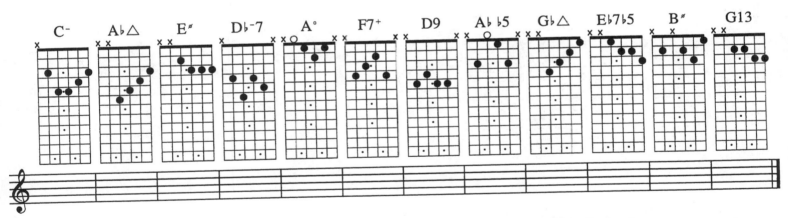

Next we then find compatible scales to work over the chords. Remember, the scale you use must contain the notes, or tones, of the chord you are soloing over. At the back of this book are chord compatibility charts, however, for a very in depth study of scale-chord compatibility it is recommended that you get the **Guitar Grimoire Chords & Voicings** volume.

On the next page is an example of three different ways you can solo over this progression. The possible combinations for soloing over this progression alone are infinite.

IMPROVING OVER SCALE TONE DEGREE PROGRESSIONS

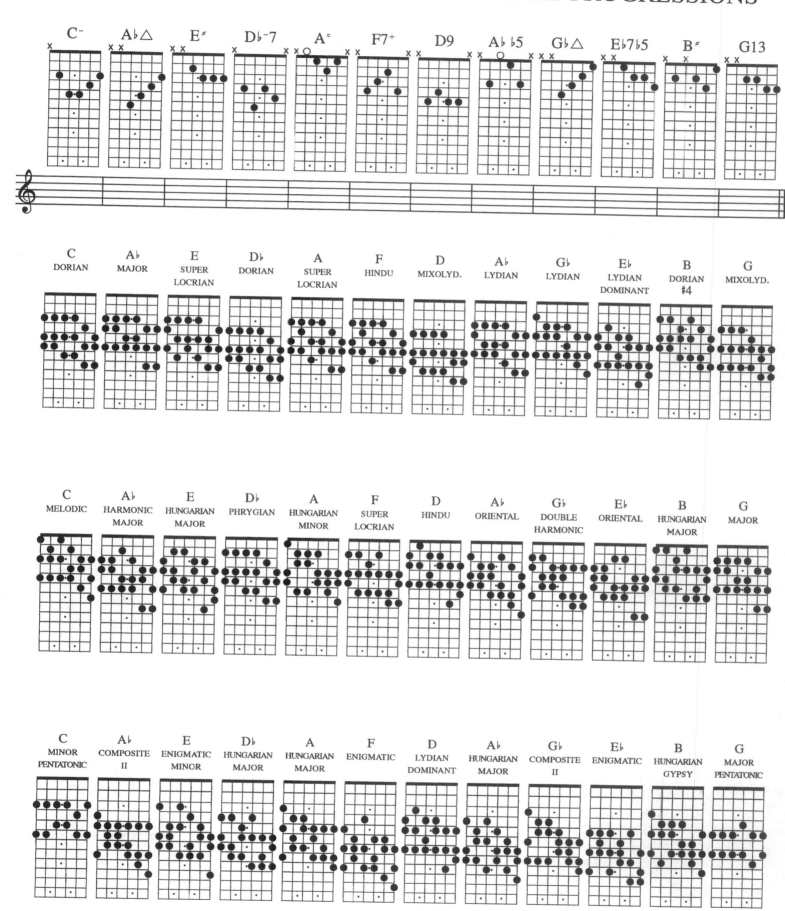

UNDERSTANDING THE NOTES

Before the advent of recording devices, such as tape recorders and now hard disk recorders, the only way to record your composition was to write it down. In order to do this a systeem of notation had to be created. The present notation system evolved from other systems. After trying to create my own "ultimate" system I then fully realized why the old Masters finally ended up with the notation system that is still in use today. If you want to know more about the history of its evolution, then scope out your school or local library. My goal is to get you to understand the system itself.

Understanding notation, or "reading music", can be quite confusing to the beginner. In fact many a "would be" excellent musician have been discouraged from pursuing music because the study of notation, "reading music", was prematurely dumped on them. That's why I teach my students how to play their instruments first, helping them develop manual dexterity and self esteem before teaching notation.

In order to understand notation you must first understand the mathematics of music. In other words harmony & theory. If you don't understand this all hope is not lost.

What makes notation so confusing to beginners is dealing with the sharps and flats. The main reason it gets so confusing is that you're dealing with the "math formula" as well as the notation. For instance, the formula for the Major scale is 1,2,3,4,5,6,7 which has no sharps or flats and works great in the key of C. But when we shift the formula, which still has no sharps or flats, to the key of C♯, we now have seven sharps of notation.

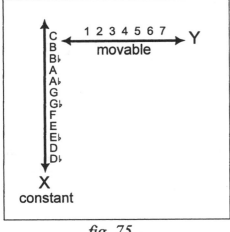

fig. 75

Figure 64 demonstrates how the pitch remains constant, while the formula moves.

You can see how impractical having a separate line for each pitch is. The amount of space wasted is great.

We can save space by using the spaces as well as the lines.

The reason for this is simple, we are dealing with a "X" and "Y" axis, in other words pitch and formula.

The "X" axis, which represent pitch degrees is constant and never moves. The "Y" axis, on the other hand, represents the formula axis and can be moved up and down along the pitch axis. This forms the basis for what we call "modulating" or changing keys (fig. 75).

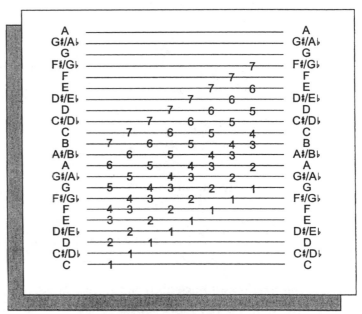

fig. 76

fig. 77

By utilizing spaces as well as lines and eliminating the sharps & flats, we come up with the diagram in figure 77.

Where did the sharps & flats go? Don't worry about that for now, we'll cover that in a moment.

Looking at figure 77, we can see that a bunch of lines & spaces could still get quite confusing. The way we get around that is by zoning or sectioning the lines & spaces. We accomplish this by using symbols known as clefs (fig. 78). This symbol ♭, is the treble clef and this symbol 𝄢, is the bass clef.

Even still, this could be quite a clutter with all the lines & spaces. So therefore, we have to single out certain lines from the rest. In figure 79, we see that the lines within the area of the clefs become constants, and the other lines are added as needed. The lines that never change are called stave lines, and the add on lines are called ledger lines.

fig. 78

The stave in the treble range is used for the keyboardists right hand and instruments such as guitar while the stave in the bass range is used for the keyboardists left hand and such instruments as the bass guitar.

Even if you just want to play guitar you should learn both clefs and their ledger lines since you need to communicate with other musicians.

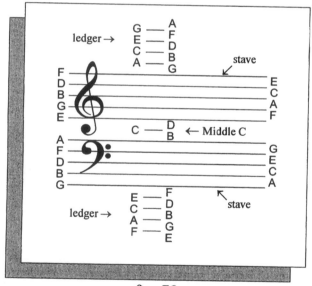

fig. 79

There is an easy way to memorize the lines and spaces. The trick is to make phrases using the pitch letter as the first letter of a word. For instance, the lines of the treble clef can be the phrase, "EVERY GOOD BOY DOES FINE". The lines of the bass clef can be the phrase, "GREAT BIG DOGS FIGHT ANIMALS". The spaces of the treble clef spell the word FACE, while the spaces of the bass clef make up the phrase of "ALL CARS EAT GAS".

Normally, the treble and bass clefs are not so close together. Remember, the first ledger line below the treble clef, and the first ledger line above the bass clef are the same note. This particular note is referred to as "MIDDLE C".

STAFF LINES & SPACES

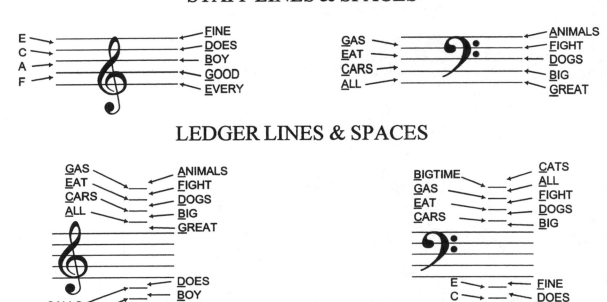

LEDGER LINES & SPACES

When we want to alter the pitch we use flat & sharp symbols on the line or space in front of the note.

Normally when writing notation, notes that have a double sharp or flat are impractical. In other words, a double flat A would simply be written as a G, and a double sharp G would be written as an A.

Beneath each set of progressions is the notated equivalent.

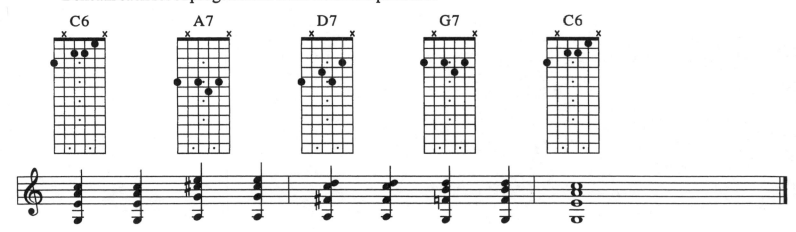

The chart on the next page shows the relationship between the written notes and the fretboard.

NOTATED FRETBOARD CHART

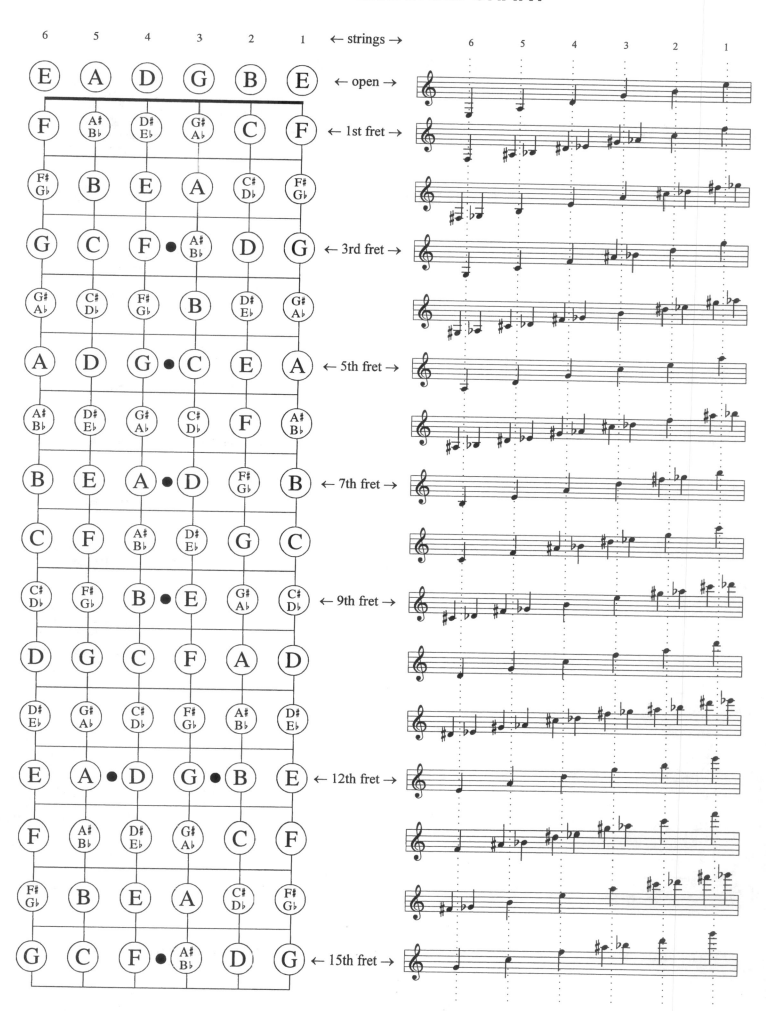

180

KEY SIGNATURES

The circle of fifths is also used for key signatures. Key signatures are located at the beginning of a score or song just after the clefs. Sometimes they are also in the middle of the composition when the song changes keys.

Key signatures tell what key you are in at a glance. This is especially important when using fake books where only the melody is written. Sonically there are only 12 keys; however, in notation there are 15 different key signatures as demonstrated in fig. 80 and fig. 81. This is because of the notes known as "the enharmonics", you know the notes such as C♯ & D♭ which sound the same but are written differently. These are the standard key signatures.

Compare the ♭II , ♭V , and VII positions of fig. 80 and fig. 81. Remember, C♯ & D♭ sound the same, in fact, they are the same. Yet when written they are very different as is the case with F♯ and G♭ and also with B and C♭.

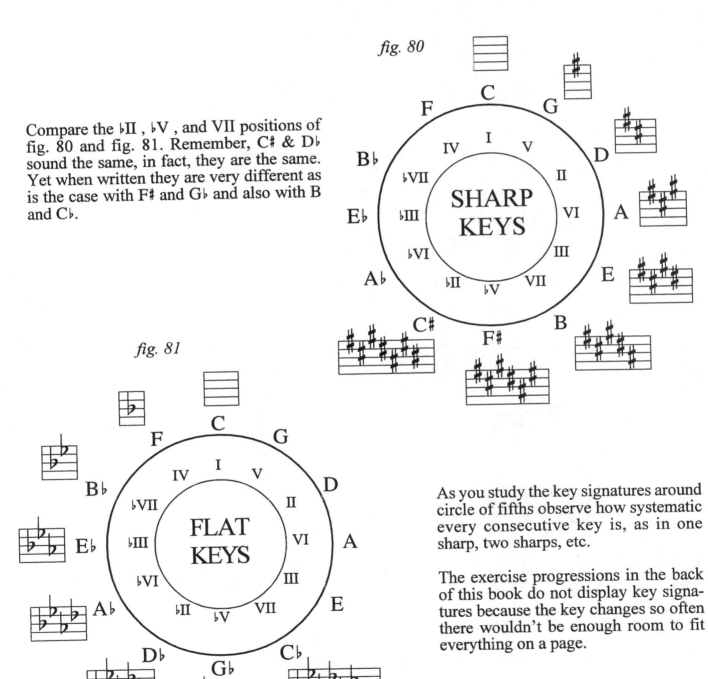

fig. 80

fig. 81

As you study the key signatures around circle of fifths observe how systematic every consecutive key is, as in one sharp, two sharps, etc.

The exercise progressions in the back of this book do not display key signatures because the key changes so often there wouldn't be enough room to fit everything on a page.

What exactly are the key signatures telling us? Let's start with the formula for the Major scale on the "C". At a glance we can see that the notes, (C,D,E,F,G,A,B), are played as is and are unaltered by sharps or flats. Therefore the key of "C" has no sharps or flats. When we take the formula for the Major scale and start it on the "G" pitch, note, or tone, we have to sharp the "F" in order to retain the intervallic spacing of the Major scale (fig.82).

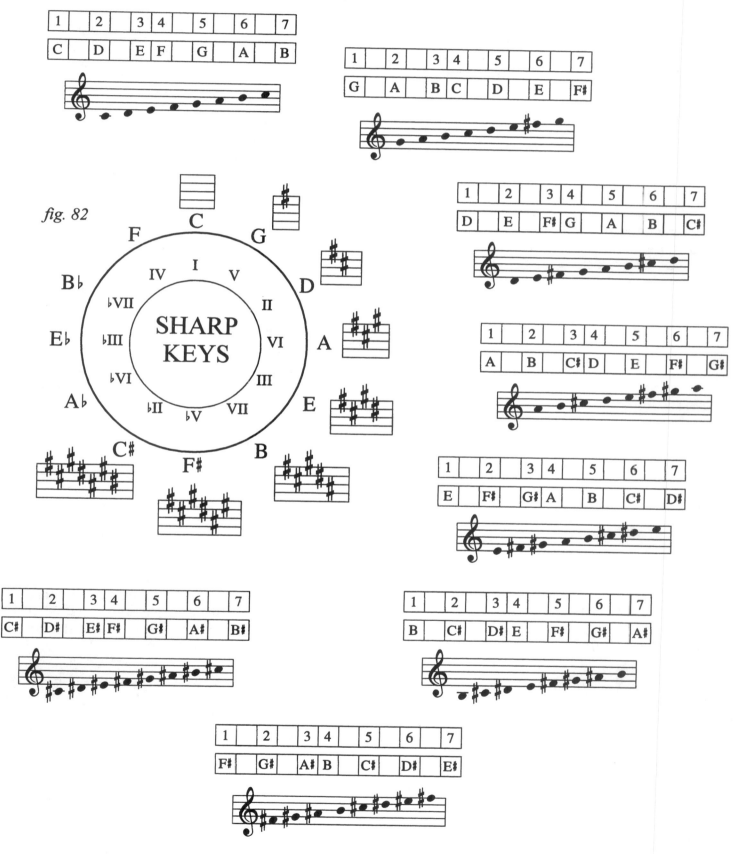

fig. 82

The same holds true for the flat keys as demonstrated below (fig. 83).

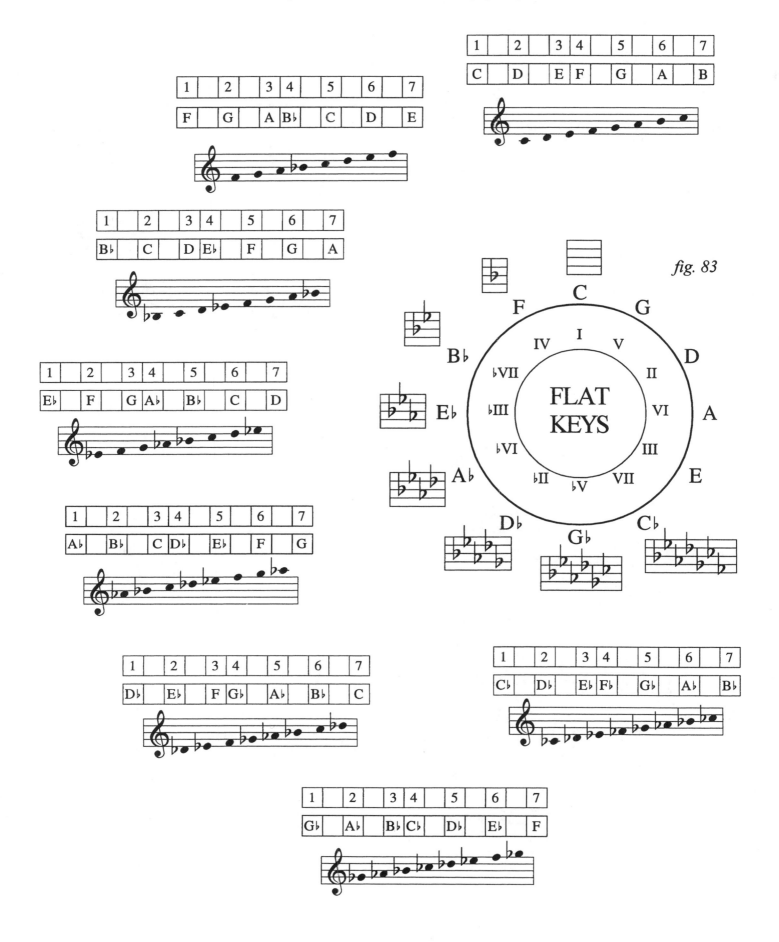

fig. 83

I once asked a guitar teacher if there was a key of G♯ or D♯ etc., and was told that there were no such keys. This was not a true statement as the diagram below demonstrates (fig. 84).

A more acurate answer would have been that we don't use or write in these keys because they are impractical and redundant. However, theoretically, these keys do exist. In fact you can get crazy keys such as C✸✸✸✸✸✸✸✸ and beyond. Something that's fun to do when you are extremely curious or absolutely bored.

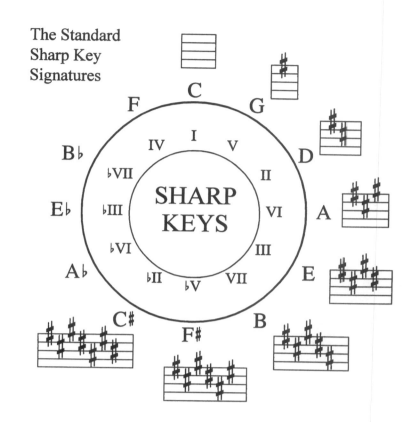

The Standard Sharp Key Signatures

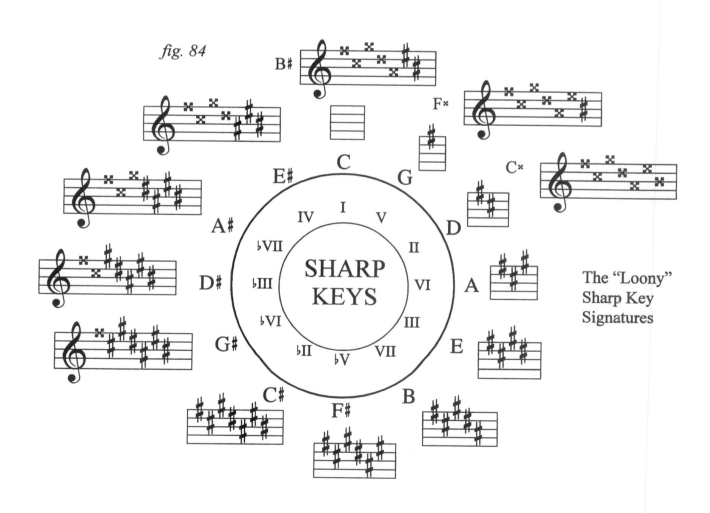

fig. 84

The "Loony" Sharp Key Signatures

The same holds true for the flat keys for those of you who are completeness freaks such as me (fig. 85).

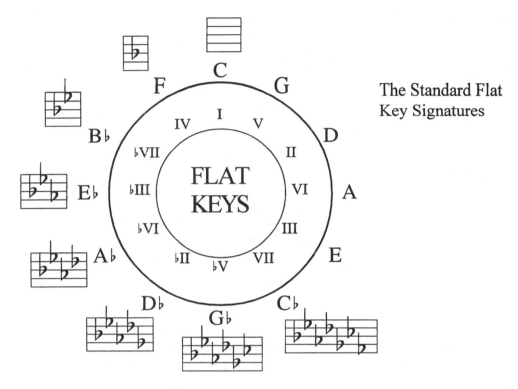

The Standard Flat
Key Signatures

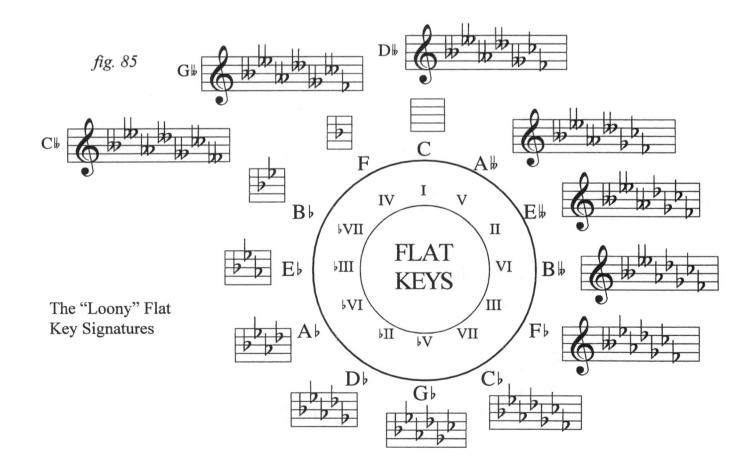

fig. 85

The "Loony" Flat
Key Signatures

CIRCLE OF FIFTHS IN ALL 15 KEYS

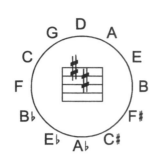
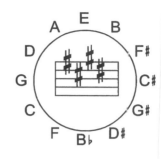
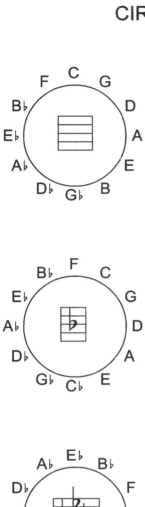
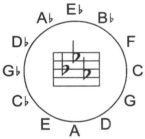
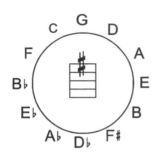
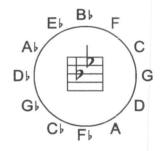
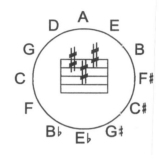
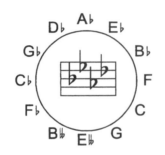
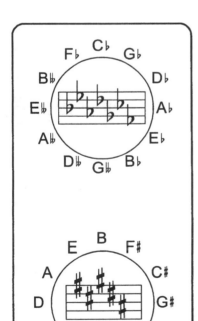
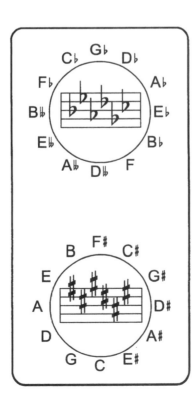
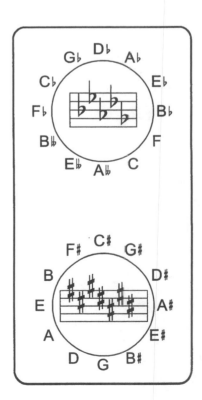

DIATONICS NOTATED

Now that we have studied basic notation and key signatures, we are ready to see what the diatonic chord progressions look like in all keys:

SUBSTITUTIONS NOTATED*

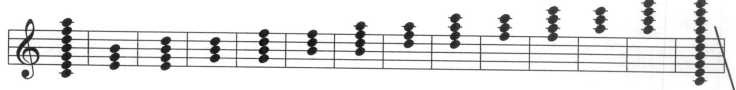

*The notation equivalent of the substitutions diagram on page 7.

Extra C, E, G added so you can see substitution compatability

188

EXERCISE PROGRESSIONS

We now come to the last section of this book called exercise progressions. The reason for the title is threefold. The exercise progressions are designed to exercise your fingers, mind, and your ear. How they exercise your fingers is obvious. Your mind is exercised by the mathematics of music. Your ear is exercised by learning to recognize all the ninths, elevenths, and thirteenths.

When I first started studying jazz, some twenty three years ago, I hated it. I knew, however, that it would make me a better player. As time progressed I learned to appreciate and understand it. I still prefer playing rock, R&R, R&B, and blues, but studying jazz has improved my playing and will do the same for you.

The first part of this section is more or less a primer, getting you started with, for example, minor seventh and minor sixth chords then moving them up chromatically. This helps familiarize you with the "jazz" chords and builds strength, or what is called building your chops.

The second section consists of basic circle progressions (II V I, VI II V I, etc.) using sixth, seventh, minor sixth, minor seventh chords. Each progression is three measures long then demonstrated chromatically four times giving you enough of an idea on how to continue the process upward yourself.

The third section moves in what might be called cycles. For instance, play a II V I, drop it down a step play a II V I, etc. This section uses sevenths, ninths, elevenths, and thirteenths. This section also teaches you how to trade off voicings while playing the cycles. The progressions in this section are six measures, twelve measures, and twenty four measures. The twenty four measure part is set up like this: a II V I then a II V I built upon the IV in relation to the first II V I, then the whole thing is dropped down a step etc. This helps you to recognize it when it happens in tunes that are commonly known as your jazz standards.

All the progressions of the entire exercise section are designed to be picked and practiced at random. In other words, you don't have to learn them consecutively, unless you want to. This works especially well if you are a rocker or metalhead, because it does take some time to get used to the sound of the jazz chords.

Also, all of the progressions in the exercise section are notated. As you advance you will naturally want to study the notation, so it is there when you need it.

I didn't include expanded chord diagrams for this sections, like I did for the four measure progression section because by the time you get to this section, you should be more than adequately familiar with how these chords are voiced, etc. If you still have trouble understanding the "big" chords it is highly recommend that you get **The Guitar Grimoire Chords & Voicings** and **The Guitar Grimoire Chord Encyclopedia.**

All the progressions in this book are in midi-file format. So, if you pester my publisher, he will make them available to you.

Publisher's Note
The MIDI Files will be available on the Web. Go to our home page,
http://www.carlfischer.com
and click on the
Guitar Grimoire bar.

The
Exercise
Progressions

EXERCISE PROGRESSIONS

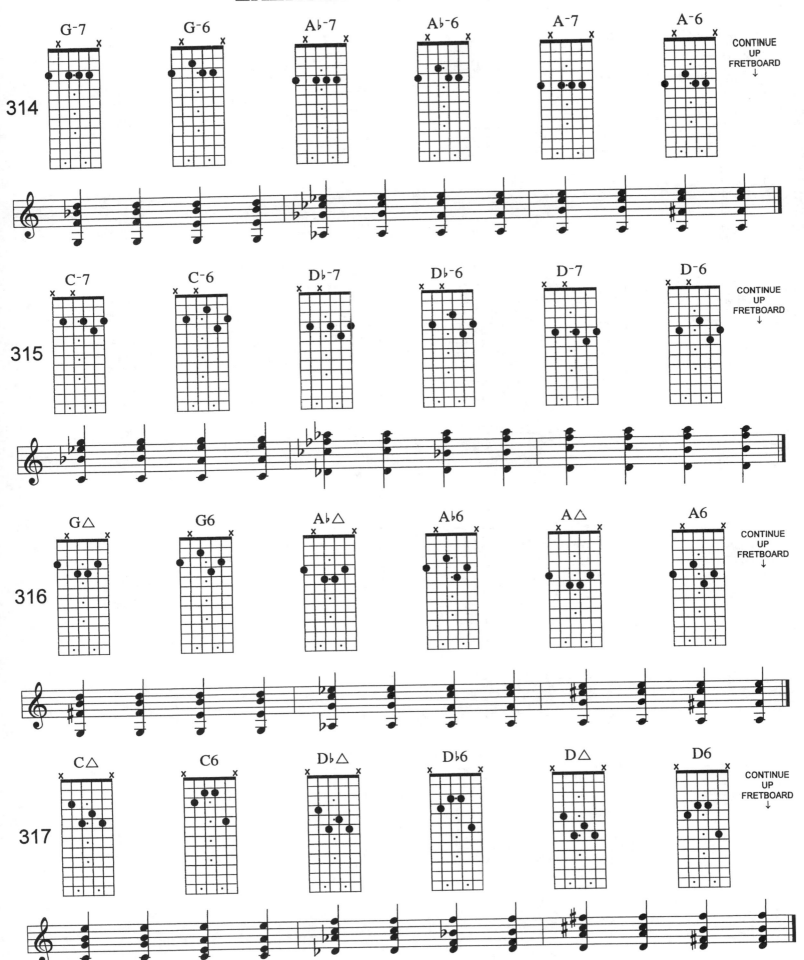

EXERCISE PROGRESSIONS

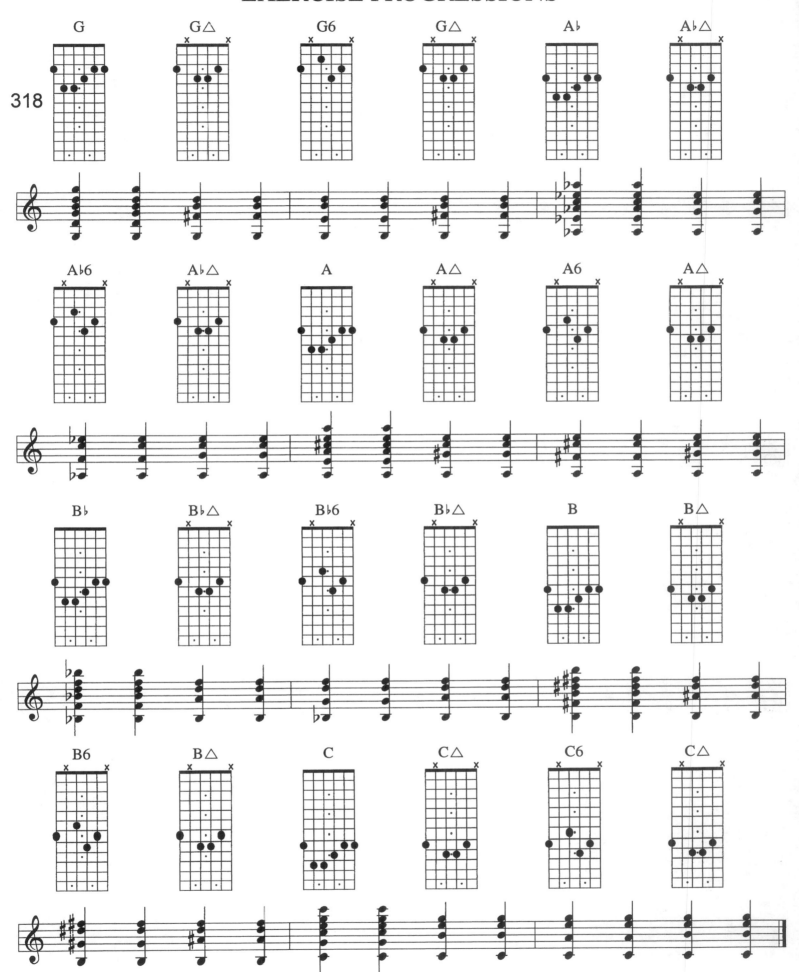

EXERCISE PROGRESSIONS

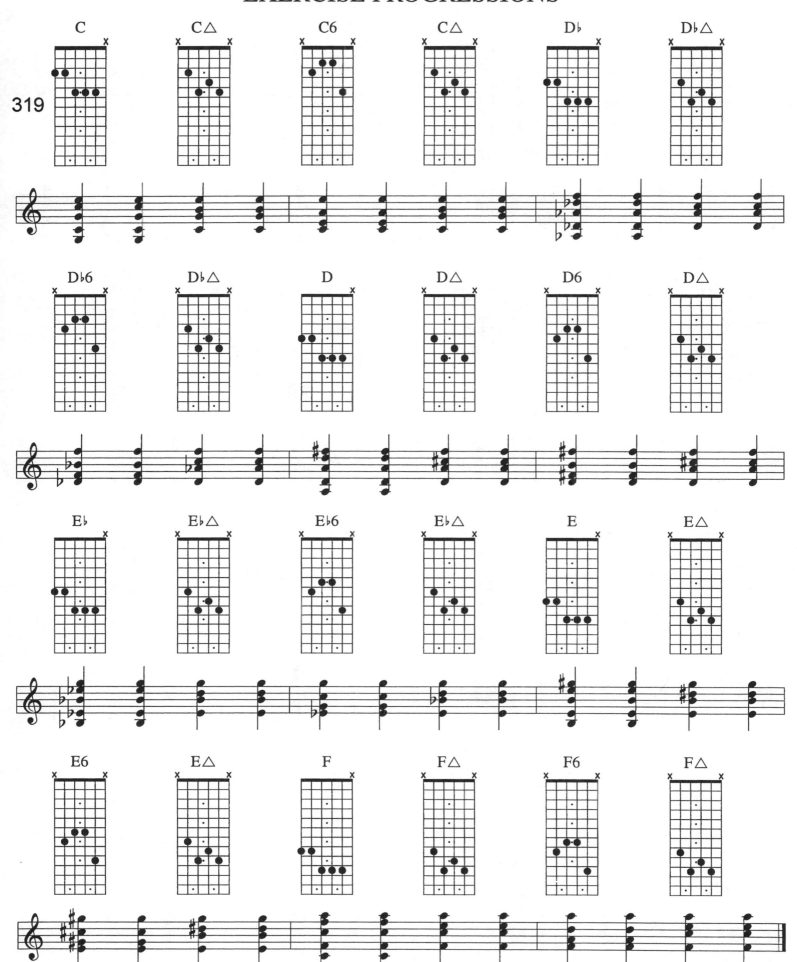

319

EXERCISE PROGRESSIONS

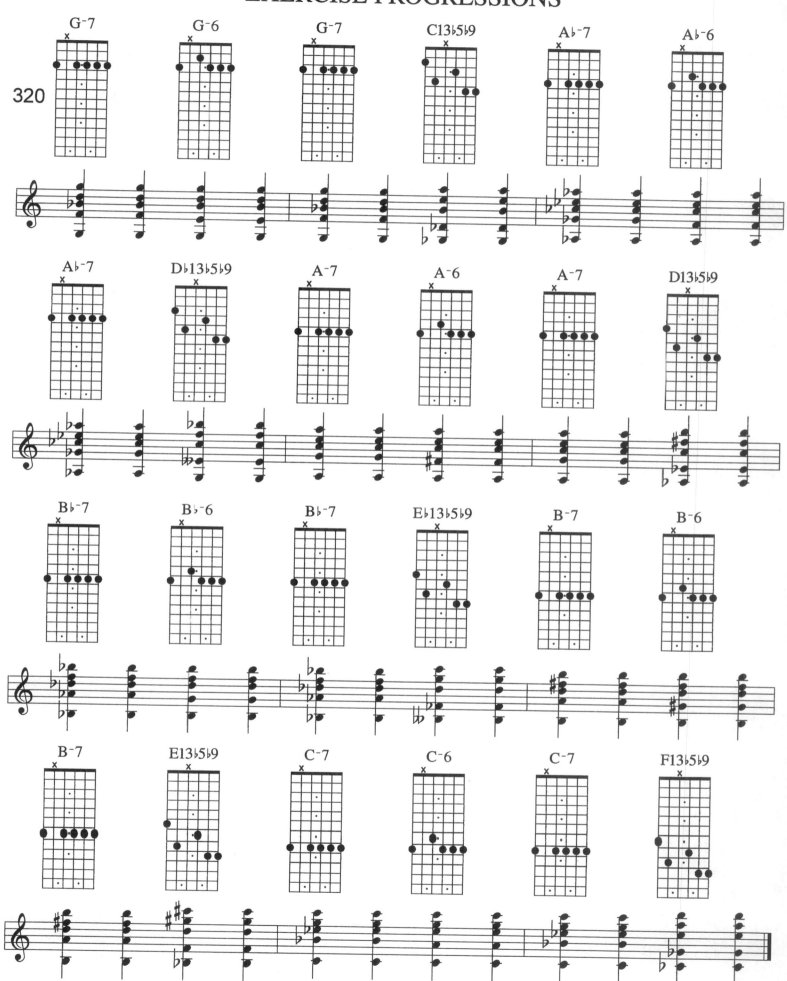

EXERCISE PROGRESSIONS

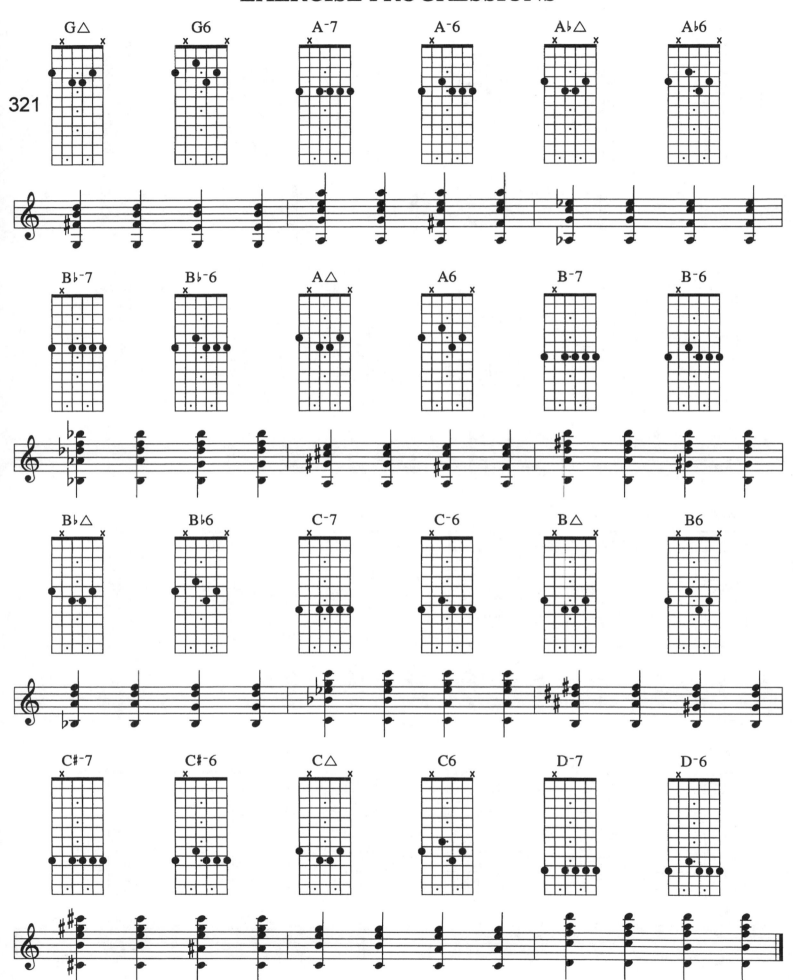

EXERCISE PROGRESSIONS

EXERCISE PROGRESSIONS

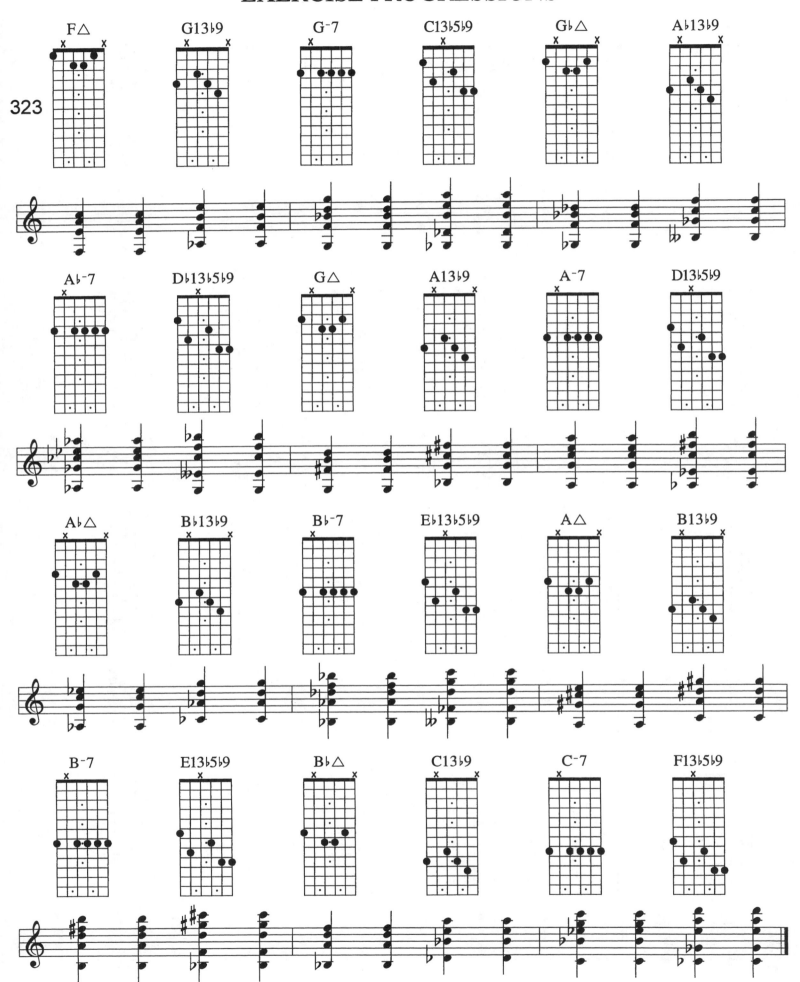

EXERCISE PROGRESSIONS

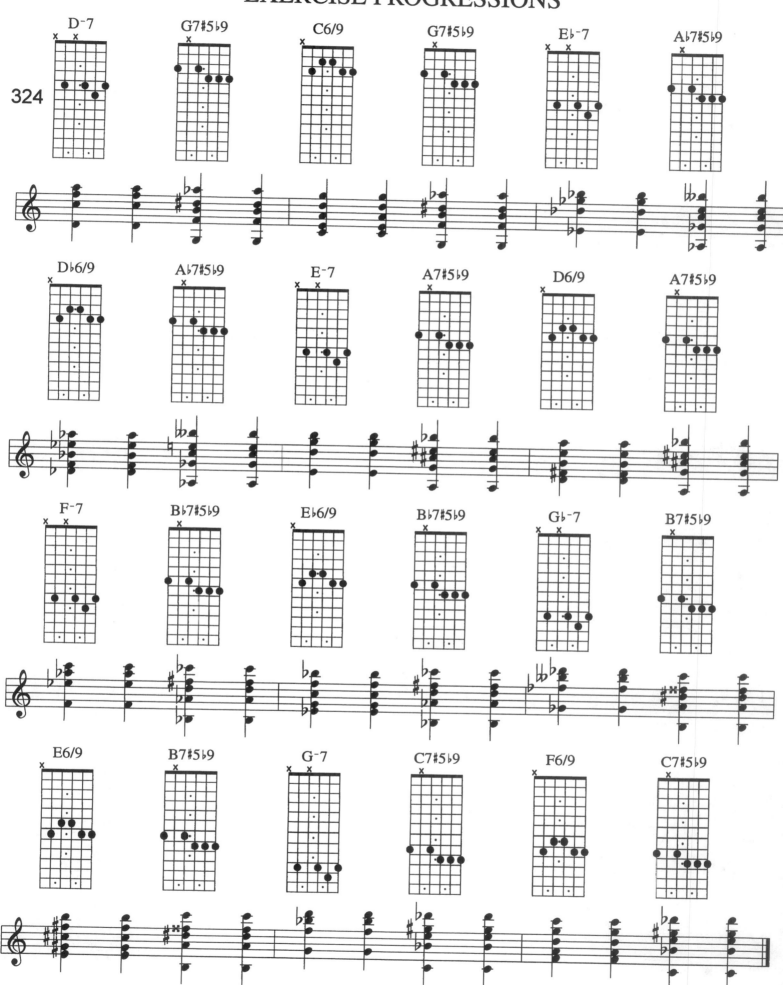

EXERCISE PROGRESSIONS

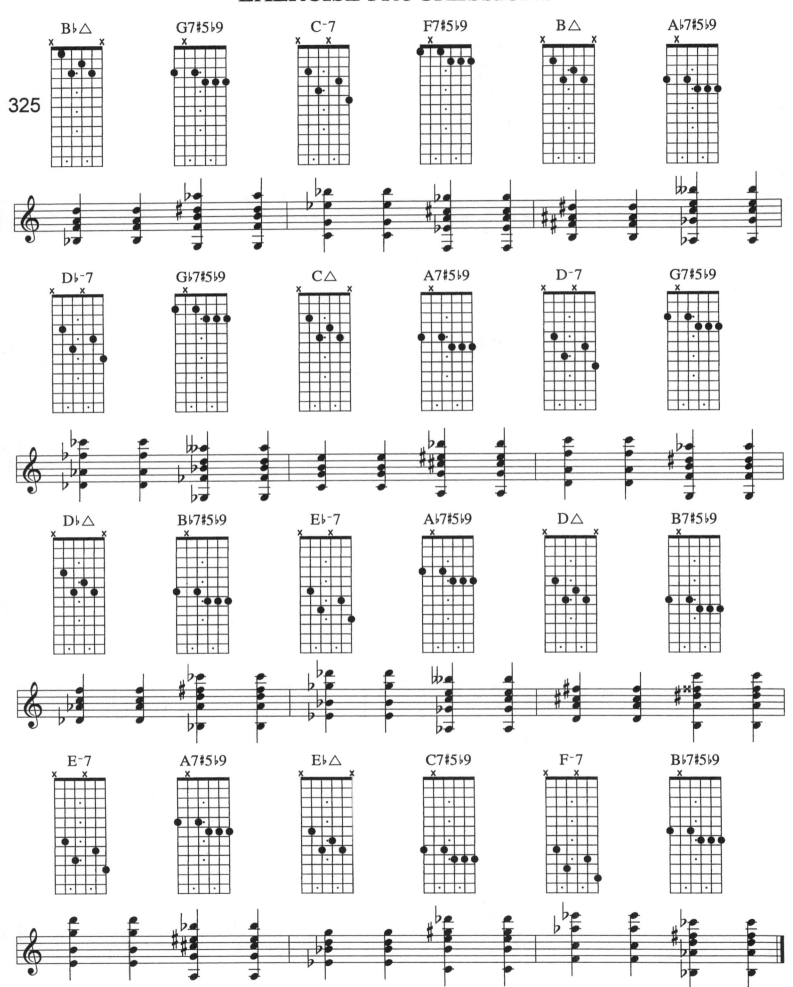

325

I - VI - II - V - I: EXERCISE PROGRESSIONS

I - VI - II - V - I: EXERCISE PROGRESSIONS

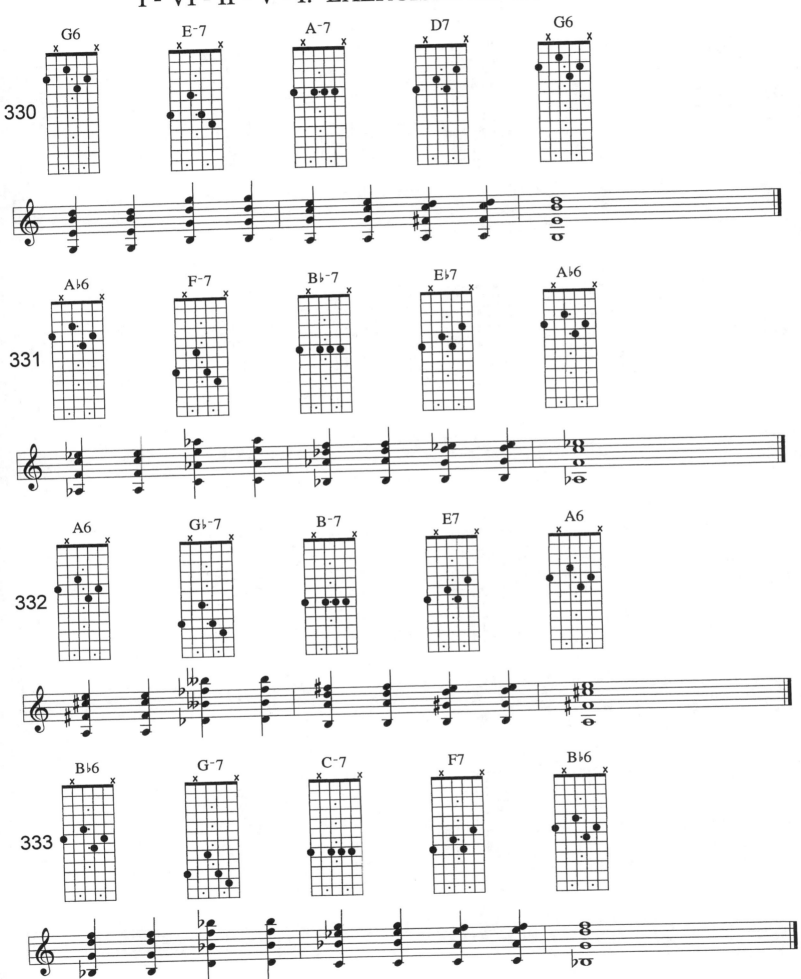

I - VI - II - V - I: EXERCISE PROGRESSIONS

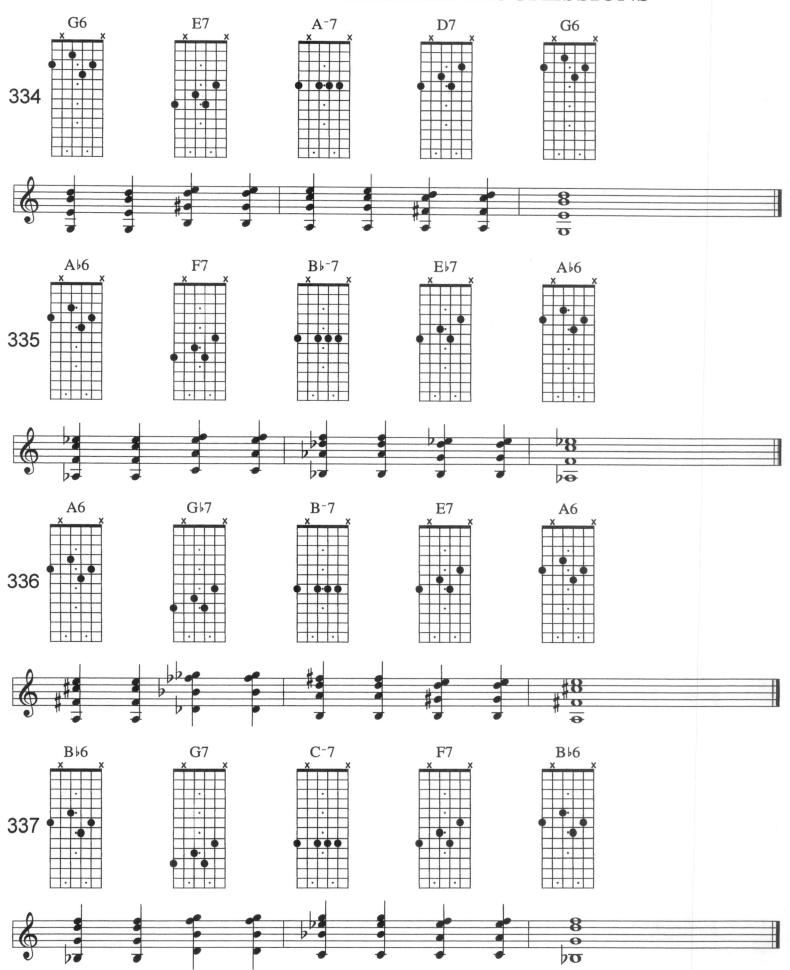

I - III - VI - II - V - I: EXERCISE PROGRESSIONS

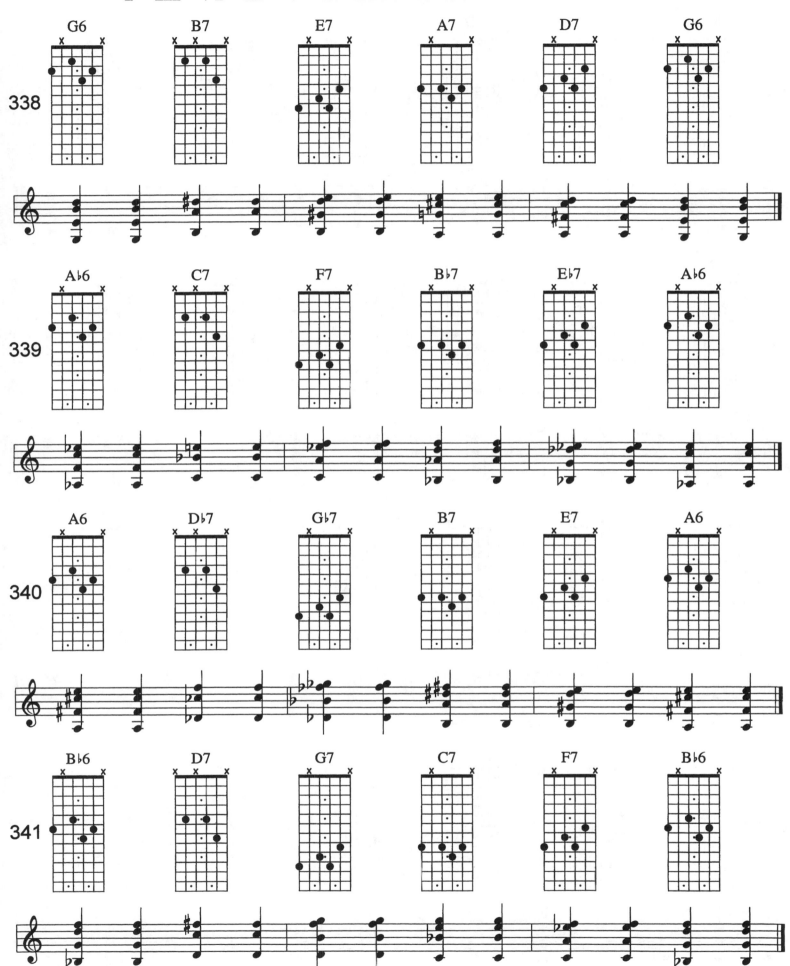

I - V - VI - II - V - I: EXERCISE PROGRESSIONS

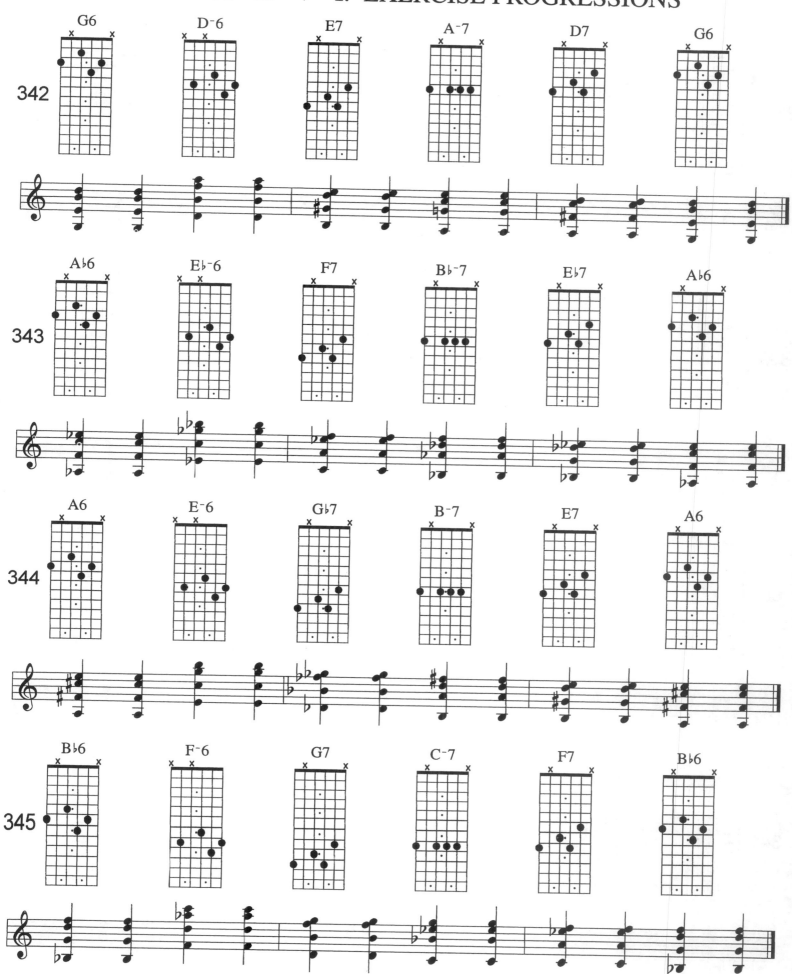

I - VI - II - V - I: EXERCISE PROGRESSIONS

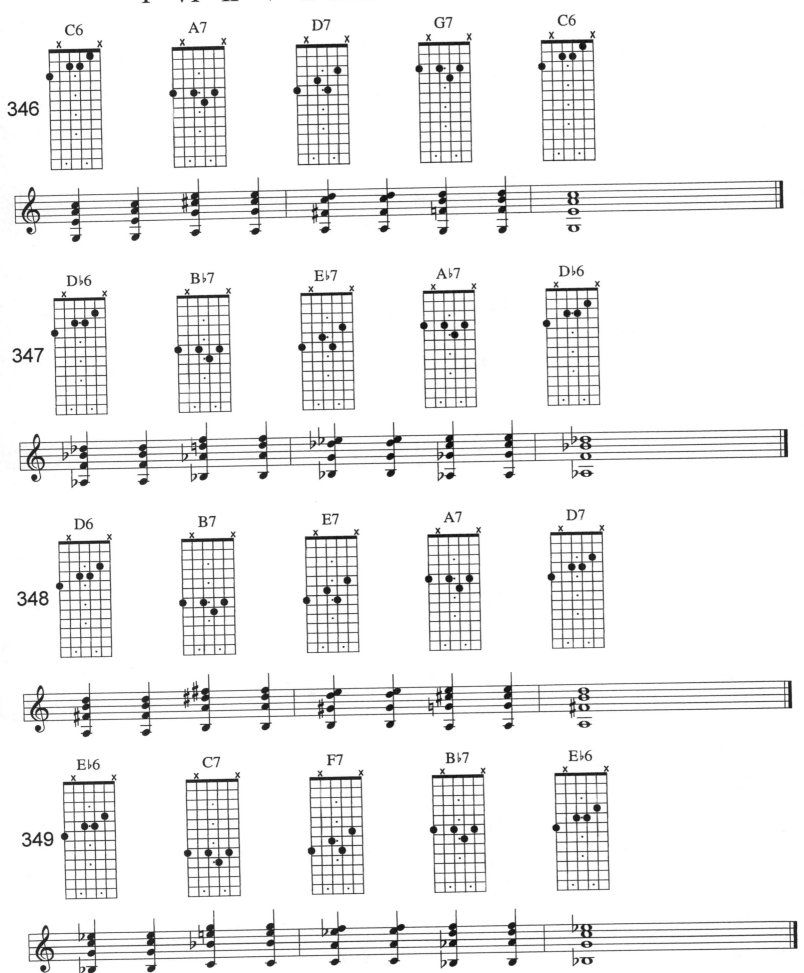

I - VI - II - V - I: EXERCISE PROGRESSIONS

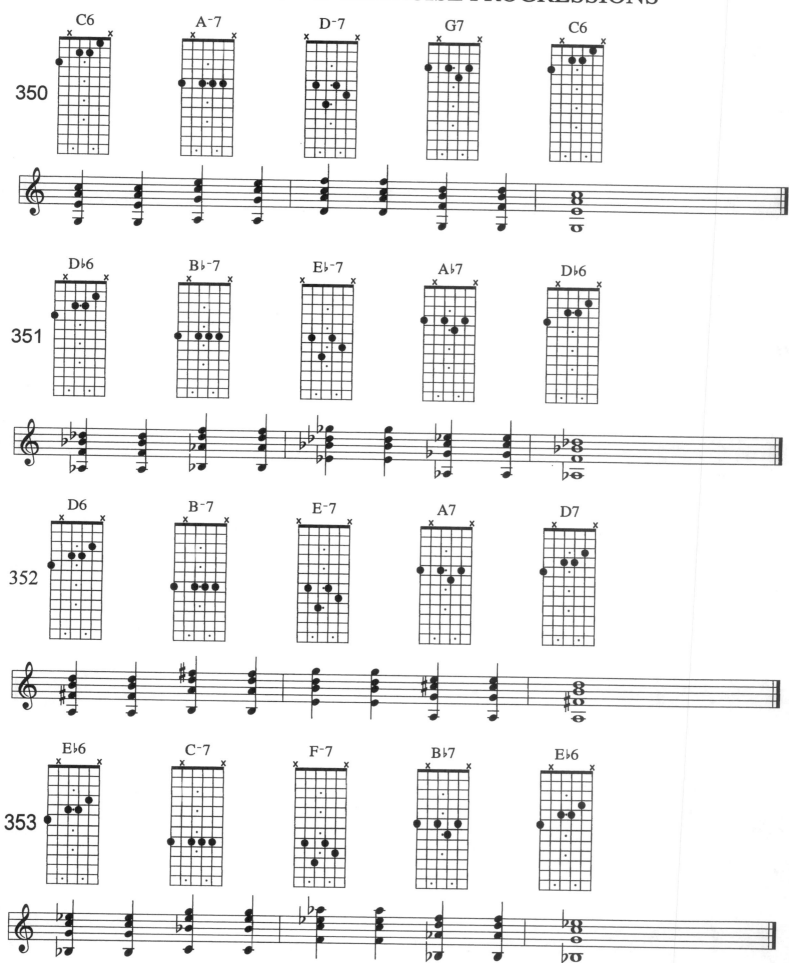

I - VI - II - V - I: EXERCISE PROGRESSIONS

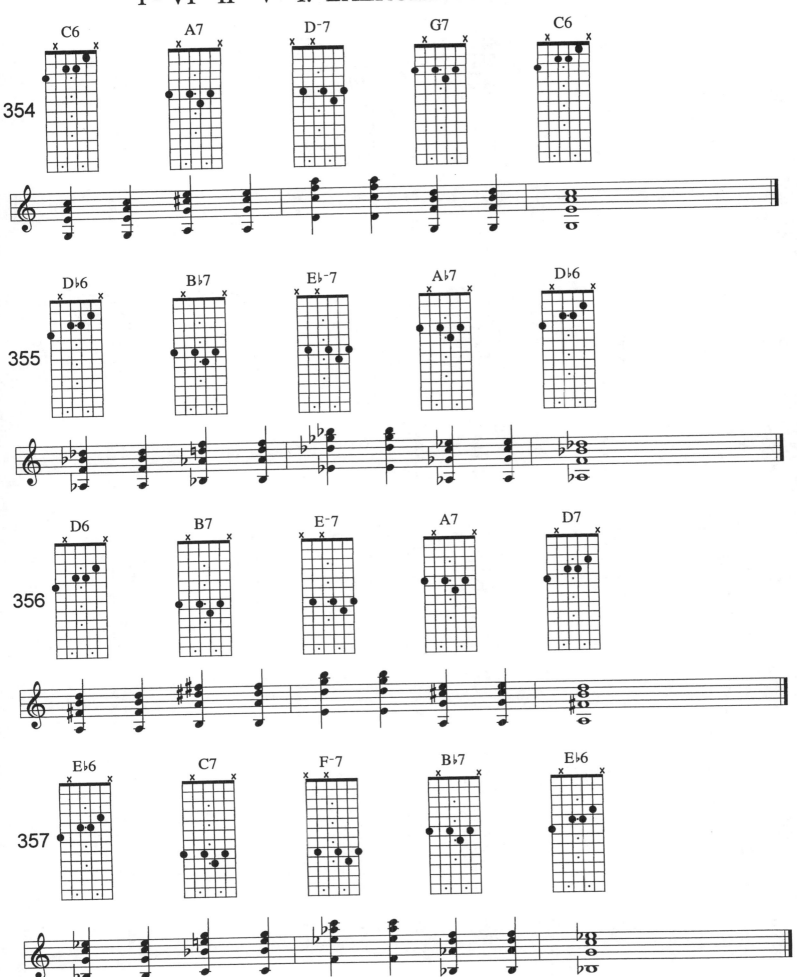

I - III - VI - II - V - I: EXERCISE PROGRESSIONS

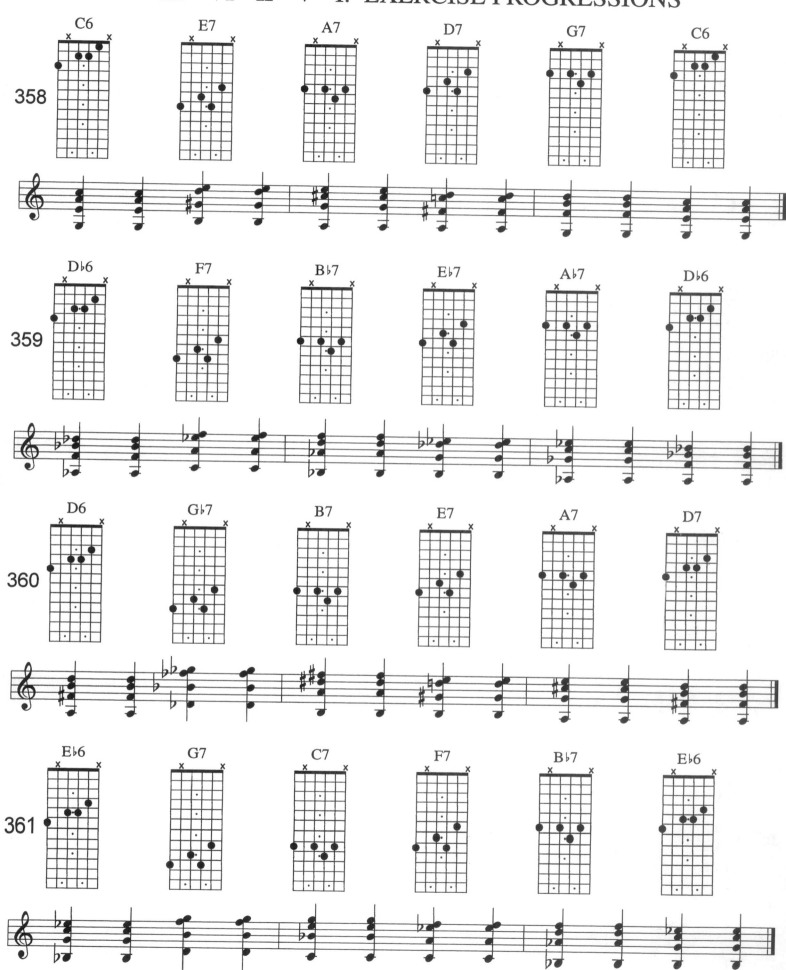

I - V - VI - II - V - I: EXERCISE PROGRESSIONS

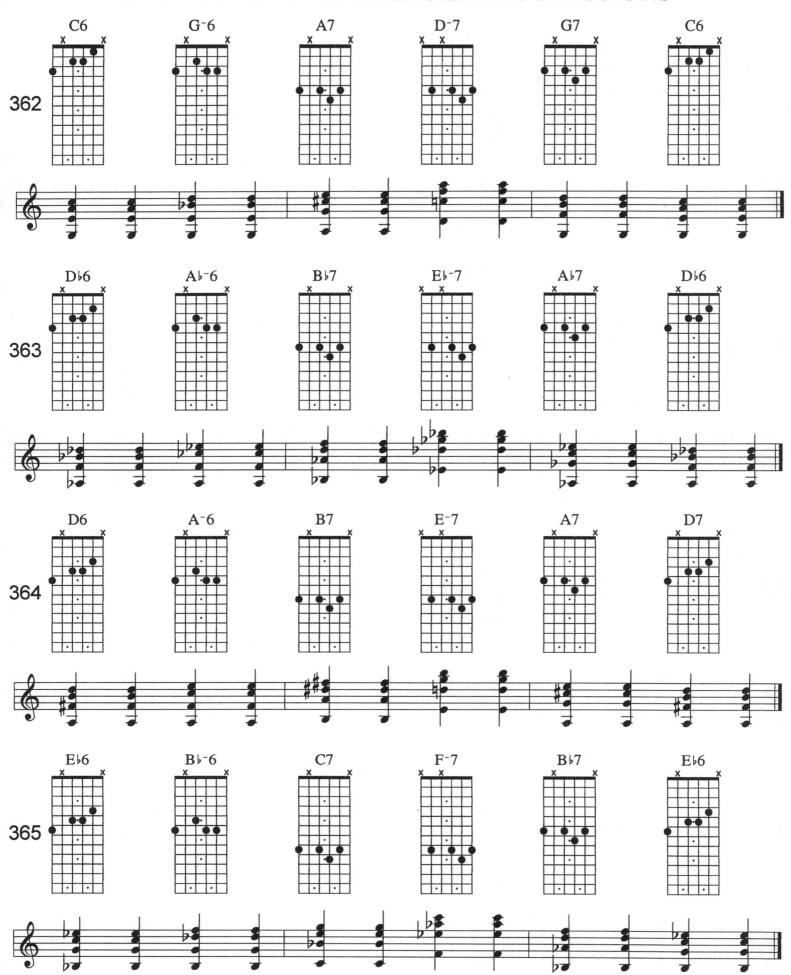

I - I - IV - IV - I: EXERCISE PROGRESSIONS

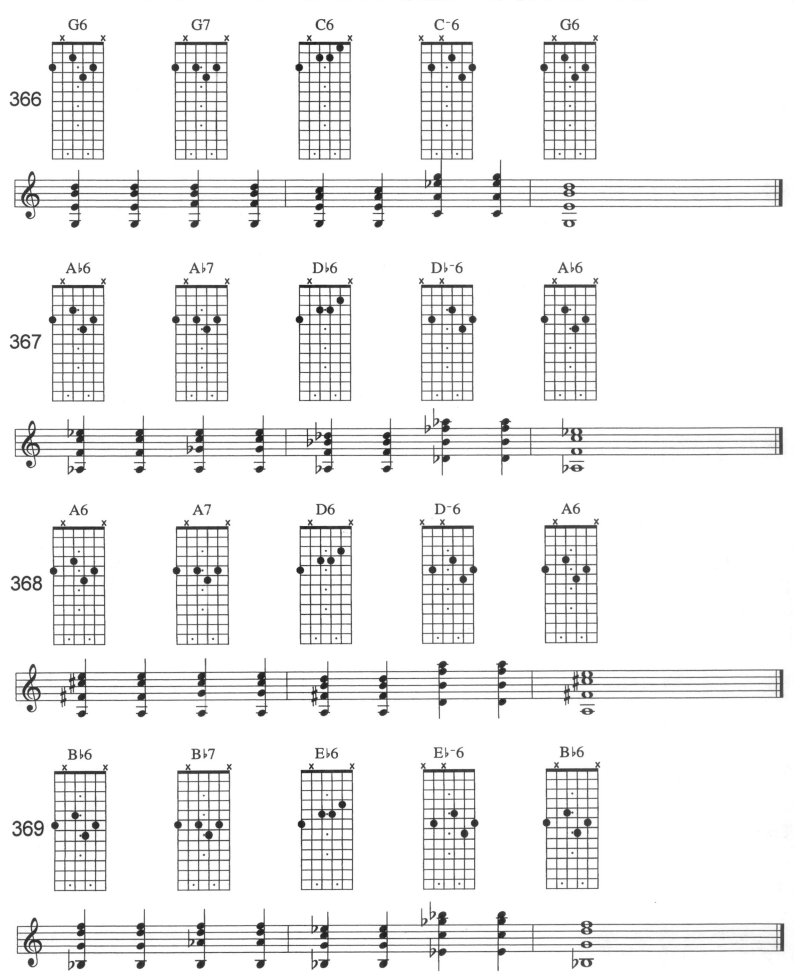

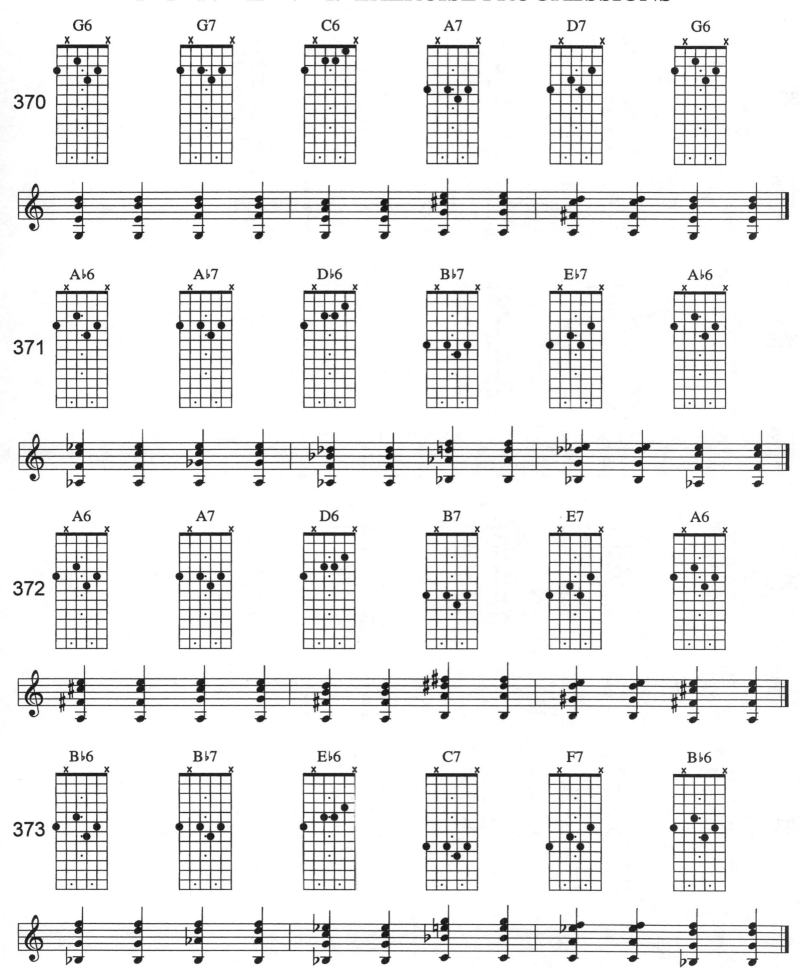

I - I - IV - IV - I: EXERCISE PROGRESSIONS

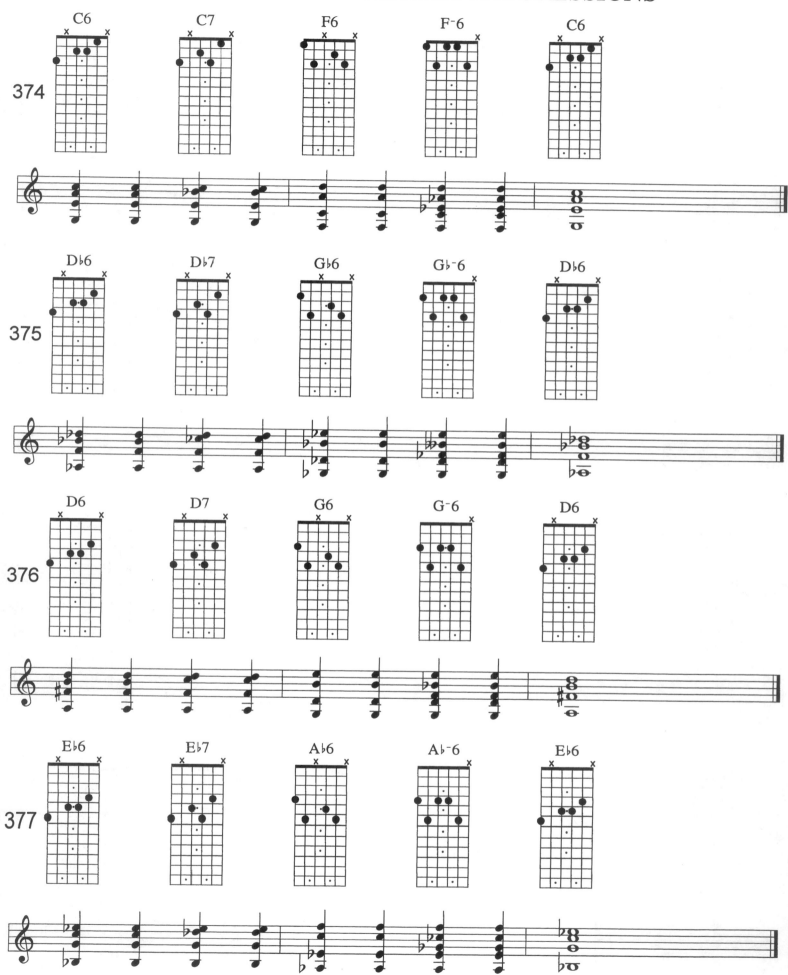

I - I - IV - II - V - I: EXERCISE PROGRESSIONS

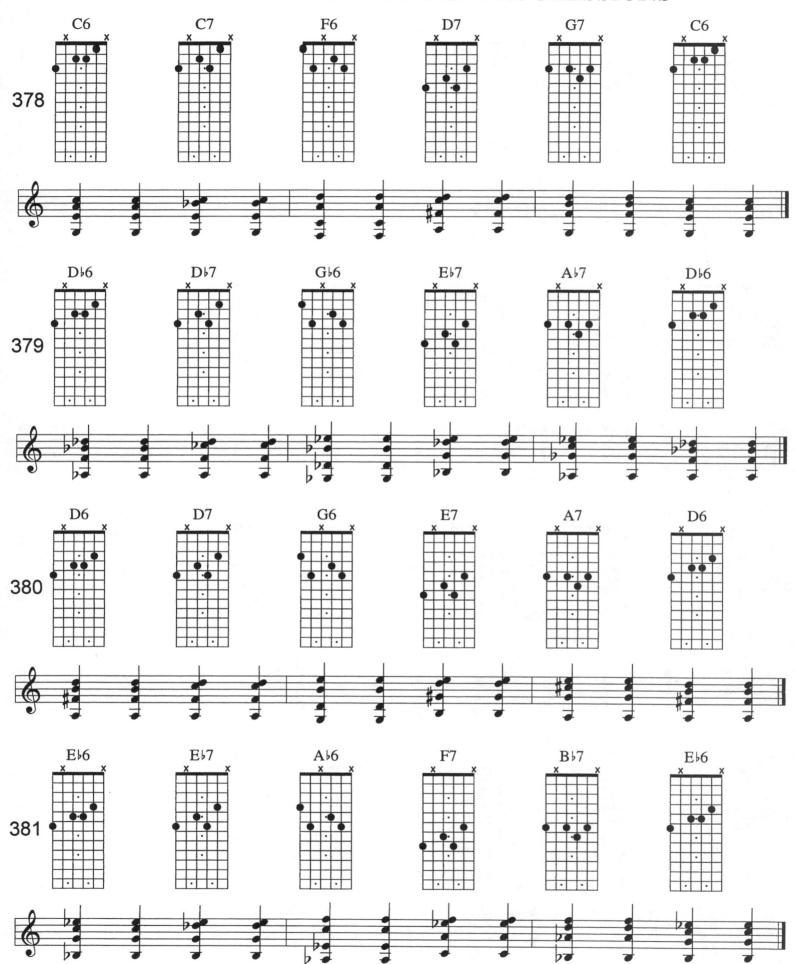

I - VI - II - V - I: EXERCISE PROGRESSIONS

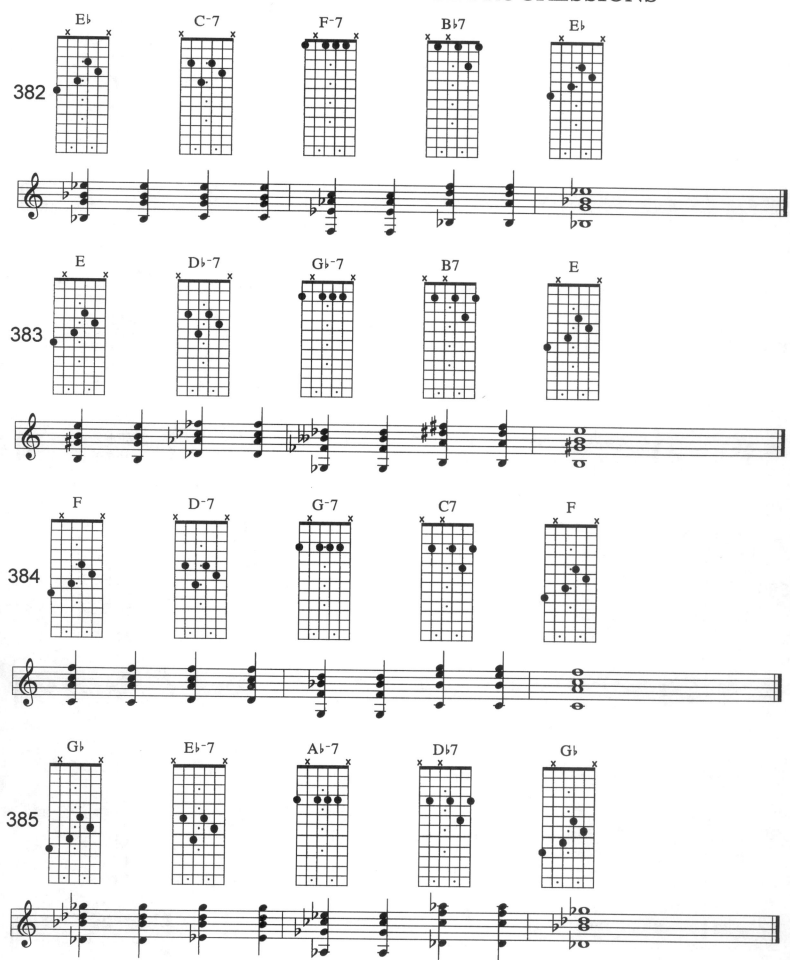

I - ♭V - II - V - I: EXERCISE PROGRESSIONS

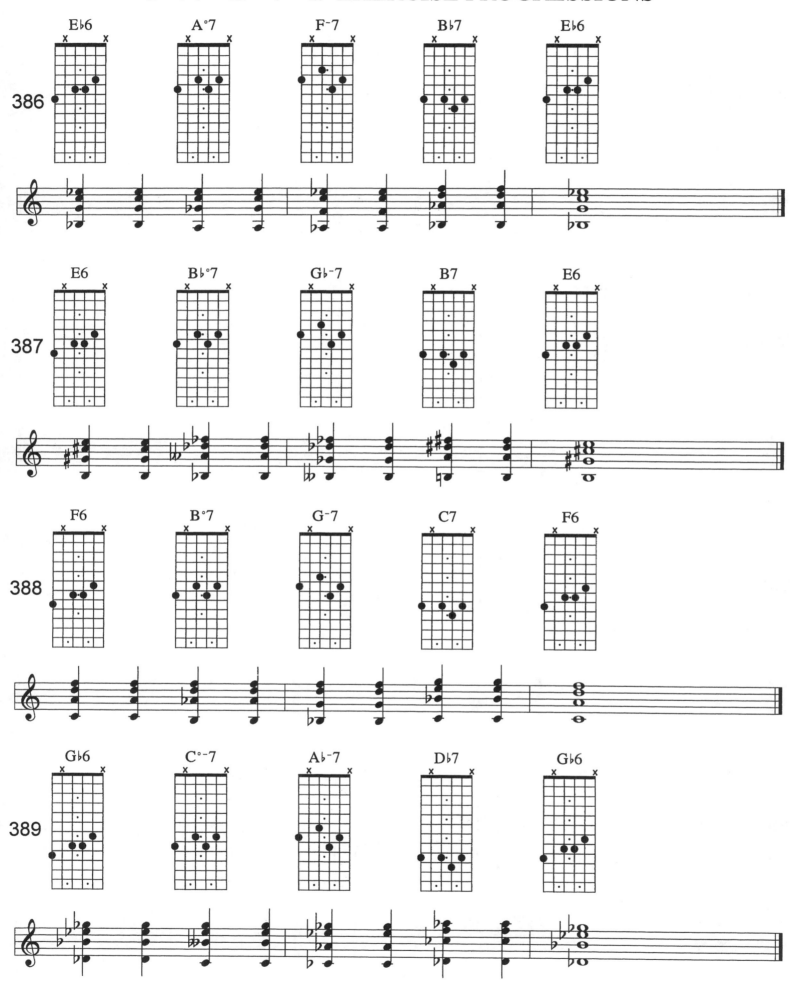

I - II - III - II - I: EXERCISE PROGRESSIONS

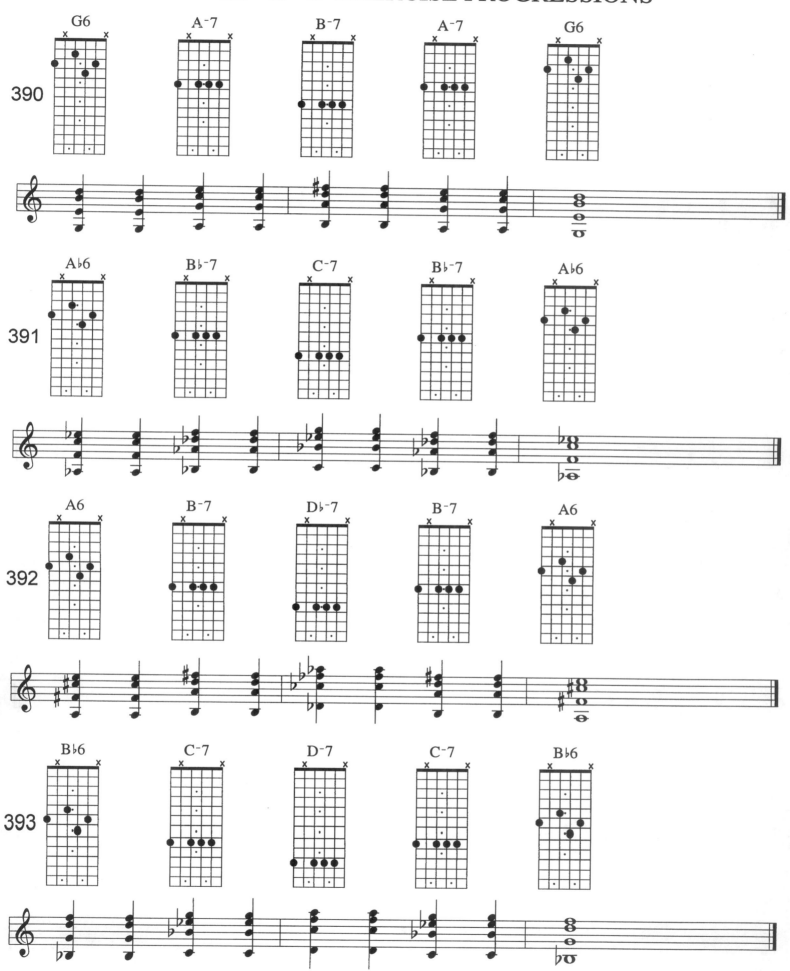

I - II - III - II - I: EXERCISE PROGRESSIONS

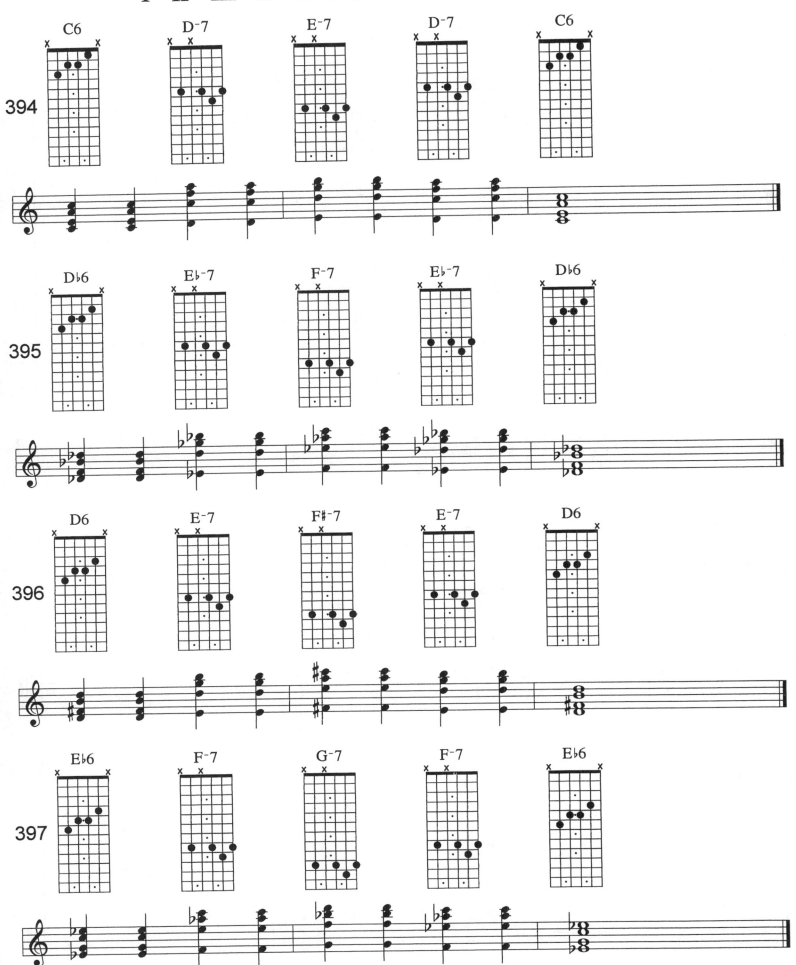

I - ♭III - II - V - I: EXERCISE PROGRESSIONS

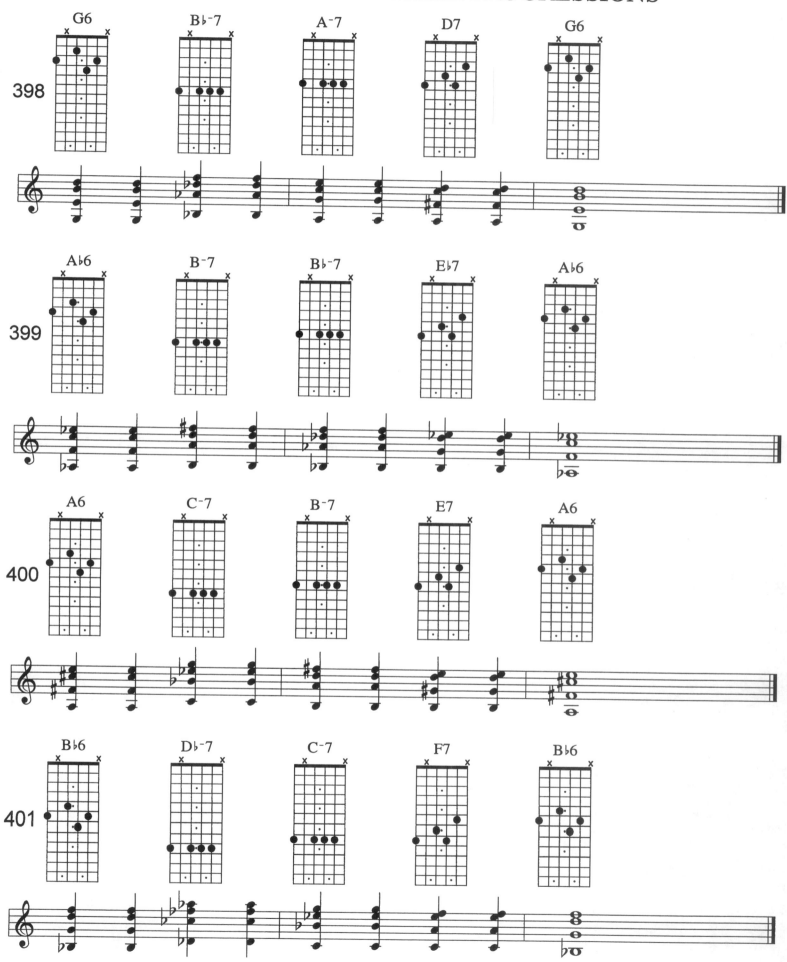

I - ♭III - II - V - I: EXERCISE PROGRESSIONS

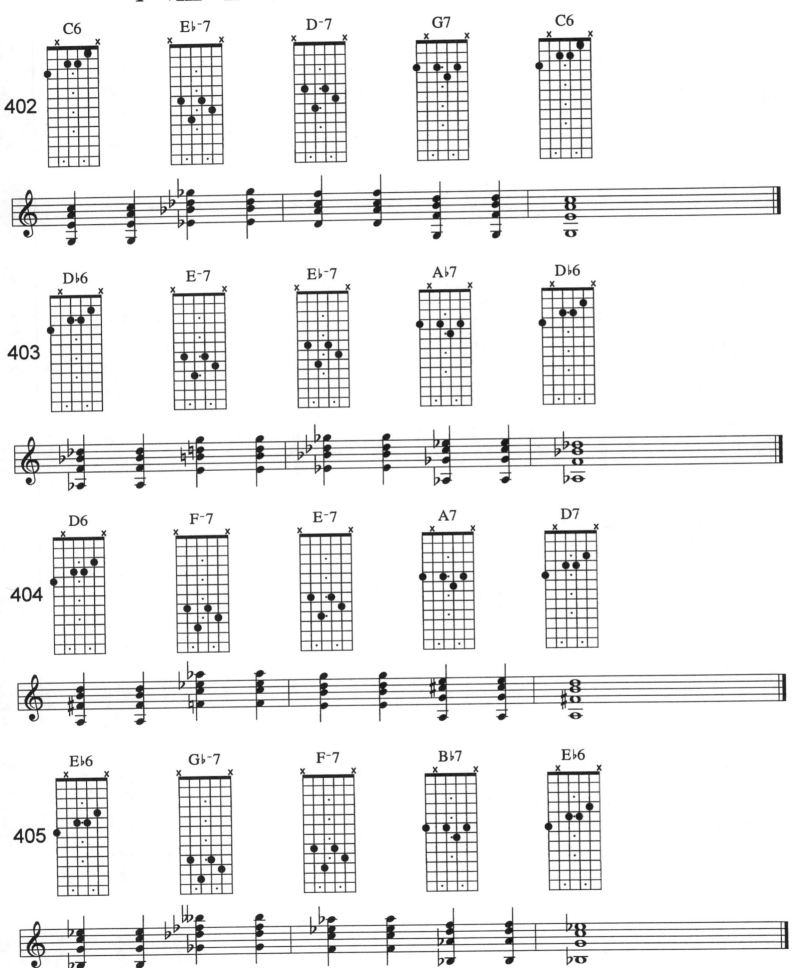

I - IV: with △

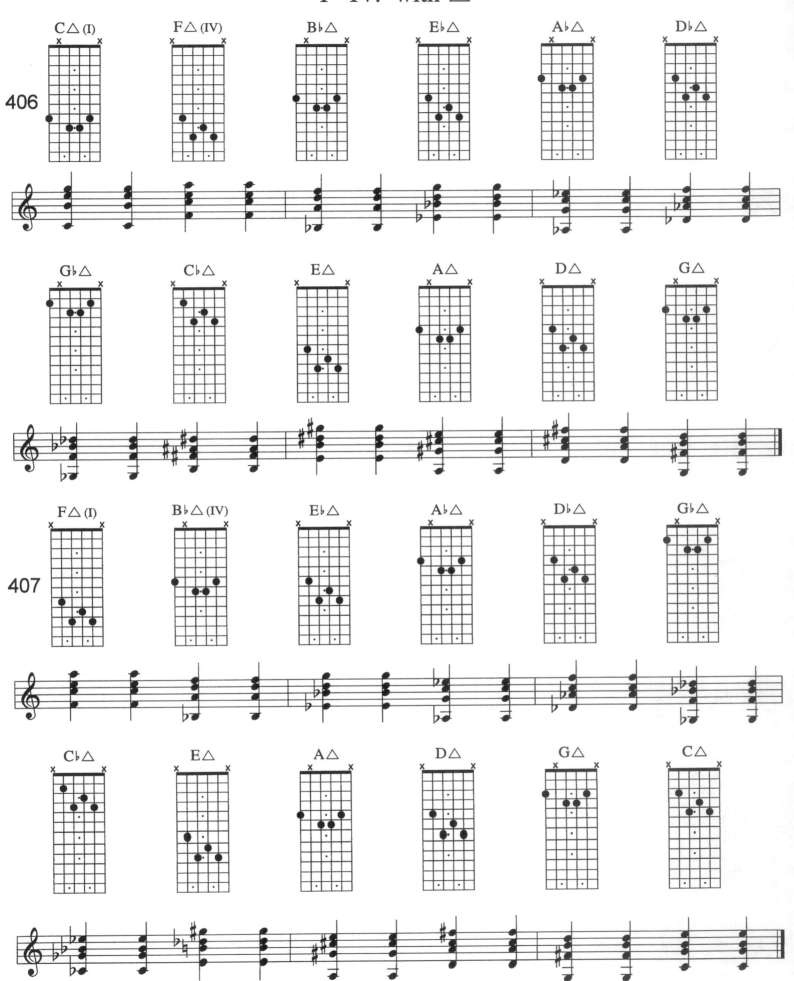

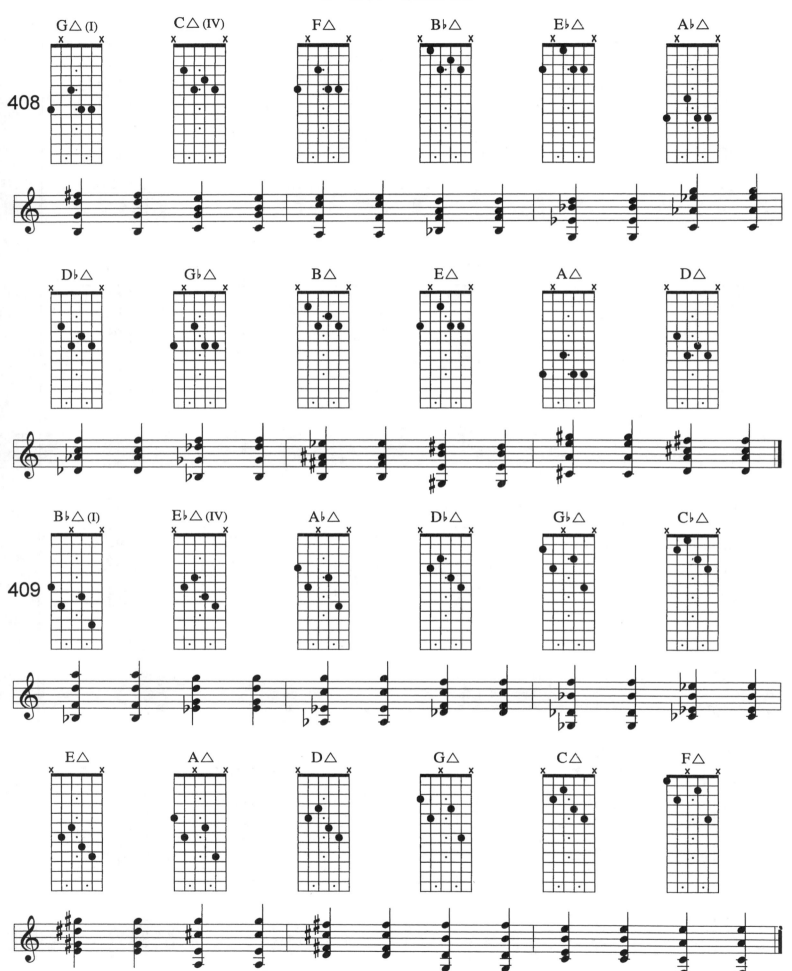

I - IV: with △

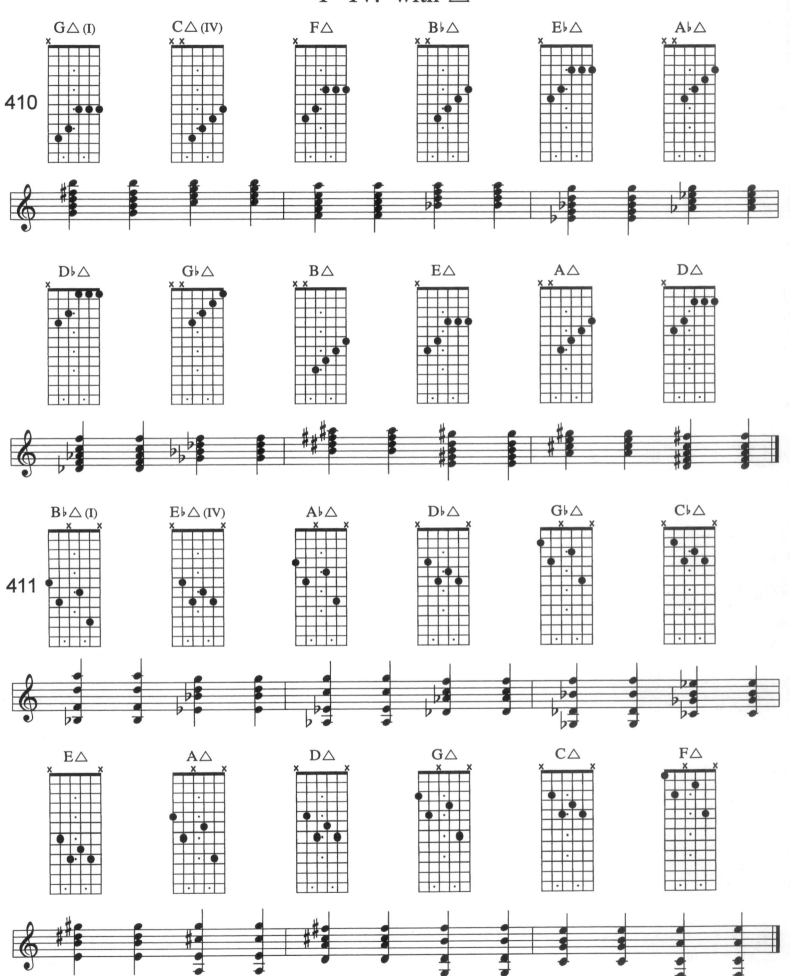

I - IV: with 6

I - IV: with △, 6

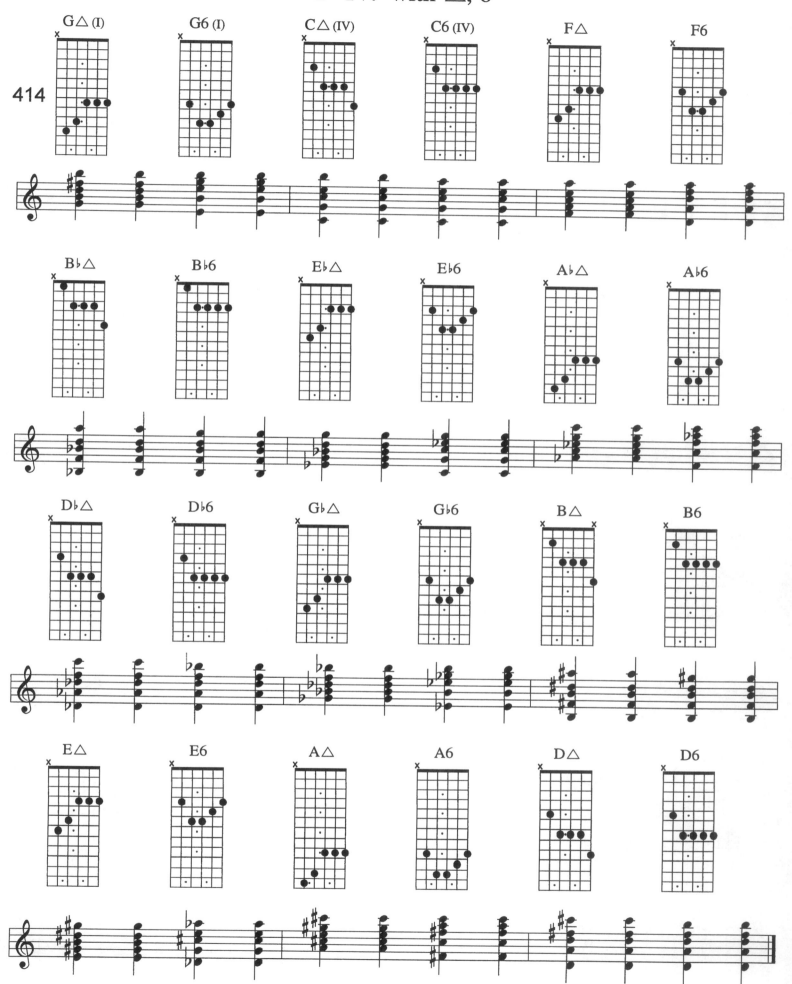

I - IV: with △, 6

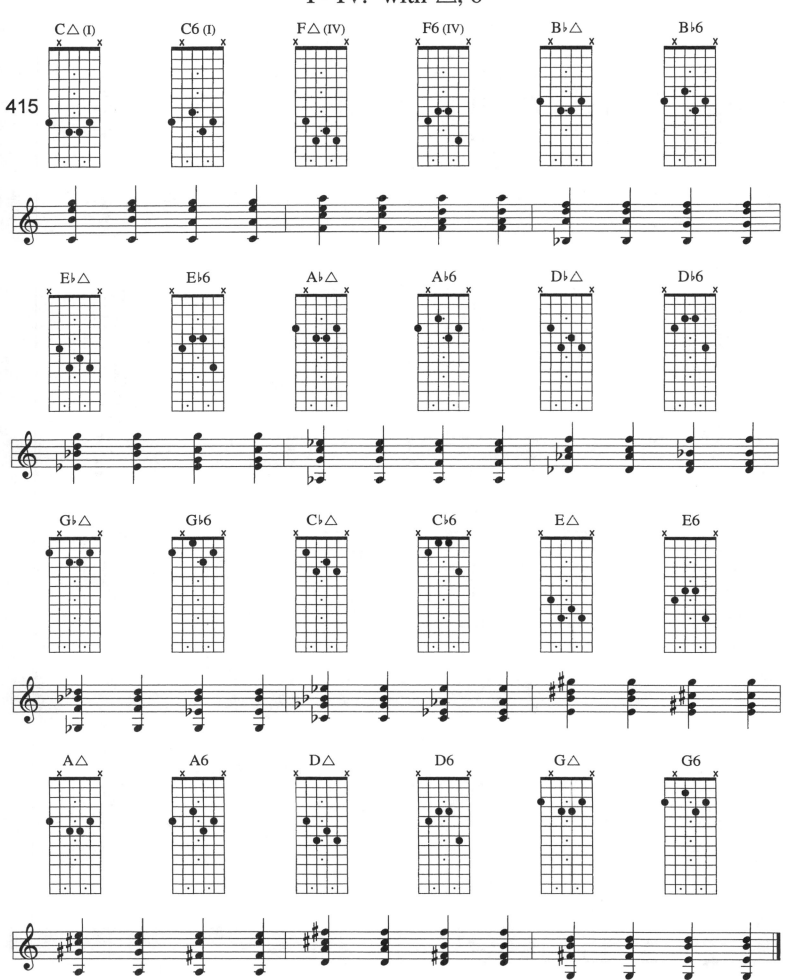

I - IV: with △, 6

I - IV: with △, 6

I - IV: with △9

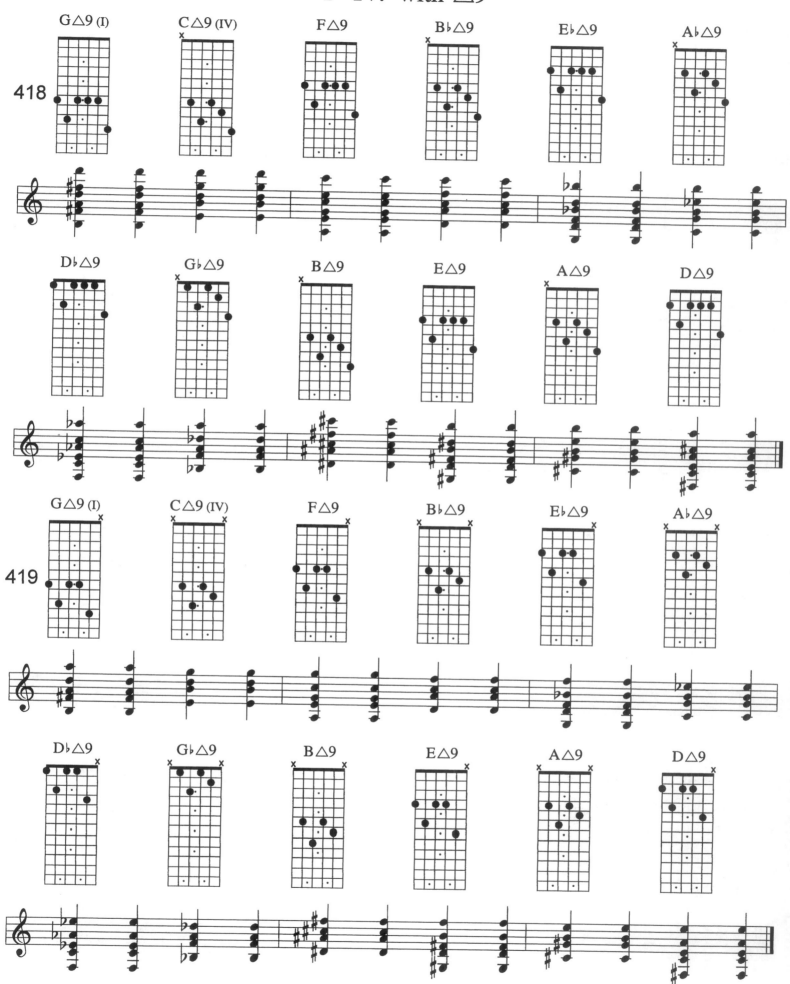

I - IV: with MINOR, 7

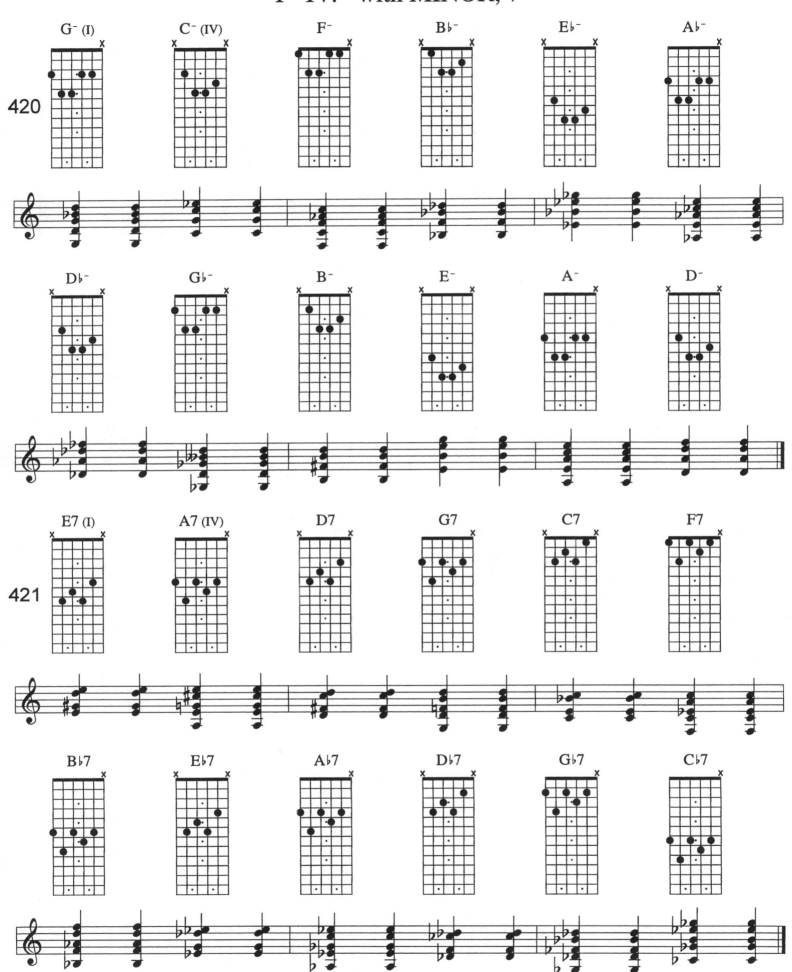

I - IV: with 7

I - IV: with ⁻7

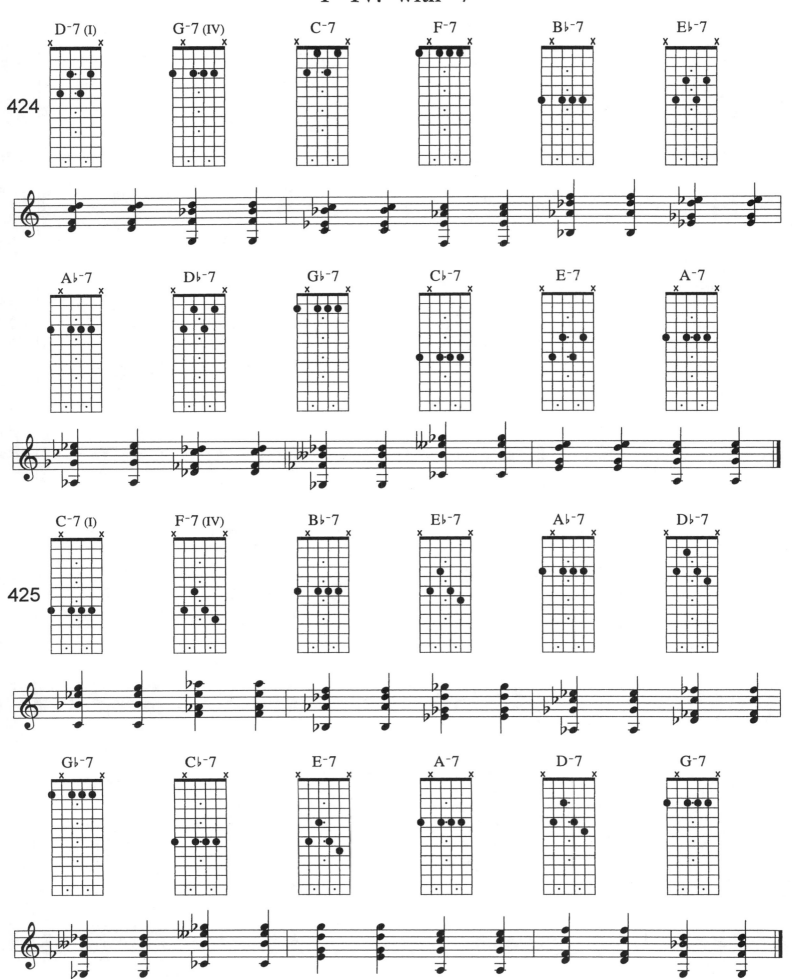

I - IV: with ⁻7

I - IV: with ⁻7

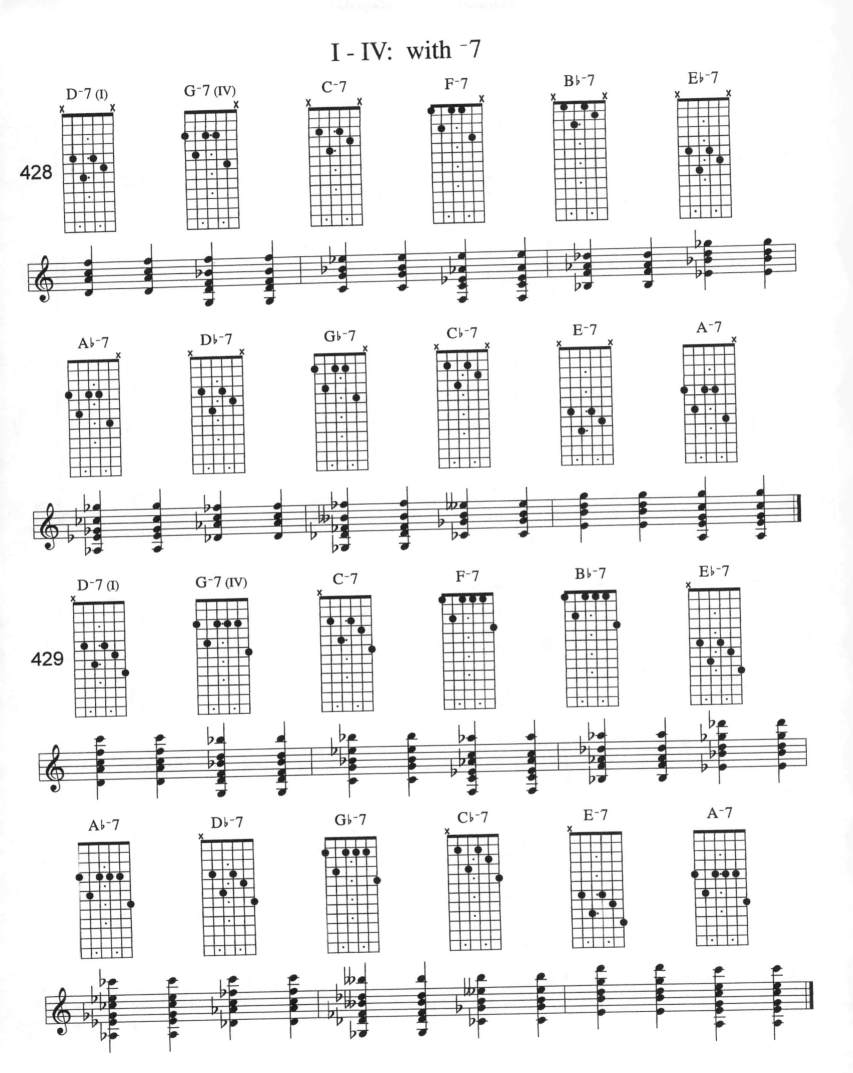

I - IV: with ⁻7

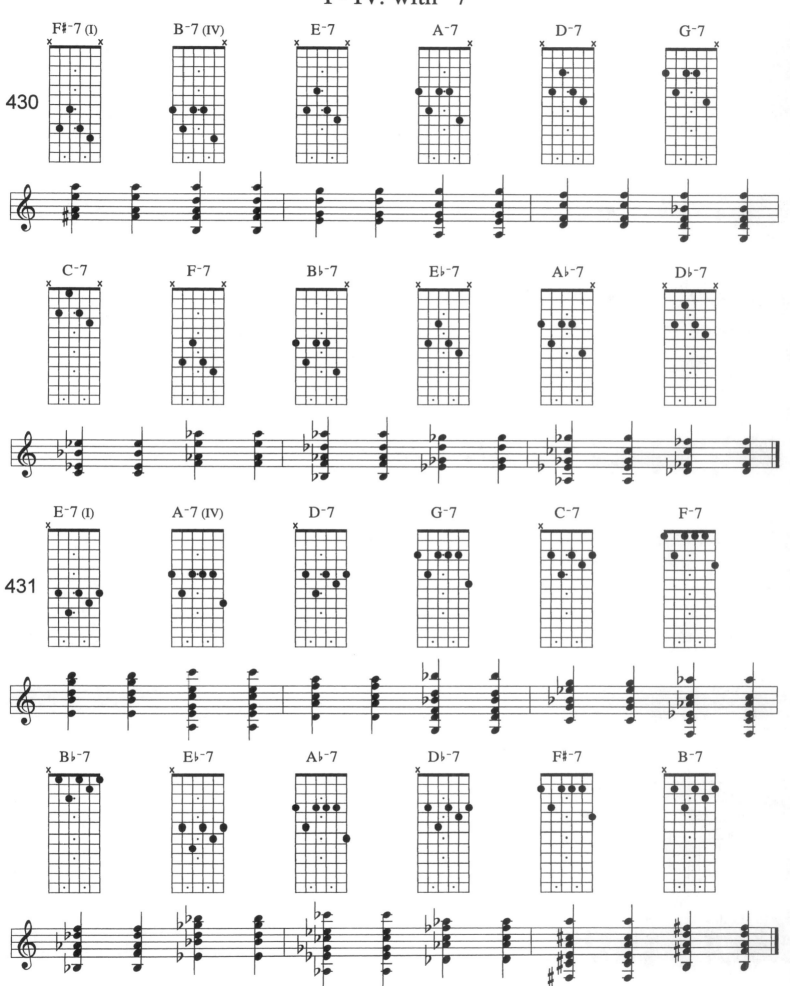

I - IV: with 7♭9

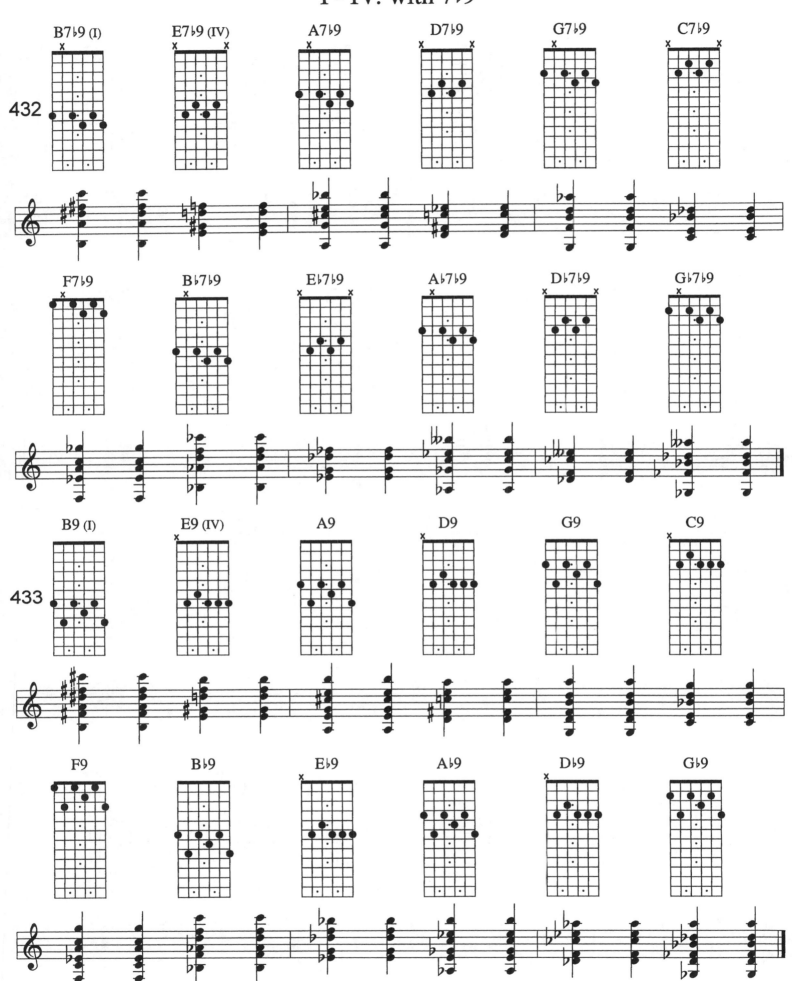

I - IV: with 7⁺ & 9

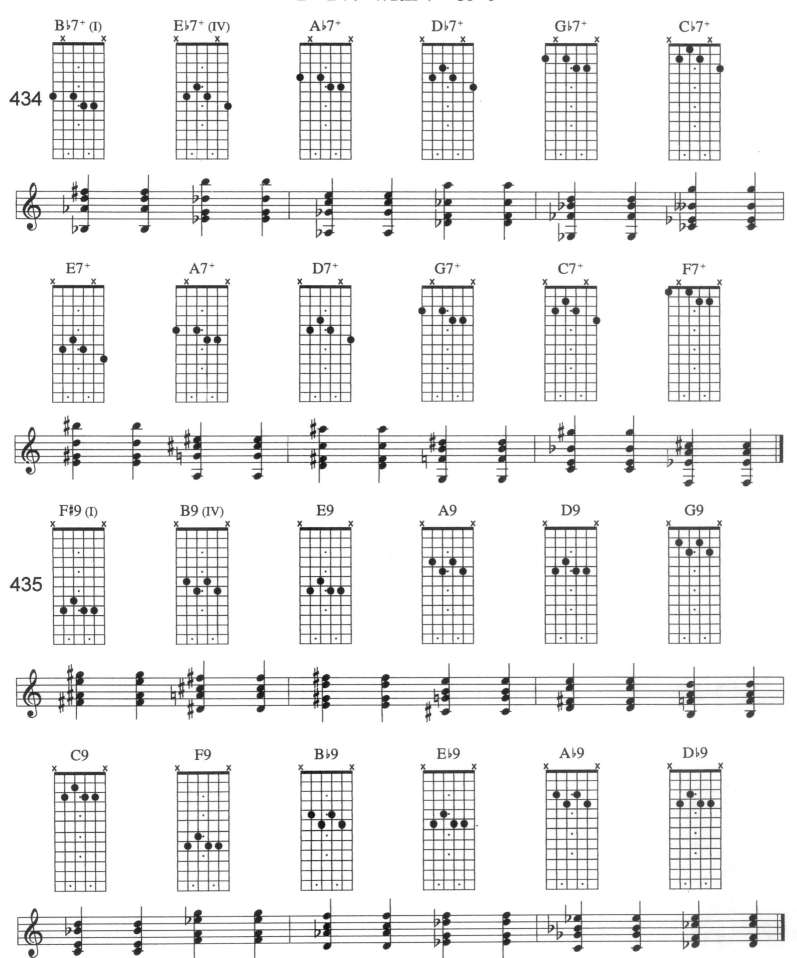

I - IV: with 7#9 & 9#11

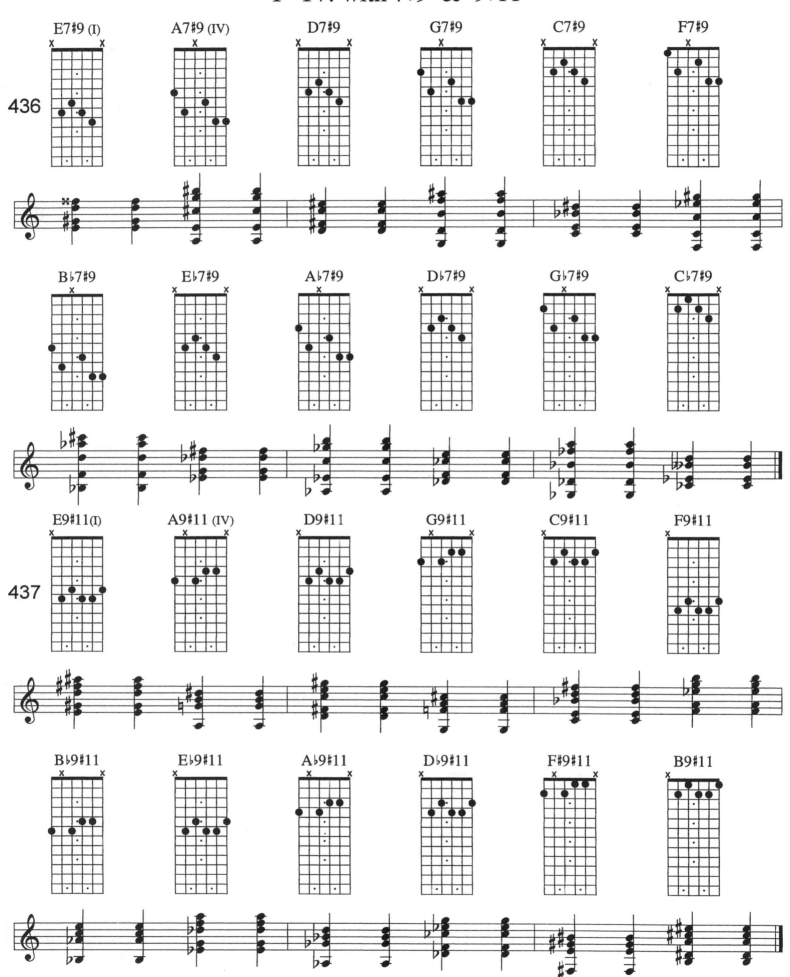

I - IV: with 13 & 13♭9

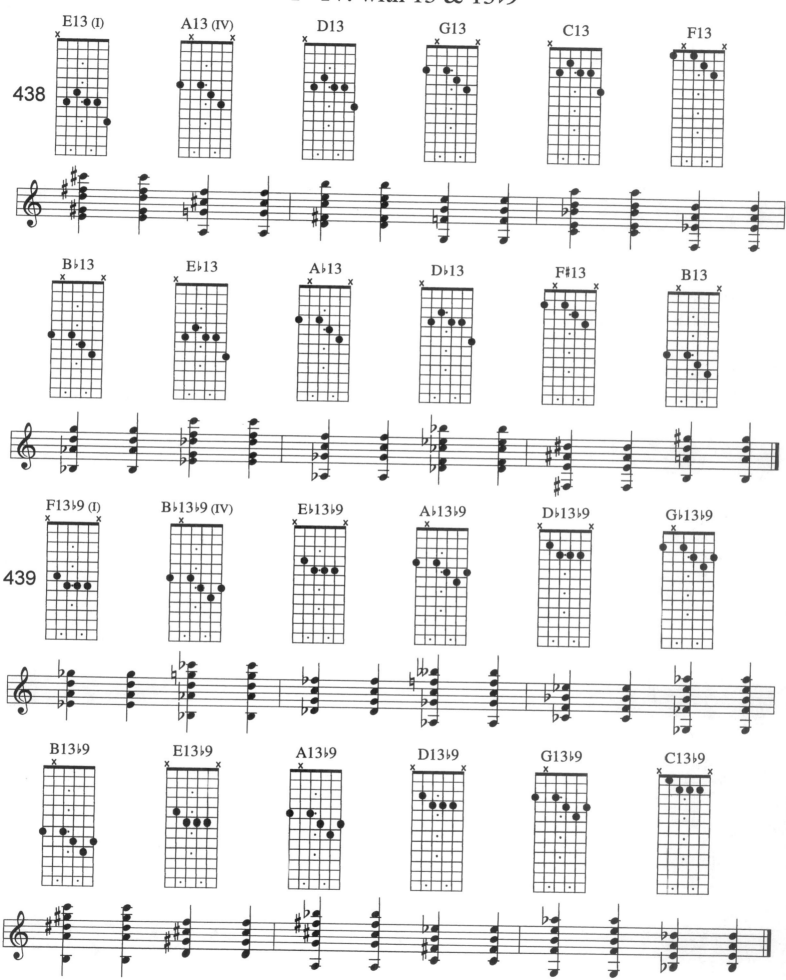

I - IV: with ⁻9

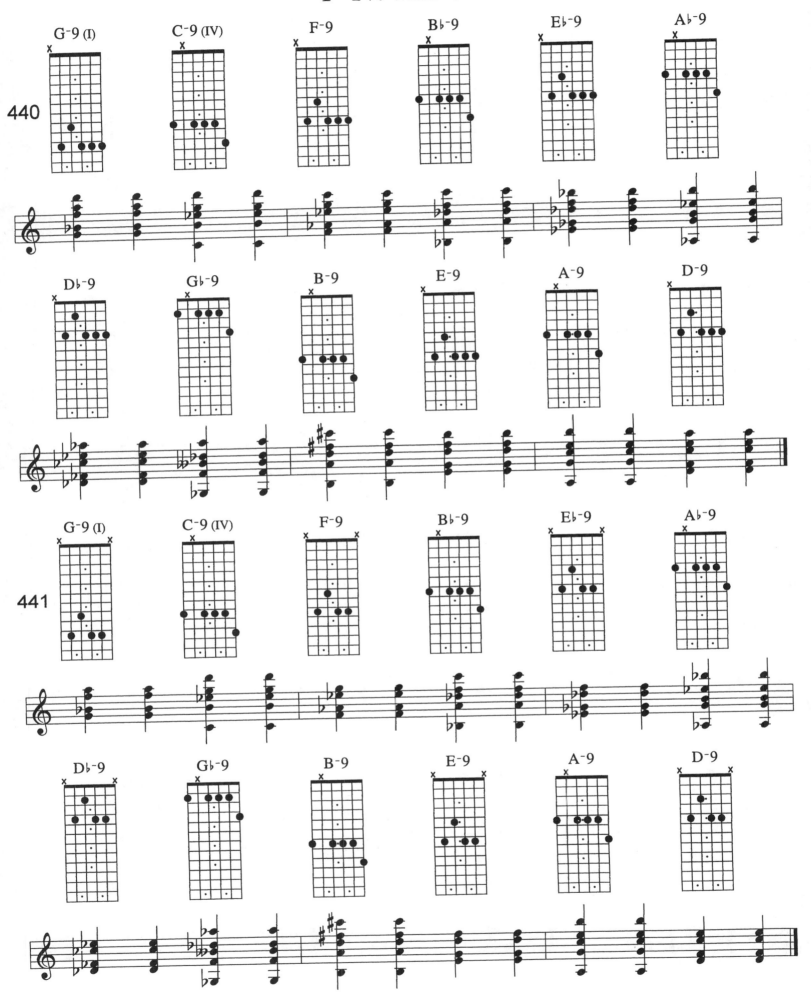

239

I - IV: with ⁻9

442

443

I - IV: 11, 7

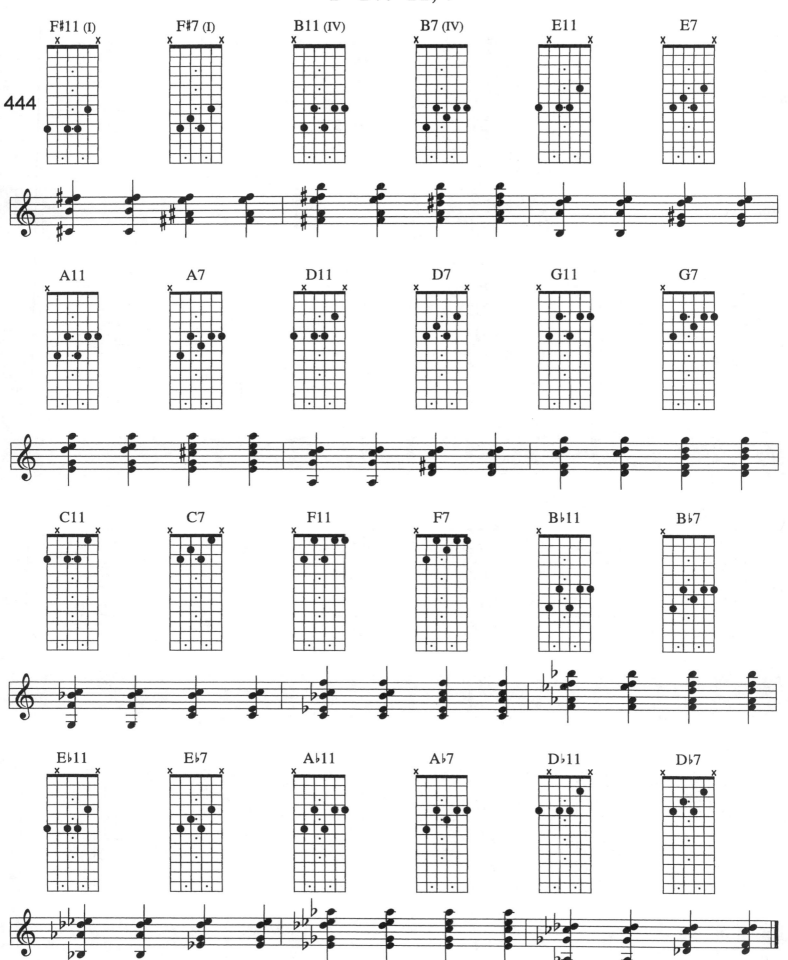

II - V - I: with ⁻7, 7, 9

445

II - V - I: with ⁻7, 7

II - V - I: with ⁻7, 7

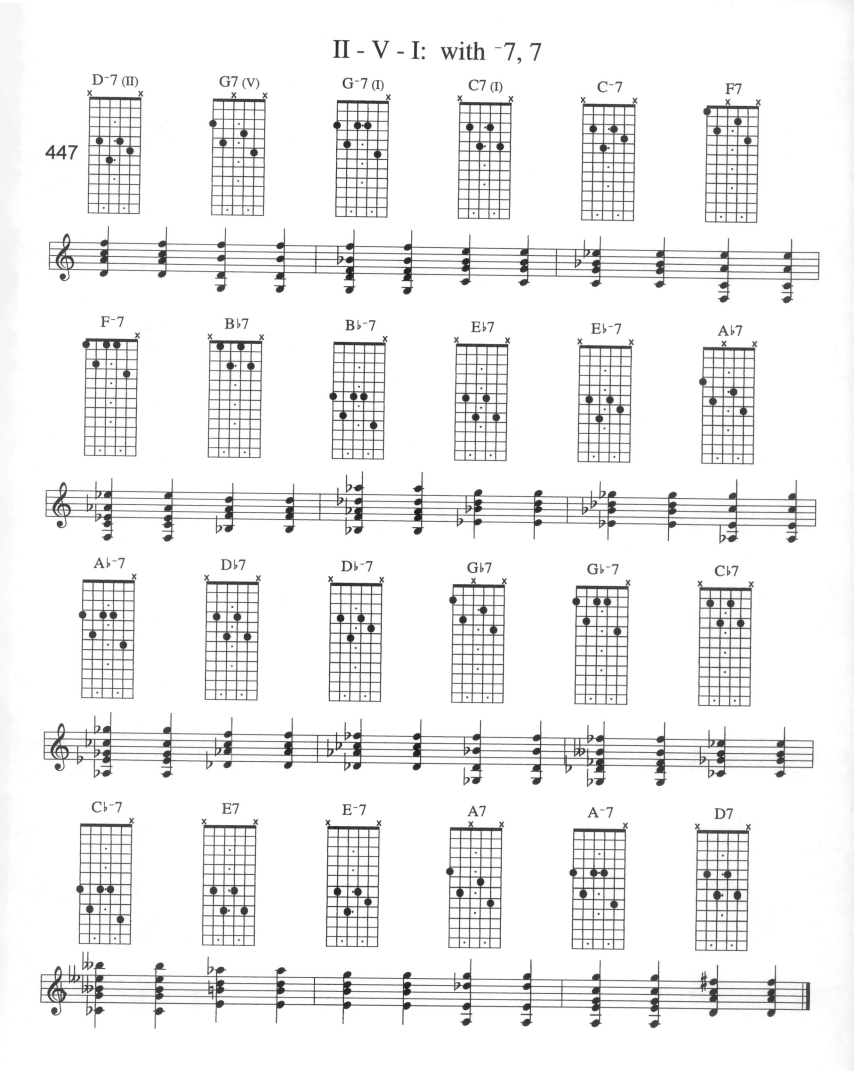

II - V - I: with ⁻7, 7

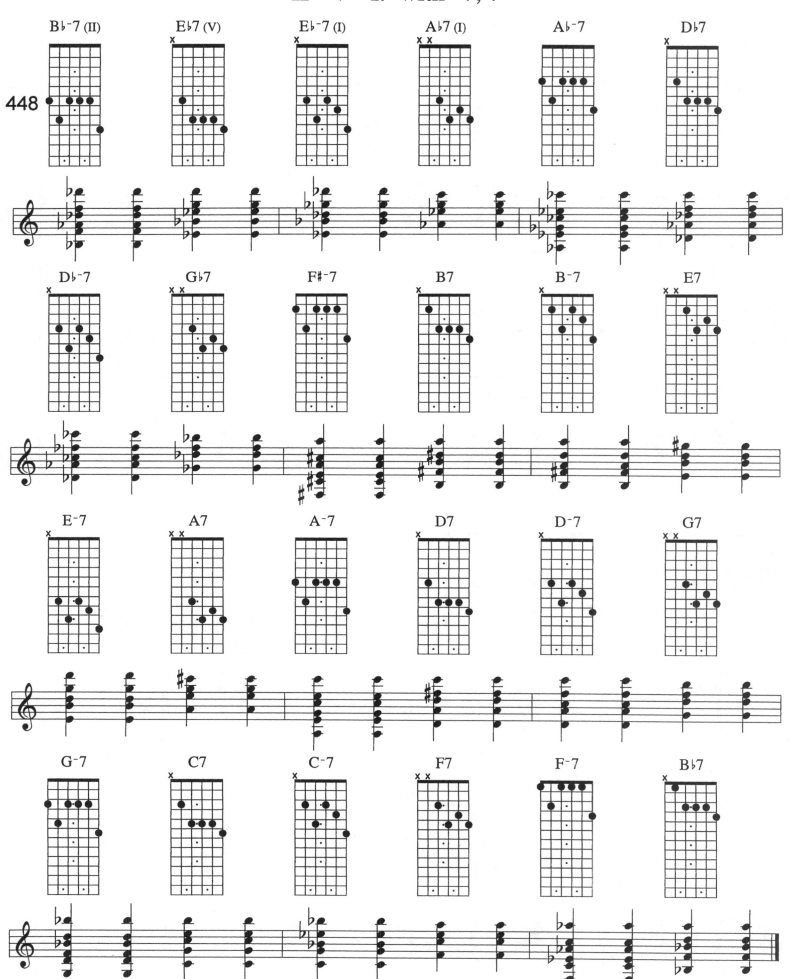

II - V - I: with ⁻7, 7

II - V - I: with ⁻7, 7

II - V - I: with ⁻7, 7, 9

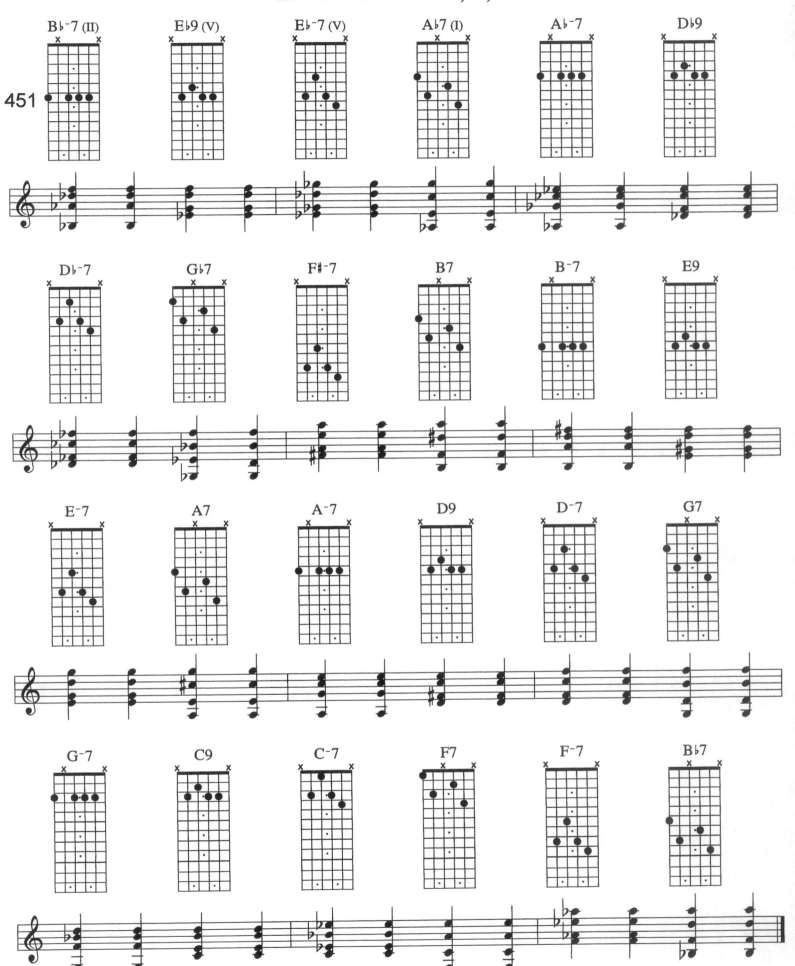

II - V - I: with 7, △

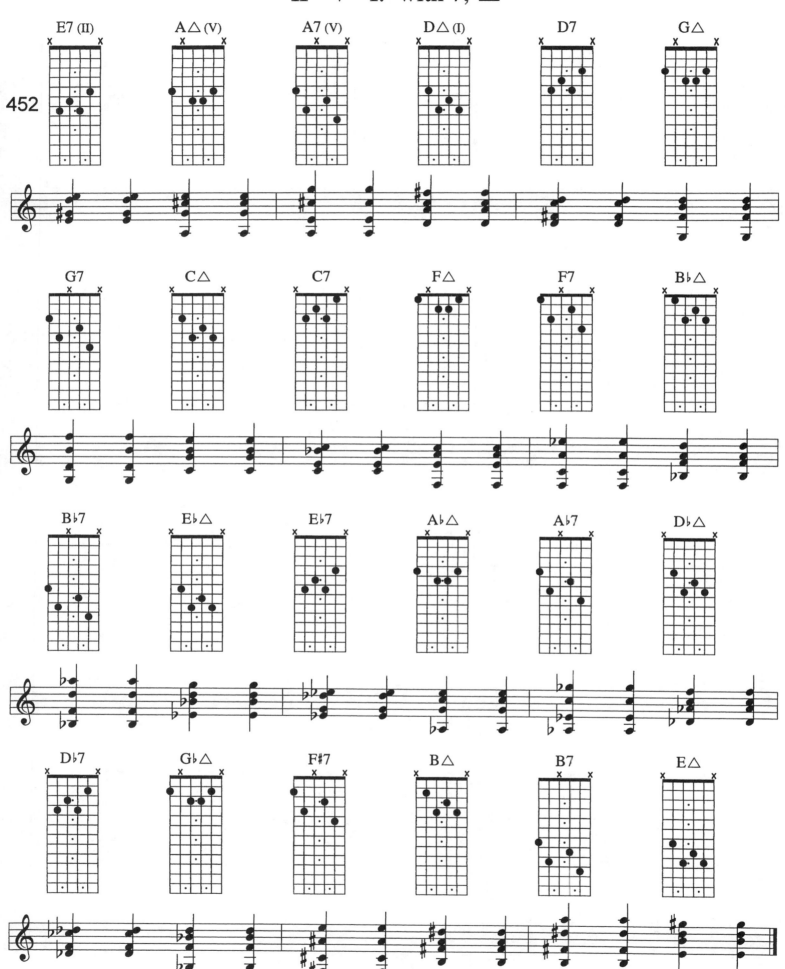

II - V - I: with ⁻11, 7

II - V - I: with ⁻9, 9#11

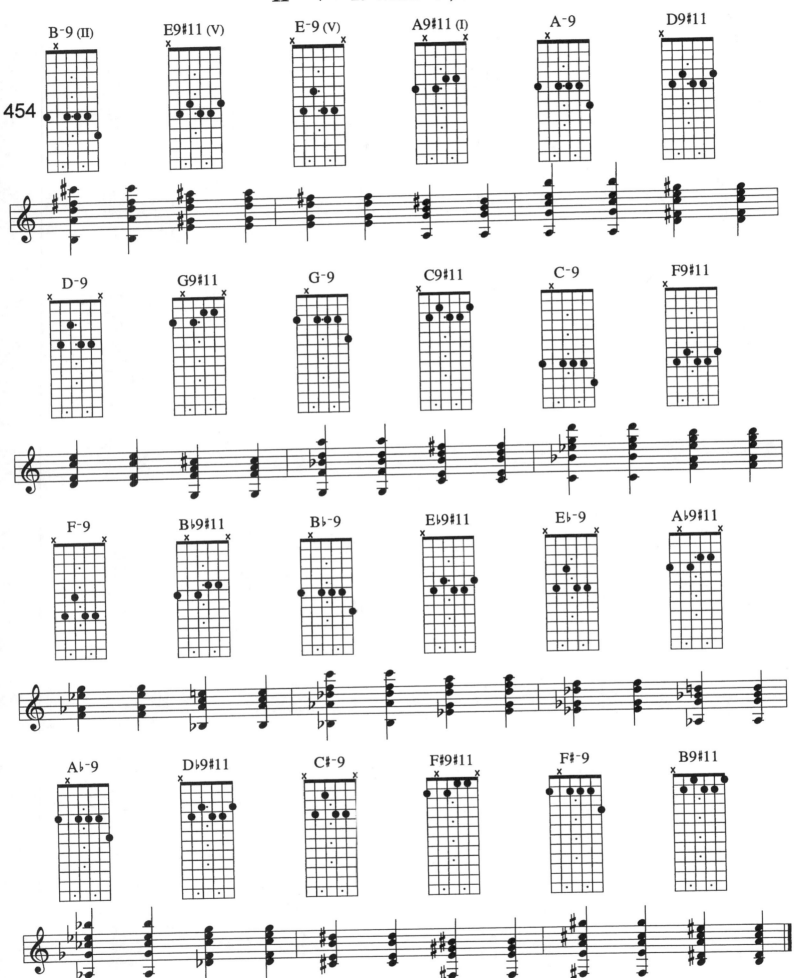

II - V - I: with ⁻9, 13

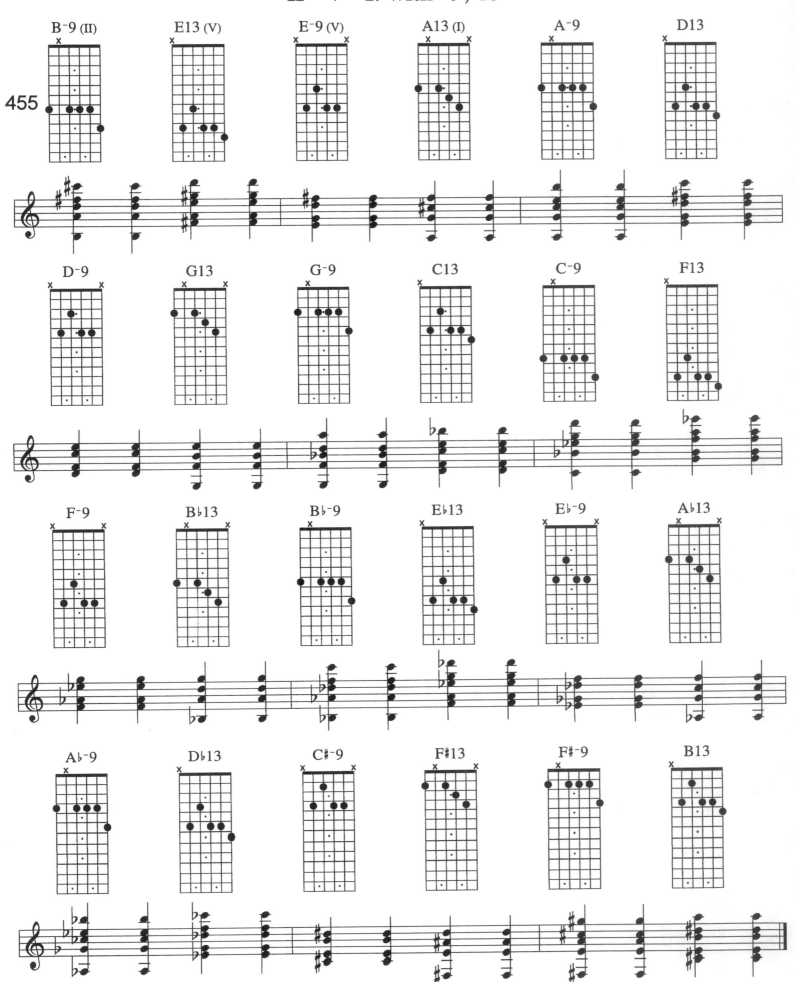

II - V - I: with ⁻9, 13

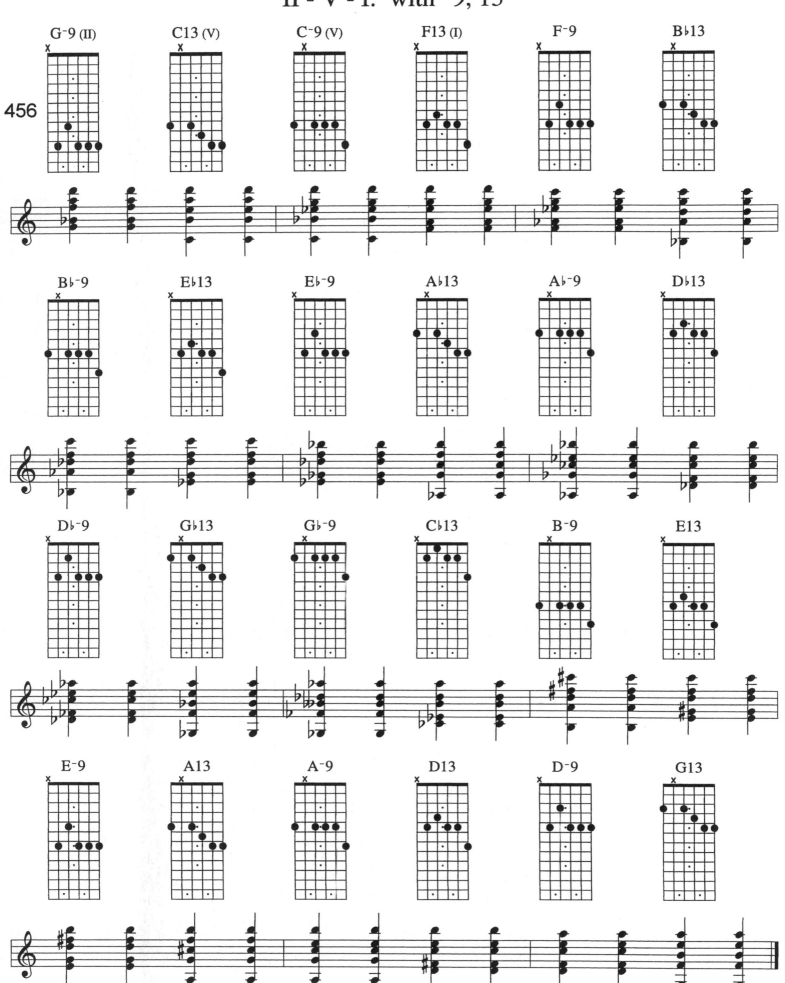

II - V - I: with -9, 13

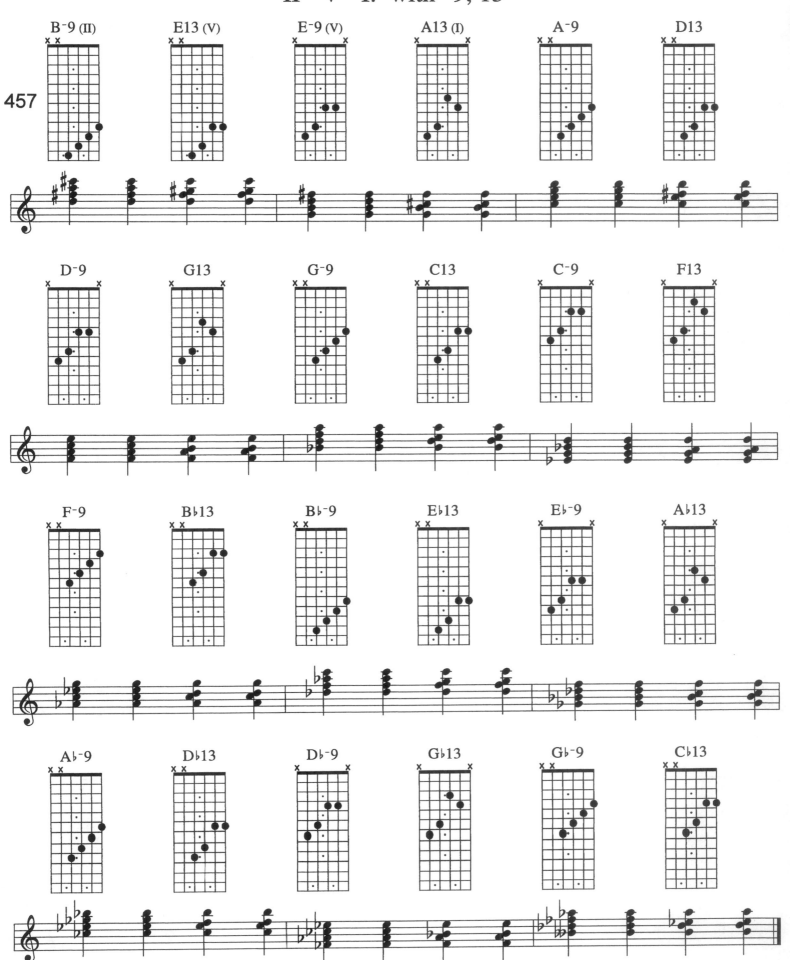

II - V - I: with ⁻9, 13

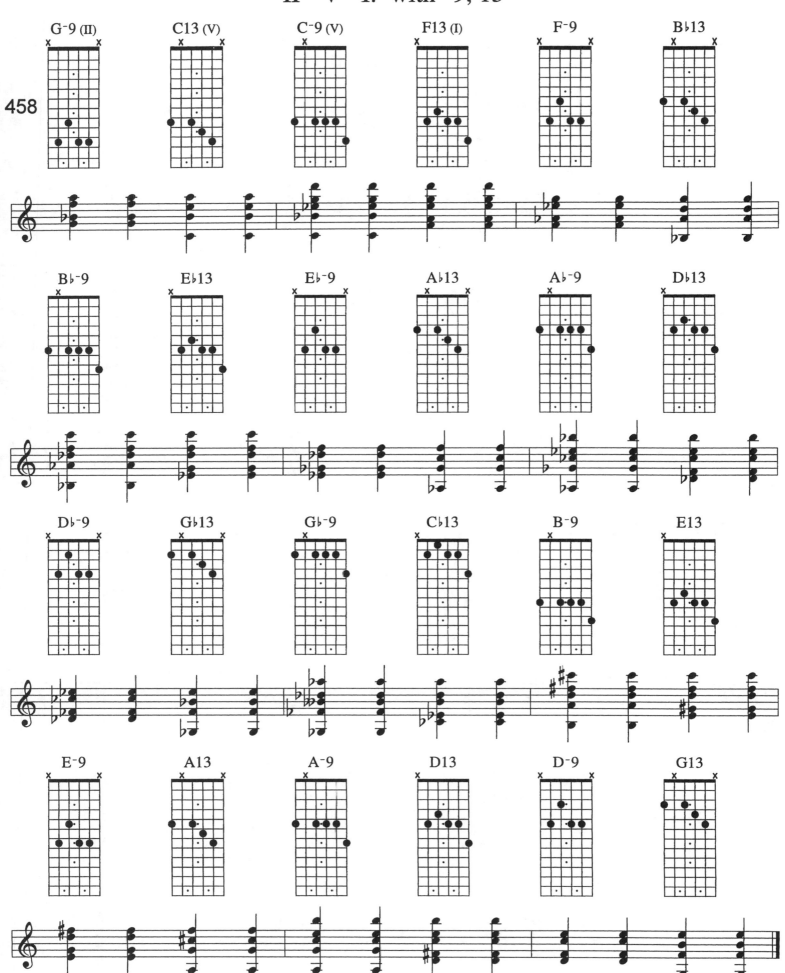

II - V - I: with ⁻7, 7, △, 6, 9

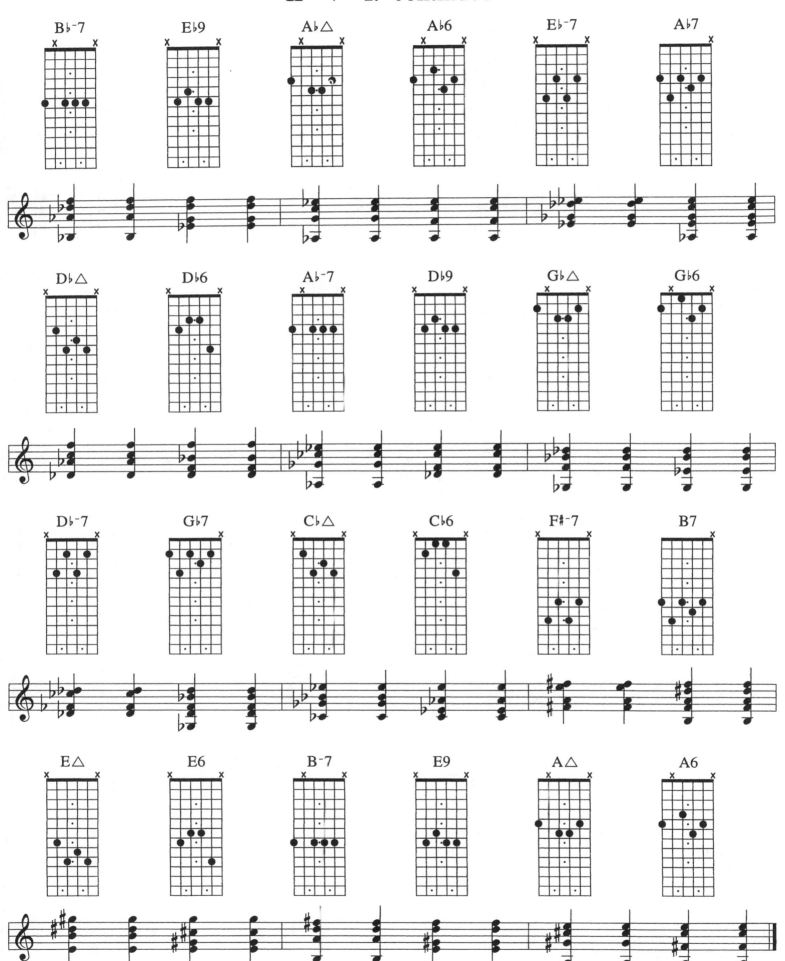

II - V - I: with ⁻7, 7, △, 6

460

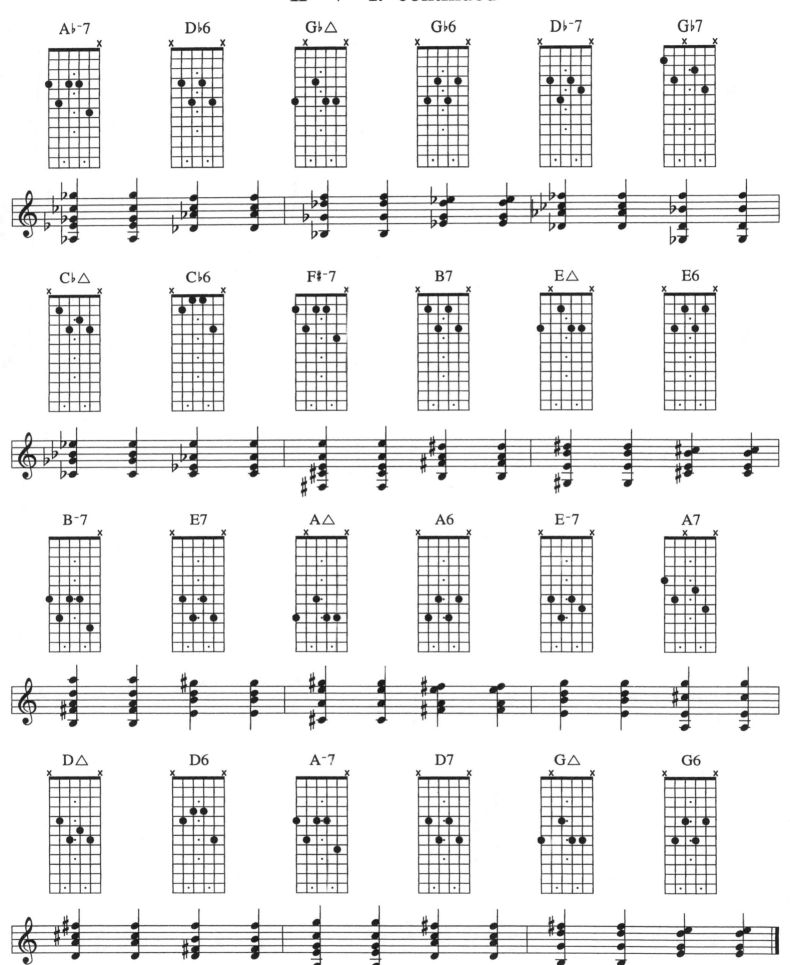

II - V - I: with ⁻7, 7, △, 6

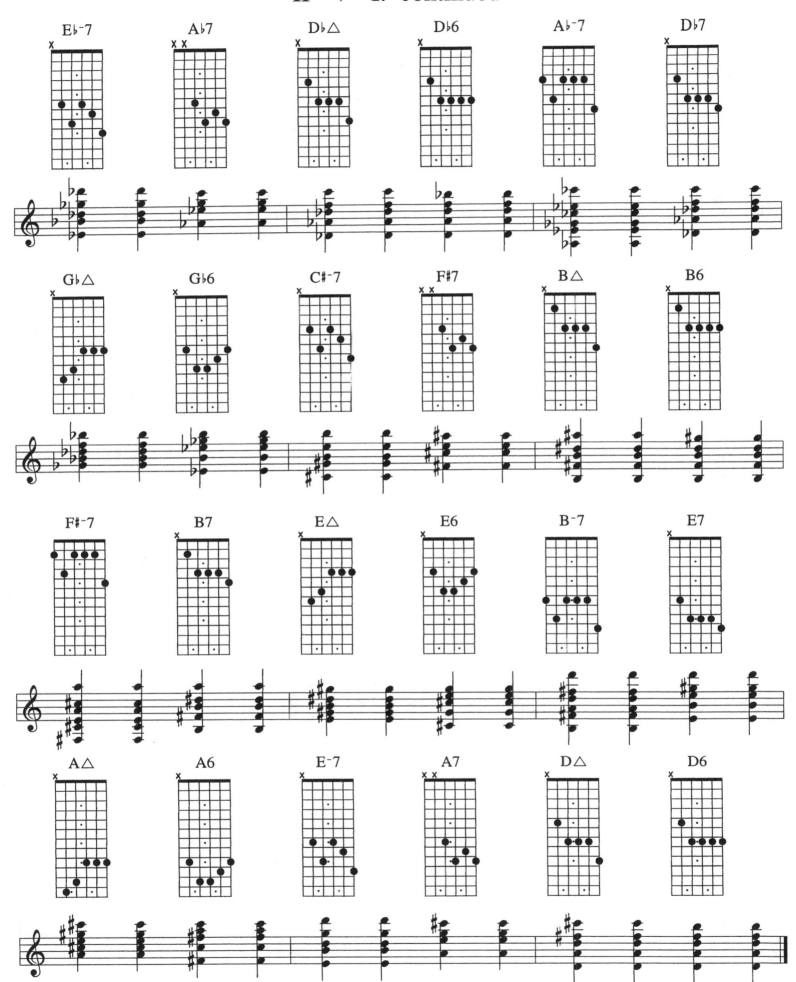

II - V - I: with ⁻7, 9, △9, 6

II - V - I: continued

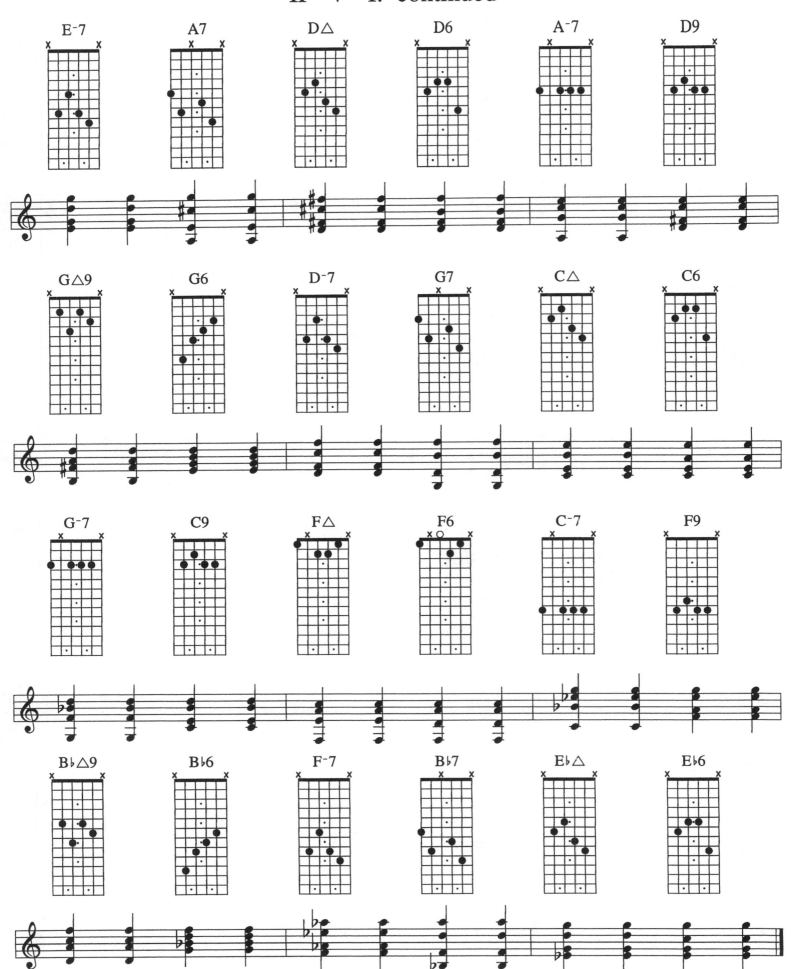

II - V - I: with ⁻7, 7, △, 6

463

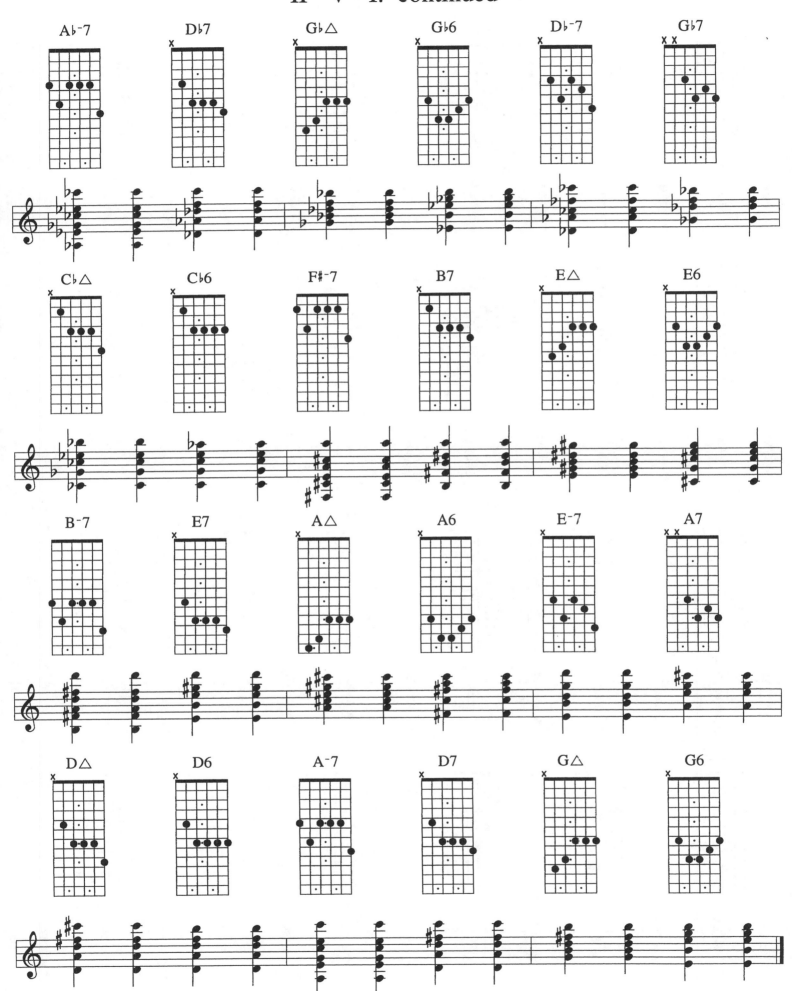

II - V - I: with ⁻7, 7, △, 6

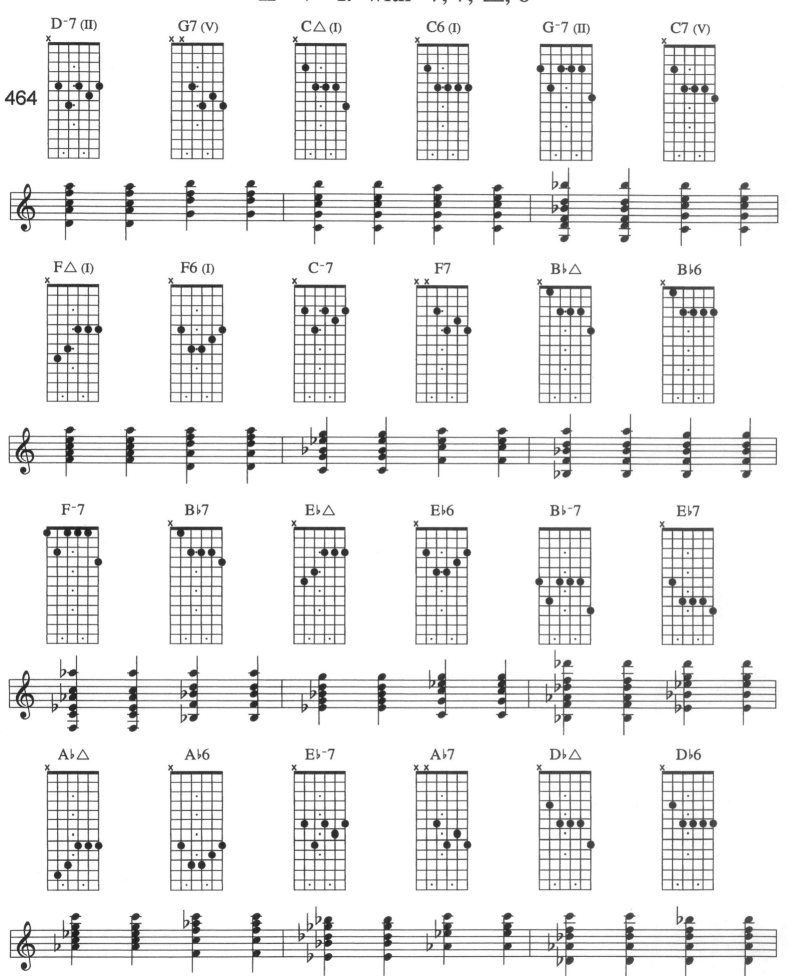

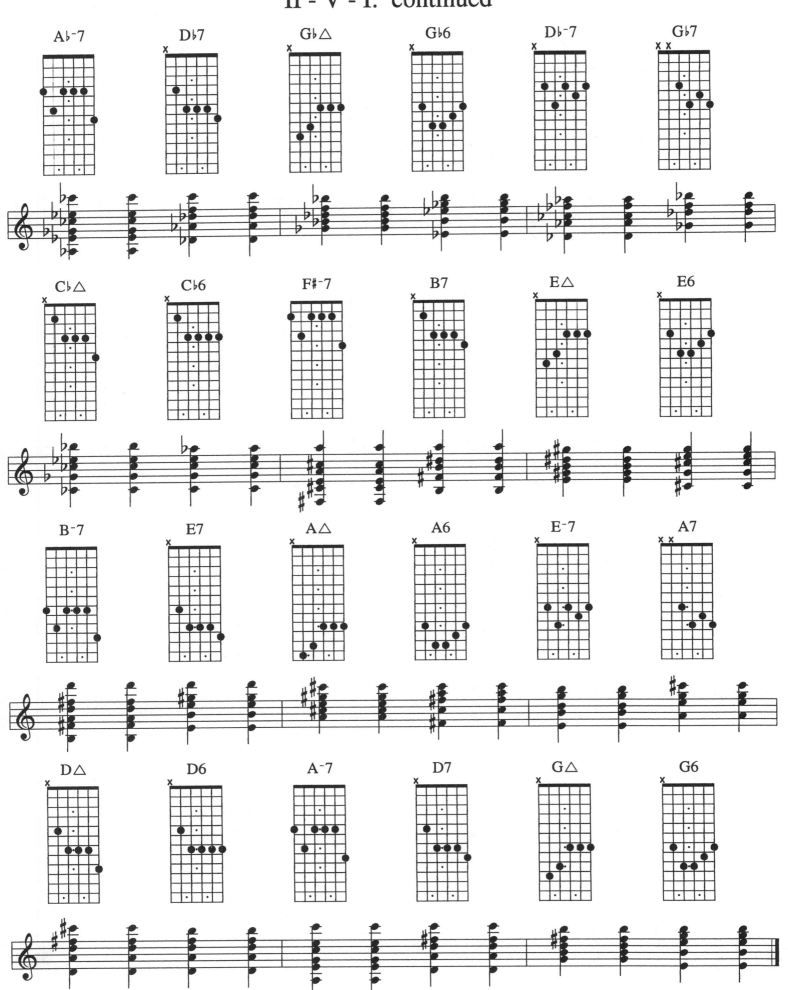

II - V - I: with $^-7$, 7, $\triangle$, 6

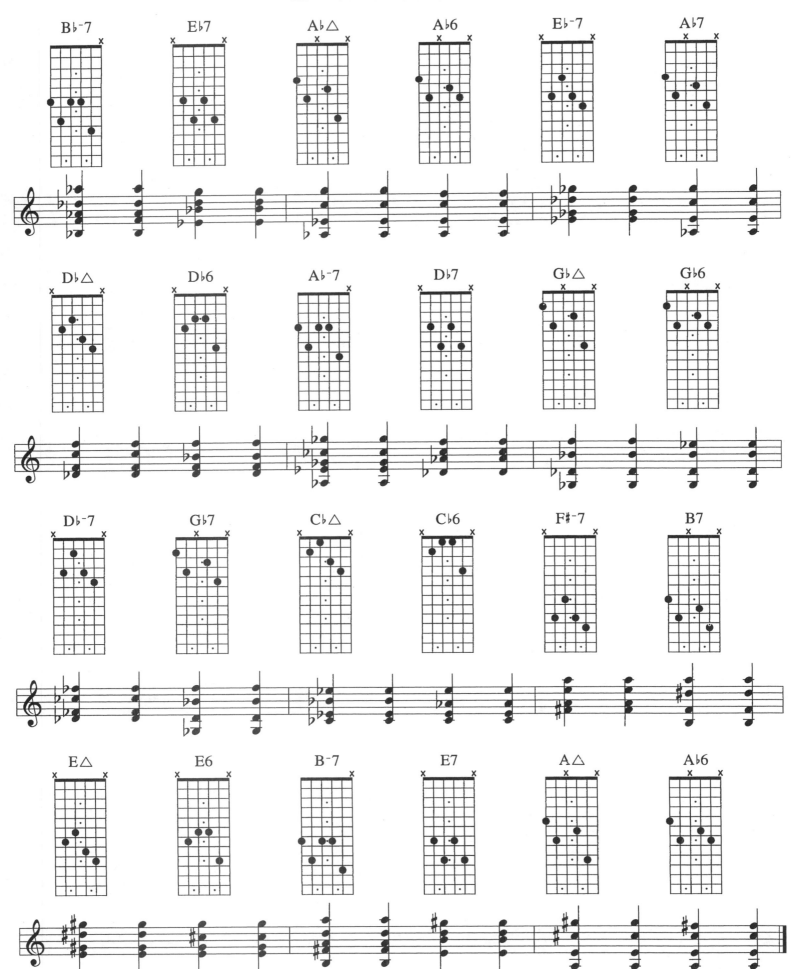

II - V - I: with ⁻9, 13, △9, 6

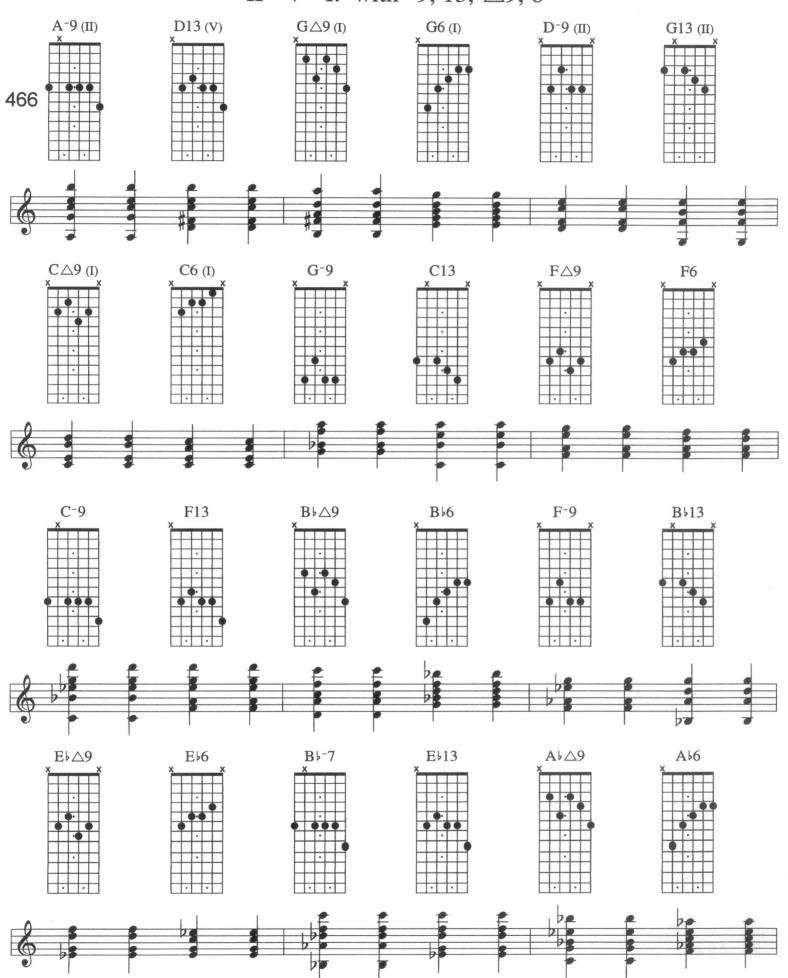

466

II - V - I: continued

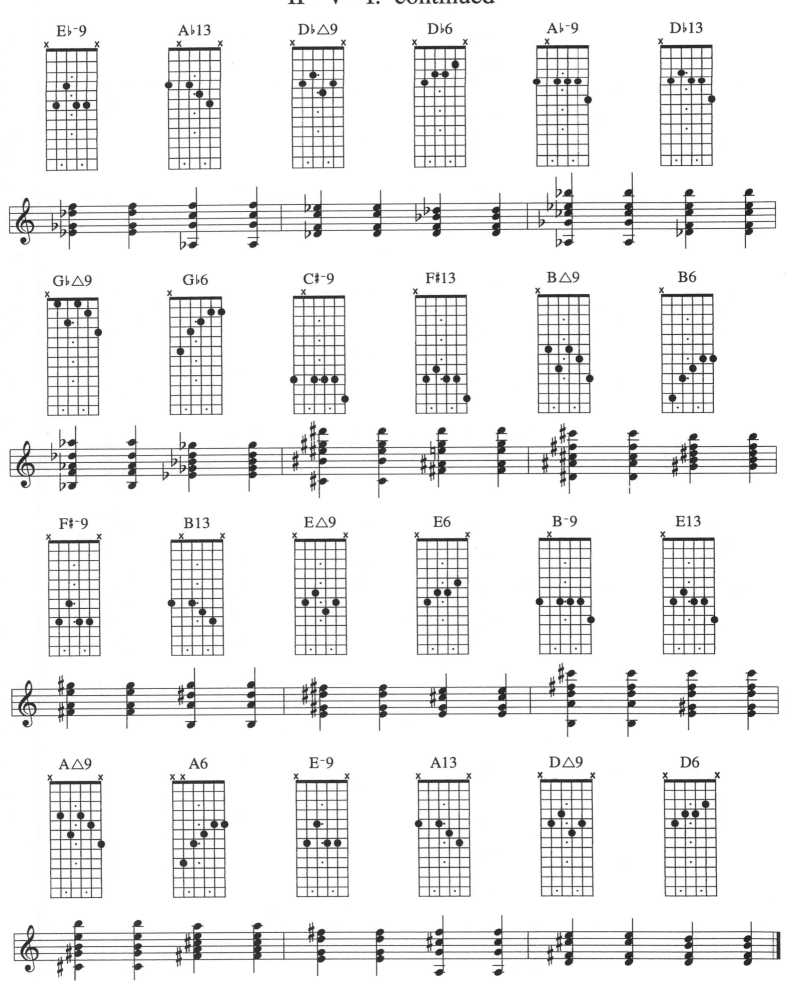

271

II - V - I: with ⁻9, 13, △, 6

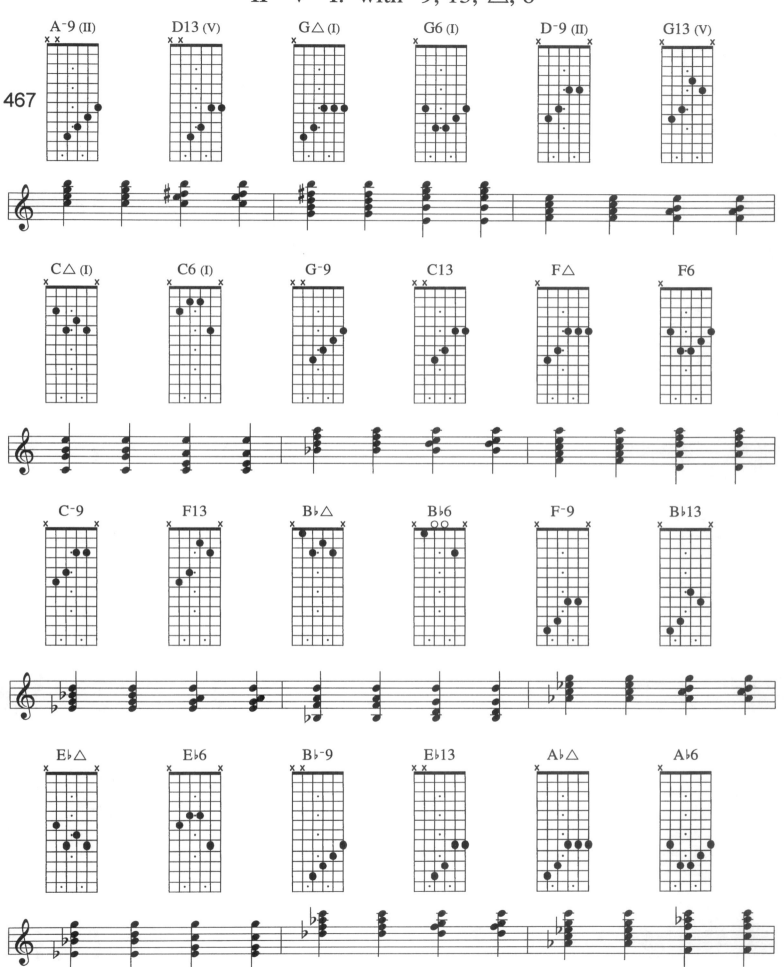

II - V - I: continued

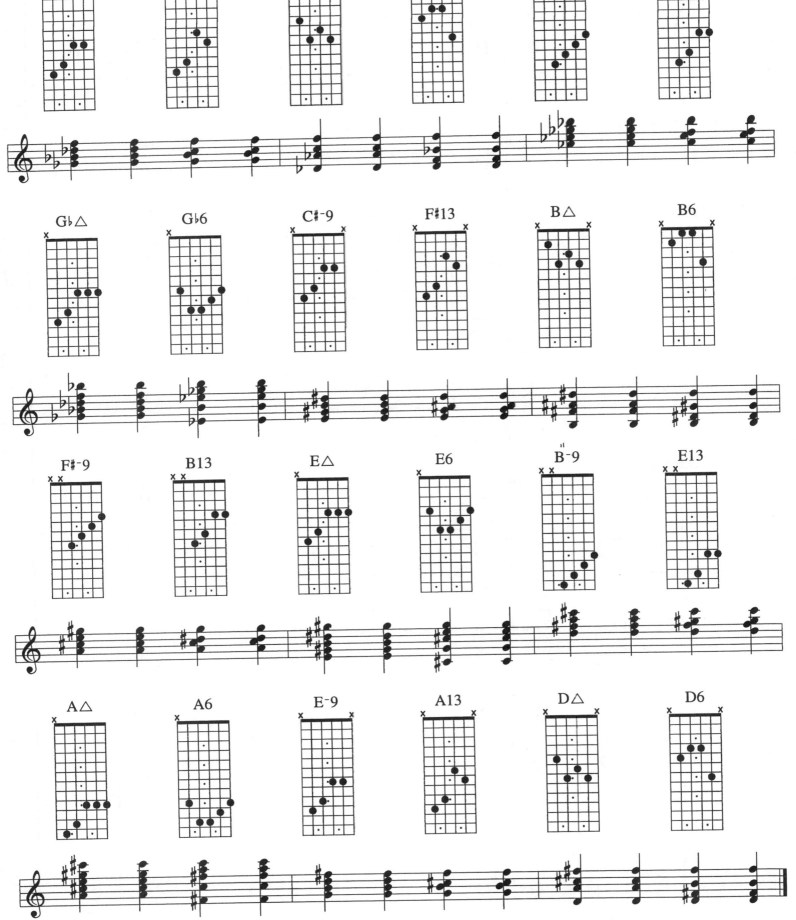

SCALE TONE DEGREES IN 15 KEYS: THEORETICAL

SCALE TONE DEGREES →

KEYS ↓	I	♭II	II	♭III	III	IV	♭V	V	♭VI	VI	♭VII	VII
	C	D♭	D	E♭	E	F	G♭	G	A♭	A	B♭	B
	C#	D	D#	E	E#	F#	G	G#	A	A#	B	B#
	D♭	E♭♭	E♭	F♭	F	G♭	A♭♭	A♭	B♭♭	B♭	C♭	C
	D	E♭	E	F	F#	G	A♭	A	B♭	B	C	C#
	E♭	E	F	G♭	G	A♭	A	B♭	C♭	C	D♭	D
	E	F	F#	G	G#	A	B♭	B	C	C#	D	D#
	F	G♭	G	A♭	A	B♭	C♭	C	D♭	D	E♭	E
	F#	G	G#	A	A#	B	C	C#	D	D#	E	E#
	G♭	A♭♭	A♭	B♭♭	B♭	C♭	D♭♭	D♭	E♭♭	E♭	F♭	F
	G	A♭	A	B♭	B	C	D♭	D	E♭	E	F	F#
	A♭	B♭♭	B♭	C♭	C	D♭	E♭♭	E♭	F♭	F	G♭	G
	A	B♭	B	C	C#	D	E♭	E	F	F#	G	G#
	B♭	C♭	C	D♭	D	E♭	F♭	F	G♭	G	A♭	A
	B	C	C#	D	D#	E	F	F#	G	G#	A	A#
	C♭	D♭♭	D♭	E♭♭	E♭	F♭	G♭♭	G♭	A♭♭	A♭	B♭♭	B♭

SCALE TONE DEGREES IN 15 KEYS: SIMPLIFIED

SCALE TONE DEGREES →

I	♭II	II	♭III	III	IV	♭V	V	♭VI	VI	♭VII	VII
C	D♭	D	E♭	E	F	G♭	G	A♭	A	B♭	B
C#	D	D#	E	F	F#	G	G#	A	A#	B	C
D♭	D	E♭	E	F	G♭	G	A♭	A	B♭	B	C
D	E♭	E	F	F#	G	A♭	A	B♭	B	C	C#
E♭	E	F	G♭	G	A♭	A	B♭	B	C	D♭	D
E	F	F#	G	G#	A	B♭	B	C	C#	D	D#
F	G♭	G	A♭	A	B♭	B	C	D♭	D	E♭	E
F#	G	G#	A	A#	B	C	C#	D	D#	E	F
G♭	G	A♭	A	B♭	B	C	D♭	D	E♭	E	F
G	A♭	A	B♭	B	C	D♭	D	E♭	E	F	F#
A♭	A	B♭	B	C	D♭	D	E♭	E	F	G♭	G
A	B♭	B	C	C#	D	E♭	E	F	F#	G	G#
B♭	B	C	D♭	D	E♭	E	F	G♭	G	A♭	A
B	C	C#	D	D#	E	F	F#	G	G#	A	A#
C♭	C	D♭	D	E♭	E	F	G♭	G	A♭	A	B♭

KEYS ↓

NUMERIC ANALYSIS OF CHORDS

	1		2		3	4		5		6		7	1		2		3	4		5		6		7
M	1				3			5																
−	1			♭3				5																
sus2	1		2					5																
sus	1					4		5																
♭5	1				3		♭5																	
°	1			♭3			♭5																	
5/8	1							5					8											
+	1				3				♯5															
♭6	1				3			5	♭6															
−♭6	1			♭3				5	♭6															
6	1				3			5		6														
−6	1			♭3				5		6														
°7	1			♭3			♭5			♮7														
Q(3)	1					4					♭7													
7	1				3			5			♭7													
−7	1			♭3				5			♭7													
7sus2	1		2					5			♭7													
7sus	1					4		5			♭7													
7♭5	1				3		♭5				♭7													
ø	1			♭3			♭5				♭7													
7+	1				3				♯5		♭7													
△	1				3			5				7												
−△	1			♭3				5				7												
△sus2	1		2					5				7												
△sus	1					4		5				7												
△♭5	1				3		♭5					7												
△°	1			♭3			♭5					7												
△+	1				3				♯5			7												
−△+	1			♭3					♯5			7												
7/6	1				3			5		6	♭7													
9/6	1				3			5		6					9									
−9/6	1			♭3				5		6					9									

276

NUMERIC ANALYSIS OF CHORDS continued

	1	2	3	4	5	6	7	1	2	3	4	5	6	7
9	1		3		5		b7		9					
-9	1		b3		5		b7		9					
b9	1		3		5		b7		b9					
-b9	1		b3		5		b7		b9					
#9	1		3		5		b7		#9					
△9	1		3		5		7		9					
-△9	1		b3		5		7		9					
△b9	1		3		5		7		b9					
-△b9	1		b3		5		7		b9					
△#9	1		3		5		7		#9					
b5 #9	1		3		b5		b7		#9					
b5 b9	1		3		b5		b7		b9					
#5 b9	1		3		#5		b7		b9					
#5 #9	1		3		#5		b7		#9					
11	1		3		5		b7		9		11			
-11	1		b3		5		b7		9		11			
#11	1		3		5		b7		9		#11			
-#11	1		b3		5		b7		9		#11			
△11	1		3		5		7		9		11			
-△11	1		b3		5		7		9		11			
△#11	1		3		5		7		9		#11			
-△#11	1		b3		5		7		9		#11			
13	1		3		5		b7		9		11		13	
-13	1		b3		5		b7		9		11		13	
13#11	1		3		5		b7		9		#11		13	
-13#11	1		b3		5		b7		9		#11		13	
△13	1		3		5		7		9		11		13	
-△13	1		b3		5		7		9		11		13	
△13#11	1		3		5		7		9		#11		13	
-△13#11	1		b3		5		7		9		#11		13	

ALT* { b5 #9, b5 b9, #5 b9, #5 #9 }

* the ALT chords can be used interchangeably

NUMERIC ANALYSIS OF SCALES

Scale	1	♭2	2	♭3	3	4	♯4/♭5	5	♭6	6	♭7	7
MAJOR (IONIAN)	1		2		3	4		5		6		7
DORIAN	1		2	♭3		4		5		6	♭7	
PHRYGIAN	1	♭2		♭3		4		5	♭6		♭7	
LYDIAN	1		2		3		♯4	5		6		7
MIXOLYDIAN	1		2		3	4		5		6	♭7	
AEOLIAN	1		2	♭3		4		5	♭6		♭7	
LOCRIAN	1	♭2		♭3		4	♭5		♭6		♭7	
MELODIC	1		2	♭3		4		5		6		7
DORIAN ♭2	1	♭2		♭3		4		5		6	♭7	
LYDIAN AUGMENTED	1		2		3		♯4		♯5	6		7
LYDIAN DOMINANT	1		2		3		♯4	5		6	♭7	
HINDU	1		2		3	4		5	♭6		♭7	
LOCRIAN ♮2	1		2	♭3		4	♭5		♭6		♭7	
SUPER LOCRIAN	1	♭2		♭3	♭4		♭5		♭6		♭7	
HARMONIC MINOR	1		2	♭3		4		5	♭6			7
LOCRIAN ♮6	1	♭2		♭3		4	♭5			6	♭7	
IONIAN ♯5	1		2		3	4			♯5	6		7
DORIAN ♯4	1		2	♭3			♯4	5		6	♭7	
PHRYGIAN ♮3	1	♭2			3	4		5	♭6		♭7	
LYDIAN ♯2	1			♯2	3		♯4	5		6		7
ALT ♮7	1	♭2		♭3	♭4		♭5		♭6	♮7		
HARMONIC MAJOR	1		2		3	4		5	♭6			7
DORIAN ♭5	1		2	♭3		4	♭5			6	♭7	
PHRYGIAN ♭4	1	♭2		♭3	♭4			5	♭6		♭7	
LYDIAN ♭3	1		2	♭3			♯4	5		6		7
DOMINANT ♭2	1	♭2			3	4		5		6	♭7	
LYDIAN AUG ♯2	1			♯2	3		♯4		♯5	6		7
LOCRIAN ♮7	1	♭2		♭3		4	♭5		♭6	♮7		
HUNGARIAN MINOR	1		2	♭3			♯4	5	♭6			7
ORIENTAL	1	♭2			3	4	♭5			6	♭7	
IONIAN AUG ♯2	1			♯2	3	4			♯5	6		7
LOCRIAN ♮3 ♭7	1	♭2		♮3		4	♭5		♭6	♮7		
DOUBLE HARMONIC	1	♭2			3	4		5	♭6			7
LYDIAN ♯6 ♯2	1			♯2	3		♯4	5			♯6	7
ALT ♭5 ♭7	1	♭2		♭3	♭4			5	♭6		♮7	
HUNGARIAN MAJOR	1			♯2	3		♯4	5		6	♭7	
ALT ♭6 ♭7	1	♭2		♭3	♭4		♭5		♭6		♮7	
LOCRIAN ♮2 ♮7	1		2	♭3		4	♭5		♭6			7
ALT ♮6	1	♭2		♭3	♭4		♭5			6	♭7	
MELODIC AUG	1		2	♭3		4			♯5	6		7
DORIAN ♭2 ♮4	1	♭2		♭3			♯4	5		6	♭7	
LYDIAN AUG ♮3	1		2			♯3	♯4		♯5	6		7

Scale	1	♭2	2	♭3	3	4	♯4/♭5	5	♭6	6	♭7	7
NEAPOLITAN MINOR	1	♭2		♭3		4		5	♭6			7
LYDIAN ♮6	1		2		3		♯4	5			♯6	7
DOMINANT AUG	1		2		3	4			♯5	6	♭7	
HUNGAR GYPSY	1		2	♭3			♯4	5	♭6		♭7	
LOCRIAN ♮3	1	♭2			3	4	♭5		♭6		♭7	
IONIAN ♮2	1			♯2	3	4		5		6		7
ALT ♮3 ♭7	1	♭2		♯3	♭4		♭5		♭6	♮7		
NEAPOLITAN MAJOR	1	♭2		♭3		4		5		6		7
LYDIAN AUG ♮6	1		2		3		♯4		♯5		♯6	7
LYDIAN DOM AUG	1		2		3		♯4		♯5	6	♭7	
LYDIAN MINOR	1		2		3		♯4	5	♭6		♭7	
MAJOR LOCRIAN	1		2		3	4	♭5		♭6		♭7	
ALT ♮2	1		2	♭3	♭4		♭5		♭6		♭7	
ALT ♮3	1	♭2		♯3	♭4		♭5		♭6		♭7	
ENIGMATIC MINOR	1	♭2		♭3			♯4	5			♯6	7
MODE 2	1		2		♯3	♯4			×5		♯6	7
MODE 3	1			♯2	3		×4		♯5	6	♭7	
MODE 4	1	♭2			3	4	♭5		♭6		♮7	
MODE 5	1			♯2	3	4	♭5		♭6			7
MODE 6	1	♭2		♯3	♭4		♭5		♭6		♭7	
MODE 7	1	♭2		♯3	♭4			5	♭6			7
ENIGMATIC	1	♭2			3		♯4		♯5		♯6	7
MODE 2	1			♯2		♯3	×4		×5		♯6	7
MODE 3	1		2		3		♯4	5	♭6		♮7	
MODE 4	1		2		3	4	♭5		♭6		♭7	
MODE 5	1		2	♭3	♭4		♭5		♭6		♭7	
MODE 6	1	♭2		♯3	♭4		♭5		♭6		♭7	
MODE 7	1	♭2		♯3		4		5		6		7
COMPOSITE II	1	♭2			3		♯4	5	♭6			7
MODE 2	1		♯2		♯3	♯4		5			♯6	7
MODE 3	1		2	♭3	♭4			5	♭6		♮7	
MODE 4	1	♭2		♯3		4	♭5		♭6		♭7	
MODE 5	1	♭2			3	4	♭5			6		7
MODE 6	1			♯2	3	4			♯5		♯6	7
MODE 7	1	♭2		♯3		4		5	♭6		♮7	
IONIAN ♮5	1		2		3	4	♭5			6		7
DORIAN ♮4	1		2	♭3	♭4			5		6	♭7	
PHRYGIAN ♮3	1	♭2		♯3		4		5	♭6		♭7	
LYDIAN ♮2	1	♭2			3		♯4	5		6		7
SUPER LYDIAN AUG	1			♯2		♯3	♯4		♯5		♯6	7
AEOLIAN ♮7	1		2	♭3		4		5	♭6		♮7	
LOCRIAN ♮6	1	♭2		♭3		4	♭5		♮6		♭7	

NUMERIC ANALYSIS OF SCALES continued

	1	♭2	2	♭3	3	4	♭5	5	♭6	6	♭7	7
LOCRIAN ♮7	1	♭2		♭3		4	♭5		♭6			7
IONIAN ♯6	1		2		3	4		5			♯6	7
DORIAN AUG	1		2	♭3		4			♯5	6	♭7	
PHRYGIAN ♯4	1	♭2		♭3			♯4	5	♭6		♭7	
LYDIAN ♯3	1		2		♯3		♯4	5		6		7
DOMINANT ♯2	1			♯2	3	4		5		6	♭7	
ALT ALT	1	♭2		♭♭3	♭4		♭5		♭♭6		♭♭7	
PERSIAN	1	♭2			3	4	♭5		♭6			7
MODE 2	1			♯2	3	4		5			♯6	7
MODE 3	1	♭2		♭♭3	♭4			5	♭6		♭♭7	
MODE 4	1	♭2		♭3			♯4	5	♭6			7
MODE 5	1		2		♯3		♯4	5			♯6	7
MODE 6	1			♯2	3	4			♯5	6	♭7	
MODE 7	1	♭2		♭♭3		4	♭5		♭♭6		♭♭7	
MINOR PENT	1			♭3		4		5			♭7	
MAJOR PENT	1		2		3			5		6		
MODE 3	1		2			4		5			♭7	
MODE 4	1			♭3		4			♯5		♭7	
MODE 5	1		2			4		5		6		
KUMOI	1		2	♭3				5		6		
MODE 2	1	♭2				4		5			♭7	
MODE 3	1				3		♭5			6		7
MODE 4	1		2			4		5	♭6			
MODE 5	1			♭3		4	♭5				♭7	
HIROJOSHI	1		2	♭3				5	♭6			
MODE 2	1	♭2				4	♭5				♭7	
MODE 3	1				3	4				6		7
MODE 4	1	♭2				4		5	♭6			
MODE 5	1				3		♯4	5				7
WHOLE TONE	1		2		3		♯4		♯5		♯6	
AUGMENTED	1			♯2	3			5	♭6			7
MODE 2	1	♭2			3	4			♯5	6		
PELOG	1	♭2		♭3	♭4			5	♭6			
MODE 2	1		2	♭3			♯4	5				7
MODE 3	1	♭2			3	4				6	♭7	
MODE 4	1			♯2	3				♯5	6		7
MODE 5	1	♭2				4	♭5		♭6		♭♭7	
MODE 6	1				3	4		5	♭6			7
DOMINANT SUS	1		2			4		5		6	♭7	
MODE 2	1			♭3		4		5	♭6		♭7	
MODE 3	1		2		3	4		5		6		
MODE 4	1		2	♭3		4		5			♭7	
MODE 5	1	♭2		♭3		4			♭6		♭7	

	1	♭2	2	♭3	3	4	♭5	5	♭6	6	♭7	7
MODE 6	1		2		3			5		6		7
DIMIN: WHOLE-HALF	1		2	♭3		4	♭5		♭6	6		7
HALF-WHOLE DIMIN	1	♭2		♭3	3		♯4	5		6	♭7	
8-TONE SPANISH	1	♭2		♭3	3	4	♭5		♭6		♭7	
MODE 2	1		2	♭3	3	4		5		6		7
MODE 3	1	♭2	2	♭3		4		5		6	♭7	
MODE 4	1	♭2	2		3		♯4		♯5	6		7
MODE 5	1	♭2		♭3		4		5	♭6		♭7	7
MODE 6	1		2		3		♯4	5		6	♭7	7
MODE 7	1		2		3	4		5	♭6	6	♭7	
MODE 8	1		2	♭3		4	♭5	5	♭6		♭7	
BEBOP LOCRIAN ♮2	1		2	♭3		4	♭5		♭6		♭7	7
MODE 2	1	♭2		♭3	3		♯4		♯5	6	♭7	
MODE 3	1		2	♭3		4		5	♭6	6		7
MODE 4	1	♭2		♭3		4	♭5	5		6	♭7	
MODE 5	1		2		3	4	♭5		♭6	6		7
MODE 6	1		2	♭3	3		♯4	5		6	♭7	
MODE 7	1	♭2	2		3	4		5	♭6		♭7	
MODE 8	1	♭2		♭3	3		♯4	5		6		7
BEBOP DOMINANT	1		2		3	4		5		6	♭7	7
BEBOP MINOR	1		2	♭3		4		5	♭6	6	♭7	
BEBOP LOC add 5	1	♭2		♭3		4	♭5	5	♭6		♭7	
MODE 4	1		2		3	4	♭5	5		6		7
MODE 5	1		2	♭3	3	4		5		6	♭7	
MODE 6	1	♭2	2	♭3		4		5	♭6		♭7	
MODE 7	1	♭2	2		3	4		5		6		7
MODE 8	1	♭2		♭3	3		♯4		♯5		♯6	7
BEBOP DORIAN	1		2	♭3		4		5		6	♭7	7
MODE 2	1	♭2		♭3		4		5	♭6	6	♭7	
MODE 3	1		2		3		♯4	5	♭6	6		7
MODE 4	1		2		3	4	♭5	5		6	♭7	
MODE 5	1		2	♭3	3	4		5	♭6		♭7	
MODE 6	1	♭2	2	♭3		4	♭5		♭6		♭7	
MODE 7	1	♭2	2		3	4		5		6		7
MODE 8	1	♭2		♭3	3		♯4		♯5		♯6	7
BEBOP MAJOR	1		2		3	4		5	♭6	6		7
MODE 2	1		2	♭3		4	♭5	5		6	♭7	
MODE 3	1	♭2		♭3	3	4		5	♭6		♭7	
MODE 4	1		2	♭3	3		♯4	5		6		7
MODE 5	1	♭2	2		3	4		5		6	♭7	
MODE 6	1	♭2		♭3	3		♯4		♯5	6		7
MODE 7	1		2	♭3		4		5	♭6		♭7	7
MODE 8	1	♭2		♭3		4	♭5		♭6	6	♭7	

CHORD - SCALE COMPATIBILITY CHART

M

MAJOR
LYDIAN = MAJOR MODE 4
MIXOLYDIAN = MAJOR MODE 5
LYDIAN DOMINANT = MELODIC MODE 4
HINDU = MELODIC MODE 5
PHRYGIAN ♭3 = HARMONIC MINOR MODE 5
LYDIAN ♯2 = HARMONIC MINOR MODE 6
HARMONIC MAJOR
PHRYGIAN ♭4 = HARMONIC MAJOR MODE 3
DOMINANT ♭2 = HARMONIC MAJOR MODE 5
DOUBLE HARMONIC = HUNGARIAN MINOR MODE 5
LYDIAN ♯6 ♯2 = HUNGARIAN MINOR MODE 6
ALT ♭5 ♭7 = HUNGARIAN MINOR MODE 7
HUNGARIAN MAJOR
ALT ♯6 ♭7 = HUNGARIAN MAJOR MODE 2
LYDIAN ♯6 = NEAPOLITAN MINOR MODE 2
IONIAN ♯2 = NEAPOLITAN MINOR MODE 6
LYDIAN MINOR = NEAPOLITAN MAJOR MODE 4
ENIGMATIC MINOR MODE 3
ENIGMATIC MINOR MODE 4
ENIGMATIC MINOR MODE 7
ENIGMATIC MODE 3
ENIGMATIC MODE 4
COMPOSITE II
COMPOSITE II MODE 3
DORIAN ♯4 = IONIAN ♭5 MODE 2
LYDIAN ♭2 = IONIAN ♭5 MODE 4
IONIAN ♯6 = LOCRIAN ♮7 MODE 2
DOMINANT ♯2 = LOCRIAN ♮7 MODE 6
PERSIAN MODE 2
PERSIAN MODE 3
MAJOR PENTATONIC = MINOR PENTATONIC MODE 2
AUGMENTED
PELOG MODE 6
DOMINANT SUS MODE 3
DOMINANT SUS MODE 6
HALF-WHOLE DIMINISHED = DIMINISHED MODE 2
8 TONE SPANISH MODE 2
8 TONE SPANISH MODE 6
8 TONE SPANISH MODE 7
BEBOP LOCRIAN MODE 6
BEBOP LOCRIAN MODE 7
BEBOP LOCRIAN MODE 8
BEBOP DOMINANT
BEBOP DOMINANT MODE 4
BEBOP DORIAN MODE 3 / MODE 4 / MODE 5
BEBOP DORIAN MODE7
BEBOP MAJOR
BEBOP MAJOR MODE 3 / MODE 4 / MODE 5

- (MINOR)

DORIAN = MAJOR MODE 2
PHRYGIAN = MAJOR MODE 3
AEOLIAN = MAJOR MODE 6
MELODIC
DORIAN ♭2 = MELODIC MODE 2
HARMONIC MINOR
DORIAN ♯4 = HARMONIC MINOR MODE 4
LYDIAN ♯2 = HARMONIC MINOR MODE 6
PHRYGIAN ♭4 = HARMONIC MAJOR MODE 3
LYDIAN ♭3 = HARMONIC MAJOR MODE 4
HUNGARIAN MINOR
LYDIAN ♯6 ♯2 = HUNGARIAN MINOR MODE 6
ALT ♭5 ♭7 = HUNGARIAN MINOR MODE 7
HUNGARIAN MAJOR
ALT ♯6 ♭7 = HUNGARIAN MAJOR MODE 2
DORIAN ♭2 ♯4 = HUNGARIAN MAJOR MODE 6
NEAPOLITAN MINOR
HUNGARIAN GYPSY = NEAPOLITAN MINOR MODE 4
IONIAN ♯2 = NEAPOLITAN MINOR MODE 6
NEAPOLITAN MAJOR
ENIGMATIC MINOR
ENIGMATIC MINOR MODE 3
ENIGMATIC MODE 2
COMPOSITE II MODE 2
COMPOSITE II MODE 3
DORIAN ♯4 = IONIAN ♭5 MODE 2
AEOLIAN ♮7 = IONIAN ♭5 MODE 6
LOCRIAN ♮6 = IONIAN ♭5 MODE 7
PHRYGIAN ♯4 = LOCRIAN ♮7 MODE 4
DOMINANT ♯2 = LOCRIAN ♮7 MODE 6
PERSIAN MODE 2
PERSIAN MODE 4
MINOR PENTATONIC
KUMOI
AUGMENTED
HALF-WHOLE DIMINISHED
8 TONE SPANISH MODE 2 / MODE 3 / MODE 5
8 TONE SPANISH MODE 8
BEBOP LOCRIAN ♭2 MODE 3
BEBOP LOCRIAN ♭2 MODE 4 / MODE 6
BEBOP LOCRIAN ♭2 MODE 8
BEBOP MINOR = BEBOP DOMINANT MODE 2
BEBOP LOCRIAN add 5 = BEBOP DOMINANT MODE 3
BEBOP DOMINANT MODE 5 / MODE 6
BEBOP DORIAN
BEBOP DORIAN MODE 2 / MODE 5
BEBOP MAJOR MODE 2
BEBOP MAJOR MODE 3 / MODE 4 / MODE 7

sus2

MAJOR
DORIAN = MAJOR MODE 2
LYDIAN = MAJOR MODE 4
MIXOLYDIAN = MAJOR MODE 5
AEOLIAN = MAJOR MODE 6
MELODIC
LYDIAN DOMINANT = MELODIC MODE 4
HINDU = MELODIC MODE 5
HARMONIC MINOR
DORIAN ♯4 = HARMONIC MINOR MODE 4
HARMONIC MAJOR
LYDIAN ♭3 = HARMONIC MAJOR MODE 4
HUNGARIAN MINOR
LYDIAN ♯6 = NEAPOLITAN MINOR MODE 2
HUNGARIAN GYPSY = NEAPOLITAN MINOR MODE 4
LYDIAN MINOR = NEAPOLITAN MAJOR MODE 4
ENIGMATIC MINOR MODE 7
ENIGMATIC MODE 3
ENIGMATIC MODE 4
ENIGMATIC MODE 7
COMPOSITE II MODE 3
COMPOSITE II MODE 4
COMPOSITE II MODE 7
DORIAN ♯4 = IONIAN ♭5 MODE 2
PHRYGIAN ♭3 = IONIAN ♭5 MODE 3
AEOLIAN ♮7 = IONIAN ♭5 MODE 6
IONIAN ♯6 = LOCRIAN ♮7 MODE 2
LYDIAN ♭3 = LOCRIAN ♮7 MODE 5
ALT ALT = LOCRIAN ♮7 MODE 7
PERSIAN MODE 3
PERSIAN MODE 5
PERSIAN MODE 7
MAJOR PENTATONIC = MINOR PENTATONIC MODE 2
MINOR PENTATONIC MODE 3 / MODE 5
KUMOI
KUMOI MODE 4
HIROJOSHI
PELOG MODE 6
DOMINANT SUS
DOMINANT SUS MODE 3 / MODE 4 / MODE 6
8 TONE SPANISH MODE 2 / MODE 3 / MODE 6 / MODE 7
8 TONE SPANISH MODE 8
BEBOP LOCRIAN ♭2 MODE 4
BEBOP LOCRIAN ♭2 MODE 6 / MODE 7
BEBOP DOMINANT
BEBOP MINOR = BEBOP DOMINANT MODE 2
BEBOP DOMINANT MODE 4 / MODE 5 / MODE 6
BEBOP DOMINANT MODE 7
BEBOP DORIAN
BEBOP DORIAN MODE 3 / MODE 4 / MODE 5 / MODE 7
BEBOP MAJOR MODE 2 / MODE 4 / MODE 5 / MODE 7

SUS

MAJOR
DORIAN = MAJOR MODE 2
PHRYGIAN = MAJOR MODE 3
MIXOLYDIAN = MAJOR MODE 5
AEOLIAN = MAJOR MODE 6
MELODIC
DORIAN ♭5 = MELODIC MODE 2
HINDU = MELODIC MODE 5
HARMONIC MINOR
PHRYGIAN ♭3 = HARMONIC MINOR MODE 5
HARMONIC MAJOR
DOMINANT ♭2 = HARMONIC MAJOR MODE 5
DOUBLE HARMONIC = HUNGARIAN MINOR MODE 5
NEAPOLITAN MINOR
IONIAN ♯2 = NEAPOLITAN MINOR MODE 6
NEAPOLITAN MAJOR
ENIGMATIC MINOR MODE 2
ENIGMATIC MODE 4 / MODE 7
COMPOSITE II MODE 2 / MODE 4 / MODE 7
PHRYGIAN ♭3 = IONIAN ♭5 MODE 3
AEOLIAN ♮7 = IONIAN ♭5 MODE 6
LOCRIAN ♮6 = IONIAN ♭5 MODE 7
IONIAN ♯6 = LOCRIAN ♮7 MODE 2
LYDIAN ♭3 = LOCRIAN ♮7 MODE 5
DOMINANT ♯2 = LOCRIAN ♮7 MODE 6
PERSIAN MODE 2 / MODE 5 / MODE 7
MINOR PENTATONIC
MINOR PENTATONIC MINOR MODE 3 / MODE 5
KUMOI MODE 2 / MODE 4
HIROJOSHI MODE 4
PELOG MODE 6
DOMINANT SUS MODE 1 / MODE 2 / MODE 3 / MODE 4
8 TONE SPANISH MODE 2 / MODE 3 / MODE 5
8 TONE SPANISH MODE 7 / MODE 8
BEBOP LOCRIAN ♭2 MODE 3 / MODE 4 / MODE 7
BEBOP DOMINANT
BEBOP MINOR = BEBOP DOMINANT MODE 2
BEBOP LOCRIAN add 5 = BEBOP DOMINANT MODE 3
BEBOP DOMINANT MODE 4 / MODE 5 / MODE 6
BEBOP DORIAN
BEBOP DORIAN MODE 2 / MODE 4 / MODE 5 / MODE 7
BEBOP MAJOR
BEBOP MAJOR MODE 2 / MODE 3 / MODE 5 / MODE 7

♭5

LYDIAN = MAJOR MODE 4
LYDIAN AUGMENTED = MELODIC MODE 3
LYDIAN DOMINANT = MELODIC MODE 4
SUPER LOCRIAN = MELODIC MODE 7
ALT ♭7 = HARMONIC MINOR MODE 7
LYDIAN AUGMENTED ♯2 = HARMONIC MAJOR MODE 6
ORIENTAL = HUNGARIAN MINOR MODE 2
LYDIAN ♯6 ♯2 = HUNGARIAN MINOR MODE 6
HUNGARIAN MAJOR
ALT ♯6 ♭7 = HUNGARIAN MAJOR MODE 2
ALT ♯6 = HUNGARIAN MAJOR MODE 4
LYDIAN ♯6 = NEAPOLITAN MINOR MODE 2
LOCRIAN ♭3 = NEAPOLITAN MINOR MODE 5
LYDIAN ♭3 ♭7 = NEAPOLITAN MINOR MODE 7
LYDIAN AUGMENTED ♯6 = NEAPOLITAN MAJOR MODE 2
LYDIAN DOMINANT AUG = NEAPOLITAN MAJOR MODE 3
LYDIAN MINOR = NEAPOLITAN MAJOR MODE 4
MAJOR LOCRIAN = NEAPOLITAN MAJOR MODE 5
ALT ♭2 = NEAPOLITAN MAJOR MODE 4
ALT ♭3 = NEAPOLITAN MAJOR MODE 7
ENIGMATIC MINOR MODE 4
ENIGMATIC MINOR MODE 5
ENIGMATIC
ENIGMATIC MODE 3 / MODE 4
COMPOSITE II
COMPOSITE II MODE 5
IONIAN ♭5
LYDIAN ♭2 = IONIAN ♭5 MODE 4
ALT ALT = LOCRIAN ♮7 MODE 7
PERSIAN
KUMOI MODE 3
HIROJOSHI MODE 5
WHOLE TONE
HALF-TONE DIMINISHED
8 TONE SPANISH
8 TONE SPANISH MODE 4
8 TONE SPANISH MODE 6
BEBOP LOCRIAN ♭2 MODE 4
BEBOP LOCRIAN ♭2 MODE 5
BEBOP LOCRIAN ♭2 MODE 6
BEBOP LOCRIAN ♭2 MODE 8
BEBOP DOMINANT MODE 4 / MODE 7
BEBOP DORIAN MODE 3 / MODE 4 / MODE 8
BEBOP MAJOR MODE 4 / MODE 6

° (DIMINISHED)

LOCRIAN = MAJOR MODE 7
LOCRIAN ♮2 = MELODIC MODE 6
SUPER LOCRIAN = MELODIC MODE 7
LOCRIAN ♮6 = HARMONIC MINOR MODE 2
DORIAN ♯4 = HARMONIC MINOR MODE 4
LYDIAN ♯2 = HARMONIC MINOR MODE 6
ALT ♭7 = HARMONIC MINOR MODE 7
DORIAN ♭5 = HARMONIC MAJOR MODE 2
LYDIAN ♭3 = HARMONIC MAJOR MODE 4
LYDIAN AUGMENTED ♯2 = HARMONIC MAJOR MODE 6
LOCRIAN ♮7 = HARMONIC MAJOR MODE 7
HUNGARIAN MINOR
LYDIAN ♯6 ♯2 = HUNGARIAN MINOR MODE 6
HUNGARIAN MAJOR
ALT ♯6 ♭7 = HUNGARIAN MAJOR MODE 2
LOCRIAN ♭2 ♭7 = HUNGARIAN MAJOR MODE 3
ALT ♯6 = HUNGARIAN MAJOR MODE 4
DORIAN ♭2 ♯4 = HUNGARIAN MAJOR MODE 6
HUNGARIAN GYPSY = NEAPOLITAN MINOR MODE 4
ALT ♭2 = NEAPOLITAN MAJOR MODE 6
ENIGMATIC MINOR
ENIGMATIC MINOR MODE 5
ENIGMATIC MODE 5
COMPOSITE II MODE 2
SUPER LYDIAN AUGMENTED = IONIAN ♭5 MODE 7
LOCRIAN ♮6 = IONIAN ♭5 MODE 7
LOCRIAN ♮7
PHRYGIAN ♯4 = LOCRIAN ♮7 MODE 4
PERSIAN MODE 4
KUMOI MODE 5
WHOLE-HALF DIMINISHED
HALF-WHOLE DIMINISHED
8 TONE SPANISH
8 TONE SPANISH MODE 8
BEBOP LOCRIAN ♭2
BEBOP LOCRIAN ♭2 MODE 2
BEBOP LOCRIAN ♭2 MODE 4
BEBOP LOCRIAN ♭2 MODE 6
BEBOP LOCRIAN ♭2 MODE 8
BEBOP LOCRIAN add 5 = BEBOP DOMINANT MODE 3
BEBOP DOMINANT MODE 8
BEBOP DORIAN MODE 6
BEBOP DORIAN MODE 8
BEBOP MAJOR MODE 2
BEBOP MAJOR MODE 4
BEBOP MAJOR MODE 6
BEBOP MAJOR MODE 8

+ (AUGMENTED)

LYDIAN AUGMENTED = MELODIC MODE 3
HINDU = MELODIC MODE 5
SUPER LOCRIAN = MELODIC MODE 7
IONIAN ♭5 = HARMONIC MINOR MODE 3
PHRYGIAN ♭3 = HARMONIC MINOR MODE 5
ALT ♭7 = HARMONIC MINOR MODE 7
HARMONIC MAJOR
PHRYGIAN ♭4 = HARMONIC MAJOR MODE 3
LYDIAN AUGMENTED ♯2 = HARMONIC MAJOR MODE 6
IONIAN AUGMENTED ♯2 = HUNGARIAN MINOR MODE 3
DOUBLE HARMONIC = HUNGARIAN MINOR MODE 5
ALT ♭5 ♭7 = HUNGARIAN MINOR MODE 7
DOMINANT AUGMENTED = NEAPOLITAN MINOR MODE 3
LOCRIAN ♭3 = NEAPOLITAN MINOR MODE 5
ALT ♭3 ♭7 = NEAPOLITAN MINOR MODE 7
LYDIAN AUGMENTED ♭6 = NEAPOLITAN MAJOR MODE 2
LYDIAN DOMINANT AUG = NEAPOLITAN MAJOR MODE 3
LYDIAN MINOR = NEAPOLITAN MAJOR MODE 4
MAJOR LOCRIAN = NEAPOLITAN MAJOR MODE 5
ALT ♭2 = NEAPOLITAN MAJOR MODE 6
ALT ♭3 = NEAPOLITAN MAJOR MODE 7
ENIGMATIC MINOR MODE 3
ENIGMATIC MINOR MODE 5
ENIGMATIC MINOR MODE 7
ENIGMATIC
ENIGMATIC MODE 3
ENIGMATIC MODE 5
COMPOSITE II
COMPOSITE II MODE 3
COMPOSITE II MODE 6
PERSIAN
PERSIAN MODE 3
PERSIAN MODE 6
WHOLE TONE
AUGMENTED
AUGMENTED MODE 2
PELOG
PELOG MODE 4 / MODE 6
8 TONE SPANISH
8 TONE SPANISH MODE 4
8 TONE SPANISH MODE 7
BEBOP LOCRIAN ♭2 MODE 2 / MODE 5 / MODE 7
BEBOP DORIAN MODE 3 / MODE 5 / MODE 8
BEBOP MAJOR
BEBOP MAJOR MODE 3 / MODE 6

♭6

HINDU = MELODIC MODE 5
PHRYGIAN ♭3 = HARMONIC MINOR MODE 5
HARMONIC MAJOR
PHRYGIAN ♭4 = HARMONIC MAJOR MODE 3
DOUBLE HARMONIC = HUNGARIAN MINOR MODE 5
ALT ♭5 ♭7 = HUNGARIAN MINOR MODE 7
LYDIAN MINOR = NEAPOLITAN MAJOR MODE 4
ENIGMATIC MINOR MODE 5
ENIGMATIC MINOR MODE 7
ENIGMATIC MODE 3
COMPOSITE II
COMPOSITE II MODE 3
PERSIAN MODE 3
AUGMENTED
PELOG MODE 6
8 TONE SPANISH MODE 7
BEBOP LOCRIAN ♭2 MODE 7
BEBOP DORIAN MODE 3
BEBOP DORIAN MODE 5
BEBOP MAJOR
BEBOP MAJOR MODE 3

-♭6

PHRYGIAN = MAJOR MODE 3
AEOLIAN = MAJOR MODE 6
HARMONIC MINOR
PHRYGIAN ♭4 = HARMONIC MAJOR MODE 3
HUNGARIAN MINOR
ALT ♭5 ♭7 = HUNGARIAN MINOR MODE 7
NEAPOLITAN MINOR
HUNGARIAN GYPSY = NEAPOLITAN MINOR MODE 4
ENIGMATIC MINOR MODE 3
COMPOSITE II MODE 3
AEOLIAN ♮7 = IONIAN ♭5 MODE 6
PHRYGIAN ♮4 = LOCRIAN ♮7 MODE 4
PERSIAN MODE 4
HIROJOSHI
AUGMENTED
PELOG
DOMINANT SUS MODE 2
8 TONE SPANISH MODE 5
8 TONE SPANISH MODE 8
BEBOP LOCRIAN ♭2 MODE 3
BEBOP MINOR = BEBOP DOMINANT MODE 2
BEBOP LOCRIAN add 5 = BEBOP DOMINANT MODE 3
BEBOP DOMINANT MODE 6
BEBOP DORIAN MODE 2
BEBOP DORIAN MODE 5
BEBOP MAJOR MODE 3
BEBOP MAJOR MODE 7

6

MAJOR
LYDIAN = MAJOR MODE 4
MIXOLYDIAN = MAJOR MODE 5
LYDIAN DOMINANT = MELODIC MODE 4
LYDIAN ♭2 = HARMONIC MINOR MODE 6
DOMINANT ♭2 = HARMONIC MAJOR MODE 5
HUNGARIAN MAJOR
ALT ♮6 ♭7 = HUNGARIAN MAJOR MODE 2
IONIAN ♯2 = NEAPOLITAN MINOR MODE 6
ENIGMATIC MINOR MODE 3
ENIGMATIC MINOR MODE 4
ENIGMATIC MODE 3
COMPOSITE II MODE 3
DORIAN ♭4 = IONIAN ♭5 MODE 2
LYDIAN ♭2 = IONIAN ♭5 MODE 4
DOMINANT ♭2 = LOCRIAN ♮7 MODE 6
ALT ALT = LOCRIAN ♮7 MODE 7
PERSIAN MODE 3
MAJOR PENTATONIC = MINOR PENTATONIC MODE 2
DOMINANT SUS MODE 3
DOMINATN SUS MODE 6
HALF-WHOLE DIMINISHED
8 TONE SPANISH MODE 2
8 TONE SPANISH MODE 6
8 TONE SPANISH MODE 7
BEBOP LOCRIAN ♭2 MODE 6
BEBOP LOCRIAN ♭2 MODE 8
BEBOP DOMINANT
BEBOP DOMINANT MODE 4
BEBOP DOMINANT MODE 5
BEBOP DOMINANT MODE 7
BEBOP DORIAN MODE 3
BEBOP DORIAN MODE 4
BEBOP DORIAN MODE 7
BEBOP MAJOR
BEBOP MAJOR MODE 4
BEBOP MAJOR MODE 5

-6

DORIAN = MAJOR MODE 2
MELODIC
DORIAN ♭2 = MELODIC MODE 2
DORIAN ♮4 = HARMONIC MINOR MODE 4
LYDIAN ♯2 = HARMONIC MINOR MODE 6
LYDIAN ♭3 = HARMONIC MAJOR MODE 2
ALT ♭5 ♭7 = HUNGARIAN MINOR MODE 7
HUNGARIAN MAJOR
ALT ♮6 ♭7 = HUNGARIAN MAJOR MODE 2
DORIAN ♭2 ♮4 = HUNGARIAN MAJOR MODE 6
IONIAN ♯2 = NEAPOLITAN MINOR MODE 6
NEAPOLITAN MAJOR
ENIGMATIC MINOR MODE 3
ENIGMATIC MODE 2
COMPOSITE II MODE 2
DORIAN ♮4 = IONIAN ♭5 MODE 2
AEOLIAN ♮7 = IONIAN ♭5 MODE 6
DOMINANT ♭2 = LOCRIAN ♮7 MODE 6
KUMOI
HALF-WHOLE DIMINISHED
8 TONE SPANISH MODE 2
8 TONE SPANISH MODE 3
BEBOP LOCRIAN ♭2 MODE 3
BEBOP LOCRIAN ♭2 MODE 4
BEBOP LOCRIAN ♭2 MODE 6
BEBOP LOCRIAN ♭2 MODE 8
BEBOP MINOR = BEBOP DOMINANT MODE 2
BEBOP DOMINANT MODE 5
BEBOP DORIAN
BEBOP DORIAN MODE 2
BEBOP MAJOR MODE 2
BEBOP MAJOR MODE 4

°7

LOCRIAN ♮6 = HARMONIC MINOR MODE 2
DORIAN ♮4 = HARMONIC MINOR MODE 4
LYDIAN ♯2 = HARMONIC MINOR MODE 6
ALT ♮7 = HARMONIC MINOR MODE 7
DORIAN ♭5 = HARMONIC MAJOR MODE 2
LYDIAN ♭3 = HARMONIC MAJOR MODE 3
LYDIAN AUGMENTED ♯2 = HARMONIC MAJOR MODE 6
LOCRIAN ♮7 = HARMONIC MAJOR MODE 7
HUNGARIAN MAJOR
ALT ♮6 ♭7 = HUNGARIAN MAJOR MODE 2
ALT ♮6 = HUNGARIAN MAJOR MODE 3
DORIAN ♭2 ♮4 = HUNGARIAN MAJOR MODE 6
WHOLE-HALF DIMINISHED
HALF-WHOLE DIMINISHED
BEBOP LOCRIAN ♭2 MODE 2
BEBOP LOCRIAN ♭2 MODE 4
BEBOP LOCRIAN ♭2 MODE 6
BEBOP LOCRIAN ♭2 MODE 8
BEBOP MAJOR MODE 2
BEBOP MAJOR MODE 4
BEBOP MAJOR MODE 6
BEBOP MAJOR MODE 8

7 (DOMINANT)

MIXOLYDIAN = MAJOR MODE 5
LYDIAN DOMINANT = MELODIC MODE 4
HINDU = MELODIC MODE 5
PHRYGIAN ♭3 = HARMONIC MINOR MODE 5
PHRYGIAN ♭4 = HARMONIC MAJOR MODE 3
DOMINANT ♭2 = HARMONIC MAJOR MODE 5
LYDIAN ♭6 ♭2 = HUNGARIAN MINOR MODE 6
HUNGARIAN MAJOR
LYDIAN ♭6 = NEAPOLITAN MINOR MODE 2
LYDIAN MINOR = NEAPOLITAN MAJOR MODE 4
ENIGMATIC MINOR MODE 3
ENIGMATIC MODE 4
DORIAN ♮4 = IONIAN ♭5 MODE 2
IONIAN ♭6 = LOCRIAN ♮7 MODE 2
DOMINANT ♭2 = LOCRIAN ♮7 MODE 6
PERSIAN MODE 3
HALF-WHOLE DIMINISHED
8 TONE SPANISH MODE 3
8 TONE SPANISH MODE 7
BEBOP LOCRIAN ♭2 MODE 6
BEBOP LOCRAIN ♭2 MODE 7
BEBOP DOMINANT
BEBOP DOMINANT MODE 5
BEBOP DORIAN MODE 4
BEBOP DORIAN MODE 5
BEBOP MAJOR MODE 3
BEBOP MAJOR MODE 5

-7

DORIAN = MAJOR MODE 2
PHRYGIAN = MAJOR MODE 3
AEOLIAN = MAJOR MODE 6
DORIAN ♭2 = MELODIC MODE 2
DORIAN ♮4 = HARMONIC MINOR MODE 4
PHRYGIAN ♭4 = HARMONIC MAJOR MODE 3
LYDIAN ♭6 ♭2 = HUNGARIAN MINOR MODE 6
HUNGARIAN MAJOR
DORIAN ♭2 ♮4 = HUNGARIAN MAJOR MODE 6
HUNGARIAN GYPSY = NEAPOLITAN MINOR MODE 4
ENIGMATIC MINOR
ENIGMATIC MINOR MODE 3
ENIGMATIC MODE 5
COMPOSITE II MODE 2
DORIAN ♮4 = IONIAN ♭5 MODE 2
LOCRIAN ♮6 = IONIAN ♭5 MODE 7
PHRYGIAN ♮4 = LOCRIAN ♮7 MODE 4
DOMINANT ♭2 = LOCRIAN ♮7 MODE 6
PERSIAN MODE 2
MINOR PENTATONIC
DOMINANT SUS MODE 3
DOMINANT SUS MODE 4
HALF-WHOLE DIMINISHED
8 TONE SPANISH MODE 3
8 TONE SPANISH MODE 5
8 TONE SPANISH MODE 8
BEBOP LOCRIAN ♭2 MODE 4
BEBOP LOCRIAN ♭2 MODE 6
BEBOP MINOR = BEBOP DOMINANT MODE 2
BEBOP LOCRIAN add 5 = BEBOP DOMINANT MODE 3
BEBOP DOMINANT MODE 5
BEBOP DOMINANT MODE 6
BEBOP DORIAN
BEBOP DORIAN MODE 2 / MODE 5
BEBOP MAJOR MODE 2
BEBOP MAJOR MODE 3
BEBOP MAJOR MODE 7

7sus2

DORIAN = MAJOR MODE 2
MIXOLYDIAN = MAJOR MODE 5
AEOLIAN = MAJOR MODE 6
LYDIAN DOMINANT = MELODIC MODE 4
HINDU = MELODIC MODE 5
DORIAN ♮4 = HARMONIC MINOR MODE 4
LYDIAN ♭6 = NEAPOLITAN MINOR MODE 2
HUNGARIAN GYPSY = NEAPOLITAN MINOR MODE 4
LYDIAN MAJOR = NEAPOLITAN MAJOR MODE 4
ENIGMATIC MODE 4
COMPOSITE II MODE 4
DORIAN ♮4 = IONIAN ♭5 MODE 2
PHRYGIAN ♭3 = IONIAN ♭5 MODE 3
IONIAN ♭6 = LOCRIAN ♮7 MODE 2
PERSIAN MODE 5
MINOR PENTATONIC MODE 3
DOMINANT SUS
DOMINANT SUS MODE 4
8 TONE SPANISH MODE 3 / MODE 6 / MODE 7
8 TONE SPANISH MODE 8
BEBOP LOCRIAN ♭2 MODE 6 / MODE 7
BEBOP DOMINANT
BEBOP MINOR = BEBOP DOMINANT MODE 2
BEBOP DOMINANT MODE 5 / MODE 6
BEBOP DORIAN
BEBOP DORIAN MODE 4 / MODE 5
BEBOP MAJOR MODE 2 / MODE 5 / MODE 7

7sus

DORIAN = MAJOR MODE 2
PHRYGIAN = MAJOR MODE 3
MIXOLYDIAN = MAJOR MODE 5
AEOLIAN = MAJOR MODE 6
DORIAN ♭2 = MELODIC MODE 2
HINDU = MELODIC MODE 5
PHRYGIAN ♭3 = HARMONIC MINOR MODE 5
DOMINANT ♭2 = HARMONIC MAJOR MODE 5
ENIGMATIC MODE 4
COMPOSITE II MODE 2
COMPOSITE II MODE 4
PHRYGIAN ♭3 = IONIAN ♭5 MODE 3
LOCRIAN ♮6 = IONIAN ♭5 MODE 7
IONIAN ♭6 = LOCRIAN ♮7 MODE 2
DOMINANT ♭2 = LOCRIAN ♮7 MODE 6
PERSIAN MODE 2
PERSIAN MODE 5
MINOR PENTATONIC
MINOR PENTATONIC MODE 3
KUMOI MODE 2
DOMINANT SUS
DOMINANT SUS MODE 2
DOMINANT SUS MODE 4
8 TONE SPANISH MODE 3
8 TONE SPANISH MODE 5
8 TONE SPANISH MODE 7
8 TONE SPANISH MODE 8
BEBOP LOCRIAN ♮2 MODE 4
BEBOP LOCRIAN ♮2 MODE 7
BEBOP DOMINANT
BEBOP MINOR = BEBOP DOMINANT MODE 2
BEBOP LOCRIAN add 5 = BEBOP DOMINANT MODE 3
BEBOP DOMINANT MODE 5
BEBOP DOMINANT MODE 6
BEBOP DORIAN
BEBOP DORIAN MODE 2
BEBOP DORIAN MODE 4
BEBOP DORIAN MODE 5
BEBOP MAJOR MODE 2
BEBOP MAJOR MODE 3
BEBOP MAJOR MODE 5 / MODE 7

7♭5

LYDIAN DOMINANT = MELODIC MODE 4
ORIENTAL = HUNGARIAN MINOR MODE 2
LYDIAN ♮6 ♮2 = HUNGARIAN MINOR MODE 6
HUNGARIAN MAJOR
ALT ♮6 = HUNGARIAN MAJOR MODE 4
LYDIAN ♮6 = NEAPOLITAN MINOR MODE 2
LOCRIAN ♮3 = NEAPOLITAN MINOR MODE 5
LYDIAN AUGMENTED ♮6 = NEAPOLITAN MAJOR MODE 2
LYDIAN DOMINANT AUG = NEAPOLITAN MAJOR MODE 3
LYDIAN MINOR = NEAPOLITAN MAJOR MODE 4
MAJOR LOCRIAN = NEAPOLITAN MAJOR MODE 5
ALT ♭2 = NEAPOLITAN MAJOR MODE 6
ALT ♭3 = NEAPOLITAN MAJOR MODE 7
ENIGMATIC / ENIGMATIC MODE 4
WHOLE TONE
HALF-WHOLE DIMINISHED
8 TONE SPANISH
8 TONE SPANISH MODE 6
BEBOP LOCRIAN ♮2 MODE 2
BEBOP LOCRIAN ♮2 MODE 6
BEBOP DORIAN MODE 4
BEBOP DORIAN MODE 8

∅

LOCRIAN = MAJOR MODE 7
LOCRIAN ♮2 = MELODIC MODE 6
SUPER LOCRIAN = MELODIC MODE 7
LOCRIAN ♮6 = HARMONIC MINOR MODE 2
DORIAN ♮4 = HARMONIC MINOR MODE 4
DORIAN ♭5 = HARMONIC MAJOR MODE 2
LYDIAN ♮6 ♮2 = HUNGARIAN MINOR MODE 6
HUNGARIAN MAJOR
ALT ♮6 = HUNGARIAN MAJOR MODE 4
DORIAN ♭2 ♮4 = HUNGARIAN MAJOR MODE 6
HUNGARIAN GYPSY = NEAPOLITAN MINOR MODE 4
ALT ♭2 = NEAPOLITAN MINOR MODE 6
ENIGMATIC MINOR
ENIGMATIC MODE 6
COMPOSITE II MODE 2
SUPER LYDIAN AUGMENTED = IONIAN ♭5 MODE 5
LOCRIAN ♮6 = IONIAN ♭5 MODE 7
PHRYGIAN ♮4 = LOCRIAN ♮7 MODE 4
KUMOI MODE 5
HALF-WHOLE DIMINISHED
8 TONE SPANISH
8 TONE SPANISH MODE 8
BEBOP LOCRIAN ♮2
BEBOP LOCRIAN ♮2 MODE 2
BEBOP LOCRIAN ♮2 MODE 4
BEBOP LOCRIAN ♮2 MODE 6
BEBOP LOCRIAN add 5 = BEBOP DOMINANT MODE 3
BEBOP DOMINANT MODE 6
BEBOP DORIAN MODE 6 / MODE 8
BEBOP MAJOR MODE 2 / MODE 8

7⁺

HINDU = MELODIC MODE 5
SUPER LOCRIAN = MELODIC MODE 7
PHRYGIAN ♭3 = HARMONIC MINOR MODE 5
PHRYGIAN ♮4 = HARMONIC MINOR MODE 3
DOMINANT AUGMENTED = NEAPOLITAN MINOR MODE 3
LOCRIAN ♮3 = NEAPOLITAN MINOR MODE 5
LYDIAN AUGMENTED ♮6 = NEAPOLITAN MAJOR MODE 2
LYDIAN DOMINANT AUG = NEAPOLITAN MAJOR MODE 3
LYDIAN MINOR = NEAPOLITAN MAJOR MODE 4
MAJOR LOCRIAN = NEAPOLITAN MAJOR MODE 5
ALT ♭2 = NEAPOLITAN MAJOR MODE 6
ALT ♭3 = NEAPOLITAN MAJOR MODE 7
ENIGMATIC MINOR MODE 3
ENIGMATIC
ENIGMATIC MODE 5
COMPOSITE II MODE 6
PERSIAN MODE 6
WHOLE TONE
8 TONE SPANISH
BEBOP LOCRIAN ♮2 MODE 2 / MODE 7
BEBOP DORIAN MODE 5 / MODE 8
BEBOP MAJOR MODE 3

△ (DELTA)

MAJOR
LYDIAN = MAJOR MODE 4
LYDIAN ♮2 = HARMONIC MINOR MODE 6
HARMONIC MAJOR
DOUBLE HARMONIC = HUNGARIAN MINOR MODE 5
LYDIAN ♮6 ♮2 = HUNGARIAN MINOR MODE 6
LYDIAN ♮6 = NEAPOLITAN MINOR MODE 2
IONIAN ♮2 = NEAPOLIAN MINOR MODE 6
ENIGMATIC MINOR MODE 7
COMPOSITE II
LYDIAN ♮2 = IONIAN ♭5 MODE 4
IONIAN ♮6 = LOCRIAN ♮7 MODE 2
PERSIAN MODE 2
HIROJOSHI MODE 5
AUGMENTED
PELOG MODE 6
8 TONE SPANISH MODE 2 / MDOE 6
BEBOP LOCRIAN ♮2 MODE 8
BEBOP DOMINANT MODE 4 / MODE 7
BEBOP DORIAN MODE 3 / MODE 7
BEBOP MAJOR
BEBOP MAJOR MODE 4

−△

MELODIC
HARMONIC MINOR
LYDIAN ♮2 = HARMONIC MINOR MODE 6
LYDIAN ♮3 = HARMONIC MAJOR MODE 4
HUNGARIAN MINOR
LYDIAN ♮6 ♮2 = HUNGARIAN MINOR MODE 6
NEAPOLITAN MINOR
IONIAN ♮2 = NEAPOLITAN MINOR MODE 6
NEAPOLITAN MAJOR
ENIGMATIC MINOR
ENIGMATIC MODE 2
COMPOSITE II MODE 2
PERSIAN MODE 2 / MODE 4
AUGMENTED
PELOG MODE 2
8 TONE SPANISH MODE 2 / MODE 5
BEBOP LOCRIAN ♮2 MODE 3 / MODE 8
BEBOP DORIAN
BEBOP MAJOR MODE 4 / MODE 7

△sus2

MAJOR
LYDIAN = MAJOR MODE 4
MELODIC
HARMONIC MINOR
HARMONIC MAJOR
LYDIAN ♮3 = HARMONIC MAJOR MODE 4
HUNGARIAN MINOR
LYDIAN ♮6 = NEAPOLITAN MINOR MODE 2
ENIGMATIC MINOR MODE 7
ENIGMATIC MODE 7
IONIAN ♮6 = LOCRIAN ♮7 MODE 2
LYDIAN ♮3 = LOCRIAN ♮7 MODE 5
PERSIAN MODE 2
PELOG MODE 2
DOMINANT SUS MODE 6
8 TONE SPANISH MODE 2 / MODE 6
BEBOP LOCRIAN ♮2 MODE 3
BEBOP DOMINANT
BEBOP DOMINANT MODE 4 / MODE 7
BEBOP DORIAN
BEBOP DORIAN MODE 3 / MODE 7
BEBOP MAJOR
BEBOP MAJOR MODE 4 / MODE 7

△sus

MAJOR
MELODIC
HARMONIC MINOR
HARMONIC MAJOR
DOUBLE HARMONIC = HUNGARIAN MINOR MODE 5
NEAPOLITAN MINOR
IONIAN ♮2 = NEAPOLITAN MINOR MODE 6
NEAPOLITAN MAJOR
ENIGMATIC MODE 7
COMPOSITE II MODE 2
IONIAN ♮6 = LOCRIAN ♮7 MODE 2
LYDIAN ♮3 = LOCRIAN ♮7 MODE 5
PERSIAN MODE 2 / MODE 5
PELOG MODE 6
8 TONE SPANISH MODE 2 / MODE 5
BEBOP LOCRIAN ♮2 MODE 7
BEBOP DOMINANT / BEBOP DOMINANT MODE 4
BEBOP DORIAN / BEBOP DORIAN MODE 6
BEBOP MAJOR / BEBOP MAJOR MODE 8

△♭5

LYDIAN = MAJOR MODE 4
LYDIAN AUGMENTED = MELODIC MODE 3
LYDIAN ♮2 = HARMONIC MINOR MODE 6
LYDIAN AUGMENTED ♮2 = HARMONIC MAJOR MODE 6
LYDIAN ♮6 ♮2 = HUNGARIAN MINOR MODE 6
LYDIAN ♮6 = NEAPOLITAN MINOR MODE 2
LYDIAN AUGMENTED ♮6 = NEAPOLITAN MAJOR MODE 2
ENIGMATIC MINOR MODE 5
ENIGMATIC
COMPOSITE II / COMPOSITE II MODE 5
IONIAN ♭5
LYDIAN ♮2 = IONIAN ♭5 MODE 4
PERSIAN
KUMOI MODE 3
HIROJOSHI MODE 5
8 TONE SPANISH MODE 4 / MODE 6
BEBOP LOCRIAN ♮2 MODE 5
BEBOP DOMINANT MODE 4 / MODE 7
BEBOP DORIAN MODE 3 / MODE 8
BEBOP MAJOR MODE 4 / MODE 6

△°

LYDIAN ♮2 = HARMONIC MINOR MODE 6
LYDIAN ♮3 = HARMONIC MINOR MODE 4
LYDIAN AUGMENTED ♮2 = HARMONIC MAJOR MODE 6
HUNGARIAN MINOR
LYDIAN ♮6 ♮2 = HUNGARIAN MINOR MODE 6
LOCRIAN ♮2 ♮7 = HUNGARIAN MAJOR MODE 3
ENIGMATIC MINOR / ENIGMATIC MINOR MODE 5
COMPOSITE II MODE 2
SUPER LYDIAN AUGMENTED = IONIAN ♭5 MODE 5
LOCRIAN ♮7
PERSIAN MODE 4
PELOG MODE 2
WHOLE-HALF DIMINISHED
BEBOP LOCRIAN ♮2 / BEBOP LOCRIAN ♮2 MODE 8
BEBOP DOMINANT MODE 8
BEBOP DORIAN MODE 8
BEBOP MAJOR MODE 4 / MODE 6

△⁺

LYDIAN AUGMENTED = MELODIC MODE 3
IONIAN ♭5 = HARMONIC MINOR MODE 3
HARMONIC MAJOR
LYDIAN AUGMENTED ♮2 = HARMONIC MAJOR MODE 6
IONIAN AUGMENTED ♮2 = HUNGARIAN MINOR MODE 3
DOUBLE HARMONIC = HUNGARIAN MINOR MODE 5
LYDIAN AUGMENTED ♮6 = NEAPOLITAN MAJOR MODE 2
ENIGMATIC MINOR MODE 5 / MODE 7
ENIGMATIC
COMPOSITE II / COMPOSITE II MODE 6
PERSIAN
AUGMENTED
PELOG MODE 4 / MODE 6
8 TONE SPANISH MODE 4
BEBOP DORIAN MODE 3 / MODE 8
BEBOP MAJOR / BEBOP MAJOR MODE 6

−△⁺

HARMONIC MINOR
LYDIAN AUGMENTED ♮2 = HARMONIC MAJOR MODE 6
HUNGARIAN MINOR
IONIAN AUGMENTED ♮2 = HUNGARIAN MINOR MODE 3
LOCRIAN ♮2 ♮7 = HUNGARIAN MAJOR MODE 3
MELODIC AUGMENTED = HUNGARIAN MAJOR MODE 5
NEAPOLITAN MINOR
ENIGMATIC MINOR MODE 5
COMPOSITE II MODE 6
SUPER LYDIAN AUGMENTED = IONIAN ♭5 MODE 5
LOCRIAN ♮7
PERSIAN MODE 4

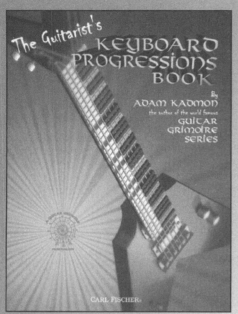

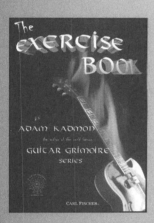

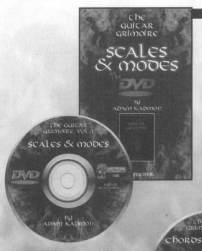

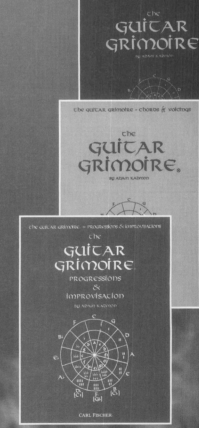